QUICK STARTS

KU-078-718

THE DAY MY INSTAGRAM ACCOUNT WAS HACKED

A couple of days ago, I woke up to loads of messages on my phone telling me that my Instagram account had been hacked.

After I'd gone to bed the night before, my account had been taken over by an unknown person who started to upload photos in my name. It was really upsetting to see strange photos of ads for phone covers in an unknown language on my Instagram feed. In just one night, I had lost my Instagram identity which I had painstakingly built over years.

I couldn't control what was being uploaded because the account had been taken over. The user settings had been tampered with so that while my feed was still viewable, I was logged out.

I tried everything I knew: changing my log-in details, requesting a password reset and reporting the user to Instagram itself. In the meantime, more and more people were messaging me about the situation, flooding my phone with screenshots of my hijacked account, making me even more anxious. Frantic, I paced up and down my room mumbling to myself, "What am I going to do?"

Our Daily Bread®

TEEN EDITION - VOLUME 5

COVER PHOTO
Milky Way over Lofoten Islands, Norway © *Denis Belitsky,* shutterstock.com

Scripture taken from Holy Bible, New International Version®, NIV®
Copyright © 1973, 1978, 1984, 2011 by Biblica, Inc.®
Used by permission. All rights reserved.

© 2020 Our Daily Bread Ministries® • Grand Rapids, Michigan, USA
ourdailybread.org • europe@odb.org
Printed in the United Kingdom.   Product Code: JZ828

Ready to explore the Bible each day with this *Our Daily Bread* Teen Edition?

Let's do this!

These readings will help you find out who God is, what the Bible's story is and where you fit into it all. But we're also going to talk about the other stuff. And you know what that is, right? Mental health, loneliness, addiction, sex, dating, bullies, guilt, social media, etc. This edition isn't just here to inspire you, but to challenge you, help you ask the right questions of your relationship with God and think about whether you agree with the Bible on the hot topics in our world right now.

I guess so . . . but is there a quick version?

Check out the *Quick Starts* reading plans on the next page. Each *Quick Starts* topic only has seven readings. You can take as long as you like to read through them; no one's going to check up on you! What really matters is that this *Our Daily Bread* Teen Edition helps you get into what God has to say in the Bible.

As much as I want to explore the Bible . . . I kinda just want to start getting answers to my burning questions right away.

I'm so up for this!

Bring it on!

Why not try to complete the "Explore the Bible's story in a year" challenge on page 378! And keep an eye out throughout this book for the "Want More . . . ?" sections with lots more stuff you can enjoy online.

And if I want more of this kind of stuff, I go where . . . ?

You can go to **ourdailybread.org/teen** to see all our Teen Editons and other resources. And make sure you check us out on Instagram: **@ourdailybreadyouth**

Then a friend came round and asked me a question that stopped me in my tracks. "What are you so anxious about? It's only an Instagram account."

My immediate reaction was to shout back, "It's not just an Instagram account!" It was *my* Instagram account! Filled with memories and my personality. I worried that I would never be able to get any of this back. And at that moment, the loss felt too big.

Yet, I knew my friend was right. It was only an Instagram account. Why was I getting so frustrated and upset?

After spending a whole day without access to Instagram, I discovered the answer. My account meant so much to me because it had become my public identity. It was a collection of photos I had directed, edited and shared that I believed represented my life. Not that this identity was false, but it was something that took a lot of work to keep up. In carefully selecting, editing and making every effort to make my feed look effortless, I had allowed the process to become a major part of who I was.

The fact that I was so upset about not being able to access my account also showed me how much time I had been spending on it, to the point where I was totally obsessed with it.

This entire episode revealed how easily I had been distracted from my walk with God. It frightened me that something seemingly harmless could use up so much of my time, emotions and energy. I had stressed over an identity that was shallow and temporary, instead of rejoicing over how I had been made right with God through Jesus' death on the cross.

A day later, Instagram restored my account. All the strange photos were removed, and I got access to my feed again. While I still don't know how my account had been hacked into, the whole thing was a glaring reminder of how my attitude towards Instagram had to change. What I had once thought of as my public identity, will now simply be a place to share my life in Jesus and appreciate what others put up.

It's great to have my account back, but what's greater is the unchanging, un-hackable, unshakable identity that I have in Jesus as God's own child!

Seven days in . . . the gospel

JESUS SAVES

BIBLE: ROMANS 4:1-8

For the Son of Man came to seek and to save the lost (LUKE 19:10).

If a friend of yours, who couldn't swim, fell into deep water, what would you do? Obviously you'd want to help rescue them. But where do you start?

You could throw a book into the water next to them called "Five Easy Swimming Lessons". Or you could just shout encouragements. Or you could jump in the water and start swimming next to them, saying, "Just copy me!" Okay, none of these are very good ideas . . .

The point is this: a drowning person doesn't need a book, a lesson or motivation. They need a saviour; someone who can get to them, pull them to safety and rescue them!

This is exactly what it's like for each of us if we don't know Jesus for ourselves. The Bible says "all have sinned" (ROMANS 3:23) and "the wages of sin is death" (6:23). Everyone born into this world fails to meet God's perfect standards, so we 'earn' death. We cannot fix ourselves by reading books about religion, by trying harder to do good stuff or by following good examples. Even the best of us don't love God as we should. Only Jesus rescues us from drowning in sin.

The Bible teaches us the gospel (which literally means "good news") that Jesus "came to seek and to save the lost" (LUKE 19:10). He rescues all who trust in Him. Just as a drowning person must stop struggling and relax in the arms of their rescuer, we too must trust in Jesus, realising we can't rescue ourselves.

RDH

THINKING IT OVER . . .

Read Ephesians 2:1-10, which is a short summary of how God has saved us. What is our role in salvation, and what Is His?

JESUS IS THE ONLY ONE WHO RESCUES US FROM SIN AND ITS PUNISHMENT.

Seven days in . . . the gospel

THE LAMB AND THE LION

BIBLE: REVELATION 5

See, the Lion of the tribe of Judah, the Root of David, has triumphed . . .
Then I saw a Lamb, looking as if it had been slain, standing at the centre
of the throne (VV.5-6).

Jesus was announced as "the Lamb of God, who takes away the sin of the world!" (JOHN 1:29). He died for our sins—in our place as our sacrifice. He saves everyone who trusts in Him. But one day that offer will expire. The Lamb sacrificed for sin will become the Lion, bringing judgement on everyone who rejected Him.

I remember a preacher telling a true story (from a long time ago) to help make sense of this. A horse bolted and ran away with a cart that had a little kid in it. A young man risked his life to catch the horse and stop it. The child was rescued, but grew up to become a violent criminal. One day he was being sentenced for a serious crime. Then the prisoner recognised the judge as the man who, years before, had saved his life, so he begged for mercy. But the judge's words silenced him: "Young man, then I was your saviour; today I am your judge, and I must sentence you to be hanged."

Today Jesus is the Lamb who died for our sins. But if we say no to Him, He will one day stand before us as our Judge, and say: "On earth I was your Saviour, but you would not believe in me. Now I am your Judge and I must sentence you to hell" (SEE MATTHEW 7:23; 10:28). Those who trust the Lamb will not have to face the Lion in judgement.

DE

COMPLETING THE PICTURE . . .

God first rescued His people from slavery in Egypt through the Passover
(SEE EXODUS 12) when the blood of lambs "without defect" was put on the doors of
Israel's houses (V.5). These lambs died instead of the Israelite firstborn males—
which was the last plague God sent against Egypt (11:4-5)—so that all of Israel could
be saved. Lambs were then sacrificed annually to remember this rescue. It was
during the celebration of Passover that Jesus had His last supper with His friends
before He was crucified. Just as the lambs died in Egypt to free the Israelites from
slavery to Pharaoh, Jesus died on the cross to rescue us from slavery to sin.

THE DECISION WE MAKE ABOUT JESUS NOW DECIDES HOW HE WILL MEET US IN ETERNITY.

Seven days in . . . the gospel

PERFECT LOVE

BIBLE: 1 JOHN 4:15-18

There is no fear in love. But perfect love drives out fear, because fear has to do with punishment (V.18).

So many Christians struggle with self-doubt, guilt and shame. They think they must do something to make God love them more. Yet we're told: "This is how love is made complete among us so that we will have confidence on the day of judgement: in this world we are like Jesus" (1 JOHN 4:17). In other words, we have the same confidence that Jesus had on earth, knowing that the Father loves us with perfect love.

Because Jesus rescued us through His death and resurrection, all judgement for sin is now completed for us. There is no judgement left for Christians to face (ROMANS 8:1)—Jesus took it all! This is what gives us joy and confidence, removing our anxiety about meeting God face to face. "There is no fear in love. But perfect love drives out fear, because fear has to do with punishment" (1 JOHN 4:18). But we know our punishment is already over!

We're forgiven for all our sins, held tightly by God's love and promised a place in His home forever—not because of anything we have done but because He has done everything for us. "This is love: not that we loved God, but that he loved us and sent his Son as [a complete and perfect] sacrifice for our sins" (V.10). That's perfect love!

DR

THINKING IT OVER . . .

Read John 3:16-18. What is God's attitude towards us and why did He send Jesus into the world (VV.16-17)? What decides whether we are under God's condemnation (judgement) or not (V.18)? How does this encourage you if you struggle with feeling guilty? And what does verse 18 tell us is the default position for everyone when it comes to judgement? Why do you think this is (SEE ROMANS 3:9-20)?

WE WON'T FEAR GOD'S JUDGEMENT WHEN WE KNOW HIS FORGIVENESS.

Seven days in . . . The gospel

AM I GOOD ENOUGH?

BIBLE: MATTHEW 7:21-23

Not everyone who says to me, "Lord, Lord," will enter the kingdom of heaven (V.21).

You're chilling after school, watching TV at home alone. There's a knock on the door. So you get up and open it. On the doorstep is someone you don't recognise—you've never seen them before in your life. They say "Hi." You reply, "Um, hello?"

They look at you like they're waiting for something. You wonder what's going on. After a long, weird pause, they finally ask, "Well, are you going to let me in?" And you say . . .

You probably say, "No way! I don't know you!" Because you don't just let random strangers into your home. Heaven is a bit like that. It's God's home! So getting into heaven isn't about what you've done or what you know. It is about who you know.

Jesus told people, "Not everyone who says to me, 'Lord, Lord,' will enter the kingdom of heaven [God's home] . . . I will tell them plainly, 'I never knew you'" (MATTHEW 7:21-23).

If we're trying to be 'good enough' to get to heaven, we'll never get there. There's no way into heaven without choosing to trust Jesus personally. Knowing about Him won't be enough. We can't get in on our own. We can't gate-crash. We can't buy tickets. We can't sit an exam. We've got to know the person who lives there for ourselves.

CW

COMPLETING THE PICTURE . . .

Heaven isn't like a city which might have hundreds of different roads leading into it. Jesus very clearly said: "I am the way and the truth and the life. No one comes to the Father except through me" (SEE JOHN 14:1-6). Not "a way", but "the way".

Why is Jesus the only way? No other religion, person or lifestyle can make us perfect (which is the standard for entering heaven). Only Jesus can make us fully clean and blameless before God: "God made him who had no sin to be sin for us, so that in him we might become the righteousness of God" (2 CORINTHIANS 5:21). That's why He is the only way. Anything else will always fall short.

JESUS WILL NEVER LET US INTO HIS HOME IF WE'RE STRANGERS TO HIM.

Seven days in . . . the gospel

IN HIS GRIP

BIBLE: ROMANS 8:31-39

I press on to take hold of that for which Christ Jesus took hold of me
(PHILIPPIANS 3:12).

I went climbing at my local gym for the first time a few days ago. The instructor climbed up the wall with me, talking me through it and showing me where to put my feet as I pushed myself higher. When I started wobbling, I grabbed for his hand. As I held on to him, I felt a lot safer. But it wasn't really my grip on him that kept me from slipping, but his grip on me.

Something similar is true in our Christian lives: it's not the tightness of our grip on God that keeps us safe, but the power of Jesus' hold on us. So Paul tells us, "Christ Jesus took hold of me" (PHILIPPIANS 3:12). Or more exactly, "Jesus has a grip on me!" No one can take us out of His hands—not the devil, not even ourselves. Once we're in His hands, He will not let go.

We have this promise: "I give them eternal life, and they shall never perish; no one will snatch them out of my hand. My Father, who has given them to me, is greater than all; no one can snatch them out of my Father's hand" (JOHN 10:28-29).

With Jesus firmly holding us, we couldn't be safer. These are the hands that shaped the mountains and oceans and flung the stars into space. Nothing in this life or the next "will be able to separate us from the love of God that is in Christ Jesus our Lord" (ROMANS 8:39).

DR

COMPLETING THE PICTURE . . .

In one sense, eternal life simply means going to heaven after we die. However, Jesus said, "Now this is eternal life: that they know you, the only true God, and Jesus Christ, whom you have sent" (JOHN 17:3). Eternal life isn't just living forever; it is being in a relationship with God. We don't have to wait for heaven to enjoy unending life with God; our life with God starts as soon as we trust Jesus!

JESUS HOLDS US AND HE WON'T LET GO.

Seven days in . . . the gospel

NEW CREATIONS

BIBLE: 2 CORINTHIANS 5:14-21

Therefore, if anyone is in Christ, the new creation has come: the old has gone, the new is here! (V.17).

Joanna Flanders-Thomas shared the message of Jesus in South Africa's most violent prison. Joanna started visiting prisoners every day, bringing them a simple gospel message of forgiveness and new life with God. She earned their trust, got them to talk about their abusive childhoods, and showed them that God could help them handle and overcome their issues. The year before her visits began, the prison had nearly three hundred acts of violence against prisoners and guards; the next year there were just two.

We're told, "If anyone is in Christ, the new creation has come: the old has gone, the new is here!" (2 CORINTHIANS 5:17). While we may not always see that newness as dramatically as that prison, the gospel's power to completely transform us is the greatest hope-providing force in the universe. New creations; brand new people! What an amazing thought! The death of Jesus launches us on a journey of becoming like Him—a journey that will be complete when we see Him face to face in total perfection (SEE 1 JOHN 3:1-3).

As Christians we celebrate our life as new, forgiven people. Yet we must never lose sight of what that cost Jesus. His death and resurrection bring us life. "Because of his great love for us, God, who is rich in mercy, made us alive with Christ even when we were dead in [sin]—it is by grace you have been saved" (EPHESIANS 2:4-5).

BC

WHAT I'M THANKFUL FOR . . .

Loving Father, I thank You that, because of what Jesus did on the cross, I am a new person. Forgive me for the times I return to my old way of life and make everything all about me. Thank You that my new life is all about Jesus and how awesome He is!

BELONGING TO JESUS BRINGS REAL CHANGE IN WHO WE ARE AND HOW WE LIVE.

Seven days in . . . the gospel

LOOKING GOOD

BIBLE: JEREMIAH 3:4-10

"Judah did not return to me with all her heart, but only in pretence," declares the LORD (V.10).

A guy accidentally bumped a parked car when he was driving. So he put a note under the car's windshield wiper that read, "I have just smashed into your car. The people who saw the accident are watching me. They think I'm writing down my name and address. I'm not."

In Jeremiah 3, the people of Judah also pretended to do the right thing. They made a show of returning to God and saying sorry for how they had lived, but in reality the hearts of the people remained far from Him. They called God "Father," but they continued doing whatever they could get away with (JEREMIAH 3:4-5).

I can't think of anything I'm more concerned about in myself than how I act towards God. Am I genuine? Do I love Him? Or is Jesus just a 'get out of jail free' card? He gets me into heaven, so I can just carry on doing whatever I want when no one is looking. That kind of attitude suggests we're not really God's people at all.

It's easy to say, "Jesus is my Lord and Saviour. He died for our sins and deserves my life and love." But it's not so easy to remember our commitment to Him when no one is watching how we live.

Let's not kid ourselves. We're smart enough to look good in youth group and say the right things to our family and church friends. But what about our personal relationship with God? Do we have one? Who are we when we're alone with God? Because in the end, looking good to others means nothing.

MDH

THINKING IT OVER . . .

Read Matthew 23. Why does Jesus reject the Pharisees and teachers of the law (the 'good', 'religious' people of His day)?

IF WE'RE LIVING TO IMPRESS OUR FRIENDS, WE'RE NOT LIVING FOR GOD.

ON OUR SIDE

BIBLE: ROMANS 8:31-39

What, then, shall we say in response to these things?
If God is for us, who can be against us? (V.31).

A Christian guy was working at his first job—a weekend shift at a warehouse—earning some money as his school life was coming to an end and he had to work out what to do next. The people he worked with were pretty rough, and he was laughed at for being a Christian. They threw jokes and abuse at him during every break.

One break time was worse than the others. They were laughing at him, swearing and making fun of Jesus. He was just about ready to quit. Then an older guy sitting at the back of the room said, "That's enough! Find someone else to pick on." They immediately backed off. Later the man said to the teenager, "I saw that you were having a difficult time, and I wanted to let you know I'm on your side."

Maybe you're a Christian and standing alone against others in your school or family who don't know God. Maybe it feels like things are only getting worse. We can definitely tell our church family about how hard things are and expect them to support us and stand with us. But even more than that, we can be confident that God is on our side. He showed His commitment and love to us when He sent His Son Jesus to die in our place on the cross. We can never be separated from His love and care (ROMANS 8:38-39).

With confidence we can say, "If God is for us, who can be against us?" (V.31).

DE

WHAT I'M THANKFUL FOR . . .

Thank You Father that no matter how hard things are, I know You are right here with me. No one can stand against Your promises to me; no one can match Your strength. Please put people in my life to help me remember this truth.

WITH GOD ON OUR SIDE WE ARE NEVER OUTNUMBERED.

HOPE

BIBLE: I PETER 1:3-9

Praise be to the God and Father of our Lord Jesus Christ! In his great mercy he has given us new birth into a living hope through the resurrection of Jesus Christ from the dead (V.3).

Sometimes life is rubbish. Let's get one thing clear: knowing Jesus doesn't change that. Nothing in the Bible promises us a free pass just because we are Jesus' followers. In fact, some of our hurts may never fully heal and some of our problems may not be corrected during our lifetime. They may even get worse. Yet our issues and weaknesses are only temporary.

Looking ahead to what God has in store for us changes our perspective on everything we have to go through. Hope (our confidence in what He promises to do) allows us live in His strength, because we know that one day we will be totally different to what we are now. We will be made perfect in Jesus (1 JOHN 3:2).

If you feel damaged in some way or defeated by sin, or if you feel like everyone else is better than you, take some time to focus on what God has in store for you. Live today with the courage God gives you. Spend time focusing more on Him than on yourself. And rejoice, because everything that gets you down about yourself is in God's hands to change—or maybe even to use in ways you'd never thought of.

With our hope in Jesus, we can deal with yesterday's regret and today's pain because of our future. God's best for us lies ahead. *HR*

THINKING IT OVER . . .

Read 1 Thessalonians 4:16-18. What promise are we to encourage each other with (V.18)? How does our certain future with Jesus impact how we're living and how we view ourselves today?

BEING A CHRISTIAN ISN'T ABOUT ESCAPING OUR CIRCUMSTANCES; JESUS GIVES US THE STRENGTH TO GET THROUGH THEM.

NOT DATING

BIBLE: 1 CORINTHIANS 12:25-13:13

[Love] always protects, always trusts, always hopes, always perseveres (V.7).

In one survey, nearly 40% of young single people said they felt isolated or cut off in their churches. It was summed up by this sentence: "Single people feel invisible and think about leaving." That doesn't surprise me. As a single person, I've felt lonely in churches filled with couples or small friendship groups who just hang out together. I've also experienced awkward silences when I say I'm not dating or looking for a boyfriend right now.

It can be easy for all of us to think romantic relationships are what we're *meant* to do, even in the church. But with that point of view, single people may find they are not invested in by their church very much.

In the Bible, Paul described church as *one* body meant to share joy and suffering together (1 CORINTHIANS 12:25-26). Each person is needed for the good of everyone else, regardless of our relationship status (VV.7,21-22). When Paul described the "most excellent way" (V.31), he didn't talk about dating or marriage, but the love we are all meant to live out (VV.12-13); a love that "never gives up, never loses faith, is always hopeful and endures through every circumstance" (13:7 NLT).

This love is about more than finding someone to date. It is about something much bigger than ourselves (12:4-6): it's about being saved by Jesus and living for God *together* as a church family! Our life with God may involve different romances, or it may not. The main thing is that we, and our church, stick close to Him.

MB

THINKING IT OVER . . .

Does your relationship status affect your church life or how people talk with you? How can you set an example to your church of living firstly for God? Read 1 Peter 4:8-10 and think about why we need to deepen our love for each other "above all".

LOVING OUR CHURCH FAMILY IS THE "MOST EXCELLENT WAY".

DARK SECRETS

BIBLE: PSALM 32:1-11

When I kept silent, my bones wasted away through my groaning all day long (V.3).

Do you have a dark secret that you've not told anybody about? Maybe it's something you are constantly day dreaming about, and think that if your friends and family found out, they'd want nothing to do with you. Or maybe you've fallen into a bad habit that you can't stop.

Some people think that it's best to keep these struggles hidden away, so no one ever finds out about them. But as one guy learned, keeping dark secrets isn't good for us.

David, one of Israel's greatest kings, chose to sleep with another man's wife and got her pregnant. When he was unable to cover it up, he arranged for the woman's husband to be killed. Soon after, he married the grieving widow (2 SAMUEL 11:1-27).

For over a year, David hid his secret. He didn't tell a single person, not even God. But keeping it hidden tore him up inside. In Psalm 32, David wrote about this time in his life, "When I kept silent, my bones wasted away through my groaning all day long" (PSALM 32:3). The torture of hiding his secret ended when he broke down and admitted what he had done. "I acknowledged my sin to you and did not cover up [what I had done] . . . And you forgave the guilt of my sin" (V.5; SEE ALSO 2 SAMUEL 12:1-13).

Are you hiding a secret that's making you sick inside? Talk to God about it and share it with your youth leader or someone in your church you feel safe with. You'll soon find out one of the 'best kept secrets' of life—the power of owning up and walking through our struggles with other Christians (JAMES 5:16).

JO

THINKING IT OVER . . .

What's stopping you from admitting your secret sins to God and other Christians? Read Psalm 51:1-12 and think about what happens when we open up to God.

SECRETS LOSE THEIR POWER OVER YOU WHEN THEY ARE BROUGHT INTO THE LIGHT.

TRAINING

BIBLE: 1 TIMOTHY 4:6-16

Physical training is of some value, but godliness has value for all things, holding promise for both the present life and the life to come (V.8).

- -

I'm not going to join the track team again! I said that to myself lots of times during school. But every track season, there I was, back on the team.

Why did I have a love/hate relationship with running? The training! During practice, we pushed ourselves really hard. After each session we'd ache for days! But we also got fitter and faster. So, even though I disliked all the training, it was good for me.

There's another kind of training that is far more important—training in godliness. Because walking with God doesn't just happen. It takes effort, like training for a race. We have to be intentional about it.

How? Firstly, just like physical training, we need to watch what we eat. What are you filling yourself up with? Reality TV? Social media feeds? Paul encouraged Timothy, who he mentored, to fill up firstly on the truth and good teaching of the Bible (1 TIMOTHY 4:6). Taking time out to be with God and think about all He says to us is great training for living with Him! In fact, it's essential!

Secondly, let's use our time well. Paul told Timothy, "Do not waste time arguing over godless ideas and old wives' tales" (V.7 NLT). We can't simply wish we had time to hang out with God—we need to actually make time and stick to it.

I take lots of walks with God. Along the way, I like to listen to sermons or simply talk with Him about what's going on. These 'workouts' have been great for my training in godliness.

PFC

THINKING IT OVER . . .

Read Psalm 1:1-3 and write down all the things here that define someone who is trained in godliness.

WE DON'T *DRIFT* WITH GOD; WE *WALK* WITH HIM!

WHAT YOU'RE WORTH

BIBLE: ZECHARIAH 11:4-13

The LORD said to me, "Throw it to the potter!" (V.13).

Caitlin blogged about the depression she battled after fighting off an assault. The emotional violence had cut her deeper than the physical struggle with her attacker. She felt it proved "how undesirable I was. I was not the kind of girl you wanted to get to know." She felt unworthy of love; like she was the kind of person others use and then throw away.

God truly understands. He lovingly looked after His people Israel, but when He asked them what He was worth, "they paid me thirty pieces of silver" (ZECHARIAH 11:12). This was the price of a slave; what masters had to be given if their slave was accidentally killed (EXODUS 21:32). God was insulted to be offered the lowest possible value—"[look at] the handsome price at which they valued me!" He said sarcastically (ZECHARIAH 11:13). And He had Zechariah throw the money away.

Jesus truly understands. He was betrayed by Judas, one of His friends. But more than that, the Jewish leaders so hated Him that they only offered Judas thirty pieces of silver—the lowest price you could put on a person—and he took it (MATTHEW 26:14-15; 27:9). Judas thought so little of Jesus he sold Him for nearly nothing.

If people undervalued Jesus, don't be surprised when they undervalue you. Your value isn't what others say. It's not even what you say. It's entirely and only what God says. He says you are worth dying for.   *MW*

TO PRAY ABOUT . . .

Dear God, please remind me just how much You love me. You sent Your Son to die in my place and make me Your own child. Help me remember this is my true identity and value.

GOD VALUES YOU SO HIGHLY, HE DID WHATEVER IT WOULD TAKE TO MAKE YOU HIS OWN.

LOSING TO GAIN

BIBLE: 2 CORINTHIANS 9:6-15

God is able to bless you abundantly, so that in all things at all times, having all that you need, you will abound in every good work **(V.8)**.

The fields on my dad's farm were sowed by hand. That meant he would strap on a canvas bag that looked like a kangaroo pouch, fill it with seeds and go out to sow. He would throw the seeds everywhere on that field.

When he did this, it looked like he was throwing the seeds away. They seemed to be lost, but they weren't really gone. After some time had passed, he got those seeds back, as fruit or grain.

When we give ourselves to Jesus, it may look to our friends and family as if we're throwing our lives away. But He said that it is only as we lose our lives in Him that we find true life **(MATTHEW 10:39)**.

Jesus teaches us to measure our lives by what we lose, rather than by what we get; by sacrifices rather than awards; by time spent for others rather than time for ourselves; by the love we give rather than the attention we get.

It's a rule of life: God gives us everything we need. So we can be people who give and serve **(2 CORINTHIANS. 9:6)**. We know that God will never leave us empty. The question is, *Do we trust Him enough to be generous? Are we prepared to rely on Him more than ourselves?* It's a learning process for sure! But from it, "others will praise God for the obedience that accompanies your confession of the gospel of Christ" **(V.13)**.

DR

THINKING IT OVER . . .

Read Psalm 145 and write down all the reasons we have to praise God for all He has given us and for how He stays with us no matter what.

FOLLOWING JESUS MEANS OUR LIVES BELONG TO HIM, NOT OURSELVES.

HITTING THE MARK

BIBLE: 1 JOHN 3:1-10

When Christ appears, we shall be like him, for we shall see him as he is (V.2).

My brother is a really good archer. He can pull back a bow and release an arrow with just the right amount of force and focus. One day he shot an arrow that hit the exact spot of another arrow, splitting it in two!

Through Jesus, we can 'hit the mark' of God's holiness—becoming more like Him. If this seems impossible to you, you're not alone. In my life, spiritual change has been a stop-and-start sort of thing.

When I mess up, it makes Jesus' perfection all the more amazing to me. Jesus never sinned (1 JOHN 3:5). Not one bad thought. Not one selfish motive. Not one wrong action. In every challenge he faced, his 'arrow' landed in the bull's eye of God's holiness.

I won't make it to Jesus' level of holiness on my own, but I can make small steps towards it with God's help. When I mess up, His Spirit lets me know, guides me back on track and helps me to avoid making the same mistake again. Over time, my way of life changes as God's Spirit works in me and changes me.

This work will continue in all Christians until Jesus returns to earth. He will then complete the Spirit's work in us and finally, "We [will] be like him for we [will] see him as he is" (v.2). When it feels like change is slow, the promise of this 'on-target' future gives us hope.

JBS

WHAT I'M THANKFUL FOR . . .

Dear God, thank You for promising to complete my holiness which started on the day I trusted Jesus. Today, I thank You that Your Spirit is at work in me, making me more like You.

EVEN ON OUR WORST DAY, WE'RE STILL HEADED TO HEAVEN TO BE WITH JESUS.

ALERT CIRCLES

BIBLE: HEBREWS 10:19-25

Encourage one another and build each other up (1 THESSALONIANS 5:11).

African gazelles instinctively make 'alert circles' while they rest. They gather in groups with each animal facing outward in a slightly different direction. This allows them to fully see the horizon that surrounds them so they can warn each other as soon as they see any dangers coming from any direction.

Instead of looking out just for themselves, the gazelles take care of one another. This is also God's plan for Christians. The Bible tells us, "Let us consider how we may spur one another on towards love and good deeds, not giving up meeting together" (HEBREWS 10:24-25).

Christians were never meant to go it alone. Together we are stronger. We are able to "[encourage] one another" (V.25), to "comfort those in any trouble with the comfort we ourselves receive from God" (2 CORINTHIANS 1:4) and to help each other stay alert to the dangers, lies and temptations from our enemy the devil, who "prowls around like a roaring lion looking for someone to devour" (1 PETER 5:8).

Being in church is about more than survival. It is to make us like Jesus: loving and clear examples of God in this world. And we are in this together, looking forward confidently to the day when Jesus returns. All of us need encouragement, and God gives us what we need to help each other stay close to Him. *JB*

WHAT I'M THANKFUL FOR . . .

Thank You for Your faithfulness, loving God. Please help me to encourage others to stay close to You and to look forward to seeing Jesus face to face!

OUR CHURCH FAMILY HELPS US STAY FAR FROM DANGER AND CLOSE TO GOD.

WHERE ARE YOU?

BIBLE: DEUTERONOMY 31:1-8

The LORD himself goes before you and will be with you; he will never leave you nor forsake you. Do not be afraid; do not be discouraged (V.8).

The girl, panicking, called her dad. She needed him to be home by 6:00 p.m. to drive her to music practice on time.

"Dad! Where are you?"

"I'm here. Just pulling up on the drive. Why don't you trust me?"

I wonder how often could our heavenly Father ask that of us? *Why don't you trust me?* In stressful moments, I too am impatient. I too struggle to trust, to believe God will keep His promises. So I shout out: "Where are you?"

In stress and uncertainty, I sometimes doubt that God is right here with me. I struggle to remember that He is good, will never leave me, and has a plan for my life. The Israelites were the same. In Deuteronomy 31, they were preparing to enter the Promised Land, knowing their leader, Moses, would stay behind. Moses reassured God's people by reminding them, "The LORD himself goes before you and will be with you; he will never leave you nor forsake you. Do not be afraid; do not be discouraged" (DEUTERONOMY 31:8).

That promise—that God is always with us—is a core part of our relationship with Him (SEE MATTHEW 1:23; HEBREWS 13:5). And Revelation 21:3 promises this is our future too: "God's dwelling place is now among the people, and he will dwell with them."

Where is God? He is right here, right now, right with us—always ready to hear our prayers.

JB

WANT MORE . . . ?

Why not read the description in Psalm 139 of God's presence with you.

GOD IS ALWAYS WITH US, ALWAYS PRESENT, ALWAYS AVAILABLE.

OUT OF CONTEXT

BIBLE: JOHN 20:13-16

She turned around and saw Jesus standing there, but she did not realise that it was Jesus (V.14).

Someone tapped my shoulder and said, "Hi!" After seeing my blank stare, she added, "It's me. Jane!" My mind flipped through a couple of different "Janes" I knew, but I couldn't place her. Was she from an old school? Did she come to youth group once? I didn't have a clue.

Then she added, "We were in the same netball club." Then I remembered! I hadn't played netball for a few years, but once I knew the context, I recognised Jane.

After Jesus' death, Mary Magdalene went to the tomb early in the morning and found the stone rolled away and His body gone (JOHN 20:1-2). She ran to get Peter and John, who returned with her to see the empty grave (VV.3-10). But Mary, full of grief, stayed outside in the garden (V.11). When Jesus appeared there, "she did not realise that it was Jesus" (V.14), thinking He was the gardener (V.15).

How could she have not recognised Jesus? Was His resurrected body so changed that He looked different? Did her tears blind her eyes? Or, perhaps, like me, was it because Jesus was 'out of context', alive in the garden instead of dead in the tomb, that she didn't recognise Him?

Are we ready and expecting to hear Jesus in any context? Not just during prayer or Bible reading, but through other conversations or situations. Or are we also in danger of not recognising Him?

EM/CW

TO PRAY ABOUT . . .

Dear God, help me to look and listen for Jesus today, both in the expected place of the Bible, and in other conversations and events.

EXPECT JESUS.

LIGHTNING AND THUNDER

BIBLE: JAMES 2:14-26

You foolish person, do you want evidence that faith without deeds is useless? (V.20).

Lightning and thunder are a good illustration of the relationship between faith (what we believe) and what we do. When lightning flashes across the sky, we know that the roar of thunder will follow. Without lightning, there would be no thunder, because one leads to the other. In the same way, doing good, loving things always goes together with faith (full trust) in Jesus, because one leads to the other.

We must always remember that we are only saved by God's love and grace. Ephesians 2:8-9 says, "For it is by grace you have been saved, through faith—and this is not from yourselves, it is the gift of God—not by works, so that no one can boast." Maybe we know that verse quite well. It's a good one to memorise. But do we know the verse that comes after? "For we are God's handiwork, created in Christ Jesus to do good works, which God prepared in advance for us to do" (EPHESIANS 2:10).

In the same way that thunder doesn't cause lightning, living a good, God-centred life adds nothing to our salvation. But that life is the 'sound' of faith. If we truly trust Jesus and have given our lives to Him, it will show. We won't be able to live in the same way anymore—our lives, actions, thoughts and motives will all be about living for Him! And it is that change in us that helps show we are really His. But 'faith' without any evidence of a changed life is not the real thing (JAMES 2:17).   *RDH*

WANT MORE . . . ?

Check out *How do I know I am a Christian?* online at
ourdailybread.org/lookingdeeper

IF WE'VE GIVEN OUR LIVES TO JESUS, IT'LL SHOW IN HOW WE LIVE.

PHOBIA

BIBLE: ISAIAH 51:1-16

I, even I, am he who comforts you. Who are you that you fear mere mortals, human beings who are but grass, that you forget the LORD your Maker, who stretches out the heavens and who lays the foundations of the earth . . . ?
(VV.12-13).

Lots of people have phobias. There are really common ones like claustrophobia (the fear of confined spaces) and arachnophobia (the fear of spiders). But have you heard of some of these more 'out there' phobias? Nomophobia (the fear of being without your smartphone), hippopotomonstrosesquippedaliophobia (the fear of long words, ironically!), cyberphobia (the fear of computers), erythrophobia (the fear of blushing) or phobophobia (the fear of phobias!).

If we're seriously affected by our phobias, they can really disrupt our lives. They might lead to things like panic attacks, difficulty breathing, dizziness and paralysing fear. Logically, phobias don't make much sense. Why are we so affected by such small things? Yet the fear is real.

Many of us have another phobia that can be equally paralysing—the fear of other people's opinions. Sometimes we think and act as if our future and wellbeing rest solely in the hands of our friends, family and classmates.

Isaiah told us how it looks to God when we become so worried about what people think of us that we panic and forget to trust Him first. He said that getting worked up over our friends' opinions is a bad idea because they are just people who have little more real strength and permanency than grass (ISAIAH 51:12). They do not compare to what God thinks of us.

God knows how other people can hurt us (VV.13-14). But He has the last word. Our future and unending wellbeing depend on Him and Him alone.   MDH

WHAT I'M THANKFUL FOR . . .

Thank You, Father, that You love me. You sent Jesus to die in my place and give me new, unending life with You as Your child. That's who I am, and that's how much I am loved by the King. No other opinion of me even begins to compare to the truth!

WHAT PEOPLE THINK OF US LASTS A MOMENT; WHAT GOD THINKS OF US LASTS FOREVER.

GOD'S GOOD ANGER

BIBLE: NAHUM 1

The LORD is a jealous and avenging God; the LORD takes vengeance and is filled with wrath . . . The LORD is good, a refuge in times of trouble (VV.2,7).

One guy became an atheist after he read the words of Jesus about hell. He apparently wanted a God who would never become angry or punish anyone. That guy definitely wouldn't like today's Bible reading, which talks about God as One who "is a jealous and avenging God" (NAHUM 1:2).

Personally, I would have trouble believing in a God who never became angry and didn't punish sin, evil and the terrible things in our world. Such a God would not be a good God. What would you think, for example, of a witness to a brutal murder who felt no emotion and didn't care about what they saw? Would you think they were good? No way!

God allows us to make our own choices, and usually doesn't stop us from doing whatever we want, right or wrong, good or bad, God-centred or selfish. But He does hold us responsible for the choices we make, and He will judge us. In Nahum's day, the Ninevites were a cruel, violent people who did unbelievably gross things. But Nahum promised God's people that God saw the wickedness of the Ninevites, was angered by it and would justly punish them.

I'm thankful that God is good. And that His anger and judgements are good. It gives me reason to trust Him to keep all His promises, and it reminds me that He will right all the wrongs of history when Jesus returns.

HVL

THINKING IT OVER . . .

Read Psalm 96. Do you praise God for His coming judgement? Why or why not? What is missing in your relationship with Him if you're not rejoicing that "he will judge the world in righteousness" (PSALM 96:13)?

GOD'S ANGER IS ALWAYS GOOD AND HOLY.

HOLD FAST

BIBLE: MATTHEW 4:1-11

So do not fear, for I am with you; do not be dismayed, for I am your God. I will
strengthen you and help you; I will uphold you with my righteous right hand
(ISAIAH 41:10).

On the day before my mum died, my brother and I sat by her bed. She was very weak, but even so, she managed to quote two verses—Isaiah 41:10 and John 10:29. She didn't just say them to comfort us, but to reinforce her own trust in God. She held tightly to what God had said; and what God said held her tight.

The Bible has tremendous holding power. When tempted in the wilderness, Jesus overcame the devil by quoting verses (MATTHEW. 4:3-10). He did this to strengthen Himself, not to intimidate His enemy. The Bible leaves no doubt that Jesus was "tempted in every way, just as we are—yet he did not sin" (HEBREWS 4:15). Jesus did not quote verses because they contained some magical power. He called them to mind to guide and strengthen Himself so that He would stay true to God's plan. Because He kept His life under the control and direction of the Bible, the devil could not defeat Him or distract Him from doing His Father's will.

Whenever we are tested—whether it's a strong temptation, a paralysing worry, a really bad habit we're struggling to break or anything else—we need to practise turning our attention to the Bible. That is where our confidence in God, and our love for Him and His ways, will grow.

DDH

THINKING IT OVER . . .

Do you have verses of the Bible you have memorised? Memorising verses can be
a really helpful way to have them at the forefront of your mind to reflect on,
especially during hard times. If you are struggling with temptations, why not
spend time thinking about and memorising these verses to start: Matthew 4:4,
1 Corinthians 10:13, 2 Timothy 1:7.

**EITHER THE BIBLE WILL HELP KEEP YOU FROM SIN;
OR SIN WILL KEEP YOU FROM READING THE BIBLE.**

LETTER OF RECOMMENDATION

BIBLE: 2 CORINTHIANS 2:17-3:6

You yourselves are our letter, written on our hearts, known and read by everyone (V.2).

Sometimes students leaving school ask their teachers to write letters of recommendation for them—for jobs, study-abroad programmes, college applications or other opportunities. In each letter, the teachers have a chance to praise each student's character and abilities.

When Christians travelled in the ancient world, they often carried with them similar letters of recommendation from their churches. A letter like that made sure that the traveller would be welcomed at any church they came to.

The apostle Paul didn't need a letter of recommendation when he spoke to the church in Corinth—they knew him. In his second letter to that church, Paul wrote that he preached the gospel out of genuine care, not for personal gain (2 CORINTHIANS 2:17). But then he wondered if his readers would think that in defending his motives in preaching, he was trying to write a letter of recommendation for himself.

He didn't need such a letter, he said, because the people in the church in Corinth were themselves like letters of recommendation. The obvious work of Jesus in their lives was like a letter "written not with ink but with the Spirit of the living God" (3:3). Their lives clearly showed the true gospel Paul had preached to them—their lives were letters of recommendation that could be "known and read by everyone" (3:2). As we follow Jesus, this becomes true of us too—our lives tell the story of how good it is to belong to God and be changed by His Spirit.

AP

TO PRAY ABOUT . . .

Jesus, I want others to see You in my life.
May I become less and You become more.

OUR LIVES ARE LETTERS FROM JESUS TO THE WORLD.

CARING PRAYERS

BIBLE: ROMANS 15:30-33

I urge you, brothers and sisters, by our Lord Jesus Christ and by the love of the Spirit, to join me in my struggle by praying to God for me (V.30).

I got a message from a friend. He set a great example we all can learn from, because his message showed how much he believed in the power of prayer.

He told me about a girl in his school who had become pregnant. Her parents were threatening to force her to get an abortion.

When my friend heard about it, he got on his phone and messaged hundreds of people, telling them about the girl's situation and asking over and over, "Please pray for this girl." His compassion for her was obvious—as well as his trust in God to answer prayer.

My friend could have used his phone to gossip about that girl. Or he could have just forgotten about her and started playing games or browsing Instagram. Instead, he used his social media to get the right kind of attention for this girl and her needs.

In Romans 15:30-33, the apostle Paul showed that he knew the value of prayer—whether it's for ourselves or for someone else in need. What a lesson! It reminds us to always come to God with the stuff that's going on. And it shows us an example of the kind of love that leads us to team up with others in caring prayer.

DB

WHAT I'M THANKFUL FOR . . .

Thank You, God, that I can bring every need to You.
Thank You for faithfully answering our prayers!

THERE'S NOT A SINGLE PERSON IN THE WORLD YOU CAN'T HELP BY PRAYING FOR THEM.

THE STRUGGLE

BIBLE: EPHESIANS 6:10-20

Our struggle is . . . against the powers of this dark world (V.12).

In 1896, an explorer named Carl Akely was in a remote section of Ethiopia. He was also being chased by an 80-pound leopard. He remembered the leopard pouncing, trying "to sink her teeth into my throat." She missed, snagging his right arm with her vicious jaws. The two rolled in the sand—a long, fierce struggle. Akely weakened, and "it became a question of who would give up first." Summoning his last bit of strength, Akely was able to suffocate the big cat with simply his bare hands.

In the Bible, Paul explained how each of us who trust Jesus will face our own fierce struggles at some point; those times when we feel overwhelmed and just want to give it all up. Instead, we must "stand firm" and take our "stand against the devil's schemes" (EPHESIANS 6:11,14). Rather than crumbling as we see our weaknesses and issues, Paul challenged us to step forward with our confidence in God, remembering that we don't rely on our own courage and strength but in His. "Be strong in the Lord and in his mighty power," he wrote (V.10). In the challenges we face, He's only a prayer away (V.18).

Yes, we have many struggles, and we will never escape them by our own power or abilities. But God is more powerful than any enemy or evil we will ever face.

WC

THINKING IT OVER . . .

Read Colossians 1:21-23. What hope do these verses give,
especially on days when the struggle is hardest?

WHEN THE STRUGGLE IS REAL, GOD IS OUR SAFETY.

THE COCKEYED SQUID

BIBLE: COLOSSIANS 3:1-4

Set your minds on things above, not on earthly thing (V.2).

The cockeyed squid lives in the ocean's 'twilight zone' where sunlight barely filters through the deep, dark waters. The squid got its nickname from its two extremely different eyes: the left eye develops over time to become considerably larger than the right—almost twice as big. Scientists studying the squid have worked out that it uses its right eye, the smaller one, to look down into the darker depths. The larger, left eye, gazes upward, towards the sunlight.

The squid is a surprising image of what it means to live in our world as Christians. We, like the squid, keep one eye on what's going on around us, while also keeping one eye fixed 'upwards' on the future certainty we wait for as people who "have been raised with Christ" (COLOSSIANS 3:1). In Paul's letter to the Colossians, he is clear that we should "set [our] minds on things above" because our lives are "hidden with Christ in God" (VV.2-3).

We live on earth, but we know "our citizenship is in heaven" (PHILIPPIANS 3:20). We belong in heaven and we "eagerly" wait for Jesus to take us there (V.20). But we also need to be involved in what's going on here and now, helping others to find their true identity in Jesus and to also look ahead to the future God has promised.

We may not have yet fully grasped what it means to be alive in Jesus, but as we look at "things above", our eyes will begin to see it more and more.   *KH*

TO PRAY ABOUT . . .

Dear God, help me to focus my thoughts, needs and wants on those things that are all about You!

WE ALWAYS HAVE ONE EYE ON HEAVEN.

BREAKING THE CYCLE

BIBLE: 2 CORINTHIANS 5:11-21

If anyone is in Christ, the new creation has come: the old has gone, the new is here! (V.17).

David's first beating came at the hands of his dad on his seventh birthday, after he accidentally broke a window. "He kicked me and punched me . . . Later he said sorry. He was an abusive alcoholic, and it's a cycle I'm doing my best to end now."

But it took a long time for David to get to this point. Most of his teen years and twenties were spent in jail or on probation, and in and out of addiction treatment centres. When it felt like his dreams were completely destroyed, he found hope when someone introduced him to Jesus.

"I used to be filled with nothing but despair," David said. "Now I'm pushing myself in the other direction. When I get up in the morning, the first thing I tell God is that I'm surrendering my will over to Him."

When we come to God with broken, messy and even abused lives, no matter whose fault it all is, God takes us just as we are and makes us brand new: "If anyone is in Christ . . . the old has gone, the new is here!" (2 CORINTHIANS 5:17). Jesus' love breaks the cycles of our past, giving us new strength and a new direction to go in (vv.14-15). And it doesn't end there! Throughout our lives, He never stops making us more like Himself (3:18).

AK

THINKING IT OVER . . .

Where were you headed before you gave your life to Jesus? How does it help to know that God continues to shape your life to make you more and more like Him?

WHATEVER CYCLES WE'RE STUCK IN —JESUS PROMISES TO BREAK THEM.

HE CHANGED ME

BIBLE: EZEKIEL 18:21-32

But if a wicked person . . . does what is just and right, they will save their life (V.27).

When John, who ran the biggest brothel in London, was found guilty of blackmail and sent to prison, he mistakenly thought, *But I'm a good guy*. He decided to go to the Bible study at the prison for the cake and coffee, thinking he could also "fill [his] pockets" when the leaders closed their eyes to pray.

But while there, he was struck by how happy the guys seemed. He started to cry during one song, and later was given a Bible. Reading Ezekiel 18 changed him, hitting him "like a thunderbolt. I realised I wasn't a good guy . . . I was wicked and I needed to change." While praying with the prison chaplain, "I found Jesus Christ and He changed me."

The words John read in the Bible came from a place of pain. They were written by Ezekiel, a priest who should have been working in the temple. But he and the Israelites had been sent away by God because He was judging their sin and selfishness. Yet Ezekiel was given God's message to His people, "Repent and live!" (EZEKIEL 18:32). God told the Israelites to stop going their own way and to "get a new heart and a new spirit" (V.31). Those words from Ezekiel helped John, although still in prison, to be set free and live a new life as a child of God (SEE JOHN 1:12-13; 8:32).

ABP

TO PRAY ABOUT . . .

Father God, thank You that the Bible and Your Holy Spirit help me realise I am not a 'good' person. I need Jesus too. Help me to find my life and freedom in knowing Him.

NONE OF US ARE 'GOOD' —THAT'S WHY WE ALL NEED JESUS SO MUCH.

SAFELY ASHORE

BIBLE: PSALM 139

Peace, be still! (MARK 4:39 NKJV).

In Papua New Guinea, the Kandas tribe awaited with excitement the arrival of New Testament Bibles printed in their language. To get there, however, both the books and their visitors had to travel on the ocean in small boats to reach the village.

What gave them the bravery to travel across such a vast amount of water in such little boats? Their seafaring skills, sure. But they also knew who created the seas. He is the One who guides all of us across life's deepest waters.

As David wrote, "Where can I go from your Spirit?" (PSALM 139:7). "If I go up to the heavens, you are there . . . if I settle on the far side of the sea, even there your hand will guide me, your right hand will hold me fast" (VV.8-10).

These words would be very meaningful for the Kandas, who live as an island nation with tropical coasts, thick rainforests and rugged mountains. They have been called "The Last Unknown." Yet as Christians there and everywhere know, no place or problem is too far away for God. "Even the darkness will not be dark to you," says Psalm 139:12, and "the night will shine like the day, for darkness is as light to you."

If we find ourselves on stormy waters, Jesus says, "Peace, be still!" and the waves and wind obey (MARK 4:39 NKJV). So, don't stress and panic about life's deep waters today. Our God leads us through them.

PR

WHAT I'M THANKFUL FOR . . .

Dear heavenly Father, You rule life's winds and waves, and we thank You for guiding us safely through each day.

NO PLACE OR PROBLEM IS TOO REMOTE FOR GOD.

HANGING ON TO GRUDGES

BIBLE: 1 CORINTHIANS 13

[Love] does not dishonour others, it is not self-seeking, it is not easily angered, it keeps no record of wrongs (V.5).

One guy once wrote, "Take away grudges from some people and you remove their reason for living." Hanging on to our grudges may seem pretty normal, but it isn't a good idea. Holding a grudge poisons our minds, damaging our relationship with Jesus and others. Yet grudges feel so right! How can we put them down? It feels just like we're letting other people off the hook, when actually they don't deserve it!

The Bible teaches us that love "keeps no record of wrongs" (1 CORINTHIANS 13:5). Love doesn't hang on to grudges. When we love others like this, we "forgive as the Lord forgave you" (COLOSSIANS 3:13). When God forgave us, He got rid of our record against Him (PSALM 130:3-4)! How can we do any less?

When we forgive, we lay down our grudges, but not so they are forgotten. We lay them down so that God can pick them up and carry them for us. Our hurts are important. They matter a great deal to God. That is why Jesus came to pay for all sin in His death—because it all matters; it must all be paid for. So when we forgive someone, we're saying we're going to leave the issue between them and God. Let's never forget this truth: if they choose to trust Jesus, He pays for all their sin too.

"Do not take revenge, my dear friends, but leave room for God's wrath, for it is written: 'It is mine to avenge; I will repay,' says the Lord" (ROMANS 12:19). By trusting our loving Father we can stop clinging to our painful grudges. Instead we have His strength to forgive and leave the matter with Him. *BC*

THINKING IT OVER . . .

Read 1 Peter 2:22-23. How did Jesus live out Romans 12:19-20? What do your grudges show about your trust of God as your good, just Judge? Why not spend time praying for the people who've hurt you, asking God to help them turn to Him for forgiveness.

IF YOU DO NOT FORGIVE OTHERS THEIR SINS, YOUR FATHER WILL NOT FORGIVE YOUR SINS. MATTHEW 6:15

Seven days with . . . Abraham

INTO THE UNKNOWN

BIBLE: HEBREWS 11:8-16

By faith Abraham, when called to go to a place he would later receive as his inheritance, obeyed and went, even though he did not know where he was going (V.8).

I hate not knowing exactly what's going to happen next. So things like new teachers, new classes and changes to my routine stress me out. I even have to flick through the last pages of books before I start reading them, so I know where the story's heading . . .

So I find the story of Abraham very challenging. "By faith Abraham, when called to go to a place he would later receive as his inheritance, obeyed and went, even though he did not know where he was going" (HEBREWS 11:8). It sounds like a total nightmare scenario!

The start of Abraham's story is Genesis 12, where God says to him: "Go from your country, your people and your father's household to the land I will show you" (GENESIS 12:1). How could Abraham just get up and leave everything? "By faith": Abraham trusted God, so His promise was all he needed. God said He was going to take him somewhere important, and get him there, and that was enough for Abraham to trust his future to God.

Honestly, we don't know how things are going to work out most of the time. We often don't really know where we're headed. The story of Abraham shows us not knowing is OK, as long as we do know God. He will always lead us the right way.

DM

COMPLETING THE PICTURE . . .

Abraham (originally called Abram) was born nearly 2,000 years before Jesus. The world was full of selfishness and godlessness. But rather than destroy the world, God was going to provide salvation and new life. And He promised to do it through Abraham's family (SEE GENESIS 12:2-3; 15:5-6). Abraham's family eventually grew into the nation of Israel, who were led by God. It was to this nation that He promised to send Jesus, who would offer salvation to the whole world, starting with the Jews.

ARE YOU WILLING TO TRUST GOD INTO THE UNKNOWN?

Seven days with . . . Abraham

COVENANT PROMISE

BIBLE: GENESIS 15:5-21

When the sun had set and darkness had fallen, a smoking brazier with a blazing torch appeared and passed between the pieces (V.17).

In the ancient Near East a covenant (a binding agreement) between a lord or king and his people was called a suzerain treaty. The ceremony required animals to be sacrificed and cut in half. The animal parts were then arranged in two rows on the ground, forming an aisle between them. As the king walked between the halves, he was publicly saying that if he did not keep the covenant, then he deserved to be killed like those animals.

When Abraham (Abram) asked God how he could be sure His promises would come to pass, God used the suzerain treaty to confirm them (GENESIS 15). When the burning torch passed through the pieces of the sacrifice, Abraham understood that God was saying it was *His* job to keep the covenant.

God's covenant with Abraham also extends to those of us who trust Jesus. That is why Paul repeatedly calls Christians children of Abraham in his teaching (ROMANS 4:11-18; GALATIANS 3:29). Once we trust Jesus Christ as our Saviour, God becomes the one responsible for upholding His covenant promise to save us and keep us securely for heaven (SEE JOHN 10:28-29).

Because God is the keeper of our salvation, we can confidently trust Him with our lives.

RK

COMPLETING THE PICTURE . . .

When Jesus ate His last supper with His followers, He gave them bread and wine as symbols of the sacrifice He was about to make: "This is my blood of the covenant, which is poured out for many for the forgiveness of sins" (MATTHEW 26:28). Just like the covenant with Abraham, this covenant required a death—Jesus' death. His blood is the symbol that He will always keep His promise of full forgiveness and salvation for those who put their trust in Him (HEBREWS 10:12-18).

OUR SALVATION IS SECURE BECAUSE JESUS DOES THE HOLDING.

Seven days with . . . Abraham
HELPING GOD

BIBLE: GENESIS 16:1-16

[Sarah] said to Abram, "The LORD has kept me from having children. Go, sleep with my slave; perhaps I can build a family through her" (V.2).

Do you sometimes want to 'help' God out? Maybe He's being a bit slow to answer your prayers and so you start taking matters into your own hands, to nudge Him along . . .

God had promised Abraham that his descendants would be as countless as the stars and that he would be a dad, despite how old he was (GENESIS 15:1-5). Abraham believed God, but Sarah ran out of patience. She talked Abraham into having kids through her servant Hagar. Ishmael was born, but he wasn't the son God had promised (17:18-21). Fourteen years later, when Abraham and Sarah were very old, God did the impossible—Sarah conceived and the son of promise, Isaac, was born.

I remember someone once telling me: "I was in trouble. I needed to act quickly, but I was totally helpless. Finally I prayed, 'God, this is impossible for me. You'll have to take over completely. I can't even help You!'" She said that God had, in His timing, guided her through the difficulty—but it started with her admitting she was helpless—and giving the situation fully to Him.

When we rely on ourselves, people see what we can do and our story is simply, "Didn't I do well!" When we rely on God, people see what He can do and our story becomes, "Isn't God awesome!" What story are you telling today? *JY*

COMPLETING THE PICTURE . . .

Abraham was seventy-five years old (GENESIS 12:4) when God first promised him and Sarah a child—and eventually a huge people-group. Both Abraham and Sarah laughed at the idea of having a child: "[Abraham] laughed and said to himself, 'Will a son be born to a man a hundred years old?'" (17:17); "Sarah laughed to herself as she thought, 'After I am worn out and my lord is old, will I now have this pleasure?'" (18:12). But ultimately they trusted God, even though they were impatient for Him to provide. Isaac was eventually born, in God's perfect timing, when Abraham was one hundred (21:1-7).

IMPOSSIBLE SITUATIONS ARE GOD'S TERRITORY!

Seven days with . . . Abraham

NOTHING'S TOO HARD FOR GOD

BIBLE: GENESIS 18:1-14

Is anything too hard for the LORD? (V.14).

God is able to meet all our needs. Nothing is too difficult for Him. Sarah needed to learn this truth. God's promise to give Abraham a son is in Genesis 17:21. In the next chapter the promise was repeated to Abraham as he talked outside his tent with three men sent from God. This time Sarah overheard the conversation. To her, having a child in her old age was impossible. So she "laughed to herself" (GENESIS 18:12). God then said to Abraham, "Why did Sarah laugh and say, 'Will I really have a child, now that I am old?' Is anything too hard for the LORD?" (VV.13-14).

As Christians, we can have the same confidence. Abraham's God is our God, and He is all-powerful. He's the Creator of the universe. Nothing is too big for Him. No problem slows Him down. No obstacle can stand against Him. Our heavenly Father is in control of every situation.

What confidence it gives us! The all-knowing, all-present, all-powerful Creator and King can do anything. When we give our lives, our problems, our doubts and our stresses to our heavenly Father in prayer, He promises us that nothing is too hard for Him. He will lead us through it all. *RDH*

WHAT I'M THANKFUL FOR . . .

Thank You, God, that nothing is too hard for You. Every challenge I face, no matter how stressful or impossible, is tiny compared to You. Thank You that I go through it all with You, my Saviour and the unrivalled King of the universe.

NOTHING IS TOO DIFFICULT FOR GOD.

Seven days with . . . Abraham

THE HILL OF SACRIFICE

BIBLE: GENESIS 22:1-19

God said, "Take your son, your only son, whom you love—Isaac—and go to the region of Moriah. Sacrifice him there as a burnt offering on a mountain that I will show you" (V.2).

Do your parents have to wake you up in the morning to get you to school on time? When I read today's story about Abraham, I wonder if waking Isaac was part of his routine—and how different it must have been on this particular day.

Abraham had waited for this promised child for over twenty years. Yet now God said to Abraham, "Sacrifice [Isaac] as a burnt offering" (GENESIS 22:2)! What?

How must Abraham have felt?! Yet, despite his questions, confusion and pain, Abraham trusted God's words more than anything else. God had said Isaac was the promised child and the first of a great nation—so somehow Abraham knew He'd keep His promise. Abraham bound his son and laid him on an altar, but then God stepped in and provided another sacrifice (VV.11-14)!

Nearly two thousand years later, God provided again—the final sacrifice—His own Son. Think of how painful it must have been for God to watch His Son suffer and die, His only Son who He loved! And He went through all of that because He loves you and wanted to save you.

If you wonder whether you are loved by God, look to Jesus on the cross and see the price He paid for you.

JS

COMPLETING THE PICTURE . . .

As Abraham went to sacrifice Isaac on Mount Moriah, he told his son, "God himself will provide the lamb for the burnt offering" (GENESIS 22:8). Many Bible teachers believe that Moriah is the same place as (or very near to) Golgotha, where Jesus was sacrificed (JOHN 19:17). Isaac didn't have to die, and we don't have to die, because God provided the Lamb to die in our place, bearing our sin for us.

GOD HAS ALREADY PROVEN HIS LOVE FOR YOU.

Seven days with . . . Abraham

RESCUED OUT OF WRATH

BIBLE: GENESIS 18:16-33

[God] is patient with you, not wanting anyone to perish, but everyone to come to repentance (2 PETER 3:9).

Fire rained down and destroyed the grim, godless cities of Sodom and Gomorrah, which had rejected God and were full of selfishness, violence and all kinds of wickedness (SEE GENESIS 18:20-21; 19:3-5).

But before judgement came, God told Abraham that He was about to destroy the cities, "For I have chosen him, so that he will direct his children and his household after him to keep the way of the LORD by doing what is right and just" (18:19). God wanted Abraham to see where sin ends up, so that he would always stick close to Him.

Abraham then asked God to save Sodom if just ten God-centred people could be found (V.32). God answered, "For the sake of ten, I will not destroy it." Could ten people be found? Nope.

Yet God is "slow to anger, abounding in love and faithfulness" (PSALM 86:15). His wrath is never without the offer of rescue. Abraham's nephew, Lot (who still trusted God), and his family lived in Sodom. But when two angels came to rescue Lot's family (GENESIS 19:12-13), his sons-in-law thought the warning was a joke (V.14) and even Lot hesitated (V.15). At that point, the angels "grasped his hand and the hands of his wife and of his two daughters and led them safely out of the city, for the LORD was merciful to them" (V.16).

What is it God wanted Abraham to see? Both His judgement of those who refuse Him *and* His incredible commitment to save those who trust Him. *CW*

COMPLETING THE PICTURE . . .

One day God's wrath will come on this earth for a final time (SEE 2 PETER 3:7-10). Christians will be rescued from this day, just as Lot was, because Jesus took all our judgement on the cross. "In keeping with his promise we are looking forward to a new heaven and a new earth" (V.13). But this final day will "be the day of judgement and destruction of [everyone who says no to Jesus]" (V.7). It is our responsibility to make sure our friends, family and classmates know where this world is headed, so they can decide now whether they are going to suffer God's wrath, or be rescued out of it.

GOD'S WRATH IS NEVER WITHOUT THE OFFER OF RESCUE.

Seven days with . . . Abraham

GOD'S FAMILY

BIBLE: JOHN 8:39-47

To those who believed in his name, he gave the right to become children of God (JOHN 1:12).

Where I'm from, family surnames don't really matter—they are just names. But in some parts of the world, family names are really important; they are part of each person's identity. In many cultures, ancestry (or, family history) is important.

The Israelites believed in the importance of their family history too. They were proud of their nation's 'father': Abraham. They thought being part of Abraham's clan earned them God's favour and made them His children.

When Jesus was talking with the Jews, He pointed out that this wasn't the case. They could say Abraham was their earthly father, but if they didn't love Jesus—the One sent by the heavenly Father—they were not part of God's family. Just being a descendent of Abraham didn't give them a free pass into heaven.

It's the same for us. We can't choose our human family, but we have decided the spiritual family we belong to. From the moment we first trusted in Jesus, God gave us the right to become His children (JOHN 1:12). It's like Jesus has made us brand new with God's own DNA! We are now unmistakably His own family, and we will be welcomed into His home after we die.

KO

COMPLETING THE PICTURE . . .

While the nation of Israel were the privileged people God chose to make Himself known through, they still needed to have a relationship with Him for themselves. The Bible calls Abraham "God's friend" because he "believed God" (JAMES 2:23). True children of Abraham follow this exact path: we trust God and become part of the true nation of Abraham—God's family. "Understand, then, that those who have faith are children of Abraham . . . [God] announced the gospel in advance to Abraham: 'All nations will be blessed through you.' So those who rely on faith are blessed along with Abraham, the man of faith" (GALATIANS 3:7-9).

EVERY PERSON NEEDS TO MEET JESUS FOR THEMSELVES.

THAT WAS AWESOME!

BIBLE: PROVERBS 12:12,24-28

Diligent hands will rule, but laziness ends in forced labour (V.24).

It was her first cross-country school race, but she didn't want to run. She'd been practising for the event for weeks, but she was afraid of running badly. Still, she started the race with everyone else.

Later, one by one the other runners all crossed the finish line—everyone except the reluctant runner. Finally, her mum, who was watching for her daughter to finish, saw a lone figure in the distance. Her mum stood by the finish line, hoping to find some encouraging words to say. Instead, when the young runner saw her mum, she shouted, "That was awesome!"

What can be awesome about finishing last? *Finishing!*

The girl had tried something difficult and finished it! In the same way, the Bible says keeping going with things that are hard is an important skill for us to learn. We often like to take the easy way—but things like training for races show that hard work and effort really do pay off.

Proverbs 12:24 says, "Diligent hands will rule, but laziness ends in forced labour." And later we read, "All hard work brings a profit, but mere talk leads only to poverty" (PROVERBS 14:23). These wise principles—not promises—can help us live well for God, and not give up on the hard roads He will sometimes ask us to walk.

God's plan for us includes work and difficult things. They are unavoidable in this world. Instead of trying to avoid them, let's make every effort to do the things God gives us "with all [our] heart" (COLOSSIANS 3:23). And then we can leave the results to Him.   *DB*

TO PRAY ABOUT . . .

Heavenly Father, whatever it is You have asked me to do today—big or small—
help me to do it. Protect me from laziness as I learn to walk closely with You.

WE WON'T SERVE GOD WELL IF WE'RE LAZY.

IT'S SLIPPERY OUT HERE!

BIBLE: PSALM 141

Do not let my heart be drawn to what is evil (V.4).

I remember having a go at skiing. I was pretty nervous, so I followed my friend down what looked like a gentle slope. With my eyes on him I didn't notice that he turned down the steepest hill on the mountain, and I found myself careening down the slope, completely out of control. I crashed of course.

Sin is like a slippery slope. Psalm 141 shows how we can easily find ourselves off course and headed for trouble. One way to avoid going off course is prayer. "Do not let my heart be drawn to what is evil" (PSALM 141:4) reminds me almost exactly of the prayer model Jesus taught: "Lead [me] not into temptation, but deliver [me] from the evil one" (MATTHEW 6:13). In His goodness, God hears and answers this prayer.

This psalm also talks about another way God keeps us on the right path: God-centred friends. "Let a righteous man strike me—that is a kindness; let him rebuke me—that is oil on my head. My head will not refuse it" (PSALM 141:5). Temptations are subtle. We're not always aware that we're going wrong. A true friend can help us see the truth. "Faithful are the wounds of a friend" (PROVERBS 27:6 NKJV). It's hard to accept when we're being corrected, but if we see their hard words as a "kindness" we'll be able to let them put us back on the path of obeying and loving God.

Let's try to be open to the things our parents, youth leaders and Christian friends say to us. And let's make sure we keep relying on God through prayer.

DR

THINKING IT OVER . . .

How do you react when other Christians give you advice? Are you open, or do you get offended? Read 1 Peter 5:5-11. What attitude are we to have to other Christians (VV.5-6)? Why is it so important that we support each other (VV.8-9)?

GOD GIVES US OTHER CHRISTIANS TO KEEP US WALKING THE RIGHT WAY.

CHATTY BUS

BIBLE: COLOSSIANS 4:2-6
Let your conversation be always full of grace (V.6).

A bus company recently launched a new project called, "Chatty Bus"! It's been a big success. The idea is that a Chatty Bus has people on board willing to talk with passengers who just fancy a chat. Chatty Buses are in response to the upsetting stat that nearly 30% of people in the UK go at least one day a week without a meaningful conversation.

Many of us have experienced the loneliness that comes from not having someone to talk to. Whether we're stood in the corner on our own at a party, or all our friends are busy and we have nothing to do. Connecting with others is an important and powerful experience; and a good conversation can be life-changing. As I think about some of the important conversations in my life, I'm especially reminded of discussions that were full of God's love and generosity. I cannot begin to describe the impact they've had on my life.

At the end of his letter to the Colossian church, Paul encouraged his readers to have the kind of conversations that would show God's love. He wrote, "Let your conversation be always full of grace" (COLOSSIANS 4:6), reminding his readers that it is not simply the amount of words but the quality of those words—"full of grace"—that bring true encouragement to others.

The next time you see someone who's on their own, or if you feel lonely, try to connect with someone with a conversation that's "full of grace". And whenever we're hanging out with friends or youth group or anyone else, let's look for ways to have a conversation that has lasting value.

LS

TO PRAY ABOUT . . .
Heavenly Father, help me to encourage everyone I speak with today,
filling my conversations with Your grace.

IF GOD IS THE CENTRE OF OUR CONVERSATIONS, THEY WILL BE FILLED WITH HIS LOVE AND GRACE.

A GOAL AND A PURPOSE

BIBLE: ACTS 20:17-24

My only aim is to finish the race and complete the task the Lord Jesus has given me (V.24).

Recently Colin O'Brady took a walk that had never been taken before. Pulling a supply sledge behind him, he trekked across Antarctica completely on his own—a total of 932 miles in 54 days. It was a hard journey which took dedication and bravery.

Later, when he talked about his time alone with the ice, the cold and the long distance, he said, "I was locked in a deep flow state [being totally focused on what he was doing] the entire time, equally focused on the end goal, while allowing my mind to recount the lessons of this journey."

His words make me think of what it is like to follow Jesus. We are to be focused on the goal of walking through life in a way that pleases God and reveals Him to others. In Acts 20:24, Paul (who was no stranger to dangerous journeys) said, "I consider my life worth nothing to me; my only aim is to finish the race and complete the task the Lord Jesus has given me—the task of testifying to the good news of God's grace."

As we walk on in our relationship with Jesus, let's remember our purpose (to make Him known) and our goal (that we will see Him face-to-face in heaven).

DB

TO PRAY ABOUT . . .

Dear heavenly Father, as we walk through life, help us to live for You in all we do. And may we encourage others to journey with You as well.

I PRESS ON TOWARDS THE GOAL TO WIN THE PRIZE FOR WHICH GOD HAS CALLED ME HEAVENWARDS IN CHRIST JESUS. PHILIPPIANS 3:14

LOVED AND IMPORTANT

BIBLE: ROMANS 8:15-17

The Spirit himself testifies with our spirit that we are God's children (V.16).

Malcolm seemed confident as a teenager. But this confidence was a mask. In reality a miserable and aggressive home left him scared and desperate for love. He felt like his family's problems were all his fault. "For as far back as I remember," he said, "every morning I would go into the bathroom, look in the mirror and say out loud to myself, 'You are stupid, you are ugly and it's your fault.'"

Malcolm's self-hatred continued until his late teens, when he felt God speak to him very clearly one night about his Christian identity. "I realised that God loved me unconditionally and nothing would ever change that," he remembered. "I could never embarrass God, and He would never reject me." After three weeks of reflection and talking it over with people in his church, Malcolm looked in the mirror and spoke to himself differently. "You are loved, you are important," he said, "and it's not your fault."

Malcolm's story shows what God's Spirit does—He frees us from fear by showing how much we are loved (ROMANS 8:15,38-39). By His Spirit, God confirms that we are His children, with all the gifts and benefits that status brings (8:16-17; 12:6-8). Knowing this truth, we can begin to see ourselves correctly as our minds are made new in this reality (12:2-3).

It's been a few years now—and Malcolm still says those words each day, reinforcing who God says he is. In the Father's eyes he is loved, important and a special child of God. And so are we. *SV*

THINKING IT OVER . . .

What words come to mind when you see yourself in the mirror?
How different are they to the Bible's description of what God sees in you
(SEE ROMANS 8:1-4,14,17)?

THE BIBLE IS THE MOST IMPORTANT MIRROR BY WHICH WE CAN SEE OURSELVES.

LOVE'S LONG REACH

BIBLE: PSALM 139:1-10

Oh, the depths of the riches of the wisdom and knowledge of God!
(ROMANS 11:33).

Mary Lee is a sixteen-foot, 3,500-pound great white shark who was tagged by researchers. The transmitter attached to one of her fins could be tracked by satellite when she surfaced. For five years Mary Lee's movements were observed online by everyone from researchers to surfers. She was tracked for nearly 40,000 miles until one day her signal stopped—probably because the battery on her transmitter died.

On the other end of the scale, David said to God, "Where can I go from your Spirit? Where can I flee from your presence? If I go up to the heavens, you are there; if I make my bed in the depths, you are there" (PSALM 139:7-8). "Such knowledge is too wonderful for me," he said with thanks (V.6).

God chooses to know us because He loves us. He cares enough not only to watch our lives but also to enter into them and make them new. He made Himself open to us through Jesus' life, death and resurrection, so we could know Him for ourselves and love Him forever. Human knowledge and technology reach only so far. Those 'following' Mary Lee lost track of her, but you and I can never escape God's attention, or His love, throughout every moment of our lives.

JB

WHAT I'M THANKFUL FOR . . .

Thank You for always seeing me, Father! Help me to live today with a strong awareness of Your perfect love.

WE'VE ALWAYS GOT GOD'S FULL ATTENTION!

GUEST LIST

BIBLE: LUKE 14:7-14

When you give a banquet, invite the poor, the crippled, the lame, the blind, and you will be blessed (VV.13-14).

Qumran was a first-century Jewish community that had cut itself off from everyone else so they could prepare for the arrival of the Messiah (God's promised Saviour). They took great care in keeping their traditions, rituals and strict rules. Ancient documents show that they would not allow the lame, the blind or the crippled into their communities. This was because they believed that anyone with a disability was unclean. During their feasts, disabled people were never on the guest list.

Ironically, at that very time the actual Messiah was at work in the cities and villages of Judea and Galilee. Jesus made His Father's kingdom known, taught the Bible clearly, comforted those who suffered, healed the disabled and opened the eyes of the blind. He cut right through tradition when He said: "When you give a banquet, invite the poor, the crippled, the lame, the blind, and you will be blessed" (LUKE 14:13-14).

It's important that we pay attention to the difference between Jesus' words and the guest list of the Qumran 'spiritual elite'. Anyone is welcome in God's home—and everyone is invited. No one is too bad; no one is disqualified! But trusting Jesus is the only way in. No one can enter heaven by their own goodness.

DF

THINKING IT OVER . . .

Read Jesus' parable in Matthew 22:1-14 (as a picture of entry into heaven). Who is invited to the wedding feast (VV.9-10)? The suggestion in the passage is that the poor, crippled and others who come to the feast are given wedding clothes (as they may only have rags to wear themselves); why is one man thrown out of the feast (VV.11-13)? What do you think verse 14 means?

GOD'S INVITE IS FOR EVERYONE; BUT WE MUST CHOOSE TO PUT OUR TRUST IN JESUS FOR OURSELVES.

PARALLEL UNIVERSE

BIBLE: LUKE 12:1-20

Our citizenship is in heaven. And we eagerly await a Saviour from there, the Lord Jesus Christ (PHILIPPIANS 3:20).

The idea of parallel universes sounds like something from sci-fi movies! But we actually live in a parallel universe ourselves. I don't mean there's another version of you in another reality who's some kind of superhero. I mean that right now we're living in two worlds.

One of those 'universes' is about what we see and do in the world around us: going to school, catching up on homework, hanging out with friends, uploading to Instagram, eating, sleeping, brushing our teeth . . .

The other 'universe' we live in is spiritual: which means we can't see it. But that doesn't make it any less real. It is a world of angels, spiritual forces and the somewhere-out-there places called heaven and hell.

These parallel universes most dramatically came together when Jesus was born in Bethlehem (LUKE 2:1-20). What Jesus went on to do on planet earth made it possible for God to make us "[citizens] of heaven", rather than just people of earth (PHILIPPIANS 3:20). We were once spiritually dead in the one universe, and headed for physical death in the other (EPHESIANS 2:1-3)—now we have been made fully alive forever by giving our lives to Jesus. He makes the two worlds one again. For now we live on earth, but "eagerly await a Saviour from [heaven], the Lord Jesus Christ" (PHILIPPIANS 3:20). We are of earth *and* of heaven!   PY

THINKING IT OVER . . .

Read Ephesians 1:1-14. What does it mean for God to have "blessed us in the heavenly realms with every spiritual blessing in Christ" (V.3)? List out every "spiritual blessing" in these verses. What difference does it make to know you have these things, no matter what you're facing today?

WE LIVE ON EARTH, BUT HEAVEN IS WHERE WE BELONG.

WHY ME?

BIBLE: JOB 7:17-21

Why have you made me your target? Have I become a burden to you? (V.20).

The Book of Odds says that one in a million people are struck by lightning. One in 25,000 suffer a medical condition called "broken heart syndrome" when they face a terrible shock or loss. Page after page in this book gives us such stats. They pile up without explanation. *What if we're the one?*

Job found himself as a "one". God Himself talked about Job, saying: "There is no one on earth like him; he is blameless and upright, a man who fears God and shuns evil" (JOB 1:8). Yet Job was chosen to suffer a series of losses that defied all odds (JOB 1-2). Of all people on earth, Job had reason to demand an answer. We can see it ourselves as we read of his struggles and his cries of, "Why me?"

Job's story helps us to think about the unexplained pain and evil in our world; including our own struggles. After Job's friends gave him bad advice (SEE 6:21 AND 42:7) "the LORD spoke to Job out of the storm" (38:1). But He didn't give Job answers to why he had suffered. Instead He said, "Brace yourself like a man; I will question you, and you shall answer me" (V.3).

Through God's questions, Job realised just how awesome God truly is. God took Job's attention away from his pain (real and devastating as it was) and put it back on the King of the universe who loved him. Job's response? "Now my eyes have seen you" (42:5).

We may not get an answer to "Why me?" when we're struggling or things are really hard. But through reading the Bible we too can 'see' God and be strengthened for the things we have to grow through.   *MDH*

THINKING IT OVER . . .

Read Job 38-42. How does God's response to Job challenge and reassure you during your own times of pain and difficulty. Do you react to God's words in the same way as Job (42:1-6)? How can Job's story help you to remember to focus on God during hard times, and to remind your friends to do the same when they are struggling?

WILL YOU CHOOSE TO TRUST GOD EVEN WHEN THINGS DON'T MAKE SENSE?

KNOWING GOD'S WORDS

BIBLE: JEREMIAH 23:16,30-40

We have renounced secret and shameful ways; we do not use deception, nor do we distort the word of God (**2 CORINTHIANS 4:2**).

I like writing. But sometimes my words get misunderstood. I feel bad when people feel pressurised or guilty because of something I've written—my aim is to encourage! And occasionally people take my words totally out of context, making them say something I never meant. What I realise is that once my writing is printed, it's out of my hands to control it or how people react to what I've said.

While my words getting confused or being misunderstood is frustrating, it's nothing compared to when God's words are misused! The false prophets in Jeremiah's day were doing this. They put their own words into God's mouth, pretending He was saying all sorts of nice, comforting things—"false hopes" for the people (**JEREMIAH 23:16**).

So the God told His people, "Do not listen to the words of the prophets who prophesy to you . . . They speak a vision of their own heart, not from the mouth of the LORD" (**V.16**). Then God warned that He punishes those who change His words and throws them away (**VV.36,39**).

Hundreds of years later, Paul made a point of saying that he did not misuse the Bible or put words in God's mouth (**2 CORINTHIANS 4:2**). He knew the danger of teaching people his own ideas rather than God's. All of us need to be careful to use the Bible for His purpose, rather than for our own agenda. We need to be ready to hear what it actually says; not just what we may want it to say. *JAL*

THINKING IT OVER . . .

Read 1 John 4:1-6. Are false teachers (those who misuse the Bible and lie about what God says) just something of the past, or are they are danger to us today as well (**V.1**)? How do we recognise false teachers and true Bible teachers (**VV.2-3**)? What is our confidence (**V.4**)? False teachers "speak from the viewpoint of the world" (**V.5**)—this is why we need to know the Bible's viewpoint to help us spot teaching that is just trying to trip us up.

NOT EVERYTHING YOU HEAR ABOUT GOD IS TRUE; EVEN IF IT SOUNDS GOOD!

BOOK BY BOOK

BIBLE: I CORINTHIANS 3:5-9
We are co-workers in God's service (V.9).

- -

More than two hundred volunteers helped a bookshop in Southampton move all its books and furniture to a different building down the street. Helpers lined the pavement between the two buildings and passed books down a "human conveyor belt". Having seen the volunteers in action, someone who worked for the shop said, "It was a really moving experience to see people helping . . . They wanted to be part of something bigger."

As Christians, we're part of something much bigger as well. God uses us to reach the world with the message of His love. Because someone shared the message with us, we can turn to another person and pass it on. Paul compared this—the building of God's kingdom—to growing a garden. Some of us plant seeds while some of us water the seeds. We are, as Paul said, "co-workers in God's service" (1 CORINTHIANS 3:9).

Each job is important, yet everything is done in the power of God's Spirit. By His Spirit, God 'wakes people up' to join His family when they hear that He loves them and sent His Son to die in their place so that they can be free from their sin (JOHN 3:16).

God does much of His work on earth through 'volunteers' like you and me. As we live out our own confidence in God, and share how He has changed our lives, His Holy Spirit will be at work in our friends, families and schools, bringing more people into His family. So let's be deliberate about joining God in this work, and make it a key part of our prayer life!   *JBS*

TO PRAY ABOUT . . .
Dear God, thank You for including me in Your plan to tell everyone about Your love. Help me to represent You well with my words and actions.

YOU ARE PART OF GOD'S PLAN FOR REACHING THE WORLD WITH THE GOSPEL.

HOW TO GET RICH

BIBLE: LUKE 12:13-21

Watch out! Be on your guard against all kinds of greed; life does not consist in an abundance of possessions (V.15).

I find it interesting that Jesus taught more about money than anything else. And He wasn't trying to get loads of donations. As far as we know, He never asked for money from anyone. The reason He taught about it is that nothing gets in the way of our relationship with Jesus like money does. We get distracted really easily wishing we had more stuff—and so wishing we had the money to get it. The 'need' for more stuff and money can tempt us to normalise stealing or simply fill our heads with daydreams about it. And suddenly Jesus doesn't seem like such an important part of our lives . . .

Just think of the guy who asked Jesus, "Teacher, tell my brother to divide the inheritance with me" (LUKE 12:13). Amazing! He had an opportunity to 'go deep' with Jesus, but instead he wanted deep pockets.

Jesus answered: "Watch out! Be on your guard against all kinds of greed; life does not consist in an abundance of possessions" (V.15). He then went on to tell the story of a rich man who was seemed to be wildly successful—having so many crops that he had to keep building bigger barns. But in God's eyes he was a "fool" (V.20). Not because he was rich, but because he was "not rich towards God" (V.21).

You'll hear a lot of advice about how to become rich, famous and successful. But only Jesus tells it to us straight. It's not about the money or what we have. It's about the richness of our relationship with Him. If we have Him, we have it all. If we don't have Him, we'll lose it all.   JS

WHAT I'M THANKFUL FOR . . .

Thank You, Jesus, that You are all I need. You give me life "to the full" (JOHN 10:10)—and life that will never end!

REAL VALUE ISN'T IN WHAT WE HAVE, BUT WHO WE KNOW.

ENDING REVENGE

BIBLE: MATTHEW 5:38-48

I tell you, do not resist an evil person. If anyone slaps you on the right cheek, turn to them the other cheek also (V.39).

The pastor of an inner-city church said in one sermon: "Some people believe in 'an eye for an eye'. But round here, it's two eyes for an eye. You can never even the score; you can only raise the stakes." The people listening nodded—that was the reality they faced each day.

We've seen it happen at school—someone does a hard tackle in a football game, the other person pushes back. It quickly grows into a fight. And we see it at home, when arguing with your brother or sister turns into insult after insult. We want to do more harm to the other person than they have managed to do to us!

In Matthew 5, Jesus challenged a lot of the ways we behave towards other people. He used this kind of wording to show that the way to please God is very different: "You have heard that it was said . . . But I tell you . . ." (MATTHEW 5:38-39). His words about turning the other cheek, going the second mile and giving to those who ask sound radical and unrealistic (VV.38-42).

Are we willing to think and pray about His teaching? Are we ready to show love, even when we are hurt? It's not about becoming a doormat—it's about ending the cycle of revenge. It's about being brave enough to trust Jesus and forgive people, rather than trying to get back at them.   *DM*

THINKING IT OVER . . .

Read Colossians 3:12-17. What do we need to "put on" (VV.12,14) if we want to be people of forgiveness (V.13)? What might revenge and grudges rob from us (V.15)? We're not left to forgive in our own strength: we have been forgiven (V.13), we have the Bible, we have our church family and we have the Holy Spirit (V.16).

TO LOVE OUR FRIENDS IS NORMAL; LOVING OUR ENEMIES IS NOT. THAT'S WHY WE NEED JESUS TO HELP US.

EVERY MOMENT COUNTS

BIBLE: 2 TIMOTHY 4:1-8

Keep your head in all situations, endure hardships, do the work of an evangelist (V.5).

- -

When the Titanic hit an iceberg, Pastor John Harper got his six-year-old daughter into one of the few lifeboats. He gave his life-jacket to another passenger and shared the gospel with anyone who would listen. As the ship sank and hundreds of people floated in the freezing water, hoping for an unlikely rescue, Harper swam from one person to another and said, "Believe in the Lord Jesus and you will be saved" (ACTS 16:31).

Years later, during a meeting for survivors of the Titanic, one man called himself "the last convert of John Harper". Having said "No" to Harper's first invitation, the man decided to trust Jesus when the pastor asked him again. He watched as Harper gave the last moments of his life to sharing Jesus before hypothermia kicked in and he sunk below the surface of the icy water.

In his second letter to Timothy, the apostle Paul encouraged a similar urgency and commitment to telling people about Jesus. After talking about God always being with us, and reminding Timothy that Jesus is coming back soon, Paul then told him to "preach the word" (2 TIMOTHY 4:2). The apostle reminded the young church leader to remain focused, even though some people will say "No" to Jesus (VV.3-5).

It might feel like the whole of our lives are before us. So what's the rush? But we don't know how much time people have. Nobody expected the Titanic disaster to happen when it did; then all of a sudden the issue of life after death was urgent! We need to get on and share the message the world needs to hear: "Jesus saves!" (VV.6-8).

XD

THINKING IT OVER . . .

Read John 3:36 and Ephesians 4:17-19. How do these verses describe people who do not yet know Jesus for themselves? How is their situation similar to that of the dying people in the icy water after the Titanic sunk? What perspective do these verses give you towards your non-Christian friends and family?

THE MESSAGE OF JESUS' SALVATION NEEDS TO BE DELIVERED URGENTLY.

SIMON OF CYRENE

BIBLE: MARK 15:16-24

A certain man from Cyrene . . . was passing by on his way in from the country, and they forced him to carry the cross (V.21).

Simon was pulled from the watching crowd and forced to help Jesus, exhausted from being beaten and whipped, to carry His cross. Mark tells us that Simon was from Cyrene, a part of North Africa that had a large population of Jews during Jesus' time. Simon had probably travelled to Jerusalem to celebrate the Passover. Then he found himself in the middle of this unjust execution. Yet he offered a small but meaningful act of service to Jesus (MARK 15:21).

Earlier in the gospel of Mark, Jesus had told His followers, "Whoever wants to be my disciple must deny themselves and take up their cross and follow me" (8:34). On the road to Golgotha, Simon literally did what Jesus figuratively told His followers to do: he took up the cross given to him and carried it for Jesus' sake.

We, too, have crosses to bear—illness, grief, selfishness we need to give up, bad habits we need to break, difficult people we have to support. As we carry on working through these things with Jesus, we give a glimpse to others of the God we live for. Because Jesus went to the cross for us and paid for our sin, we have a brand new, unbreakable relationship with God. Now He is with us and gives us the strength to carry our crosses, and to never give up. *LS*

TO PRAY ABOUT . . .

Jesus, thank You that You understand the pain I feel as I take up my cross and follow You. Please be my strength, especially when the journey is difficult.

SAYING "YES" TO JESUS MEANS SAYING "NO" TO MYSELF.

THE KNIFE ANGEL

BIBLE: ISAIAH 2:1-4

Nation will not take up sword against nation, nor will they train for war anymore (V.4).

With knife crime on the rise across the United Kingdom, the British Ironwork Centre came up with an idea. Working with local police forces, the Centre put 200 boxes around the country and asked people to give up their knives. About 100,000 knives were anonymously dropped in the boxes—some still with blood on their blades. These were then passed to an artist who blunted them and wrote on them the names of young knife-crime victims, plus messages of regret from ex-offenders. All 100,000 weapons were then welded together to create the Knife Angel—a 27-foot figure with shimmering steel wings. It is the National Monument against violence and aggression.

Standing in front of the Knife Angel I wondered how many thousands of people it's protecting as a symbol of peace. I thought too of Isaiah's vision of the new heaven and earth (ISAIAH 65:17), a place where children won't die young (V.20) or grow up in crime-filled poverty (VV.22-23); and a place where knife crime is gone because all blades have been reshaped for bringing life, not death (2:4).

That new world isn't yet here, but we can pray that we will see more and more examples of heaven on earth (MATTHEW 6:10). In its own way, the Knife Angel gives us a glimpse of God's promised future. How can we be examples of God's love today, showing His offer of peace through Jesus to the people around us?

SV

TO PRAY ABOUT . . .

Dear God, there is so much violence in the world and even in my community. Please help me to be an example of Jesus' love and welcome. Use me to show people a picture of Your good kingdom.

WE CAN BE EXAMPLES OF TRUE PEACE IN A WORLD OF FIGHTING AND VIOLENCE.

SURPRISE ME!

BIBLE: EPHESIANS 3:14-21

"My thoughts are not your thoughts, neither are your ways my ways," declares the LORD (ISAIAH 55:8).

When our family went out for ice cream, my dad would ask my mum what she'd like. Often she would just reply, "Surprise me!" She told me she was never disappointed in his choice.

Do you like surprises? Would you ever dare say, "Surprise me!" to God? A lot of us are a little scared to do that. Yes, we may believe that God is good and that He loves us. Yet we're afraid we won't like what He chooses for us.

Throughout the Bible we see how God often does the unexpected. Sometimes it's holding back the waters for His people to cross a sea on dry ground (EXODUS 14:21-22). Or forgiving and embracing those who admit their sin and turn back to Him (PSALM 130:1-4). Jesus' time on earth was filled with amazing events that pointed people to His Father—He turned water into wine, calmed storms, healed the sick and raised the dead.

What kind of God is He? One who is not restricted by our small understanding and limited imagination (EPHESIANS 3:20). God's thoughts and ways are not like ours (ISAIAH 55:8), and He wants to give us far more than a special flavour of ice cream. He loves it when we a willing to trust Him—really trust Him—by saying, "Surprise me! Let Your will be done today, not mine."   CHK

TO PRAY ABOUT . . .

Father, I know that You are good and that You love me. So please help me to trust You with everything today, letting You lead me through it and relying on You for the challenges.

GOD IS FULL OF AMAZING SURPRISES FOR THOSE WHO GIVE THEMSELVES COMPLETELY TO HIM.

THE DANGER OF DOING WELL

BIBLE: DEUTERONOMY 8:6-18

Be careful that you do not forget the LORD your God, failing to observe his commands, his laws and his decrees that I am giving you this day (V.11).

Have you ever done really well at something? Maybe winning an award at school, making your parents proud or acing an exam? The thing with doing well is that it can make us think we've got everything sorted. The danger of doing well is that we forget just how much we need God for everything!

The Israelites learned the daily habit of depending on God in the Sinai wilderness where they had no choice; they needed His daily provision just to eat and drink. But when they finally stood on the banks of the Jordan River, they awaited a more difficult test. After they entered the land of plenty, which God had promised to give them, would they quickly forget about Him?

Having spent many years in the desert, they didn't know how easily they'd be distracted by the nations around them who did what they wanted and ignored God. But Moses knew the danger. He was more afraid of the land of plenty than of the empty desert—the alluring obsession of sex; the exotic, self-centred religions; the money and possessions. The Israelites might just put God behind them and enjoy living for themselves, thinking: "My power and the strength of my hands have produced this wealth for me" (DEUTERONOMY 8:17).

Sometimes doing well and having lots of stuff makes it harder to rely on God. The Israelites quickly got distracted from God after they moved into the Promised Land. Again and again they chased other gods and selfish ways of living.

It can be quite dangerous to get what we want—and to forget who we need.

PY

THINKING IT OVER . . .

What are the dangers of forgetting God (PSALM 50:22)? Read all of Psalm 50 and think about all the ways God is described. Why is thankfulness (VV.14,23) a good way to avoid forgetfulness?

I CONSIDER EVERYTHING A LOSS BECAUSE OF THE SURPASSING WORTH OF KNOWING CHRIST JESUS MY LORD. PHILIPPIANS 3:8

HAPPINESS AND HOLINESS

BIBLE: I PETER 1:13-21

Just as he who called you is holy, so be holy in all you do; for it is written:
"Be holy, because I am holy" (VV.15-16).

At one university, you can take a course in happiness. Apparently this class helps students discover "How to get happy."

That's not a bad idea. In fact, the Bible suggests several times the importance of being happy or joyful. King Solomon (King David's son) tells us that happiness is a gift from God (ECCLESIASTES 3:12; 7:14; 11:9).

Sometimes, though, we take the search for happiness too far. We see it as the most important thing, and even believe that our happiness is God's highest goal for us. That's when our thinking gets confused.

The fullest and richest way of life comes by keeping God's ways (PSALM 1:1-2; PROVERBS 16:20; 29:18). God demands holiness and wants us to live a holy life—which means we are set apart for Him and show His perfect, loving ways to the world around us (1 THESSALONIANS 4:7; 2 PETER 3:11). In Peter's first letter we read, "Just as he who called you is holy, so be holy in all you do; for it is written: 'Be holy, because I am holy'" (1 PETER 1:15-16).

When we face big decisions, our friends are pressurising us to do something we know we shouldn't, or things feel hard for any reason, we must remember God's command to us. He didn't say, "Be happy" but "Be holy"! That doesn't mean He isn't interested in our happiness, but that holiness is our first priority. Happiness is then the natural result of holiness.

DB

THINKING IT OVER . . .

One of the most miserable feelings in life is knowing that we've done wrong. Whereas the best feeling is when we know we've done things well and have nothing to hide! The world tells us that following our own desires is the path to happiness; but that happiness is shallow and short-lived. Being right with God is the best feeling in the world.

HOLINESS IS THE SUREST PATH TO HAPPINESS.

INNER STRUGGLE

BIBLE: I SAMUEL 1:9-18

I am a woman who is deeply troubled. I have not been drinking wine or beer; I was pouring out my soul to the LORD (V.15).

Sometimes I feel as if I'm in a bad relationship—with myself! Whenever I want to take on a new challenge or sign up to a team or club at school, a voice in my head starts saying, "No way! You can't do that! People will just laugh at you if you try!"

Sometimes, before I've even begun to think about a new idea or something I want to try, my alter ego has torn it to shreds. It really gets me down. It's also something that I think a lot of us struggle with.

The devil loves to distract us with criticism, and he tries to get us to use it on others as well as ourselves. We judge quickly and try to correct others before we know what they're saying. That's what Eli the priest did when Hannah was crying out to God. He interrupted her prayer and accused her of being drunk (1 SAMUEL 1:12-14).

But God lets us talk to Him in full honesty (PSALM 62:8). In fact, the psalms show again and again that it is when we are sharing our doubts and fears that God gives us peace. Many psalms that begin in misery end in praise (SEE PSALM 22; 42; 60; 69; 73).

When a battle is raging inside, "pour out [your] soul to the LORD" (1 SAMUEL 1:15). He can make sense out of our struggles.

JAL

TO PRAY ABOUT . . .

Dear God, please help me to pour out my soul to You in prayer. I want to go through everything knowing You are right here with me. Help me to be honest with You and to look firstly for the peace only You give.

PRAYER DOES NOT MAKE GOD SEE THINGS AS WE SEE THEM; IT HELPS US SEE THINGS AS GOD SEES THEM.

TRANSFORMED AND TRANSFORMING

BIBLE: 2 CHRONICLES 33:9-17

[Manasseh] restored the altar of the LORD and sacrificed fellowship offerings and thank-offerings on it, and told Judah to serve the LORD, the God of Israel (V.16).

Tani and Modupe grew up in Nigeria and went to the UK to study. Having been transformed by God's love, they never imagined that they would be used to transform a poor, cut-off community in the UK. As Tani and Modupe shared the love and welcome of God with their community, many people came to them to find out more about Jesus. They lead a lively church and continue to run lots of community projects that have led to a significant transformation of the whole area.

Manasseh changed his community, first for evil and then for good. Crowned king of Judah at the age of twelve, he led his people down bad paths and they did great evil for many years (2 CHRONICLES 33:1-9). They paid no attention to God's warnings and so He allowed Manasseh to be taken prisoner to Babylon (VV.10-11).

In his suffering, the king cried out to God who heard his prayer and gave him back his kingdom (VV.12-13). The now reformed king rebuilt the city walls and got rid of the fake gods (VV.14-15). "He restored the altar of the LORD and . . . told Judah to serve the LORD, the God of Israel" (V.16). As the people saw the radical transformation of Manasseh, they also turned back to God and were transformed (V.17).

As we get to know God better, may He transform us and our friends, families and communities through us.

ROR

TO PRAY ABOUT . . .

Heavenly Father, transform our lives that we may be used by You to bring transformation to others.

YOUR TRANSFORMATION BY GOD BRINGS TRANSFORMATION TO OTHERS.

LINED UP TO LOVE

BIBLE: MARK 10:46-52

Jesus stopped and said, "Call him" (V.49).

A guy wanted to end his life by jumping from a bridge onto the motorway below. So the police stopped some lorries and trucks, and asked the drivers to help. The lorry drivers stopped and lined up their lorries under the overpass to shorten the guy's fall if he jumped. This gave the police time to help the man, and the situation thankfully ended without anyone getting hurt. Each of the thirteen drivers had a responsibility to deliver their cargo, yet they stopped to help save a man's life.

About two thousand years ago, on a different kind of road, another guy needed help. Blind Bartimaeus heard about Jesus, believed He could give him his sight back and shouted for mercy (MARK 10:46-52). I've always been amazed at this passage because Jesus—though He walked towards Jerusalem that day knowing an unfair trial and crucifixion awaited Him—stopped. Jesus arguably had "more important" things to do—the most important thing in all of history—offering Himself as a sacrifice for Bartimaeus and all who would trust in Him. Yet He stopped and showed love and kindness to the man, giving him sight.

As we walk the roads of life, we'll become aware of the needs of those in our path. We may have many important things to do and places to be. Yet as we do life, we should always ask ourselves whether we're keeping our eyes open for the people who need help. And are we prepared to stop for them? Dear God, please use us to care for others!

KH

THINKING IT OVER . . .

Who has God put in your path to care for today?
What simple way can you help?

LOOK FOR OPPORTUNITIES TO SHARE JESUS WITH OTHERS EVERYWHERE YOU GO.

LAST BREATH

BIBLE: PSALM 139:1-16

All the days ordained for me were written in your book before one of them came to be (V.16).

Mum, my sisters and I waited by Dad's bed as his breaths became shallower and less frequent—until they were no more. Dad was a few days shy of eighty-nine when he slipped quietly into the life beyond, where God awaited him. His leaving left us feeling a great emptiness—we had great memories, but not Dad. Yet we knew that one day we'd be reunited with him in God's home.

We have that certain hope because we believe Dad is with God, who knows and loves him. When Dad breathed his first breath, God was there breathing breath into his lungs (ISAIAH 42:5). Yet even before his first—and with every breath in between—God was intimately involved in each detail of Dad's life, just as he is in yours and mine. It was God who designed him and "knit" him together in the womb (PSALM 139:13-14). And when Dad breathed his last breath, God's Spirit was there, holding him in love and carrying him to be with Him (VV.7-10).

The same is true for everyone who gives their lives to Jesus. Every moment of our life on earth is known by God (VV.1-4). With each day remaining, and as we look forward to the life beyond, let's join with "everything that has breath" to praise Him. "Praise the LORD" (150:6)! AK

WHAT I'M THANKFUL FOR . . .

Dear Father, thank You for creating us and giving us breath—and for giving us certain hope for the future. In the sadness and losses of life, help us to cling to You.

OUR LAST BREATH ON EARTH IS NOT OUR LAST BREATH.

Seven days in . . . Genesis
THE GOOD EARTH

BIBLE: GENESIS 1

God saw all that he had made, and it was very good (V.31).

While orbiting the moon in 1968, Apollo 8 astronaut Bill Anders described the crew's close-up view of the moon. He called it "a foreboding horizon . . . a stark and unappetising-looking place." Then the crew took turns reading to a watching world from Genesis 1:1-10. After Commander Frank Borman finished verse 10, "And God saw that it was good," he signed off with, "God bless all of you, all of you on the good earth."

The opening chapter of the Bible makes two things very clear: the universe, our earth and everything in it is God's work. The phrase "and God said . . ." (GENESIS 1:3) is all the way through the chapter. The entire world we live in was created by the power of His words. The Bible reinforces the message of Genesis 1 in every page: behind all of history, there is God.

The other thing that we are meant to see from this chapter is that what God made was good. Again and again we read: "And God saw that it was good" (V.4). Much has changed since that first moment God created the world. Genesis 1 describes the world as God wanted it, before anything got broken. Whatever goodness we see around us today is a faint echo of the perfect world God created.

The Apollo 8 astronauts saw earth as a brightly coloured ball hanging alone in space. It looked at once awesome and fragile. It looked like the view from Genesis 1.

PY

COMPLETING THE PICTURE . . .

The detailed design of the universe demands an explanation. Where there is design, there must be a designer. Yet some people say the universe just came from nothing—without needing God. But if there is no God, there can be no miracles (things happening outside the natural laws). And if there are no miracles, something cannot come from nothing. And if something cannot come from nothing, then our universe can't exist . . .

The Bible's retelling makes much more sense, "In the beginning God . . ." (GENESIS 1:1). The Bible tells us the proof of God's existence is all around us! "The heavens declare the glory of God; the skies proclaim the work of his hands" (SEE PSALM 19). Which is why we are told that only "the fool says in his heart, 'There is no God'" (PSALM 14:1).

HOLY, HOLY, HOLY IS THE LORD ALMIGHTY; THE WHOLE EARTH IS FULL OF HIS GLORY. ISAIAH 6:3

Seven days in . . . Genesis
GOD IS GOOD

BIBLE: GENESIS 3:1-7

Good and upright is the LORD; therefore he instructs sinners in his ways (PSALM 25:8).

I often repeat the phrase "God is good, all the time; all the time, God is good" to myself. I don't just repeat the words as a chant. I say them, particularly when I'm struggling or my prayers don't seem to be being answered, to remind myself of a really important truth about God. Despite how things look or feel, God is good!

In the Garden of Eden, the snake put a doubt in Eve's mind about whether God had been good to her and had her best interest at heart. He said, "God knows that when you eat [the forbidden fruit] your eyes will be opened, and you will be like God, knowing good and evil" (GENESIS 3:5). The devil (who was the snake) tried to convince her that God was holding out on her and not giving her something really good—more knowledge.

Do you feel as though God isn't answering your prayers? Are you doubting His goodness? When I feel this way, I have to remind myself that my circumstances aren't a reliable way to measure God's love and goodness—the cross is. He has shown how good He is by giving His only Son Jesus to die for our sin. We can't rely on our feelings. But day by day as we choose to trust Him more, we learn to believe with confidence that God is good—all the time. *AC*

COMPLETING THE PICTURE . . .

The tree of the knowledge of good and evil and the tree of life (GENESIS 2:9) represent our options: either we enjoy living life with God in charge (the tree of life); or we take control ourselves, using our own knowledge to decide what is best and to live by our own code (the tree of the knowledge of good and evil). Adam and Eve decided to be their own bosses, cutting God out. So they lost the tree of life—and sin and death entered the world (3:22).

The good news is that if we trust Jesus, we can look forward to a future where we will live with God (just as Adam and Eve had done) and eat from the tree of life again (REVELATION 22:1-5).

CIRCUMSTANCES AREN'T THE WAY TO MEASURE GOD'S LOVE AND GOODNESS—THE CROSS IS.

Seven days in . . . Genesis

NOT MUCH TO OFFER

BIBLE: GENESIS 6:9-18

[Noah] walked faithfully with God (v.9).

An app development company hired me after I finished school, even though I couldn't write a single line of code. I learned that the company didn't place high value on work experience. Things like problem solving, good judgement and teamwork were more important. The company said new staff could be trained for the job as long as they were the right kind of people.

God was "deeply troubled" as He "saw how great the wickedness of the human race had become" since Adam and Eve first got things wrong (GENESIS 6:5-6). So God wiped the earth clean with a great flood, saying: "I am going to put an end to all people" (v.13).

Yet Noah stood out because "he walked faithfully with God" (v.9). Noah did not let himself become like the world around him, who ignored God and did whatever they wanted. He trusted God and followed His ways. And so God rescued him and his family, telling Noah to build a boat to hide in during the coming flood.

Noah was most probably a farmer, not a ship builder. Yet "Noah did everything just as God commanded him" (v.22). When God asks us to do things, or gives us opportunities to stand up for Him, we may not have the right 'work experience'. Thankfully, God is not limited by our skill set. He simply asks that we love and trust Him. As God's Spirit grows this attitude in us, we will realise He can use us in big or small ways—because the strength and the result always comes from Him!

JBS

THINKING IT OVER . . .

Read Hebrews 11:7. What did Noah have that allowed him to build the ark?
Read Hebrews 11:1 for definition of "faith". Does that describe your relationship with God?

WE NEVER HAVE MUCH TO OFFER GOD —SO WE JUST HAVE TO TRUST HIM!

Seven days in . . . Genesis

THE BABEL PROJECT

BIBLE: GENESIS 11:1-9

Unless the LORD builds the house, the builders labour in vain (PSALM 127:1).

Working with classmates on group projects can be hard—especially if you don't get to choose your own teammates! It's easy to miscommunicate and wind each other up when a deadline is coming up fast.

This wasn't a problem in Babel. The people had "one language", and said to themselves, "Come, let us build ourselves a city, with a tower that reaches to the heavens, so that we may make a name for ourselves" (GENESIS 11:1,4).

But God didn't want them working on a grand, self-centred plan based on the idea that they could rise to the heights of God and solve all of their own problems without Him. So He came down (V.7), scattered the people "over all the earth" and gave them different languages (VV.8-9).

God alone has the solution to humanity's problems. He revealed His plan to Abraham (12:1-3). Through Abraham's family, God promised to bring a Saviour. So Abraham didn't need to try to make something great of himself; God told him, "*I* will make your name great" (12:2).

It's not what we can do with our lives that matters. It's what God builds that actually lasts. Are we trusting in God alone to make something great of our lives? Or are we trying to "make a name for ourselves"? *MDH*

COMPLETING THE PICTURE . . .

Even after God cleaned the earth with the flood, people still instinctively rejected God. The tower of Babel helps show us that the world doesn't just need a clean on the outside; the inside is where the real problem lies. Jesus explained: "For it is from within, out of a person's heart, that evil thoughts come" (MARK 7:21). When we trust Jesus, He makes us a "new creation" (2 CORINTHIANS 5:17)—we're brand new people, with new hearts that can love Him. And He gives us His Holy Spirit who undoes the scattering of Babel, uniting God's people again in His family (SEE ACTS 2:5-12; EPHESIANS 4:1-6).

WE DON'T NEED TO BUILD ANYTHING FOR GOD; WE JUST NEED TO MAKE OURSELVES AVAILABLE TO HIM.

Seven days in . . . Genesis

WRESTLING WITH GOD

BIBLE: GENESIS 32

If you remain in me and I in you, you will bear much fruit; apart from me you can do nothing (JOHN 15:5).

When the staff of George Müller's orphanage told him it was impossible to raise enough money to keep it going, George praised God. He said their helplessness would make them rely more fully on God. They did, and He provided the money they needed.

Completely relying on God is the only way for us to live if we want to be confident in His love, provision and promises. But it seems like this is a hard lesson for all of us to learn.

Jacob didn't learn it easily. For many years he had lived by his own plans and lies. When he heard that his brother Esau, (who he had tricked years before), was coming with 400 men, Jacob made a plan. He tried to make sure that if he was attacked, half of his family would survive (GENESIS 32:7). That night, a "man" (God in human form) wrestled with Jacob (V.24). Just before dawn, the Man touched Jacob's hip and put it out of joint. All Jacob could do was cling to the Man, demanding a blessing (GENESIS 32:26; HOSEA 12:4). This was a turning point in Jacob's life. He limped for the rest of his life; but that was the day he became a man who trusted God, not himself. God weakened his body but made him strong on the inside, because now he relied on God. *HVL*

COMPLETING THE PICTURE . . .

Jacob (whose name literally means "deceiver") was Abraham's grandson. After he wrestled with God, God gave him a new name: "Israel". Jacob now had a new identity! And he's an illustration of what Jesus does for us when we trust Him—He makes us brand new children of God.

We hear about Jacob again in the New Testament, where we read: "By faith Jacob . . . worshipped as he leaned on the top of his staff" (HEBREWS 11:21). God had "wrenched" Jacob's hip (GENESIS 32:25), weakening him for the rest of his life as he needed a staff to walk and stand. Yet in his weakness, Jacob praised God. He had learnt to rely on God, not himself!

GOD IS ALWAYS AT WORK, TEACHING US TO RELY ON HIM FOR EVERYTHING.

Seven days in . . . Genesis

GOD'S PLANS

BIBLE: GENESIS 39:6-12,20-23

But while Joseph was there in the prison, the LORD was with him; he showed him kindness and granted him favour (VV.20-21).

Joseph had no idea what would happen to him after his angry brothers faked his death and sold him to slave traders who took him to Egypt and sold him to Potiphar, an Egyptian official (GENESIS 37:36). He found himself in a culture surrounded by people who believed in thousands of gods. To make things worse, Potiphar's wife tried to get Joseph to go to bed with her. When Joseph kept saying no, she framed him, which got him sent to prison (39:16-20).

Things were looking worse than ever for Joseph. He had done nothing wrong, yet he found himself in prison in another country. God had given him dreams when he was a teenager; dreams that he would one day be in a position of power, even over his family (37:5-7). But now, it seemed like God had forgotten him.

But God had not forgotten Joseph. He was making him the man He needed him to be. Not only was God with Joseph, but He also "gave him success in everything he did" and even "showed him kindness and granted him favour" with those in authority (39:3,21).

Imagine how scared Joseph must have felt. But he kept trusting God and living by His ways. God was with Joseph in his difficult journey and had a plan for him. He has a plan in mind for you too. Keep focused on Him and His promises in the Bible. His eyes are turned towards you (PSALM 11:4) and no one can snatch you from His hands (JOHN 10:28-29).

EPE

COMPLETING THE PICTURE . . .

Jacob's family was seriously complicated. He had twelve sons through two wives and two maidservants. They didn't exactly get on. Joseph was Jacob's favourite son, which made the other brothers jealous. That's why they came up with a plan to get rid of him. However, God used this troubled family to continue His story of salvation (GENESIS 50:20). Jacob's twelve sons became the heads of the twelve tribes of Israel—God's people.

IF GOD CAN USE JACOB'S FAMILY, HE CAN USE ANYONE!

Seven days in . . . Genesis

GOD IS WORKING FOR OUR GOOD

BIBLE: GENESIS 45:1-8

You intended to harm me, but God intended it for good to accomplish what is now being done, the saving of many lives (GENESIS 50:20).

God is so wise and powerful that absolutely nothing can stop His plans. In fact, He is able to use even bad things and make them work for good.

Joseph's brothers hated him so much that they had plotted his murder before deciding to sell him as a slave. But in Egypt, Joseph gained the favour of Pharaoh, who made Joseph his right hand man (he effectively became Egypt's prime minister). During a famine, his brothers came to Egypt for food, not realising Joseph was alive, let alone in charge there. Joseph had the perfect opportunity to get even with his brothers. But he didn't. He forgave them.

When Joseph finally identified himself to his brothers, he said: "Do not be distressed and do not be angry with yourselves for selling me here, because it was to save lives that God sent me ahead of you" (GENESIS 45:5). Later he told them, "You intended to harm me, but God intended it for good to accomplish what is now being done, the saving of many lives" (50:20).

To me, that's both exciting and encouraging. It's amazing to think that no matter what someone might do to hurt me, God is able to use it for my good and His glory.

When we're upset because of things that are happening in our lives, we can still be thankful. In God's wisdom, power and love, He is working all things for our good (ROMANS 8:28).

RDH

COMPLETING THE PICTURE . . .

While Joseph was in charge in Egypt, "There was famine in all the other lands" (GENESIS 41:54). "All the world came to Egypt to buy grain from Joseph, because the famine was severe everywhere" (V.57). This is what made Joseph's brothers come to Egypt. Joseph became a saviour-like figure during a global crisis, giving us a picture of Jesus who is the true Saviour for the real global crisis: sin. Through Joseph, God provided a worldwide rescue, but also saved Jacob's family which became the nation of Israel (and God promised to provide our Saviour through this nation). The people of Israel lived in Egypt for 430 years (EXODUS 12:40-41), but during that time they became enslaved (EXODUS 1:8-14).

GOD CAN BRING GOOD OUT OF BAD.

THERE IS HOPE

BIBLE: I KINGS 19:1-13

"I have had enough, LORD," he said. "Take my life" (V.4).

We're all affected by depression at some point, either because we're going through it or someone close to us is.

Some common signs and symptoms of depression include hopelessness, a loss of interest in life, struggling to engage with things and feeling worthless and helpless. Alongside depression, many of us battle suicidal thoughts during our darkest days. But isn't Jesus meant to fix this kind of stuff in our lives?

Knowing Jesus doesn't change the fact that many of us will still struggle to some extent with depression, mental and emotional issues, and suicidal thoughts. In 1 Kings 19, Elijah was so physically and emotionally exhausted that he asked God to take his life. Although that's not suicide, he was clearly feeling helpless and like his life was too hard. But God brought Elijah out of his depression. He strengthened him with food and sleep, listened to his complaint, reassured him in a still, small voice—and gave him new work to do.

Are you feeling hopeless and desperate today? Do things feel too hard for you to handle? Just as God was ready to meet Elijah's needs, He is ready to meet yours. Realising we haven't got what it takes is no reason to give up—it shows us our reality; we can't do life without God (JOHN 15:5).   *DDH*

WANT MORE ... ?

Check out *What difference does God make when I feel depressed?* online at
ourdailybread.org/teen

WHEN WE GET TO THE END OF OUR STRENGTH, WE'RE READY TO RELY ON GOD'S.

BURYING OUR HEADS

BIBLE: 2 SAMUEL 12

I gave you all Israel and Judah. And if all this had been too little, I would have given you even more. Why did you despise the word of the LORD by doing what is evil in his eyes? (V.8).

Lots of people believe the myth that ostriches bury their heads in the sand to ignore danger. An ostrich can run at a speed of 45 miles per hour, kick powerfully and peck aggressively with its beak. As the largest and fastest bird in the world, it doesn't need to bury its head!

"Burying your head in the sand" is something we can all be guilty of. A difficult, awkward situation comes up . . . and we just hope it goes away by itself! The prophet Nathan, however, did not allow King David to forget his sins of adultery and murder (2 SAMUEL 12:1-14). It took a brave man to confront a king about the mess he had made. Yet Nathan trusted God's leading, and went to talk to David about what he had done wrong.

In a similar way, the apostle Paul teaches us to confront sin: "If someone is caught in a sin, you who live by the Spirit should restore that person gently. But watch yourselves, or you also may be tempted" (GALATIANS 6:1). This doesn't mean we go looking for mistakes our friends are making, just to point them out. It means that we are looking out for them and caring about how they are doing with God.

If we see friends at youth group starting to drift away from God, let's not bury our heads in the sand. Like Nathan, let's talk to them and remind them that their relationship with God is the most important thing they have! *AL*

TO PRAY ABOUT . . .

Dear God, please help me to care as much about my friends' relationships with You as I care about my own relationship with You. When I'm tempted to ignore their drifts from You, show me instead how I can encourage them to come close to You.

WE LOVE OUR FRIENDS BEST WHEN WE HELP THEM STAY CLOSE TO GOD.

GOT YOUR NOSE

BIBLE: EXODUS 12:12-20
I will bring judgement on all the gods of Egypt (V.12).

"Why are the statues' noses broken?" That's the number one question visitors ask at the Ancient Egyptian part of one museum.

The broken noses can't be blamed on normal wear and tear; even two-dimensional painted figures are missing noses. One expert explains that the statues and paintings must have been attacked, and the noses deliberately removed. Enemies meant to kill Ancient Egypt's gods. It's as if they were playing a game of 'got your nose' with them. Invading armies broke off the noses of these fake gods so they couldn't breathe.

Really? That's all it took? With gods like this, Pharaoh should have known he was in trouble. Yes, he had an army and led a powerful nation. Whereas God's people were just worn-out slaves being led by a fugitive called Moses. But Israel had the living God, and Pharaoh's gods were pretenders. Ten plagues later, their imaginary lives were over (EXODUS 7-11).

Israel were to celebrate their rescue from Egypt with the yearly Festival of Unleavened Bread. In this festival, they would eat bread without yeast for a week (EXODUS 12:17-20). Yeast symbolised sin, and God wanted his people to remember their rescued lives belong entirely to Him.

Our God says to idols, "Got your nose," and to us, His people, "Got your life." Choose the God who gives you breath, and know the confidence of belonging to Him.
MW

THINKING IT OVER . . .
We may not have many statue-like idols in our day-to-day lives, but what 'modern' fake gods might still be trying to distract you from the real, living God? How might things like social media, boyfriends or girlfriends, exam grades and even serving in church become idols? How can you make sure you're only trusting in and living for Jesus?

THE SON OF GOD HAS COME AND HAS GIVEN US UNDERSTANDING, SO THAT WE MAY KNOW HIM WHO IS TRUE. 1 JOHN 5:20

LIGHTING UP A DARK WORLD

BIBLE: ROMANS 16:1-5

All the churches of the Gentiles are grateful to them (V.4).

A refugee who ran away from his war-torn country told the nightmarish story of his journey to freedom.

Separated from his family, he was abandoned in the middle of the ocean by a smuggler and only just escaped being shipwrecked. When he finally made it to land again, he was imprisoned for a time, where he was starved and beaten. Just when he thought it was all over, he met some Christians who gave him food and somewhere to stay. Eventually, he found a church family who cared for him with a place to live in a new country he could call home.

This story shines a light on the role played by Christians who bring hope and kindness to a hurting world. When writing to Christians in Rome, Paul finished his letter by giving little messages about a few individuals. Among them was Phoebe who had "been the benefactor of many people, including me." And of Priscilla and Aquila he wrote, "They risked their lives for me. Not only I but all the churches of the Gentiles are grateful to them" (ROMANS 16:1-4).

Priscilla and Aquila also made space for their church family to meet in their home (V.5), and mentored new Christians (ACTS 18:24-26). And they did this in a time when the church was under a lot of attacks.

Christians like Phoebe, Priscilla and Aquila were examples of being lights for Jesus in a dark world. Let's look to follow in their footsteps, even when it costs us something.

RO

TO PRAY ABOUT . . .

Heavenly Father, I pray for the many Christians around the world being attacked and hated for Your sake. Please give them the strength to keep trusting Jesus. And please help me to stay true to You, even when things are hard and I feel rejected by friends and family.

GOD'S PEOPLE LIGHT UP A DARK WORLD.

LYING DOWN DEAD

BIBLE: JAMES 4:7-17
You are a mist that appears for a little while and then vanishes (V.14).

A primary school teacher asked her class to draw a picture of what they'd be doing one hundred years from now. The kids drew the sort of pictures you would expect: firemen, princesses and so on. One of them, Aaron, very practically drew a stick man along the bottom of the page and explained, "In 100 years . . . I'll be lying down dead."

None of us knows where we'll be in five, ten or fifteen years. But in a hundred years, like Aaron, we can be fairly certain we'll no longer be walking this earth. James talked about this in his letter: "What is your life? You are a mist that appears for a little while and then vanishes" (JAMES 4:14). We don't know what tomorrow will bring, but because we belong to Jesus we can know that God is with us and guiding us by His Spirit every step of the way.

James told us to "come near to God." As we do, He comes near to us (V.8). When we are completely God-centred and relying on Him for everything, we can trust our hopes, dreams and plans to Him, knowing He holds our lives in His hands (VV.13-16)—no matter how short or long! When we're focused on Him, He won't waste a single moment.

AK

WHAT I'M THANKFUL FOR . . .
Heavenly Father, thank You that no matter how short or long my life is on the earth, and no matter what each day brings, as Your child You are with me and promise me a place in Your home forever!

WE DON'T KNOW WHAT TOMORROW WILL BRING —BUT WE KNOW GOD WILL BE WITH US.

THE RIGHT PLACE

BIBLE: ROMANS 11:33-36

Oh, the depth of the riches of the wisdom and knowledge of God! How unsearchable his judgements, and his paths beyond tracing out! (V.33).

I was stressed out and got up during the night to pace the floor and pray. To be honest, my attitude wasn't great—even though I was praying. I was full of frustration towards God. *What was He doing? Why was this even happening?*

Not getting any answers, I slumped down by the window and stared out at the night sky. I found myself looking up at Orion's belt—those three bright stars which are often easy to spot on clear nights. I remembered that those three stars, forming a perfect line in the sky, are actually hundreds of light-years apart.

I realised that if I were to get closer to those stars, they would look less and less like they were in a line. Yet far away as I was, they looked carefully placed in the heavens. At that moment, I realised I was too close to my life to see what God sees. In His big picture, everything is in its right place.

The apostle Paul, as he wrote a summary of the purposes of God, broke into a hymn of praise (ROMANS 11:33-36). His words lift our eyes to our King, whose ways are far better and way beyond our small ability to understand Him (V.33). The One who holds all things together in the heavens and on earth is totally involved with every detail of our lives (MATTHEW 6:25-34; COLOSSIANS 1:16). "The plans of the LORD stand firm for ever" (PSALM 33:11), even when our days—and nights—feel chaotic and overwhelming. *EM*

THINKING IT OVER . . .

Read Psalm 33. What do you learn about God's plans and ways (VV.4-5,11)? Are any parts of the universe outside of His reach or control? What is better, trying to fix our own problems or relying on God (VV.16-22)? What encourages you most from this psalm?

GOD'S PLANS MIGHT BE HARD TO UNDERSTAND, BUT THEY ARE ALWAYS GOOD.

FOMO

BIBLE: PHILIPPIANS 4:10-19

I have learned the secret of being content in any and every situation (V.12).

I think our cat Heathcliff has a bad case of FOMO (the fear of missing out). When I come home, Heathcliff rushes over to inspect my bag to see what I've been doing. When anyone is in the kitchen, he stands up on his back paws trying to see if there is anything worth eating on the side and begging for a little bit of it. But when we actually give Heathcliff whatever's caught his attention, he quickly loses interest, walking away with bored disinterest. But I can't be too hard on him . . . I'm just the same.

Paul tells us that contentment (being satisfied) isn't natural—it is learned (PHILIPPIANS 4:11). On our own, we chase after whatever we think will make us feel good, moving on to the next thing the minute we realise it won't. Other times, this 'chasing' gets us down; making us anxiously shield ourselves from others because we can't deal with the feeling of emptiness.

The surprising thing is that sometimes we need to face our fears (like missing out or somehow messing up) in order to find real satisfaction. These things can help us finally realise that we won't find lasting contentment on our own!

Having gone through many of the worst things life has to offer, Paul could say first-hand that he had finally learned "the secret" of true contentment (VV.11-12). We have to give up our chase for happiness and satisfaction entirely, and give our needs to God. It is only in knowing Him and making Him the very centre that we find true peace (VV.6-7). Where are you looking for your satisfaction today?

MB

THINKING IT OVER . . .

Is contentment something you are aiming for? Is it something you are learning as you get to know God better? What do you think Paul means when he says, "I can do all this through him who gives me strength" (PHILIPPIANS 4:13)? Where do you draw strength from during your good days and bad days?

CONTENTMENT DOESN'T MEAN GETTING EVERYTHING YOU WANT; IT MEANS BEING SATISFIED WITH WHAT GOD HAS PROVIDED.

DARK THOUGHTS

BIBLE: PHILIPPIANS 4:4-9

Whatever is true, whatever is noble, whatever is right, whatever is pure, whatever is lovely, whatever is admirable—if anything is excellent or praiseworthy—think about such things (V.8).

I watched a reality TV show where different people talked about something they owned that was so important to them that they'd never give it up. So I tried to think about the things in my life that mean the most to me.

There are some keepsakes my parents have given me; special moments with my friends which we videoed on our phones; even encouragements people at church have said to me. There are lots of things like this that make me happy.

Most of us, however, also have a store of things that make us really unhappy; things we keep inside. Anxiety, anger, regret or bitterness can fill our lives with pain and misery. Why do we hang on to these things? What good do they do for us? Nothing. They only bring fear, resentment and selfishness, and yet they are so hard to give up. Paul gave a more positive way to 'think' in a letter to the church at Philippi. He said we are to actively choose what thoughts we set our minds on. He encouraged us to always rejoice, to be gentle and to bring everything to God in prayer (PHILIPPIANS 4:4-9).

Paul's words help us see that it's possible to push out dark thoughts. It's not about 'emptying' our minds. It's about filling our minds—with God's good, pure, excellent words and ways (VV.8-9). When we focus on God and bring our dark thoughts to Him, the peace of God will "guard [our] hearts and minds in Christ Jesus" (V.7).

CHK

THINKING IT OVER . . .

What unwelcome, dark thoughts stubbornly take up space in your mind and heart? What's one way you can daily fill up your mind with good things? What might it look like to put Colossians 3:1-3 into practice? Why not use these verses to reflect on this week.

SET YOUR MINDS ON THINGS ABOVE, NOT ON EARTHLY THINGS. COLOSSIANS 3:2

ANCIENT PROMISES

BIBLE: NUMBERS 6:22-27

The LORD bless you and keep you (V.24).

In 1979, Dr. Gabriel Barkay and his team discovered two silver scrolls in a burial ground outside the Old City of Jerusalem. In 2004, after twenty-five years of careful research, scholars confirmed that the scrolls were the oldest biblical texts in existence, having been buried in 600 BC. What I really love is the words of the Bible on the scrolls—the blessing that God wanted spoken over His people: "The LORD bless you and keep you; the LORD make his face shine on you" (NUMBERS 6:24-25).

God showed Aaron and his sons (through Moses) how to bless the people on His behalf. The leaders were to memorise the words God gave so they could speak them to the people just as God wanted (6:24-26). Notice how these words emphasise that God is the one who blesses! Three times they say, "the LORD". And six times He says, "you," showing just how personal and close our God is. He wants His people to know His love and favour.

Think about it for a moment: the oldest existing bits of the Bible tell us about how God wants to bless. What a reminder of God's love and how He wants to be in a relationship with us. If you feel far from God today, hold tightly to the promise in these ancient words. May God bless you; may He keep you.

ABP

WANT MORE ... ?

Check out *Can we really trust the Bible?* online at
ourdailybread.org/lookingdeeper

THE BIBLE IS THE STORY OF GOD'S LOVE FOR US.

THE HARDEST PLACES

BIBLE: GENESIS 41:46-52

Joseph stored up huge quantities of grain, like the sand of the sea (V.49).

Geoff is a youth pastor today in the same city where he once was addicted to heroin. God transformed him and his life in an amazing way. "I want to keep kids from making the same mistakes and suffering the pain I went through," Geoff said. "And Jesus will help them." Over time, God set him free from addiction and has given him a really important mission, despite his past.

God has a way of bringing unexpected good out of hopeless situations. Joseph was sold into slavery in Egypt, then he was falsely accused and finally he was sent to prison. For years, he was forgotten about. But God rescued him at just the right time and put him in a position of authority directly under Pharaoh. God used him to save many lives—including the lives of his brothers who'd sold him.

In Egypt Joseph married and had children. He named the second Ephraim (from the Hebrew term for "twice fruitful"), giving this reason: "It is because God has made me fruitful in the land of my suffering" (GENESIS 41:52).

Geoff's and Joseph's stories, while separated by three or four thousand years, show the same unchanging truth: even the hardest places in our lives can be used by God to help and save others. Jesus' love and power never change, and He's always faithful to those who trust in Him.   JB

WHAT I'M THANKFUL FOR . . .

All-powerful Father, I praise You that nothing is too hard for You!
Thank You for Your perfect faithfulness today and forever.

GOD CAN USE EVERYTHING WE GO THROUGH FOR GOOD.

CENTRE OF THE WORLD

BIBLE: PSALM 48

Your praise reaches to the ends of the earth (V.10).

You can often tell where a map was made by what sits in its middle. We tend to think our home is the centre of the world, so we put a dot in the middle and sketch out from there. Nearby towns might be fifty miles to the north or half a day's drive to the south, but all are described in relation to where we are. The psalms draw their 'map' from God's earthly home in the Old Testament, so the centre of biblical geography is Jerusalem.

Psalm 48 is one of many psalms that praise Jerusalem. This "city of our God, his holy mountain" is "beautiful in its loftiness, the joy of the whole earth" (PSALM 48:1-2). Because "God is in her citadels," He "makes her secure forever" (VV.3,8). God's fame begins in Jerusalem's temple and spreads outwards to "the ends of the earth" (VV.9-10).

Unless you're reading this in Jerusalem, your home is not in the centre of the biblical world. Yet your country, town and home matters because God will not rest until His praise reaches "to the ends of the earth" (V.10). Would you like to be part of the way God reaches His goal? Spend time with God's family each week at church and openly live each day for Him. A true knowledge of God will continue spreading "to the ends of the earth" as we also give all that we are to Him. *MW*

TO PRAY ABOUT . . .

Father, use me to spread the gospel and the truth of who You are to the people I know—and even to the ends of the earth.

THE GOSPEL IS MEANT TO SPREAD —ARE YOU SHARING IT?

DOES WHAT WE DO MATTER?

BIBLE: COLOSSIANS 3:12-17

Whatever you do, do it all for the glory of God (1 CORINTHIANS 10:31).

I dropped my forehead to my hand with a sigh, "I don't know how I'm going to get it all done." My friend's voice crackled through the phone: "Give yourself some credit. You're doing a lot." He then listed the things I was trying to do—preparing for my final exams, writing and leading a Bible study for my youth group, balancing family time, seeing friends and trying to keep myself fit. I wanted to do all these things for God. But I was more focused on *what* I was doing than *how* I was doing it—or that perhaps I was trying to do too much.

Paul reminded the church in Colossae that they were to live in a way that pleased God and made Him known. Ultimately, what they specifically did on a day-to-day basis was not as important as how they did it. They were to do their work with "compassion, kindness, humility, gentleness and patience" (COLOSSIANS 3:12), to be forgiving and above all to love (VV.13-14). They were to "do it all in the name of the Lord Jesus" (V.17). What they did wasn't to be separated from Jesus-like living.

What we do matters, but how we do it, why we do it and who we do it for matters more. Each day we can choose to run around like headless chickens, or live in a way that puts God first, follows His priorities and relies on Him.   JS

THINKING IT OVER . . .

How does Ephesians 2:10 help you understand the right perspective we should have on the things that we do?

GOD ISN'T JUST INTERESTED IN WHAT WE DO, BUT WHY WE DO IT.

HOW TO STAY ON TRACK

BIBLE: 1 JOHN 2:18-27

The Spirit teaches you everything you need to know, and what he teaches is true—it is not a lie (V.**27** NLT).

As the world's fastest blind runner, David Brown says his wins are all down to God, his mum's early advice ("no sitting around") and his running guide—Jerome Avery. Attached to Brown by a string tied to their fingers, Avery guides Brown's races with words and touches.

"It's all about listening to his cues," says Brown, who says he could "swing out wide" on 200-metre races where the track curves. "Day in and day out, we're going over race strategies," Brown says, "communicating with each other—not only verbal cues, but physical cues."

In our own 'races' in life, we're given a Divine Guide. Our Helper, the Holy Spirit, leads our steps when we follow Him. "I am writing these things to you about those who are trying to lead you astray," wrote John (1 JOHN 2:26). "But you have received the Holy Spirit, and he lives within you, so you don't need anyone to teach you what is true. For the Spirit teaches you everything you need to know" (V.27 NLT).

John stressed this to the Christians of his day who faced "antichrists"—people who denied that Jesus is God's promised King (V.22). We face people like that today as well—perhaps even in our churches. But the Holy Spirit, our Guide, helps us keep following Jesus. We can trust His 'touches' through the Bible to keep us on track.

PR

TO PRAY ABOUT . . .

Dear God, help me to listen to Your guidance through the Bible and the Holy Spirit living within me. Help me to avoid lies about You and to stick close to the truth.

THE HOLY SPIRIT HELPS US SEE AND AVOID LIES ABOUT GOD.

THE GOD-MAN

BIBLE: COLOSSIANS 1:15-22

The Son is the image of the invisible God, the firstborn over all creation (V.15).

Before I decided to give my life to Jesus, I'd heard about His story and wrestled with His identity. How could He offer forgiveness for my sins when the Bible says only God can forgive sins? I discovered I wasn't alone in my struggles after reading something from a Christian author. He suggests that for many non-Christians the "really staggering Christian claim is that Jesus of Nazareth was God made man . . . as truly and fully God as He was human." Yet this is the truth that makes salvation possible.

When Paul talks about Jesus as "the image of the invisible God," he's saying that Jesus is completely and perfectly God—Creator and Sustainer of all things in heaven and earth—but also fully human (COLOSSIANS 1:15-17). Because of this truth, we can be confident that Jesus' death and resurrection has fully paid for our sin and take the judgement we deserve. As a human, He could take our place; as God, He's perfect and had no sin of His own to pay for. He is the only One who meets this 'job description'! He is the only One who could save us (VV.19-22)!

God the Father reveals Himself in and through the Bible by the power of the Holy Spirit and through the life of His Son. Those who believe in Jesus are saved because He is "God with us" (MATTHEW 1:23). Praise God!   XD

THINKING IT OVER . . .

Do you wrestle with Jesus' identity? Take some time to read and think about Philippians 2:5-11. How does this help describe who Jesus is, what He has done and what our response to Him should be?

THE WORD BECAME FLESH AND MADE HIS DWELLING AMONG US. JOHN 1:14

FULL ATTENTION

BIBLE: ISAIAH 46:3-10

I have made you and I will carry you (V.4).

Sometimes when my family's Labrador wants attention, he'll take something that belongs to one of us—like a shoe, sock or bag—and parade it in front of us. One morning as I was watching TV, Max snatched my wallet and ran off. But realising I hadn't seen him do it, he returned and nudged me with his nose—wallet in mouth, eyes dancing, tail wagging, asking me to play.

Max's behaviour made me laugh, but it also reminded me how much I am in my own little world; unaware of others. So often I've intended to spend time with family or friends, but other things take up my time; and before I know it the day slips away and I've missed lots of opportunities to show love to the people in my life.

It's good to know that our heavenly Father is so great that He's able to focus on each of us perfectly. He gives every breath in our lungs for as long as we live. He promises His people, "Even to your old age and grey hairs I am he, I am he who will sustain you. I have made you and I will carry you" (ISAIAH 46:4).

God always has time for us. He understands every detail of our lives—no matter how complex or messy—and He's there whenever we talk to Him in prayer. We never have to wait in line for our Saviour's unlimited love and attention.

JB

TO PRAY ABOUT . . .

You always have time for me, Jesus.
Please help me to live every moment for You!

**WE DON'T HAVE TO GET GOD'S ATTENTION
—WE ALREADY HAVE IT!**

WAITING WITH THE TURTLE

BIBLE: PSALM 40:1-5,14-17

I waited patiently for the LORD; he turned to me and heard my cry (V.1).

Every autumn, when the painted turtle senses winter coming, she dives to the bottom of her pond, burying herself in the muck and mud. She pulls into her shell and goes still: her heart rate slows, almost stopping. Her body temperature drops, staying just above freezing. She stops breathing, and she waits. For six months she stays buried, and her body releases calcium from her bones into her bloodstream, so that she slowly begins even to lose her shape.

But when the pond thaws, she will float up and breathe again. Her bones will reform, and she will feel the warmth of the sun on her shell.

I think of the painted turtle when I read the description of waiting for God in Psalm 40. The psalm-writer is in a "slimy pit" of "mud and mire," but God hears him (PSALM 40:2). God lifts him out, and gives him a firm place to stand. God is "my help and my deliverer," he sings (V.17).

Perhaps it feels like you've been waiting forever for something to change—for things to get easier with your parents, for the end of the school year, for the end of your exams, for an end to the bullying or for the strength to break a bad habit. The painted turtle and Psalm 40 are here to remind us to trust in God: He hears and He will rescue us.

AP

TO PRAY ABOUT . . .

God, sometimes it's hard to wait. But I trust in You and in Your timing, Your plans for me and Your rescue. Please give me patience as You show Your greatness in my life.

WAIT FOR THE LORD; BE STRONG AND TAKE HEART AND WAIT FOR THE LORD. PSALM 27:14

STORM CHASERS

BIBLE: PSALM 107:23-32

He stilled the storm to a whisper; the waves of the sea were hushed (V.29).

"Chasing tornadoes," says Warren Faidley, "is often like a giant game of 3D-chess played out over thousands of square miles." The photographer and storm chaser adds: "Being in the right place at the right time is a mix of forecasting and navigation while dodging everything from football-sized hailstones to dust storms and slow-moving farm equipment."

His words make my palms sweaty with nervousness! I admire his raw courage and scientific hunger as a storm chaser. But I go a bit faint at the idea of throwing myself into the middle of some of the most dangerous and unpredictable weather conditions.

In my experience, however, I don't have to chase storms in life—they seem to be chasing me. That's what Psalm 107 describes too, as it talks about sailors trapped in a storm. They were being chased by the results of their wrong choices, but the psalm-writer says, "They cried out to the LORD in their trouble, and he brought them out of their distress. He stilled the storm to a whisper; the waves of the sea were hushed. They were glad when it grew calm" (PSALM 107:28-30).

Whether the storms of life come from our own mess or just because we live in a broken world, our God is greater. When we are being chased by storms, He is able to calm them—or to calm the anxious storm within us.   BC

THINKING IT OVER . . .

Read the story of Jesus literally calming a storm for His followers (MARK 4:35-41). How dangerous was this storm (V.37)? What did the disciples' question show about their trust of Jesus (V.38)? How difficult was it for Jesus to calm the storm (V.39)? What stops you believing Jesus is as in control of your storms? What is your answer to Jesus' question in verse 40?

NO STORM IS OUTSIDE OF JESUS' MIGHTY POWER!

SLOWING DOWN TIME

BIBLE: PSALM 90:4-15

Teach us to number our days, that we may gain a heart of wisdom (V.12).

A lot has changed since the electric clock was invented in the 1840s. We now keep time on smart watches, smart phones and just about everything else. The pace of our lives seems to be set by speed and time. "We're just moving faster and faster and getting back to people as quickly as we can," one researcher said. "That's driving us to think everything has to happen now."

Moses, the writer of one of the oldest psalms in the Bible, had a few things to say about time. He reminds us that God controls life's pace. "A thousand years in your sight are like a day that has just gone by, or like a watch in the night," he wrote (PSALM 90:4).

So the secret to managing our time well isn't about going faster or slower. It's about trusting the stuff we have to do to God, and firstly spending more time with Him. That will allow us to trust our days and the things we're doing to Him. Then we can get in step with each other as we look out for others before ourselves. But it starts with getting in step with Him—the One who made us (139:13) and knows our purpose and plans (V.16).

Even if we get to live on earth for a long, long time—it won't last forever. So it is important that we use our time, even now. Not by watching the clock or trying to fit in as much as we can, but by giving each day to God. As Moses said, "Teach us to number our days, that we may gain a heart of wisdom" (90:12). Then, with God we'll always be on time, now and forever.

PR

THINKING IT OVER . . .

What's your pace in life? Do you fit in as much as you can, or do you feel like you have lots of empty hours? How could you spend more time with God, getting in step with Him?

NO TIME IS EVER WASTED WHEN WE'RE WAITING ON GOD.

RUN TOWARDS YOUR CHALLENGE

BIBLE: 2 KINGS 6:8-23

He looked and saw the hills full of horses and chariots of fire all round Elisha (V.17).

Tom chased the guys who were stealing a bike. He didn't have a plan. He only knew he needed to get that bike. To his surprise, the three thieves looked his way, dropped the bike and backed away. Tom was both relieved and impressed with himself as he picked up the bike and turned around. That's when he saw Jeff, his huge, muscly friend who had been following close behind.

Elisha's servant panicked when he saw his town surrounded by an enemy army. He ran to Elisha, "Oh no, my lord! What shall we do?" Elisha told him to relax. "Those who are with us are more than those who are with them." Then God 'opened' the servant's eyes to the reality, and he "saw the hills full of horses and chariots of fire all round Elisha" (2 KINGS 6:15-17).

If you want to follow Jesus, you may find yourself in some difficult situations. Kids at school might make fun of you; your family may not like you going to church; you might have to stand up for the weird people in your class who get bullied. You may lose sleep wondering how it will all turn out. Remember you're not alone. You don't have to be stronger or smarter than the things you face or the people who are making life hard for you. Jesus is with you, and His power is completely unmatched. Ask yourself Paul's question, "If God is for us, who can be against us?" (ROMANS 8:31). Really, who? No one. Run towards your challenge—with God.

MW

THINKING IT OVER . . .

What wakes you up at night? How can you give your worries to God?
Read John 16:33, Hebrews 13:5-6 and 1 John 5:4-5.
What encouragement do these verses give you?

GOD IS WITH US IN EVERY STRUGGLE.

STAY ON THE WAY

BIBLE: JOHN 14:1-7

Lord, we don't know where you are going, so how can we know the way? (V.5).

It was getting dark as I followed Li Bao along the tops of walls cut into the mountains of central China. I had never been this way before, and I couldn't see more than one step ahead—or how steep the drop was to our left. I gulped and stuck close to Li. I didn't know where we were going or how long it would take, but I trusted my friend.

I was in the same position as Thomas, the disciple who always seemed to need reassurance. Jesus told His followers that He must leave to prepare a place for them, and that they knew "the way to the place where I am going" (JOHN 14:4). Thomas asked a logical follow-up question: "Lord, we don't know where you are going, so how can we know the way?" (V.5).

Jesus didn't answer Thomas's doubt by explaining every little detail of heaven and how He was going to get them there. He simply promised Thomas that He was the way there. And that was enough.

We too have questions about our future. None of us know the details of what lies ahead. Life is full of twists we don't see coming. That's okay. It's enough to know Jesus, who is "the way and the truth and the life" (V.6). He will lead us the right way—and at the end, bring us safely into heaven. *MW*

WHAT I'M THANKFUL FOR . . .

Thank You, Jesus, that You are the way to heaven. And You are the way every single day until then. I know I am heading the right way when I stick close to You.

**JESUS KNOWS WHAT'S NEXT.
HE ONLY ASKS THAT WE WALK CLOSE TO HIM.**

THE FLIP SIDE OF LOVE

BIBLE: 2 JOHN 1:1-11

Grace, mercy and peace from God the Father and from Jesus Christ, the Father's Son, will be with us in truth and love (V.3).

The Roman inns during Jesus' time had a reputation so bad that rabbis (Jewish religious teachers) wouldn't even allow cattle to be left at them. Faced with such bad conditions, travelling Christians usually looked out for other Christians they could stay with.

Among those early travellers were false teachers who said that Jesus wasn't God's promised King (the Messiah). This is why John said in his letter of 2 John that there is a time to *not* be hospitable. John had said before that these false teachers were an "antichrist—denying the Father and the Son" (1 JOHN 2:22). In 2 John he expanded on this, telling his readers that whoever trusts Jesus as God and King "has both the Father and the Son" (2 JOHN 1:9).

Then he warned, "If anyone comes to you and does not bring this teaching, do not take them into your house or welcome them" (V.10). To welcome someone spreading a false message about Jesus would actually keep people separated from God. It would encourage people to believe in a fake-Jesus, which would do them no good at all!

John's second letter shows us a 'flip side' of God's love. We belong to a God who welcomes everyone with open arms. But genuine love won't stand for people who harm themselves and others by spreading fake news about Jesus. God wraps His arms around those who genuinely trust Jesus for themselves, but He never allows a lie.   TG

THINKING IT OVER . . .

Where do you get your information and teaching about Jesus from? Church leaders, youth pastors and Christian friends are really helpful—but we need to be spending time with Jesus in the Bible. This is where Jesus makes Himself known to us most clearly. Jesus asked His followers, "Who do you say I am?" (MARK 8:29). What's your answer?

THERE IS ONLY ONE JESUS —AND HE'S FOUND IN THE BIBLE.

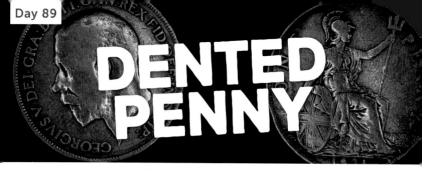

DENTED PENNY

BIBLE: EPHESIANS 6:10-18

Stand firm then . . . with the breastplate of righteousness in place (V.14).

Private John Trickett kept a penny in the top breast pocket of his uniform during World War I. He kept it as a reminder of home. But it became much more valuable than that! John got hit by a bullet in 1914, but the penny—tucked away in his pocket, and covering his heart—deflected the bullet and saved his life. The dented coin was passed down through generations of his family—generations that wouldn't have existed if it weren't for that penny.

That dented penny reminds us why armour is so important. And so Paul told the Ephesians to put on "the full armour of God" every day (EPHESIANS 6:11). The breastplate in the armour, which would have covered most of the soldier's body, including his vital organs, is likened to "righteousness" (V.14). Our right relationship with God is our best protection for whatever we face today. We are covered in Jesus' perfection. All our past and future wrongs have been paid for. We cannot be accused of anything (ROMANS 8:33), no matter what guilty feelings the devil tries to fire our way. Now nothing can separate us from God's love (VV.38-39). The breastplate and the other pieces of God's armour allow us to "stand [our] ground" when we face temptations and problems (EPHESIANS 6:13).

We are in a battle against an enemy who wants to distract us from God, even today (VV.11-12). When we wear the armour of God, through prayer and reading the Bible, God gives us His unfailing strength and "mighty power" (V.10).

KH

WANT MORE . . . ?

Check out *What is the armour of God?* online at
ourdailybread.org/lookingdeeper

OUR RELATIONSHIP WITH GOD IS OUR BEST PROTECTION FOR WHATEVER WE FACE TODAY.

UNSEEN REALITIES

BIBLE: EPHESIANS 6:10-20

Our struggle is not against flesh and blood, but . . . against the spiritual forces of evil in the heavenly realms (V.12).

In 1876, men drilling for coal in central Indiana thought they had found the gates of hell. Historian John Barlow Martin reports that at six hundred feet down, "foul fumes issued forth amid awesome noises." Afraid they had "bitten into the roof of the devil's cave," the miners plugged the well and ran back to their homes.

The miners, of course, were mistaken—and some years later, they would drill again and be rich in natural gas. Even though they got it wrong, I find myself a little challenged by them. These miners lived with an awareness of the spiritual world that is often missing from my own life. It's easy for me to live as if the supernatural and the natural rarely come together. I get so distracted by what I see around me, that I forget "our struggle is not against flesh and blood, but . . . against the spiritual forces of evil in the heavenly realms" (EPHESIANS 6:12).

When we see things going wrong or when we're having a hard time, we shouldn't give in or try to fight it all in our own strength. Instead, we are to put on "the full armour of God" (VV.13-18). It is His strength and protection we need, because ultimately our enemies are not the people we see or the bullies in class. Our enemies are "the spiritual forces of evil" hiding behind and using the people we see.

Studying the Bible, meeting regularly with our church family for encouragement and praying for the people we're struggling with can help us "stand against the schemes of the devil" (V.11). Strengthened by the Holy Spirit, we'll be able to stand firm in the face of anything (V.13). *AP*

THINKING IT OVER . . .

How can you keep reminding yourself that "our struggle is not against flesh and blood, but against . . . the spiritual forces of evil in the heavenly realms" (EPHESIANS 6:12)? Why not spend some time reflecting on Jesus' words in Matthew 5:43-48.

WHO IS IT THAT OVERCOMES THE WORLD? ONLY THE ONE WHO BELIEVES THAT JESUS IS THE SON OF GOD. 1 JOHN 5:5

Seven days with . . . Moses

WHO AM I?

BIBLE: EXODUS 3:10-17
I AM WHO I AM (V.14).

Dave was about to fulfil a dream and start as a full time Christian worker, sharing the gospel in his community. But then he started to have serious doubts.

"I don't deserve this," he told a friend. "The church supporting me doesn't know the real me. I'm not good enough."

Dave isn't alone. Mention the name of Moses and we might think of leadership, strength and the ten commandments. We often forget that Moses ran away to the desert after murdering a man (EXODUS 2:11-15). We lose sight of his forty years as a fugitive (ACTS 7:23). We don't often hear about his anger problem and his rejection of God's plan at first (EXODUS 4:13-14).

When God showed up with marching orders (3:1-10), Moses played the 'I'm-not-good-enough' card. He even got into a lengthy argument with God, asking Him: "Who am I?" (V.11). Then God told Moses who He was: "I AM WHO I AM" (V.14). It's impossible for us to explain that incredible and deep name. God is indescribable and awesome—yet there is something powerful and comforting in knowing "I AM".

A sense of our own weaknesses is healthy. But if we use them as an excuse to keep God from using us, we insult Him. What we're really saying is that God isn't good enough.

The question isn't *Who am I?* The question is *Who is the I AM?*

TG

COMPLETING THE PICTURE . . .

Moses was born while Israel was enslaved in Egypt. He was hidden from the Egyptians, who were killing all the Israelite baby boys (EXODUS 1:22; 2:1-4). He ended up being raised in Pharaoh's palace (VV.5-10). As an adult he still knew he was an Israelite, and fought back when an Egyptian was "beating a Hebrew, one of his own people" (V.11). This led to Moses running away and living in the wilderness for forty years (ACTS 7:30), before God then spoke to him from the burning bush, telling him it was time to set God's people free.

IT'S NOT ABOUT WHO YOU ARE, BUT WHO GOD IS.

Seven days with . . . Moses

KEEP ON GOING

BIBLE: EXODUS 10:21-29

By faith [Moses] left Egypt, not fearing the king's anger (HEBREWS 11:27).

There was one teacher at school who always seemed like she was just waiting for me to get things wrong. It didn't matter how much work I put into my essays, or how many questions I answered in class, it was never good enough. Sometimes I just wanted to quit her lessons.

The Bible tells us Moses wasn't mad keen on the idea of being the person to tell Pharaoh to let the people go (EXODUS 3:10; 4:13). As part of God's rescue of His people from Egypt, He sent ten plagues on the land. I wonder if Moses felt like quitting when he talked with Pharaoh during the plague of darkness (the second to last plague). Pharaoh finally exploded, "[Moses,] get out of my sight! Make sure you do not appear before me again! The day you see my face you will die" (10:28).

Despite this threat, Moses was used by God to free the Israelites. "It was by faith that Moses left the land of Egypt, not fearing the king's anger. He kept right on going because he kept his eyes on the one who is invisible" (HEBREWS 11:27 NLT). Moses didn't give up because he trusted God to keep His promise of rescue (EXODUS 3:17).

We can also rely on the promise that God is with us in every situation, supporting us through His Holy Spirit. He helps us keep going through His power, love and self-control (2 TIMOTHY 1:7). The Spirit provides the strength we need to be people of love, even in difficulties.

CW

COMPLETING THE PICTURE . . .

God finally rescued His people after the tenth plague (the death of the firstborn males) where lambs died instead of the Israelite firstborn males (check out the reading on Day 2). When Pharaoh then changed his mind and chased the Israelites, God parted the Red Sea, led His people through and brought the waters back down on Pharaoh and his army, washing them away (SEE EXODUS 14:26-31). All of this showed the people of Israel (and the world) that God is the only God (SEE EXODUS 6:7; 18:11; JOSHUA 2:8-10).

WE CAN KEEP GOING BECAUSE GOD IS OUR STRENGTH EACH DAY.

Seven days with . . . Moses

GO-BETWEEN

BIBLE: EXODUS 20:18-26

The people remained at a distance, while Moses approached the thick darkness where God was (V.21).

Imagine standing at the bottom of a mountain, elbow-to-elbow with thousands of others. Thunder and lightning flash; you hear an ear-splitting trumpet blast. God comes down to the mountaintop in fire. The mountain is covered in smoke; the whole thing begins to shake, and so do you (EXODUS 19:16-20).

When the Israelites had this terrifying experience near Mount Sinai, they begged Moses, "Speak to us yourself and we will listen. But do not let God speak to us or we will die" (20:19). The Israelites were asking Moses to mediate (or, be the go-between) between them and Almighty God. "The people remained at a distance, while Moses approached the thick darkness where God was" (V.21). After meeting with God, Moses brought God's messages and commands back down the mountain to the people below.

Today, we worship the same God who showed His staggering greatness on Mount Sinai. Because God is perfectly holy and we are so selfish and sinful, we cannot come to Him on our own (19:20-25). Left to ourselves we too would (and should) shake in fear. But Jesus made it possible for us to know God when He took our sins on Himself, died and rose again (1 CORINTHIANS 15:3-4). Even now, Jesus is the go-between for us to a holy and perfect God (ROMANS 8:34; 1 TIMOTHY 2:5).

JBS

COMPLETING THE PICTURE . . .

Moses went up Mount Sinai several times to speak with God, get His messages to the people and give their reply (SEE EXODUS 19:2-9,20-25; 20:21; 24:1 FOR SOME EXAMPLES). This is where God gave Moses the ten commandments (EXODUS 20), various laws (EXODUS 21-23) and details on how to make the ark of the covenant and the tabernacle—the tent where God's presence would be with His people (EXODUS 25). The books of Leviticus, Numbers and Deuteronomy contain the details of the laws, rituals and ways the people were to live as God's special people (as well as more of the story of their time in the wilderness).

BECAUSE OF JESUS WE CAN COME TO THE ALMIGHTY GOD WITH CONFIDENCE AND IN PEACE!

Seven days with . . . Moses

GOLDEN GOD

BIBLE: EXODUS 32

When the people saw that Moses was so long in coming down from the mountain, they gathered round Aaron and said, "Come, make us gods who will go before us" (V.1).

God hadn't let the Israelites leave Egypt emptyhanded. They had asked their former masters for silver, gold and clothing, and they got them. "The LORD had made the Egyptians favourably disposed towards the people, and they gave them what they asked for; so they plundered the Egyptians" (EXODUS 12:36).

It wasn't long, however, until God's people used their gold to make a golden calf. On Moses' longest trip up the mountain, he was gone for forty days (24:18). While he was gone, the people came to Moses' brother Aaron, the priest, and said, "Make us gods who will go before us. As for this fellow Moses who brought us up out of Egypt, we don't know what has happened to him" (32:1). Aaron did what they said, and they bowed down to their golden 'god' while Moses was on Mount Sinai receiving the law from the real God (32:1-4).

This story gives us a hard truth to face up to. There is so much around us to distract us from God—even the things we own (which God has given us). God gave the Israelites the Egyptians gold as a gift, and they used it to make a new god. What about the things God has given you? Do you use them to please Him, or to replace Him? Are you all about the stuff you can get here and now, or are you a "foreigner and stranger on earth" (HEBREWS 11:13), looking forward to being in heaven? Let's be like Moses who "regarded disgrace for the sake of Christ as of greater value than the treasures of Egypt, because he was looking ahead to his reward" (V.26).

HR

COMPLETING THE PICTURE . . .

God saw the Israelites rejection of Him while He was giving Moses the law (EXODUS 32:7-8). So He sent Moses back down to them. When Moses saw the golden image, he broke the ten commandments (written on stone tablets) in anger (32:19). This breaking was an image of the people of Israel having already broken the covenant (binding agreement) they had made with God (24:6-7). Amazingly, after this God gave Moses new stone tables (remaking the covenant) saying, "The LORD, the LORD, the compassionate and gracious God, slow to anger, abounding in love and faithfulness" (34:6).

I AM THE LORD YOUR GOD . . . YOU SHALL HAVE NO OTHER GODS BEFORE ME. EXODUS 20:1-2

Seven days with . . . Moses

FRIENDSHIP BENCH

BIBLE: EXODUS 33:9-11

The LORD would speak to Moses face to face, as one speaks to a friend (V.11).

Zimbabwe has a thing called friendship benches. People who are feeling down, sad or overwhelmed can go there to talk with 'grandmothers'—older women who are ready to listen to anyone struggling with depression, known in their language as *kufungisisa*, or "thinking too much".

The Friendship Bench Project is being started in other places, like Zanzibar, London and New York. "We were thrilled to bits with the results," said one person. "Before you know it, you're not just on a bench, you're just inside a warm conversation with someone who cares."

This is something of what it is like to talk with God. Moses didn't make a bench but a tent to spend time with God, calling it the tent of meeting. There, "the LORD would speak to Moses face to face, as one speaks to a friend" (EXODUS 33:11). Joshua, his assistant, wouldn't even leave the tent, seemingly because he so enjoyed his time with God (V.11).

Today we no longer need a tent of meeting. Jesus has brought us right into God's presence all the time. As He told His followers, "I have called you friends, for everything that I learned from my Father I have made known to you" (JOHN 15:15). Yes, our God knows us and is with us. He's our best Helper, our closest Friend. Spend some time talking with Him today!

PR

WHAT I'M THANKFUL FOR . . .

Dear God, thank You for encouraging me with these truths about You. When I'm sick with worry, point my mind back to You, my caring and amazing Friend.

DON'T MISS OUT ON SPENDING TIME WITH GOD!

Seven days with . . . Moses

GIANTS IN THE LAND

BIBLE: NUMBERS 13:25-14:9

Caleb silenced the people before Moses and said, "We should go up and take possession of the land, for we can certainly do it" (V.30).

After being camped near Mt. Sinai for two years, the people of Israel were about to enter Canaan—the land God had promised them. God told them to send twelve spies to check out the land and the people living there. When the spies saw how strong the Canaanites were, and the size of their cities, ten of them said, "We can't!" Two said, "We can!"

What made the difference? When the ten compared the giants with themselves, the giants loomed large. But the two—Caleb and Joshua—compared the giants with God, and the giants were cut down to size. "The LORD is with us," they said. "Do not be afraid of them" (NUMBERS 14:9).

When we're focused on ourselves and our abilities, the hard things we face can quickly become impossible.

Trusting God, on the other hand, means we're focused firstly on Him. This doesn't minimise the issues and giants we face—but it does put them in their place. They are not in charge. They do not have the final say.

What are your 'giants'? A habit you can't break? A temptation you can't resist? A person at school? Your home life? If we compare ourselves with them, we will always be overwhelmed. Let's look away from the size of our challenges to the size of the awesome God who leads us through them. *DR*

COMPLETING THE PICTURE . . .

Moses led the people to the edge of the Promised Land—but they didn't trust God to provide it. God was angry with the people for their rejection of Him (NUMBERS 14:11). While God did forgive them (V.20), there were big consequences: "No one who has treated me with contempt will ever see [the Promised Land]" (V.23). God turned them around to wander in the wilderness for forty years, "one year for each of the forty days you explored the land—you will suffer for your sins and know what it is like to have me against you" (V.34). God would bring the next generation of Israelites to the Promised Land (along with people like Caleb and Joshua, who had trusted Him) for them to enter it instead.

WHEN WE'RE AFRAID OF THE THINGS WE FACE, WE NEED TO TURN TO FACE GOD INSTEAD.

Seven days with . . . Moses

A LONGING IN STONE

BIBLE: DEUTERONOMY 34:1-5

I have let you see it with your eyes, but you will not cross over into it (V.4).

I read one poem that talked about piers as "a longing in stone". The poem describes that feeling of a boat sailing away, but the people on the pier being left behind. They can only watch it disappear—and ache for what's now out of reach.

We could say that Mount Nebo was Moses' "longing in stone". From Nebo he saw the Promised Land after forty years in the desert—a land he would never reach. God's words to Moses—"I have let you see it with your eyes, but you will not cross over into it" (DEUTERONOMY 34:4)—might seem harsh. But if that's all we see, we miss everything that's going on in the story. God was reassuring Moses: "This is the land I promised on oath to Abraham, Isaac and Jacob when I said, 'I will give it to your descendants'" (V.4). God had kept His promise! And very soon, Moses would leave Nebo for a land far better than Canaan (V.5; SEE HEBREWS 11:16).

Life often finds us standing on the pier. Dreams fade, friends move away, school changes, exams go badly, life happens—and things we might have been hoping for drift out of reach. When we ache for these things, let's bring them to God. He is our comfort (2 CORINTHIANS 1:3-4) and our life (JOHN 10:10) who promises us an amazing future (REVELATION 21:1-5). He is never out of reach. *TG*

COMPLETING THE PICTURE . . .

Moses was not allowed into the Promised Land because of what happened at Meribah Kadesh. The people turned against Moses because they had no water. So God told Moses to speak to the rock, and water would come out. Being angry with the people, Moses instead hit the rock with his staff (NUMBERS 20:10-11) as he had done once before (SEE EXODUS 17:6). Water came, as God promised, but Moses had not trusted in God enough to "honour [him] as holy" (V.12). Being kicked out of the Promised Land may sound harsh—but in his anger Moses had disobeyed God and apparently taken the credit for the miracle himself (V.10). Moses never complained about his punishment—he accepted it and continued to trust God. And God continued to love him, work through him and lead him.

GOD'S COMFORT, LOVE AND GOODNESS ARE ALWAYS WITHIN REACH FOR US TO HOLD ON TO.

TALKING TABLES

BIBLE: ACTS 2:42-47

Every day they continued to meet together in the temple courts (V.46).

Loneliness is one of the greatest threats to our mental health. When we feel lonely or cut off, it affects how we act, how much we eat, how we treat our families, how depressed we feel, and stuff like that. Apparently nearly two-thirds of us—across all ages and genders—feel lonely at least some of the time. One supermarket has come up with "talking tables" in their cafés as a way to offer a connection between people. Anyone who needs a bit of company can simply sit at a talking table and start a conversation with the other people who join them.

The people in the early church were committed to connecting with each other too. Without continually meeting up together, they would probably have felt very alone in their life with Jesus, which was still new to the world. Not only did they "[devote] themselves to the apostles' teaching" to learn what following Jesus meant, they also "[met] together in the temple courts" and "broke bread in their homes" for encouragement and to look out for each other (ACTS 2:42,46).

We need human connection; God designed us that way! Painful times of loneliness show how much we need other people. Like those first Christians in the early church, it's important for us to meet up with our youth group and church families. They can encourage us, share our worries, pray for us, care for us . . . and we can do the same for them! We all need each other as we walk this journey with God.

KH

THINKING IT OVER . . .

How can you intentionally connect with someone in your church or youth group today? How can you help make praying together and talking about God a bigger part of your church friendships?

IT'S IMPORTANT TO STAY WELL CONNECTED WITH OUR CHURCH FAMILIES.

MORNING PRAYERS

BIBLE: DEUTERONOMY 6:1-9

These commandments . . . are to be on your hearts. Impress them on your children (VV.6-7).

A boy was having a hard time at school. So his dad began to teach him to pray each morning before school. While the prayers weren't the same words every day, his dad suggested some things he could pray regularly, to help give him a God-centred view for the day ahead: "Thank You God for waking me up today. I am going to school so I can learn . . . and to be the leader that You have created me to be."

In a way, by teaching his son to pray like that, the dad is helping him to know and live by God's ways. It is similar to what God commanded His people when He was leading them through the desert: "These commandments . . . are to be on your hearts. Impress them on your children" (DEUTERONOMY 6:6-7).

After wandering in the wilderness for forty years, the next generation of Israelites was about to enter the Promised Land. God knew it would not be easy for them to succeed—unless they kept their focus on Him. And so, through Moses, He told them to remember His words and to obey Him—and to help their children to know and love God by talking about His ways and His words "when you sit at home and when you walk along the road, when you lie down and when you get up" (V.7).

Talking with God is a great way to start each day. It allows us to trust the day, and its lessons, to Him. And it means we'll be more ready to live by His ways, thank Him for His provision and be looking for what He's doing in our lives.   AK

THINKING IT OVER . . .

Do your parents "impress" God's ways on you, teaching you to know Him and trust Him for yourself? If they're not Christians, who can you look to in your church to support and teach you in this way?

STARTING THE DAY WITH GOD HELPS US LIVE THE DAY WITH GOD.

SMALL PRINT

BIBLE: PSALM 119:17-24

Open my eyes that I may see wonderful things in your law (V.18).

Do you ever read through the terms and conditions when you take out a new phone contract? Sometimes there can be pages and pages of small print! That didn't stop Amy from reading through the details of a new contract she had. And her reading paid off—literally! On page seven of the small print, she found out the company was giving away £10,000 to the first person to read that far into the contract. They also gave thousands of pounds to local schools as part of their "It Pays to Read" competition.

Amy said, "I've always been that nerd who reads contracts. I was the most surprised of anyone!"

One psalm-writer wanted his eyes opened to "see wonderful things" about God in the words of the Bible (PSALM 119:18). He knew there were exciting and life-changing truths about God to find out, and he wanted to get to know Him better. I imagine he was looking to see more of who God is, what He has already given, and how to follow Him closely (VV.24,98). He wrote, "Oh, how I love your law! I meditate on it all day long" (V.97).

We too can take our time to read and think about the Bible's stories and teaching. Every bit of it will help us get to know God better and grow in our life with Him. God wants to teach us, guide us and open our eyes to find out awesome things about Him. We'll find that it pays to read because it's the best way to get to know Him better.   *AC*

WANT MORE . . . ?

Check out *How do you read the Bible?* online at
ourdailybread.org/lookingdeeper

IF WE WANT TO KNOW GOD BETTER, WE NEED TO SPEND TIME READING HIS WORDS.

TAUGHT BY TURKEYS

BIBLE: MATTHEW 6:25–34

Look at the birds of the air; they do not sow or reap or store away in barns, and yet your heavenly Father feeds them (V.26).

Do you know what a group of turkeys is called? It's called a rafter. Why am I writing about turkeys? Because I've just returned from a weekend at a farm. Each day, I stopped to watch the train of turkeys that went parading past.

I'd never turkey-watched before. They scratched fiercely with spectacular talons. Then they hunted and pecked at the ground. Eating, I assume (since I'd never watched turkeys before, I wasn't 100% sure!). The scrawny bits of grit they ate didn't look like very filling. Yet here were these turkeys, a dozen of them, all of which looked plump and happy.

Watching those well-fed turkeys brought to mind Jesus' words in Matthew 6:26: "Look at the birds of the air; they do not sow or reap or store away in barns, and yet your heavenly Father feeds them. Are you not much more valuable than they?" Jesus uses God's provision for seemingly worthless birds to remind us of His care for us. If a bird's life matters, how much more does ours? Jesus then contrasts worrying about our daily needs (vv. 27–31) with a life in which we "seek first his kingdom and his righteousness" (v. 33), one in which we're confident of His generous provision for our needs. Because if God can care for that rafter of wild turkeys, He can certainly look after you and me.   *AH*

TO PRAY ABOUT . . .

Father, sometimes I get scared. I worry. I struggle to trust. Thank You for Your care for me. Help me to remember Your provision in the past so I'm better able to trust You with future fears.

IF GOD CARES FOR THE CREATURES HE HAS MADE, HE WILL CERTAINLY PROVIDE FOR THE PEOPLE HE LOVES.

READY FOR THE WEDDING

BIBLE: MATTHEW 25:1-13

Therefore keep watch, because you do not know the day or the hour (V.13).

I'll be honest: we were bored and hungry. We had been waiting over an hour for the bride to arrive at the church for what was meant to be a 12 o'clock wedding. I was getting really fidgety and starting to wonder, *Maybe I could just pop outside for a few minutes and stretch my legs. I'm sure there'll be a corner shop somewhere where I could quickly get a snack . . .*

As we waited, I felt like we were living out a parable (the type of story Jesus often told). I knew if I went outside for a quick walk or to buy snacks, the bride could come at any moment and I would miss her entrance. As I toyed with the idea, I also thought about Jesus' parable about the ten virgins (MATTHEW 25:1-13). Five came prepared with enough oil for their lamps to stay lit as they waited for the bridegroom, but five did not. Just as it was too late for me to go and get snacks, so it was too late for the girls in the story to go and buy more oil for their lamps.

Jesus told this parable to make the point that we need to be prepared for when He comes again. When He comes back we will give an account of ourselves to Him. Are we trusting Him for ourselves? Are we waiting and ready for Him? Or are we distracted with other things?   *ABP*

THINKING IT OVER . . .

What does waiting for Jesus' return look like in your life?

ARE WE WAITING FOR JESUS' RETURN?

SCAR STORIES

BIBLE: JOHN 20:24-29

See my hands. Reach out your hand and put it into my side. Stop doubting and believe (**V.27**).

The butterfly flew in and out of the flowers my mum had planted in our garden. Being a young child, I really wanted to catch it. I raced from our back garden into our kitchen and grabbed a glass jar, but because I was rushing, I tripped and hit the concrete patio hard. The jar smashed under my wrist and left an ugly slash that needed eighteen stitches. Today the scar crawls like a caterpillar across my wrist.

When Jesus appeared to the disciples after His death and resurrection, He brought His scars. John tells us Thomas wanted to see "the nail marks in his hands". Jesus told Thomas to "put your finger here; see my hands. Reach out your hand and put it into my side" (**JOHN 20:25,27**). In order to show He was the same Jesus, He rose from the dead with the scars of His suffering still visible.

The scars of Jesus prove Him to be our Saviour—the only One who has beaten death—and tell the story of our salvation. The holes through His hands and feet and the cut in His side tell the story of the pain He went through—for us. He did it so that we can be made whole and know God for ourselves.

Have you ever thought about the story told by Jesus' scars? *EM*

THINKING IT OVER . . .

Read Isaiah 53. In this promise of Jesus (written about 700 years before He was born), highlight all the times it talks about the pain and suffering He would go through. What is the result of "His wounds" (**V.5**)?

JESUS' SCARS TELL US THE STORY OF HIS SUFFERING FOR OUR SALVATION.

A LIGHT IN THE DARKNESS

BIBLE: JOHN 1:5; 16:1-11,33

In this world you will have trouble. But take heart! I have overcome the world
(JOHN 16:33).

M r. Bae's grandfather, parents and his own family were all persecuted, attacked and hated for talking about Jesus. They live in a country that hates Jesus and has made Christianity illegal. But an amazing thing happened when Mr. Bae was imprisoned for telling a friend about God: his trust in Jesus actually grew. The same was true for his parents when they were sentenced to a concentration camp—they continued to share Jesus' love even there. Mr. Bae found the promise of John 1:5 to be true: "The light shines in the darkness, and the darkness has not overcome it."

Before His arrest and crucifixion, Jesus warned His followers about the trouble and dangers they'd face. They would be rejected by people who "will do such things because they have not known the Father or me" (JOHN 16:3). But Jesus offered words of comfort: "In this world you will have trouble. But take heart! I have overcome the world" (V.33).

While many Christians haven't experienced the same kind of persecution as Mr. Bae and his family, we can expect to face trouble. Maybe you are already facing it. Your family might be making it hard for you to go to church. Your classmates might bully you for being different.

But we don't have to give in or become hateful ourselves. Remember Mr. Bae's example. In the pain and the attacks we face, let's come even closer to Jesus for protection, strength and opportunities to keep sharing Him. We are not on our own; we have a Helper—the Holy Spirit Jesus promised to send. We can turn to Him for all our needs (V.7). The power of God will hold us steady in dark times.

LW

THINKING IT OVER . . .

What trouble are you going through because you belong to Jesus? How do you handle persecution? Who can you share this difficult journey with in your church family?

IF YOU SUFFER AS A CHRISTIAN, DO NOT BE ASHAMED, BUT PRAISE GOD THAT YOU BEAR THAT NAME. 1 PETER 4:16

JOIN THE STREET TEAM

BIBLE: MARK 2:13-17

I have not come to call the righteous, but sinners (V.17).

Health workers in one part of the world are taking medical care to the streets to help homeless people who are suffering from addictions. The project started because the amount of homeless people there was on the rise, along with an increase in drug use.

Normally doctors wait for patients to come to them. But by taking medicine out to the streets, homeless people don't have to worry about making appointments or getting themselves to the hospital.

The willingness of this medical team to go to those in need reminds me of the way Jesus came to us in our need. Jesus always looked for the people who the proud religious leaders were quick to ignore. He ate with "sinners and tax collectors" (MARK 2:16)—the lowest, most hated people in ancient Israel. When asked why He would do that, Jesus replied, "It is not the healthy who need a doctor, but the sick" (V.17). Jesus didn't come for the people who think they've got it all together; He came to help, heal and save the people who've made a real mess of things and know they need rescuing!

When we realise that we're all 'sick' and in need of a doctor (ROMANS 3:10), we can better understand Jesus's willingness to eat with the "sinners and tax collectors"—people just like us. Now that we have trusted Jesus, we're a bit like those health workers. We're Jesus' street team, taking His saving love to others who need to be rescued—other people just like us! *KH*

WHAT I'M THANKFUL FOR . . .

Thank You, Jesus, for coming to find me as I am and for saving me and bringing me into Your family. All praise and thanks go to You! Thank You that I can now be part of Your rescue mission.

ALL OF US ARE "SICK" AND IN NEED OF RESCUE—THAT'S WHY JESUS CAME.

HANG IN THERE

BIBLE: ISAIAH 41:8-13

I will strengthen you and help you; I will uphold you with my righteous right hand (V.10).

- -

An older guy in our church reached seventy-eight recently. So we had a little birthday party after one of the Sunday morning services for him. Someone asked him, "What's the most important thing you've learned in your life so far?" His answer? "Hang in there!"

Hang in there. We might be tempted to ignore those words as simplistic. But the guy in our church wasn't telling us to just hope for the best. He's gone through some really tough things in nearly eight decades. His determination to keep going wasn't based in some vague hope that things might get better, but in Jesus' work in his life.

"Hanging in there"—the Bible uses words like perseverance, endurance and longsuffering—isn't possible through trying harder. We keep going because God promises, over and over, that He's with us, that He'll give us strength and that He'll use us for His plans, no matter what. That's the message He spoke to the Israelites through Isaiah: "So do not fear, for I am with you; do not be dismayed, for I am your God. I will strengthen you and help you; I will uphold you with my righteous right hand" (ISAIAH 41:10).

What does it take to "hang in there"? According to Isaiah, it's all about knowing who God is: His goodness, love, faithfulness. By making the time every day to have some space with Him and read the Bible, we will grow in our confidence of who He is. And as we hold onto His promises, we'll be less afraid of the challenges we face, and more secure that He is with us through them all. Knowing God is what makes it possible to "hang in there".

AH

THINKING IT OVER . . .

Read 2 Corinthians 1:8-11. How bad were some of the trials and troubles Paul went through (V.8)? What was the purpose of these trials (V.9)? What was Paul's confidence for future trouble he might face (V.10)? What help could the church at Corinth give Paul (V.11)?

WE CAN "HANG IN THERE" WHEN WE ARE HANGING ON TO GOD!

WATER WHERE WE NEED IT

BIBLE: JOHN 4:7-14

Whoever drinks the water I give them will never thirst (V.14).

Lake Baikal is the world's deepest lake. Measuring one mile deep, nearly four hundred miles long and forty-nine miles across, it holds one-fifth of all the surface fresh water in the world. But this water is mostly inaccessible. Lake Baikal is in Siberia—one of the most remote areas of Russia. With water so desperately needed across much of our planet, it is ironic that such a huge supply of water is tucked away in such a far-off place.

Lake Baikal may be remote and unusable, but there is another endless source of life-giving water available and accessible to those who need it most. When sitting at a well in Samaria, Jesus talked to a woman about a different kind of water.

She had come to draw water from the well, but Jesus told her that she would soon get thirsty again. However, Jesus said, "Whoever drinks the water I give them will never thirst. Indeed, the water I give them will become in them a spring of water welling up to eternal life" (JOHN 4:13-14).

Many things in our world promise satisfaction, but they never fully meet our needs. They never fully meet the "thirst" we have. Jesus alone can truly satisfy us! That's what He promised to the woman at the well; that's what He promises us. And He is available to everyone, everywhere.   BC

THINKING IT OVER . . .

Read Ephesians 3:16-21. Why do you think that understanding the "love of Christ" (V.18) is key to our Christian lives? What does it mean to be "filled to the measure of all the fullness of God" (V.19)? Is this where you look for your satisfaction? Or what are you trying to 'fill' yourself with?

OUR NEEDS ARE TRULY MET IN JESUS.

STAY TOGETHER

BIBLE: EPHESIANS 4:1-6

Keep the unity of the Spirit through the bond of peace (V.3).

Dewberry Baptist Church split in the 1800s over a chicken leg. A few versions of the story exist, but a current member of the church said it like this: two men fought over the last drumstick at a church lunch. One man said God wanted him to have it. The other said God didn't care, and he really wanted it. The men became so angry that one moved a couple of miles down the road and started Dewberry Baptist Church #2. Thankfully the churches managed to sort things out and become one church again. Today, everyone agrees the reason for this split was a bit crazy!

Jesus agrees. The night before His death He prayed that His followers would "be one, Father, just as you are in me and I am in you." May they "be brought to complete unity. Then the world will know that you sent me" (JOHN 17:21-23).

Paul agrees. He tells us: "Make every effort to keep the unity of the Spirit through the bond of peace. There is one body and one Spirit" (EPHESIANS 4:3-4), and these cannot be split up.

Hopefully we'll never find ourselves in the sort of strange situation Dewberry Baptist Church did in the 1800s. But we still have a role to play in our churches to be part of the unity of Christians. Do we spend Sunday mornings or youth group meet ups talking to and sitting with the same people? Or do we realise we are "one body and one Spirit" with every Christian? Once we realise we are the same and specially joined together with *everyone* in our church family, we'll be ready to "make every effort" with them. MW

THINKING IT OVER . . .

What do you think Galatians 3:28 means? How does this verse help you work out your own identity? And how does it help you think about your identity as part of your church family? What might it mean for you to "make every effort to keep the unity" with the people in your church family (EPHESIANS 4:3)?

WE'RE NOT JUST "ONE" WITH THE CHRISTIANS WE LIKE, BUT WITH *EVERY* CHRISTIAN!

EASILY ENTANGLED

BIBLE: HEBREWS 2:17-18; 12:1-2

Throw off everything that hinders and the sin that so easily entangles
(HEBREWS 12:1).

Soldiers in a humid and dense jungle came across an unusual problem. Without warning, a prickly vine would attach itself to the soldiers' bodies and gear, trapping them in its grip. As they struggled to get free, even more of the plant's tentacles grabbed hold of them. The soldiers named the plant the "wait-a-minute" vine because once it caught them, they had to shout out to others, "Hey, wait a minute, I'm stuck!"

As Christians we are in a similar situation. It's hard for us to move forward with Jesus when we're tangled up in sin. Hebrews 12:1 tells us to "throw off everything that hinders and the sin that so easily entangles" and "run with perseverance". But how do we throw off the sinful habits and selfishness weighing us down?

Jesus is the only One who can free us from sin's grip on our lives. So "fixing our eyes on Jesus" (HEBREWS 12:2) means spending time with Him in the Bible, understanding the salvation He has given us, reflecting on His teaching and praising Him for all He has done.

Because the Son of God became "fully human in every way," He knows what it's like to be tempted—yet not sin (2:17-18; 4:15). By our own efforts, we will get more tangled up in our own mess, but God wants us to overcome temptation and move on. It's not through our own strength, but His, that we can "throw off" sin and grow in His good ways (1 CORINTHIANS 10:13).   *CHK*

WANT MORE . . .

Check out *How do I fight temptation?* online at
ourdailybread.org/lookingdeeper

SIN HAS LESS OPPORTUNITY TO TANGLE US UP WHEN WE'RE FOCUSED ON JESUS.

WHAT'S YOUR 'CQ'?

BIBLE: 1 CORINTHIANS 9:19-23

I have become all things to all people so that by all possible means I might save some (V.23).

Do you know your IQ? Apparently the UK's average IQ score is 107. Which sounds reasonable. Although I found out the other day that Koko, a gorilla who was taught sign language amongst other things, had an IQ of approximately 95. So maybe 107 isn't that impressive after all!

Along with an IQ (Intelligence Quotient), people have an EQ (Emotional Quotient—our ability to read and understand emotions). But I wonder if we could add another one: CQ (Christ-like Quotient). This is something the apostle Paul lived out.

Paul wanted to bring as many people to Jesus as possible. His first priority was showing Jesus to the world. And so Paul adapted to each person he met to show them Jesus in a way that made sense to them. Paul's 'CQ' is most obvious in this statement: "I have become all things to all people so that by all possible means I might save some" (1 CORINTHIANS 9:22).

All things. To *all* people. So that by all possible means some might be saved. Though he was free, Paul made himself like a slave (v.19). To the people who lived by the law, Paul lived by the law (v.20). To those without God's law, Paul didn't use the law as his starting point. Paul gave up his rights, preferences and demands for the sake of bringing people to Jesus—that's great CQ!

For us, this might mean talking to the lonely, quiet kids in class during lunchbreak. Or going to a football match with your football-mad friend who doesn't know Jesus yet— even though you couldn't care less about sport. Being Christ-like to these people means putting their needs first so they can see Jesus in us!

EM

TO PRAY ABOUT . . .

Dear God, I pray that You would increase my 'CQ' so that like Paul, I might "become all things to all people so that by all possible means I might save some."

SHOW JESUS TO OTHER PEOPLE, IN EVERY PLACE AND IN EVERY SITUATION.

THE PRAYER COIN

BIBLE: LUKE 22:39-44

Father, if you are willing, take this cup from me; yet not my will, but yours be done (V.42).

Every coin has two sides. Heads and tails. Coins showing the "head" of a country's king or queen started in Roman times. The "tail" side seems to have come from our British ten pence piece, which originally showed the tail of a lion.

Like a coin, Jesus' prayer in the garden of Gethsemane, had two sides to it. In the darkest hours of His life—the night before He went to die on the cross—Jesus prayed, "Father, if you are willing, take this cup, yet not my will but yours be done" (LUKE 22:42). When Jesus says, "take this cup," that's the raw honesty of prayer. He was saying, "This is what I want."

Then Jesus flips the coin, praying "not my will,"—the side of surrendering to what God's doing. Surrender is saying to God, "But I will do what You want, Lord."

This two-sided prayer is included in Matthew 26, Mark 14 and Luke 22, and mentioned in John 18. Jesus prayed both sides of prayer: take this cup (what I want, God), yet not my will (what do you want, God?). It is a good pattern for us to follow in our prayers too. We can come with complete honesty about what we are struggling with and what we want. But we also come to trust God's plans and surrender to Him with confidence in His love for us. These are the two sides of prayer; the 'prayer coin'.

EM

THINKING IT OVER . . .

What might it look like if we prayed both sides of the 'prayer coin'—with both honesty and surrender like Jesus? What things are you facing right now where you can copy Jesus' prayer example?

BOTH SIDES OF THE 'PRAYER COIN' ARE IMPORTANT IN OUR CONVERSATIONS WITH GOD.

PERFECTLY PLACED

BIBLE: JOB 38:4-11

Where were you when I laid the earth's foundation? (V.4).

Scientists know our planet is exactly the right distance from the sun. A little closer and all the water would evaporate, like on Venus. Only a little bit further and everything would freeze like it does on Mars. Earth is also just the right size to create the right amount of gravity. Less would make everything weightless like on our moon, while more gravity would trap suffocating poisonous gases that suffocate life as on Jupiter.

The detailed physical, chemical and biological specifics that make up our world show there must be a Designer behind it all. What I mean is this: there's no way this world just happened by accident! We catch a glimpse of God's work to make the universe when He talks to Job about things beyond our understanding. "Where were you when I laid the earth's foundation?" God asks. "Who marked off its dimensions? Surely you know! Who stretched a measuring line across it? On what were its footings set, or who laid its cornerstone?" (JOB 38:4-6).

This glimpse of God as our Creator should fill us with awe. He is the only One who "shut up the sea behind doors when it burst forth from the womb . . . [who said] 'This far you may come and no further'" (VV.8-11). In thanks and praise let's sing to Him with the morning stars and shout for joy with the angels (V.7). This complex, detailed, exciting world was made for us that we might know and trust the God who created it for us.   *RO*

WANT MORE . . . ?

Is God real? Did God create evil? Check out answers to questions like this in
Big questions about . . . God online at **ourdailybread.org/teen**

OUR WORLD IS SO WELL BALANCED BECAUSE SOMEONE BALANCED IT ON PURPOSE.

LIFE CHANGES

BIBLE: EPHESIANS 4:20-24

Put on the new self, created to be like God in true righteousness and holiness (V.24).

Stephen grew up in a rough part of East London and got into gang life and crime by the age of ten. He said, "If everyone's selling drugs and doing robberies and fraud, then you're going to get involved. It's just a way of life." But when he was twenty, he had a dream that changed him: "I heard God saying, Stephen, you're going to prison for murder." This vivid dream shook him up so much that he started to find out about God for himself. It wasn't long before he decided to give his life to Jesus; and the Holy Spirit transformed him!

Stephen set up an organisation that teaches inner-city kids discipline, morality and respect through sports. He gives praise and thanks to God for the way he has been able to share Jesus with lots of kids as he prays with them and teaches them during their training sessions. He says he's, "rebuilding misguided dreams".

When we choose to follow God and leave behind our past, we—like Stephen—follow Paul's command to the Ephesians to take hold of a new way of life. Although our old self is "corrupted by its deceitful desires", we can be active every day to "put on the new self" that's created to be like God (EPHESIANS 4:22,24). All Christians take part in this every day as we ask God through His Holy Spirit to make us more like Jesus.

Stephen said, "Trusting Jesus is the foundation for me changing my life around." How has this been true for you?   ABP

TO PRAY ABOUT . . .

Jesus, You're alive and working in the world and in my life. Help me become more like You each day as I leave my old self behind.

WHEN WE CHOOSE TO FOLLOW JESUS, THERE'S NO WAY LIFE CAN EVER STAY THE SAME.

THE ENVELOPE

BIBLE: MATTHEW 6:19-21

Store up for yourselves treasures in heaven, where moths and vermin do not destroy, and where thieves do not break in and steal (V.20).

We were on the way home from our holiday when I found it. We were taking a break in a motorway services when I noticed a brown envelope lying on the ground. I picked it up and flicked it open. I nearly dropped it again in surprise! There was a hundred pounds inside!

One hundred pounds that someone had lost. They were probably frantically searching for it. We gave our house phone number to the staff in the services in case anyone came back looking for it. But no one ever called.

Someone had that money and then lost it. "Treasures on earth" are often like that (MATTHEW 6:19). They can be lost, stolen or wasted. So much of the stuff we own and money we have is not really in our control. All it takes is for our phone provider to up our contract payments—and suddenly we've got a lot less "treasure"!

That's why Jesus told us, "store up for yourselves treasure in heaven" (V.20). The heavenly treasure we have in Jesus is our right relationship with God and the promise of eternal life. It can't be taken away from us or lost—it is kept safe by Him (JOHN 10:28-29).

And we build up our "treasure in heaven" as we grow "rich in good deeds" (1 TIMOTHY 6:18) or "rich in faith" (JAMES 2:5)—trusting God more and more, looking out for others and sharing Jesus where we can. Let's look to build up our treasure in heaven, not on earth.

DB

THINKING IT OVER . . .

"Where your treasure is, there your heart will be also" (MATTHEW 6:21). Where would you say your treasure is? Or, what is the most valuable thing in your life? What does that tell you about where your "heart" is? Why not spend some time talking to God about it this week so that you can put your heart (your focus and love) more firmly on Jesus.

WHEN JESUS IS OUR TREASURE, WE WILL HAVE EVERYTHING WE NEED.

HEALING WORDS

BIBLE: PROVERBS 16:20-24

Gracious words are a honeycomb, sweet to the soul and healing to the bones (V.24).

A test was done recently to see if the way doctors spoke to their patients actually helped them cope with illness better. The test itself was pretty simple: two groups of people were given something to make their skin really itchy. Then one group was left to cope on their own, while the other group had regular visits from their doctor who gave them lots of reassuring and kind words. The results were clear: the people who were regularly encouraged by their doctor coped better with the itching than the people who had to get on with it on their own.

The writer of Proverbs seemed to know how important encouraging words are. He says that "gracious words" bring "healing to the bones" (PROVERBS 16:24). The positive effect of words isn't limited to our health: when we listen to the advice of older Christians or our youth leader, we're also more likely to make good God-centred decisions (V.20). And encouragement helps us face the challenges that come our way.

Isn't it amazing what difference a word of encouragement makes? Doesn't it feel great when someone tells us they care about what we're going through? In the same way the Bible is God's encouragement to us. It tells us He cares more than we can imagine about how we're doing and what we're going through. Let's spend time reading His words and listening to His encouragement and reassurance. And then we can be ready to share those healing words with the people we meet today.

KH

WHAT I'M THANKFUL FOR . . .

Thank You, God, for how the Bible uplifts me, reassures me and gives me loads of reasons to praise You. Thank You for the people You have put in my life who encourage me and show me what it means to look out for others.

EVERY WORD OF GOD IS FLAWLESS; HE IS A SHIELD TO THOSE WHO TAKE REFUGE IN HIM. PROVERBS 30:5

HYPOCRITES

BIBLE: GENESIS 38:16-26

She is more righteous than I (V.26).

"I'd be very disappointed if one of our team members did that," said a cricket player, talking about a South African cricketer who'd cheated in a match. But only two years later, that same player was caught doing the same thing!

Most of us hate hypocrisy: people making themselves out to be better, but actually being just as bad as everyone else. But in the story of Judah in Genesis 38, Judah's hypocritical behaviour nearly got someone killed. After two of his sons died soon after marrying Tamar, Judah had ignored his duty to provide for her, seeing as she was his daughter-in-law (GENESIS 38:8-11). In desperation, Tamar disguised herself as a prostitute, and Judah slept with her (VV.15-16).

When Judah learned that his widowed daughter-in-law was pregnant, he was murderous. "Bring her out and have her burned to death!" (V.24). But Tamar had proof that Judah was the father (V.25).

Judah could have lied. Instead he admitted his hypocrisy, and also accepted his responsibility to care for her, saying, "She is more righteous than I" (V.26).

And God used this dark chapter of Judah and Tamar's story in His story of our salvation. Tamar's children (VV.29-30) would become part of the family line that led to Jesus (MATTHEW 1:2-3).

Why is Genesis 38 in the Bible? One reason is because it shows how hypocritical we can be. The other is that is shows God can use even the worst moments of human history (and our own lives) for His good purposes.   *TG*

THINKING IT OVER . . .

How aware are you of your own hypocrisy? Do you talk a big talk, or look down on others in school, even though you struggle with stuff too? What would it be like if you were more open about your issues and struggles, rather than trying to cover them up?

JESUS CHANGES US FROM PROUD HYPOCRITES TO PEOPLE WHO ARE HONEST ABOUT HOW MUCH WE NEED HIM.

LETTING GO

BIBLE: EPHESIANS 4:25-32

In your anger do not sin: Do not let the sun go down while you are still angry (V.26).

When someone told me off for something I hadn't done wrong, I was annoyed for hours. I wanted to get back at them somehow and prove they were wrong. When I bumped into him again later, he met me with a smile—almost as if to say, "no offence meant"—I bit my tongue and forced myself to smile back.

I asked God to help me not take offence, but the indignation burned deep. It was only after I'd made the decision to not strike back that my anger began to cool off—very slowly.

While anger itself may not be wrong, Ephesians 4:26 tells us not to hang on to it, because it often only makes things worse. It is hard to do this, of course. But this little incident reminded me that letting go isn't just about trying to control my feelings. It's about making the decision to release someone from my judgement and stop thinking of getting even. It's learning to forgive as a daily habit of my life.

That's why Paul links forgiveness with action—and not emotions. Our emotions want to get even. But we forgive and let things go because we know "in Christ God forgave you" (EPHESIANS 4:32). God's forgiveness didn't let things go in the sense that they didn't matter—our sin clearly does matter; Jesus had to die for it! So we let things go in the same way; realising it does matter when people hurt us, but that their sin is also dealt with on the cross, just as ours is. This truth, rather than our feelings, is the basis for dealing with our anger well—because God completely understands our pain. Jesus went to the cross to pay for the pain we cause, but also to pay for the pain caused to us. *LK*

THINKING IT OVER . . .

How does realising Jesus' death was to pay for all sin, including the stuff done to you, help you to "be kind and compassionate" to unkind people (EPHESIANS 4:32)? How does Romans 12:19 help you let things go in a way that trusts God's judgement, rather than your own?

WE CAN LET THINGS GO WHEN WE KNOW GOD IS THE "RIGHTEOUS JUDGE" (PSALM 9:4).

A PLANNED WEAKNESS

BIBLE: ISAIAH 22:8-11

You did not look to the One who made it, or have regard for the One who planned it long ago (V.11).

There's a natural spring that rises on the east side of the city of Jerusalem. In ancient times it was the city's only water supply and was placed outside the walls. So it was the point of Jerusalem's greatest weakness. The spring meant that the city, otherwise impossible to invade or destroy, could be forced to surrender if an attacker were to stop the water supply from the spring.

King Hezekiah sorted this weakness by driving a tunnel through 1,750 feet of solid rock from the spring into the city where it flowed into the "Lower Pool" (SEE 2 KINGS 20:20; 2 CHRONICLES 32:2-4). But in all of this, Hezekiah "did not look to the One who made it, or have regard for the One who planned it long ago" (ISAIAH 22:11). Planned what?

God Himself "planned" the city of Jerusalem in such a way that its water supply was unprotected. The spring outside the wall was a constant reminder that the people of the city must rely completely on Him for their safety and provision.

Could it be that our weaknesses exist for our good? The apostle Paul said that he would "boast" in his limitations, because it was through weakness that the strength and power of Jesus was most clearly seen in him (2 CORINTHIANS 12:9-10). Could you start to see each weakness you have as an opportunity to trust God as your strength?

DR

WANT MORE . . . ?

Check out *Is it ever OK to not be OK?* online at
ourdailybread.org/lookingdeeper

I WILL BOAST ALL THE MORE GLADLY ABOUT MY WEAKNESSES, SO THAT CHRIST'S POWER MAY REST ON ME. 2 CORINTHIANS 12:9

WE ARE SEEN

BIBLE: GENESIS 16:7-16

She gave this name to the LORD who spoke to her: "You are the God who sees me," for she said, "I have now seen the One who sees me" (V.13).

Until a couple of years ago *The Experience Project* was one of the largest online communities where tens of millions of people simply shared things they had been through in life. Many were raw and painful. As I looked through some of the stories, I thought about how we all want someone to see—to really understand—the stuff we're going through.

In Genesis, the story of a young servant girl shows just how important it is to be seen and known.

Hagar was an Egyptian slave girl in Abram's camp—later called Abraham (SEE GENESIS 12:16; 16:1). When Abram's wife Sarai was unable to have a baby, she told Abram to have a child with Hagar—a normal practice back then, even though it seems odd to us today. But when Hagar got pregnant, things got tense, until Hagar ran away into the wilderness to escape Sarai's abuse (16:1-6).

But Hagar's situation—pregnant and alone in a hot, endless desert—didn't go unnoticed. After "the angel of the LORD" met with Hagar (VV.7-12), she said, "You are the God who sees me" (V.13).

God sees more than just the facts. He gets how we feel, who we are and what we're going through. We see this in Jesus as well, who, "when he saw the crowds, he had compassion on them, because they were harassed and helpless" (MATTHEW 9:36). Hagar met a God who understood.

The One who saw and understood Hagar's pain sees ours as well (HEBREWS 4:15-16). Knowing that God completely gets the stuff we're going through helps make it just a little more bearable. *JO*

THINKING IT OVER . . .

How does it reassure you to know God understands the challenges you face?
How can you remind others of this truth today?

GOD FEELS OUR PAIN AS IF IT WERE HIS OWN.

ADRIFT

BIBLE: LUKE 19:1-10
The Son of Man came to seek and to save the lost (V.10).

A man needing work agreed to spend six months miles from shore on a tiny fishing hut—lighting lamps to attract fish he could then catch. The only person he saw during that time arrived once every week to drop off supplies before disappearing again.

Things went bad when the hut's mooring broke and he drifted hundreds of miles out to sea. He lost all hope of rescue as he watched ten ships pass and his cooking fuel ran out. Finally, after nearly fifty days adrift, the man was spotted by a ship's crew and rescued!

While we may never be stranded in the ocean, most of us have felt adrift, lost and in need of help. Perhaps like Zacchaeus in today's Bible reading, we're on our own and yet somehow know Jesus is the One we need (LUKE 19:3-4). The Bible repeatedly tells us how God comes to rescue us from our mess. In Eden, God found Adam and Eve hiding and confused (GENESIS 3:8-9). And the people of Israel ran away again and again (PSALM 78:40), but God always brought them back. Finally, Jesus, God's promised Rescuer, came not for those who have life figured out but for those who are in a mess. Jesus "came to seek and to save the lost" (LUKE 19:10).

While we face challenges in the choppy seas of life, God promises to be with us throughout. And confidence grows as we remember that Jesus has provided our ultimate rescue—from sin and death (V.9; EPHESIANS 2:4-8).   *wc*

TO PRAY ABOUT . . .
God, I'm out on my own, in deep trouble. I don't think anyone can help me. But You say You come for the lost. I'm here. Please show me the way.

NO ONE IS TOO FAR ADRIFT TO BE RESCUED BY JESUS.

THREE REASONS WHY WE GOSSIP

One of my earliest memories as a child was waiting for a doctor's appointment with my mum. Across from us was a little girl with her mum. When I looked up, I caught her staring at me as she cupped her hands around her mum's ears and whispered. I don't quite remember what I felt—maybe a bit of fear, uncertainty, confusion—but I decided to copy her. I cupped my hands to my mum's ears to whisper something fairly meaningless, just to show her that she hadn't won, and that I, too, could make her feel afraid and reduce her to what my words made her out to be. That was my very first encounter with gossip. At the age of six—before I even knew what gossip was.

As a teenager, gossiping about others became a daily life. In school, my friends and I would eyeball our target's every move, anticipating her next misstep. When it happened, we'd glance at each other with knowing smirks, and gather later to whisper and laugh about what we'd just seen. And we didn't just gossip about people we disliked; we also backstabbed each other.

It was only after I trusted my life to Jesus that I began to realise the impact of my 'harmless' gossiping—on others as well as on myself. Over time, I started to understand why gossiping has such a big appeal to us:

1. We gossip because we're proud and judgemental.

Though we may like to think otherwise, every single one of us is selfish and sinful by nature. We judge others because of our pride, which tells us that we are better than them. When we think that someone is ugly, stupid, annoying or weird, it is because we think that we are more attractive, smarter, cooler or just a better person.

Quickly pointing out the faults of others, we fail to recognise our own faults—faults which Jesus chose to pay for when He died for us on the cross. Knowing that we are forgiven, accepted and loved by God's grace alone, how can we not show the same love and kindness to others?

We are in no position to judge others; only God is (ROMANS 2:16). Instead, we are meant to show grace and kindness, just as Jesus has to us: "Do not let any unwholesome talk come out of your mouths, but only what is helpful for building others up according to their needs, that it may benefit those who listen . . . Be kind and compassionate to one another, forgiving each other, just as in Christ God forgave you" (EPHESIANS 4:29-32).

2. We gossip to protect and empower ourselves.

Many of us badmouth others because we feel insecure and afraid of what others may think about us. We try to find ways to look and feel better about ourselves, and the most popular way by far is to diss others. Like a seesaw, we put others down to lift ourselves up. Gossiping inflates our self-esteem and hides our insecurities.

When our identity is found in Jesus, however, there is no need for us to protect or empower ourselves through gossip. We can find true meaning, acceptance and confidence in Him. As children of God, we are called to "put off your old self", and to "put on the new self, created to be like God in true righteousness and holiness" (EPHESIANS 4:22-24).

3. We gossip because everyone else is.

Gossiping is a social activity; for some, it is a means of making friends. Dissing others can also be 'entertaining': "The words of a gossip are like [tasty snacks]; they go down to the inmost parts" (PROVERBS 26:22).

How can we stop ourselves from taking part in gossip? Here are four things I've tried to do to help myself steer clear of gossiping:

1. Change the topic. The best way to stop ourselves from gossiping is to steer the conversation in the right direction. We can bring up other subjects or talking points that our friends would also be interested in. There are certainly far better options and more meaningful topics to chat over than badmouthing!

2. Be quick to listen and slow to speak. James 1:19 tells us that "everyone should be quick to listen, slow to speak". So, if our friends are ranting about someone to let off steam, we would do well just to listen, and not add anything. Sometimes, our friends don't expect us to say anything, but to listen, sympathise and offer some comfort where necessary (EPHESIANS 4:29).

3. Avoid those who live on gossip. I used to have a friend who was a gossip queen. From the moment we first met to the last conversation we ever had, making fun of others was the foundation of our friendship. However, a relationship built on gossip isn't built to last. If we're surrounded by friends who love gossiping, we should ask ourselves if we want to be in that environment. We may even want to prayerfully consider spending less time with them, in case we fall into this way of living and thinking ourselves. As 2 Timothy 2:16 advises: "Avoid godless chatter, because those who indulge in it will become more and more ungodly."

4. Lastly, do not judge those who gossip. We must not fall into the trap of believing that we are better than gossipers, like the Pharisees in Jesus' time who looked down on others who messed up. The reality is that we are no less sinful than others. It is by grace alone that we are saved, and grace alone that we need to be showing in what we say and do.

Although it may be hard to stop gossiping, especially when everyone else is doing it, we can trust that with God, everything is possible (MATTHEW 19:26). When we belong to Jesus, God gives us the strength and power to overcome the stuff in our lives that causes harm, no matter how deep-rooted it is (1 CORINTHIANS 10:13).

Seven days in . . . The Law

HIGHLIGHT OR DELETE?

BIBLE: ROMANS 3:19-26

Righteousness is given through faith in Jesus Christ to all who believe (V.22).

When I worked on essays or wrote up homework, I would sometimes feel like I used the highlight function and the delete button the most. I'd highlight sections that still needed work—and delete bits that weren't working.

In some ways the Mosaic Law (The law Moses was given from God—sometimes called the Old Testament law) is a bit like a highlighter. We're told, "no one will be declared righteous in God's sight by the works of the law; rather, through the law we become conscious of our sin" (ROMANS 3:20). Although the law is perfect and holy, showing God's people how to live God-centred lives—it is not able to save. In the end, its perfection simply highlights our mess. The people of Israel received God's law willingly (EXODUS 24:3). But they would soon discover that God's law was also the standard by which they would be judged.

Yet now we are promised: "My friends, I want you to know that through Jesus the forgiveness of sins is proclaimed to you. Through him everyone who believes is set free from every sin, a justification you were not able to obtain under the law of Moses" (ACTS 13:38-39). The law of God's holiness highlights our sin—demanding judgement. But Jesus, bearing our sin, takes the judgement for us, deleting it from our account. Now perfection and "righteousness is given through faith in Jesus Christ to all who believe" (ROMANS 3:22)!

CW

COMPLETING THE PICTURE . . .

Our best efforts always fall short of God's standards, "For whoever keeps the whole law and yet stumbles at just one point is guilty of breaking all of it" (JAMES 2:10). The only way we can be made righteous (fully right with God) is through trusting Jesus. He fulfils God's requirements for us, pays for our mess and gives us His own righteousness (MATTHEW 5:17; EPHESIANS 1:7; 2 CORINTHIANS 5:21). Now we live with His Spirit within us, so God's ways aren't just written as a law—they're now written on our hearts (2 CORINTHIANS 3:3). We can actually start to live as holy people for real! But we can't do it ourselves; we have to rely on Him (GALATIANS 3:1-6).

THE LAW HIGHLIGHTS OUR SIN; JESUS REMOVES IT.

Seven days in . . . the Law

OPEN THE BOOK

BIBLE: JOSHUA 1:1-9

Keep this Book of Law always on your lips; meditate on it day and night (V.8).

T*sundoku*. It's the word I've always needed! It's the Japanese word for the stack of books on your bedside table (or on your eReader) that are still waiting to be read. Books offer learning, adventure and an escape into another world. But we have to actually open them to enjoy these things!

This truth is even more important when it comes to the book of books—the Bible. I see the encouragement to dive into God's words in His instructions to Joshua, the new leader of Israel who took the people into the Promised Land (JOSHUA 1:8).

Knowing the difficulty ahead, God promised Joshua, "I will be with you" (V.5). His help would come, in part, through Joshua's obedience to God's commands. So God told him to "Keep this Book of the Law always on your lips; meditate on it day and night, so that you may be careful to do everything written in it" (V.8). It was not enough for Joshua to simply have the Book of the Law; Joshua needed to regularly open and search it to get understanding into who God is and what His ways look like.

Like Joshua, as we take time to read, reflect on and live out the Bible's teaching, we will benefit from all of it (2 TIMOTHY 3:16)—including the Old Testament law.

LS

COMPLETING THE PICTURE . . .

What was true for Joshua is true for us today. Although Jesus fulfilled the law—something we could never do—it is still part of the Bible. It is there for us to learn more about God's ways, what "love" really looks like (ROMANS 13:8-10; GALATIANS 5:14), and see all that Jesus actually did to make us right with God (SEE GALATIANS 3:10-14).

THE BIBLE TEACHES US EVERYTHING WE NEED TO KNOW ABOUT GOD AND HIS WAYS. BUT WE DO NEED TO READ IT!

Seven days in . . . The Law
IT IS WELL

BIBLE: NEHEMIAH 8:1-12

This day is holy to our Lord. Do not grieve, for the joy of the LORD is your strength (V.10).

- -

Horatio G. Spafford's four daughters all died when their ship crashed into another boat, leaving their mum as one of the few survivors. As Horatio later sailed to meet his wife, he wrote the hymn "It Is Well with My Soul". In his deep pain, he still found strength from the joy of knowing God was with him and looking after him.

The Jewish people returned to Judah after exile in Babylon. With Nehemiah's help, they'd managed to rebuild Jerusalem's wall, but there was still work to do (NEHEMIAH 7:4). As they tried to plan for their future, the people asked Ezra to bring out the Book of the Law. "[So Ezra] read it aloud from daybreak till noon . . . in the presence of the men, women and others who could understand. And all the people listened attentively to the Book of the Law" (8:1-3). While the people listened and had the words explained by the priests, they began to cry (V.9), probably with the realisation of how they had fallen so far short of God's ways.

In that moment, Nehemiah called out, "Do not grieve, for the joy of the LORD is your strength" (V.10). Then all the people celebrated "with great joy, because they now understood the words that had been made known to them" (V.12). Jerusalem was still being rebuilt, but God's words brought great joy. And so the people were strengthened to continue living for God and to keep on rebuilding. No matter our situation, we are also strengthened when we spend time in God's words, knowing His promises, love and salvation for us. *RO*

COMPLETING THE PICTURE . . .

The people of Israel had become so distant from God in their relationship with Him, that He allowed them to be taken captive by Babylon. They were exiles in Babylon for 70 years, returning back to Israel around 500 years before Jesus was born. They rebuilt Jerusalem (after Babylon had destroyed it) and that's when three key leaders—Ezra, Zerubbabel and Nehemiah—reintroduced them to the law. Ezra was a priest and teacher of the law who helped the people renew their relationship with God: "Ezra had devoted himself to the study and observance of the Law of the LORD, and to teaching its decrees and laws in Israel" (EZRA 7:10).

SOMETIMES GOD'S OWN PEOPLE NEED TO BE REMINDED OF HIS TRUTH.

Seven days in . . . the law

THROWING STONES

BIBLE: JOHN 8:1-11

Let any one of you who is without sin be the first to throw a stone (v.7).

Jesus once said to the Pharisees and teachers of the law: "Let any one of you who is without sin be the first to throw a stone" (JOHN 8:7). Jesus was teaching in the temple courts when He made that statement. A group of religious leaders had just dragged a woman (caught in adultery) in front of Him and challenged, "In the Law Moses commanded us to stone such women. Now what do you say?" (v.5). Jesus was a threat to their authority and their way of life. So their question was "a trap, in order to have a basis for accusing him" (v.6)—and getting rid of Him. They thought, *If Jesus says she can go free, He's broken the law. If He agrees to stone her, He's not merciful like He's been saying.*

Yet when Jesus replied, "Let any one of you who is without sin . . ." not one of the woman's accusers could pick up a stone. One by one, they walked away. The law shows we *all* fail, and none of us has the right to point a finger at anyone else.

Before we judge a friend or criticise someone at church, let's remember that all of us "fall short of the glory of God" (ROMANS 3:23). Instead of judgement, our Saviour showed this woman—and you and me—grace and hope (JOHN 3:16; 8:10-11). How can we not do the same for others?

AK

COMPLETING THE PICTURE . . .

Because the Pharisees knew the law and were better at following it than most people in Israel, they thought they were good enough for God. This is the danger of judging ourselves by how we live and the good stuff we do. The law was there for the people to realise how badly they compared to God's holiness! Our friends are not our benchmark for what's good enough—He is! The Pharisees' study of the law should have made them realise just how much they needed Jesus' rescue. Instead their knowledge made them proud. So they forced the people to follow their complicated rules for living a 'good' life, and forgot to help them come to God. Jesus said to them: "You shut the door of the kingdom of heaven in people's faces" (MATTHEW 23:13).

ONLY JESUS MAKES US GOOD ENOUGH FOR GOD

Seven days in . . . The Law

THE WAY OF SORROWS

BIBLE: HEBREWS 10:1-10

We have been made holy through the sacrifice of the body of Jesus Christ once for all (V.10).

The road Jesus travelled to the cross through the streets of Jerusalem is known as "The Way of Sorrows". But the writer of Hebrews viewed the road Jesus took as more than just a path of sadness and loss. Yes Jesus went to a painful death on the cross. But He willingly walked that road to make a "new and living way" into the presence of God for us (HEBREWS 10:20). It was the way of suffering, but also the way to victory.

For centuries the Jewish people had tried to know God and be right with Him through animal sacrifices and by keeping the law He had given them. But the law was "only a shadow of the good things that are coming", for "it is impossible for the blood of bulls and goats to take away sins" (VV.1,4).

Jesus' journey down The Way of Sorrows led to His death and resurrection. Because of His sacrifice, we can be made holy "just as he who called you is holy" (1 PETER 1:15) when we put our trust in Jesus for the forgiveness of our sins. Even though we aren't able to keep the law perfectly, we can now know God without fear, fully confident that we are welcomed and loved (HEBREWS 10:10,22).

Jesus' way of sorrow opened for us a new and living way to God. *AP*

COMPLETING THE PICTURE . . .

Jesus fulfilled the law, including all the animal sacrifices it required (SEE LEVITICUS 1:1-3; 3:1; 4:1-3; 5:15 FOR EXAMPLE) when He sacrificed Himself for us. This is most clearly seen in the yearly Day of Atonement sacrifices, which made the people right with God again (LEVITICUS 16). A goat would be killed "for the sin offering for the people" (V.15) and "all their sins" would be put on another goat's head, which would "carry on itself all their sins to a remote place" in the wilderness (VV.21-22). Jesus fulfils this because He pays for our sin as the sacrificed 'goat' and He is our "scapegoat" (V.26). He's literally our *escape* goat; He takes our sins on Himself in His one, completed sacrifice (HEBREWS 10:11-14), so we escape punishment and instead receive forgiveness.

FOR BY ONE SACRIFICE HE HAS MADE PERFECT FOR EVER THOSE WHO ARE BEING MADE HOLY. HEBREWS 10:14

Seven days in . . . The Law

CURTAINED OFF

BIBLE: HEBREWS 10:19-25

Since we have confidence to enter the Most Holy Place by the blood of Jesus,
by a new and living way . . . let us draw near to God (VV.19,22).

As my flight reached cruising speed, the flight attendant pulled back the curtain that hid business class, and I was given a clear reminder of the big differences between areas on aeroplanes. Some travellers get to board first, enjoying premium seating with extra legroom and personalised service. The curtain was a reminder of my separation from those perks.

Lots of things offer better service to people who can pay more, like music streaming services. If you pay, you don't get adverts. If you don't pay—it feels like that's all you listen to!

The temple in Jerusalem had different distinctions too. Non-Jewish people (gentiles) were only allowed to worship in the outer court. Next came the women's court, and even further in was an area for the Jewish men. Finally, the inner room was called the Holy of Holies. This was only accessible to one priest each year who would enter the very presence of God. And it was hidden behind a thick curtain (HEBREWS 9:1-10).

Thankfully this separation no longer exists. Jesus has completely removed any barriers that might stop anyone coming to God for themselves—even our sin (10:17). Just as the temple curtain was torn in two at the moment of Jesus' death (MATTHEW 27:52), His crucified body has torn away all obstacles to God's presence. The law contained many legitimate barriers to God because of our sin. Now there is no barrier that need separate any Christian from living confidently in the presence of God—in His very throne room (HEBREWS 4:16). LS

THINKING IT OVER . . .

How does the truth that Jesus' death provides access to God give you confidence, especially when you're struggling?

LET US THEN APPROACH GOD'S THRONE OF GRACE WITH CONFIDENCE, SO THAT WE MAY RECEIVE MERCY AND FIND GRACE TO HELP US IN OUR TIME OF NEED. HEBREWS 4:16

Seven days in . . . the Law

MORE THAN WATER

BIBLE: GALATIANS 3:23-29

All of you who were baptised into Christ have clothed yourselves with Christ (V.27).

One of my earliest childhood memories of church was a pastor walking down the aisle, telling us to "remember the waters of our baptism." *Remember the waters?* I asked myself. *How can you remember water?* He then splashed everyone with water, which was fun . . . but also weird.

Why should we think about baptism? When someone is baptised, there's so much more to it than water. Baptism symbolises how through trusting in Jesus, we've become "clothed" with Him (GALATIANS 3:27). Or in other words, it's celebrating that we now belong to Him and that He lives in and through us.

As if that weren't significant enough, today's reading in Galatians tells us that if we've been clothed with Jesus, our identity is found in Him. We're the very children of God (V.26). We've been made right with God through Him—not by following the Old Testament law (VV.23-25). We're not divided against one another by gender, culture and status. We're set free and brought together through Jesus and everything He has already done for us. We now belong to Him (V.29).

So there are very good reasons to remember baptism and all it represents. We aren't simply focusing on the act itself, but that we belong to Jesus and have become children of God. Our identity, future and freedom are found in Him.

PC

WANT MORE . . . ?

Check out *What is baptism all about?* online at
ourdailybread.org/lookingdeeper

WE WERE THEREFORE BURIED WITH HIM THROUGH BAPTISM INTO DEATH IN ORDER THAT, JUST AS CHRIST WAS RAISED FROM THE DEAD THROUGH THE GLORY OF THE FATHER, WE TOO MAY LIVE A NEW LIFE. ROMANS 6:4

DYING FOR LIFE

BIBLE: HEBREWS 11:32-40

There were others who were tortured, refusing to be released so that they might gain an even better resurrection (V.35).

"Some men can't be bullied or negotiated with. Some men just want to watch the world burn." If you've ever watched the Batman movie *The Dark Knight*, you'll probably recognise that quote straightaway!

It's a great line, describing the bad guy of the movie: the Joker. But I can't help thinking it might apply to real life as well. What makes terrorists hate the world so much that they'll kill random people in the street or at a pop concert? What makes suicide bombers blow themselves up, taking as many innocent people as possible with them? Some extremists call what they do "martyrdom".

The writer of Hebrews has a different take on what being a martyr (being killed because of your beliefs, rather than taking your own life) is all about. He writes about people who were killed because they loved Jesus: "These were all commended for their faith" (HEBREWS 11:39) because they refused "to turn from God" (V.35 NLT) and preferred death to rejecting their Saviour.

Jesus is the supreme example of martyrdom. He stayed silent and allowed Himself to go through the horror of crucifixion (ISAIAH 53:7; MATTHEW 26:63). This is true martyrdom—a selfless act that leads to life. Jesus didn't die to bring death (like a terrorist) but to bring life to all who would trust Him (1 CORINTHIANS 15:54-57)!

One Bible teacher wrote: "Should we be most amazed at the wickedness of humans, who are capable of such awful cruelties, or at the excellence of God's grace, that is able to hold us up faithfully against such cruelties, and to carry us safely through all?"

TF

WANT MORE . . . ?

Check out *How should we respond to terrorism?* online at
ourdailybread.org/lookingdeeper

OUR SACRIFICES ARE TO COPY JESUS': THEY SHOULD BRING LIFE AND LOVE TO OTHERS.

DEATH ROW JOY

BIBLE: 1 PETER 1:3-9

Though you do not see him now, you believe in him and are filled with an inexpressible and glorious joy (V.8).

In 1985 Anthony Ray Hinton was charged with the murders of two restaurant managers. It was a set up—he'd been miles away when the crimes happened—but he was found guilty and sentenced to death. At the trial, Ray forgave those who lied about him, adding that he still had peace even in the injustice. "After my death, I'm going to heaven," he said. "Where are you going?"

Life on death row was hard for Ray. Prison lights flickered whenever the electric chair was used for others, a grim reminder of what was waiting for him. Ray passed a lie detector test but the results were ignored, one of many injustices he faced getting his case reheard.

Finally Ray's conviction was overturned. He'd been on death row for nearly thirty years. His life is a powerful example of the difference God makes in impossibly hard times. Because of his trust in Jesus, Ray had a confidence that was able to see beyond what he was going through in the here and now (1 PETER 1:3-5). He even knew real joy and peace in his terrible (and painfully long) trial (V.8). "This joy that I have," Ray said after his release, "they couldn't ever take that away in prison." He is a great example of what trusting Jesus in hard times looks like (VV.7-8).

Joy on death row? That's hard to fake. Stories like this are another proof to us that God exists, loves us, strengthens us and is with us even though we can't see Him.

SV

TO PRAY ABOUT . . .

Dear God, fill me with Your joy and peace as I trust in You even when things are hard. Help me to remember that You are with me even though I can't see You. Thank You for speaking to me and reassuring me through the Bible!

THE ONLY WAY TO HAVE PEACE IN HARD TIMES IS TO PUT ALL OUR CONFIDENCE IN JESUS.

SQUEEZING THE LIFE OUT OF US

BIBLE: ISAIAH 64:1-9

You come to the help of those who gladly do right, who remember your ways. But when we continued to sin against them, you were angry. How then can we be saved? (V.5).

Recently I read about the unimaginable killing force of pythons. These snakes have been known to kill things much bigger than they are: crocodiles, hyenas and sometimes even humans. Pythons kill their prey by cutting off the blood flow—a quick but painful death. "The heart . . . doesn't have enough strength to push against the pressure," one expert said. The deadly snake literally squeezes the life out of its victims.

Sin also squeezes the life out of us. The prophet Isaiah wrote about sin's stranglehold on God's people. "We continued to sin," he said (ISAIAH 64:5). No matter how hard we try to rescue ourselves, change the things we do or cover up our selfishness and mess, "all of us have become like one who is unclean" (V.6). Sin is deadly, and it will not easily let us out of its grip.

You would think that when we find ourselves in sin's life-squeezing grip, we would call out to God for help. Yet, "No one calls on your name" (V.7). This is sin's web of lies: it is all about what we want, ignoring God and living as we think is best. Even when things are going wrong, we believe we are the ones who can fix it. We don't realise how near we are to God's help—if we'd only ask.

Thankfully, no matter how far we've run or how much we've said "No" to Him, God doesn't give up on us. His forgiveness is always available, because Jesus went to the cross to pay for all sin in full (HEBREWS 9:26). It means God is always ready to free us from sin's grip. *wc*

THINKING IT OVER . . .

Read Romans 6:15-23. Is God's grace an excuse to just keep on sinning, knowing we'll be forgiven (V.15)? How would you describe the differences shown here of belonging to sin and belonging to God? What is the command of verse 19? What do we get from belonging to sin or belonging to God (V.23)?

SIN WANTS TO SQUEEZE GOD'S LIFE OUT OF US; JESUS IS THE ONLY ONE WHO CAN SET US FREE.

A LEADER WHO SERVES

BIBLE: NEHEMIAH 5:14-19

Those preceding me placed a heavy burden on the people . . . But out of reverence for God I did not act like that (V.15).

A youth pastor was leading a group of teenagers on a short-term mission trip to a poor community in Peru. The nicest room available was given to the pastor, but he turned it down.

When it came to doing the work, which included pouring concrete in the burning heat of the day, he didn't stand under a tree and drink lemonade—he took his turn pushing the wheelbarrow up the ramp and shovelling out the concrete. He was greatly respected by both the Peruvian community and his youth group—because he joined in the hard work with them.

When Israel was rebuilding the wall of Jerusalem—hard work to do when surrounded by enemies—their leader Nehemiah took his turn at both building and standing guard. Special food was offered to him as the leader, but he refused to accept it, unlike the leaders who had come before him. He ate from the same rations that were offered to everyone else (NEHEMIAH 5:18).

Two options come with leadership: the temptation to serve yourself in your position, and the opportunity to look after the people you lead. Nehemiah chose to be a servant-leader, and it earned him huge respect.

If God ever places you in a leadership position—whether at church, in class leading a project or in some other way—ask for His help to be a leader who serves.

DCE

WHAT I'M THANKFUL FOR . . .

Thank You, God, for the example of Jesus, who "did not come to be served, but to serve, and to give his life as a ransom for many" (MARK 10:45). Thank You that He shows us what it looks like to love and serve Your people, even when it costs us something.

LEADERS WHO SERVE WILL SERVE AS GOOD LEADERS.

IS THERE HOPE?

BIBLE: ROMANS 8:31-39

If God is for us, who can be against us? (V.31).

Edward Payson (1783–1827) had a really tough life. The death of his younger brother shook him to his core. He struggled with bipolar disorder, and he was affected by extreme migraine headaches for days. If this wasn't enough, a fall from a horse paralysed one of his arms, and he almost died from tuberculosis! That's a rough deal, right? Yet he never gave up, felt hopeless or despaired. His friends said that before Edward died, his joy was intense. How could that be?

In his letter to Christians in Rome, the apostle Paul talked about his complete confidence in the reality of God's love—despite how things sometimes look. He said, "If God is for us, who can be against us?" (ROMANS 8:31). If God gave His very own Son, Jesus, to save us, then He will provide everything we need to live for Him and make it through all our problems. Paul listed the sort of things he had faced: hardships, attacks for his love of Jesus, lack of food, nakedness, danger and the sword (V.35). The Bible never says that Jesus' love for us means bad things will never happen. But Paul explains, "In all these things we are more than conquerors through him who loved us" (V.37).

In the uncertainty of this world, God can be trusted completely, knowing that nothing, absolutely nothing, "will be able to separate us from the love of God that is in Christ Jesus our Lord" (V.39).

EPE

WHAT I'M THANKFUL FOR . . .

Faithful heavenly Father, thank You for Your love for me. Thank You for Your Son's sacrifice so that I can have eternal life. Thank You that, no matter how bad things may seem right now, I can trust in Your promises.

EVEN OUR WORST DAYS ARE NO MATCH FOR GOD'S LOVE FOR US.

WHEN GOOD TURNS BAD

BIBLE: 2 KINGS 18:1-8

He broke into pieces the bronze snake Moses had made, for up to that time the Israelites had been burning incense to it (v.4).

- -

People often find ways to turn something good into something bad. It even happens in churches and our lives. Like youth group prayer meetings becoming places for gossiping. Or spending time reading the Bible becoming less about knowing God and more about feeling like a good person.

When things like this happen, someone needs to be brave enough to say that God is no longer the centre.

The people of Judah found out how true that was. In their case, the good-thing-turned-bad was the bronze serpent that Moses had made years earlier to help the people when they were in the wilderness. Back then, the people had come under God's judgement because of their attitude towards Him (NUMBERS 21:5). So God "sent venomous snakes among them; they bit the people and many Israelites died" (v.6). But because of His love for them, He told Moses to make a bronze snake. Anyone who looked at the snake (and trusted God's command) would live (vv.8-9).

But by King Hezekiah's time, the bronze snake was being worshipped instead of God! It took bravery and a clear understanding of who God is for Hezekiah to destroy the serpent and to direct people back to God (2 KINGS 18:4).

We need to be able to spot when good things in our lives stop being about God. Then we can face up to them, and with God's help, put Him back at the centre.

DB

THINKING IT OVER . . .

Read John 3:14-18. In Jesus' teaching He compared His sacrifice to the story of the bronze snake. Why do you think the bronze snake is a good illustration of Jesus? Why are the Israelites in Numbers 21:5-9 a good illustration of us?

THE THINGS IN OUR LIVES ARE GOOD IF THEY HELP US KEEP GOD AT THE CENTRE.

FASTING

BIBLE: ZECHARIAH 7:1-10

The fasts . . . will become joyful and glad occasions and happy festivals for Judah. Therefore love truth and peace (ZECHARIAH 8:19).

Hunger pangs gnawed away at me. Someone at church had recommended fasting as a way to focus on God. But as the day wore on, I thought: *How did Jesus do this for forty days?* I struggled to concentrate and to rely on the Holy Spirit for peace, strength and patience. Especially patience.

If we're physically able, fasting can teach us the importance of our most important 'food'. As Jesus said, "Man shall not live on bread alone, but on every word that comes from the mouth of God" (MATTHEW 4:4). Yet, as I discovered, fasting on its own doesn't necessarily draw us closer to God!

In fact, God once told His people through the prophet Zechariah that their fasting was useless since it wasn't leading to changed lives. "Was it really for me that you fasted?" God asked pointedly (ZECHARIAH 7:5).

God's question showed that the real problem wasn't their stomachs; it was their lack of love for Him. By continuing to serve themselves, they were staying away from Him. So He told them to live by His good ways again: "Administer true justice; show mercy and compassion to one another. Do not oppress the widow or the fatherless, the foreigner or the poor" (VV.9-10).

Our point in any spiritual discipline (praying, reading the Bible, going to church, meditating, fasting) is to get to know Jesus better. As we become like Him, we'll also grow in love for His people.   *TG*

THINKING IT OVER . . .

Have you ever tried fasting? Why or why not? Why do you think fasting is so closely linked with looking out for others (ISAIAH 58:6-9)?

FASTING IS A REMINDER TO SERVE GOD FIRST AND HIS PEOPLE—NOT OURSELVES.

NEVER ALONE

BIBLE: JOHN 14:15-18

He will give you another advocate to help you and be with you forever—the Spirit of truth (VV.16-17).

While writing a Bible teaching guide for pastors in Indonesia, a friend got really involved with that nation's culture of togetherness. Go*tong royong*—meaning "mutual assistance"—is practised in villages, where neighbours might work together to fix someone's roof or rebuild a bridge or path. In cities too my friend said, "People always go places with someone else—to a doctor's appointment, for example. It's the way of life here. So you're never alone."

As Christians we know that we are also never alone. The Holy Spirit, the third person of God, is always with us. Far more than just a loyal friend, the Spirit of God is given to everyone who trusts Jesus to "help you and be with you for ever" (JOHN 14:16).

Jesus promised God's Spirit would come after His own time on earth ended. "I will not leave you as orphans," Jesus said (V.18). Instead, the Holy Spirit—"the Spirit of truth" who "lives with you and will be in you"—is in every Christian (V.17).

The Holy Spirit is our Helper, strength and encourager—always with us in a world where loneliness can be felt by all of us, even in a crowd. May we always be aware of His comforting love and presence.   *PR*

THINKING IT OVER . . .

As a follower of Jesus, how does it encourage you to know that the Holy Spirit lives inside of you? In what part of your life are you most aware of His presence? And when do you struggle to believe God is with you? Why not talk to your youth leader about this.

JESUS PROMISED THAT THE HOLY SPIRIT WILL NEVER LEAVE US.

MORE THAN JUST WAITING

BIBLE: ACTS 1:4-11

[Jesus] gave them this command: "Do not leave Jerusalem, but wait for the gift my Father promised, which you have heard me speak about" (V.4).

Police arrested a woman for dangerous driving after she veered off the road and drove down the pavement because she didn't want to wait behind a bus at the bus stop!

While it's true that waiting can make us impatient, there are also good things to do and learn while we have to wait. Jesus knew this when He told His disciples to "not leave Jerusalem" (ACTS 1:4). They were waiting to "be baptised with the Holy Spirit" (V.5).

As they met together in an upper room, the disciples seemed to understand that when Jesus told them to wait, He didn't say for them to do nothing. They spent time praying (V.14); and through the Bible's direction, they also chose a new disciple to replace Judas (V.26). When they were joined together in worship and prayer, the Holy Spirit came upon them (2:1-4).

The disciples hadn't simply been waiting—they'd also been preparing. As we wait on God, it doesn't mean doing nothing or impatiently rushing forward. Instead we can pray, praise Him and enjoy spending time with other Christians as we expect His answers and provision. The waiting prepares us for what's to come.

Yes, when God asks us to wait, we can be excited—knowing that we can trust Him and the plans He has for us!

PC

TO PRAY ABOUT . . .

God, when I'm struggling, remind me that times of waiting aren't for nothing. They help me to look for You and be ready for what You are doing in my life.

WAITING ISN'T A TIME TO DO NOTHING, BUT TO GET READY.

LIVING EVERY DAY

BIBLE: PROVERBS 15:13-33

All the days of the oppressed are wretched, but the cheerful heart has a continual feast (V.15).

When Tamer Lee Owens celebrated her 104th birthday, she said her long life was down to "Laughter, God and the little things." She still finds enjoyment each day in talking with people, taking a walk and reading the Bible. "I don't know how long He'll let me stay here," she said. "I just thank God for what He's given me already."

Most of us won't live 104 years, but we can learn from Tamer Lee how to enjoy each day that we're given.

Laughter—"A happy heart makes the face cheerful, but heartache crushes the spirit" (PROVERBS 15:13). True happiness begins deep inside us because of our relationship with Jesus—and then shows on our faces.

God—"Wisdom's instruction is to fear the LORD, and humility comes before honour" (V.33). When God is the centre of who we are and what we do, He can teach us His ways in every experience.

The Little Things—"Better a dish of vegetables with love than a fattened calf with hatred" (V.17). Living in love and peace with the people we know is far better than having lots of stuff. Being in stressful relationships is miserable. If that's your situation, ask God to help you be a person who brings generosity and peace, not more fighting and tension.

Not all of us will live to 104, but we can all live well each day—with laughter, God and the little things in life.

DM

THINKING IT OVER . . .

Read Philippians 2:1-4. Why should our unity with other Christians give us such an encouraging, joyful, compassionate way of life (VV.1-2)? Why is valuing "others above [yourself]" such a positive way to live (V.3)?

LIVING WELL ISN'T ABOUT WHAT WE GET BUT WHO WE LIVE FOR.

INTO THE DESERT

BIBLE: EXODUS 15:22-27

He said, "If you listen carefully to the LORD your God and do what is right in his eyes . . . I will not bring on you any of the diseases I brought on the Egyptians, for I am the LORD, who heals you" (V.26).

After God rescued the Israelites from Egypt by leading them through the Red Sea, He then took them into the desert. It seems strange that God would lead them from a place of victory and power to a place of disappointment and need!

But God wanted to show them that life is a combination of bitter and sweet, good and bad. When the Israelites arrived at Marah, they complained because the water was bitter (EXODUS 15:23). After Moses talked with God (V.25), God reminded them to keep His commandments (V.26). Then He brought them to the refreshment of the water at Elim (V.27).

God wanted them to realise that every experience on their journey would show them more about themselves. This test in particular proved that they didn't yet trust God to provide for them.

They also learned that God was involved in even the smallest details of their lives. He wanted them to know that He could not only part the sea, but He would also meet their every need.

If you feel like you're being led into a place of disappointment, questions and bitterness right now, trust your situation to God—make sure you talk to Him about it. He knows exactly where you are and what you need. As you trust Him, He will lead you out of the desert and into an even deeper relationship with Him as you focus more on Him and less on yourself. *MW*

THINKING IT OVER . . .

Read Micah 6:6-8. What is God looking for in our lives? Gifts to please Him (V.6)? Good works to prove ourselves and make up for our mistakes (V.7)? Or an active, dependent and close relationship with Him (V.8)?

GOD WANTS TO TEACH US TO DEPEND ON HIM IN ALL THE SITUATIONS HE LEADS US THROUGH.

GIVE ME A SIGN

BIBLE: LUKE 11:29-32

This is a wicked generation. It asks for a sign, but none will be given it except the sign of Jonah (V.29).

A friend once told me, "I'll believe in Jesus if He comes down and stands in front of me." Well, that may sound like it makes sense. But the Bible paints a very different picture.

The religious leaders said more or less the same thing to Jesus Himself. "Then some of the Pharisees and teachers of the law said to [Jesus], 'Teacher, we want to see a sign from you'" (MATTHEW 12:38). But they said this after Jesus had already given everyone plenty of signs: healing the sick, giving sight to the blind, casting out demons and even bringing the dead back to life. What else did they need?

So Jesus called them "a wicked generation" (LUKE 11:29). He said that the only sign they would be given was the sign of Jonah, who had been thrown into a stormy sea (JONAH 1:2-3). When the Ninevites heard Jonah's message after he had spent three days in the belly of a fish, they believed God had sent him and they trusted God for themselves.

Likewise, the religious leaders who already knew of Jesus' words and works would soon see Him crucified and buried in the 'belly' of the earth for three days. And in the following weeks they would hear personal stories from those who had seen Him alive, and had even touched Him—but they still wouldn't believe.

Today we have in the Bible a record of what Jesus said and did, written by people who knew Him. If we are open to the truth, we have all the evidence we need to believe. We don't need to be sign-seekers. The religious leaders show us that signs will never be enough for people who are closed off to God anyway.

HVL

WANT MORE . . . ?

Did Jesus really do miracles? Will God do a miracle to help me believe in Him? Check out answers to questions like this in *Big questions about . . . miracles* online at **ourdailybread.org/teen**

SIGN-SEEKERS ARE NOT THE SAME AS GOD-SEEKERS.

WALKING WITH THE SPIRIT

BIBLE: GALATIANS 5:13-26

Walk by the Spirit, and you will not gratify the desires of the flesh (V.16).

Ten thousand hours. That's how long one expert thinks it takes to become really good at a new skill. Even the best singers, footballers and writers weren't just born talented. They had to work hard and spend many hours getting as good as they are at what they do.

As strange as it might seem, we need a similar mentality when it comes to learning to live in the power of the Holy Spirit. In Galatians, Paul encouraged the church to be set apart for God. But Paul explained that this wouldn't just happen by obeying a set of rules. Instead we're to "walk" with the Holy Spirit (GALATIANS 5:16). The Greek word that Paul uses for "walk" literally means to walk around and around something. So for Paul, walking with the Spirit meant journeying with the Spirit each day—it's not just a one-time experience of His power. Just like a great singer has to spend time every day practising to be that good, if we want to be "in step with the Spirit" (V.25) we need to spend time with Him. It isn't something that 'just happens'.

Let's look to be filled with the Spirit each day, giving space to read the Bible and talk with God. As we allow ourselves this time with Him, He will guide us, strengthen us and change us. And as we're "led by the Spirit" in this way (V.18), we'll become better at hearing His voice and following His leading. *PC*

TO PRAY ABOUT . . .

Father, help me to experience the presence and leading of the Holy Spirit today so that I might walk with You and live in a way that pleases You.

WALKING WITH THE SPIRIT IS A LIFE-LONG JOURNEY.

GOING GOING, GONE

BIBLE: PROVERBS 23:1-5

Cast but a glance at riches, and they are gone (V.5).

The artist Banksy pulled off another clever stunt. His painting *Girl with Balloon* sold for one million pounds at an auction house in London. Moments after the auctioneer yelled "Sold," an alarm sounded and the painting slipped halfway through a shredder mounted inside the bottom of the frame. Banksy tweeted a picture of bidders gasping at his ruined masterpiece, with the words, "Going, going, gone."

Banksy loved pulling one over on the rich people at the auction, but he didn't need to bother. Money pulls plenty of pranks itself. God says, "Do not wear yourself out to get rich . . . Cast but a glance at riches, and they are gone, for they will surely sprout wings and fly off to the sky like an eagle" (PROVERBS 23:4-5).

It may feel good to have money to spend, but it's one of the least secure things in this world. Maybe your parents give you a bit of money each month. Maybe you've got a weekend job. Whatever one or two ways we get money, there are loads of ways to lose it. We buy stuff we then regret; people can steal our money; we can easily misplace it; our phone contract suddenly increases and takes yet more money . . . Money is just one of the things of this world that is always going, going, gone.

So what should we do? God tells us a few verses later: "Always be zealous for the fear of the LORD. There is surely a future hope for you, and your hope will not be cut off" (VV.17-18). The only real security is found in Jesus; He alone keeps us safe forever and promises us a certain future.   *MW*

THINKING IT OVER . . .

Read 1 Timothy 6:12-19. What is the most important thing for us to "take hold of" (V.12)? What is the problem/limit of money (V.17)? Why can being generous and "rich in good deeds" help us stay focused on going to heaven rather than on just living for the 'here and now' (VV.18-19)?

ONLY JESUS CAN OFFER US A SECURE FUTURE.

DEBT REMOVED

BIBLE: REVELATION 1:4-7

[Jesus Christ] loves us and has freed us from our sins by his blood (V.5).

The speaker at one university graduation ceremony announced that he would be giving millions of pounds to pay for the student fees of the entire year. Their debts were completely removed! One student—with thousands of pounds of debt in student loans—was too overwhelmed to speak!

Have you ever owed a debt? It might have been some money you borrowed from a brother or sister. Or maybe you owed your friend a favour after they spent an evening helping you with some homework you just didn't get. Whatever form they take, we know what it is to be indebted to someone else. But have you ever had the relief of hearing that person say, "It's fine. You don't owe me anything." Effectively they're saying, "The debt is paid."

After calling Jesus "the faithful witness, the firstborn from the dead and the ruler of the kings of the earth," John talked about His debt-removing work: "To him who loves us and has freed us from our sins by his blood" (REVELATION 1:5). This statement is simple but its meaning is huge. It's the good news that the death of Jesus frees us from the penalty that our sinful actions and attitudes deserve. Jesus cried from the cross, "It is finished!" (JOHN 19:30)—or in other words, "The debt is paid in full!" There is nothing left to pay. Our every sin and rejection of God was emptied into Jesus' account on the cross, where He took on the full judgement of God for us.

Because our debt has been paid, those who trust in Jesus are forgiven and become a part of God's kingdom family (REVELATION 1:6). This is the best news ever!

AJ

THINKING IT OVER . . .

If you haven't trusted Jesus for yourself, what's keeping you from accepting His free gift? When was the last time you thanked God that your debt has been "paid in full" because of Jesus?

JESUS' DEATH REMOVES OUR SIN, OUR DEBT, OUR GUILT!

HE IS NOT HERE

BIBLE: LUKE 24:1-18

He is not here; he has risen! (V.6).

As I bent down to enter the small opening of the Garden Tomb outside the old city walls in Jerusalem, I could imagine how several of Jesus' female disciples felt early on the Sunday morning following Jesus' death.

They had come to prepare Jesus' crucified body for burial. As I looked at the empty ledge in the tomb, I could envision the women's confusion. As their eyes adjusted to the dim light, slowly the reality would dawn on them that there was no body or stink of death—just empty strips of linen.

Turning to exit the burial room, my eyes were immediately drawn to the words "He is not here; he has risen!" (LUKE 24:6) written on the wall. Those simple but life-changing words were announced to the women by two angels whose dramatic appearance terrified the already confused and grieving women. But even in their confusion, the angels reminded them of Jesus' own words that He "must be delivered over to the hands of sinners, be crucified and on the third day be raised again" (V.7).

"Then they remembered his words" (V.8). For the women, the empty tomb proved all of Jesus' claims, turning their sadness into rejoicing as they realised all they had believed was actually true. For us, the empty tomb also gives us confidence about our unending life with our risen Saviour. It is proof that we can live a new life now with Him and in His power (ROMANS 6:5-10).   LS

THINKING IT OVER . . .

What ways does Jesus' resurrection impact your life?
Does His empty tomb give you confidence?

JESUS IS RISEN!

RUNNING TO TELL

BIBLE: MATTHEW 28:1-10

So the women . . . ran to tell his disciples (v.8).

- -

The modern-day marathon is based on the story of a Greek messenger, Pheidippides. According to legend, in 490 BC he ran approximately twenty-five miles from Marathon to Athens to announce the Greeks' victory against their enemies, the invading Persians. Today, people run marathons for charities, to tick it off their bucket lists and for lots of other reasons. But Pheidippides ran for a very unique reason: each of his steps was for the joy of delivering good news to his people!

Around 500 years later, two women also ran to deliver good news—the most crucial news in all of history. When Mary and Mary Magdalene arrived at the tomb where Jesus had been laid after His crucifixion, they found it empty. An angel told them that Jesus had "risen from the dead" and to "go quickly and tell his disciples" (MATTHEW 28:7). The women, "afraid yet filled with joy," ran to tell the disciples what they'd found out (v.8).

Do we have the same excited reaction to the resurrection of Jesus? Does it inspire us to tell others the good news that He is alive and King forever?

We may not even need to 'run' further than next door or to a classmate to find someone who needs to know about our Saviour. He won the battle against death so we might live victoriously with Him forever!

KH

THINKING IT OVER . . .

Who shared the good news of Jesus' resurrection with you? Who can you share it with this week? Why not ask God for an opportunity to talk about Jesus' resurrection.

JESUS' RESURRECTION IS NEWS WORTH RUNNING TO SHARE.

A CHANGED MAN

BIBLE: 1 JOHN 1:5-10

He is faithful and just and will forgive us our sins and purify us from all unrighteousness (V.9).

One night, when John Wesley (1703-1791) was travelling on horseback, a robber jumped in front of the horse and grabbed the bridle. Wesley gave the few coins in his pockets to the thief, and even allowed the man to search through his saddlebags for more. As the robber left, Wesley said, "Stop! I have something more to give you!" Saying that one day the robber might regret his actions, John Wesley quoted 1 John 1:7: "The blood of Jesus Christ cleanses us from all sin!"

Wesley quoted from the first letter of the ageing disciple John, who wrote to a divided church where some said that Jesus hadn't died for the forgiveness of sins. John explained that "God is light" (1 JOHN 1:5) and that we cannot walk in darkness while claiming to walk in truth (V.6). Only when we admit our sins will God forgive us and "purify us from all unrighteousness" (V.9).

Years after the robbery, the thief realised he needed a rescue and he chose to trust Jesus for himself. The changed man walked up to John Wesley after a church service, saying, "I owe it all to you." John Wesley quickly replied, "Oh no, my friend! Not to me, but to the precious blood of Jesus!"

No matter what we've done wrong, from stealing to gossip to envy or something else, we can be forgiven and made brand new through Jesus' sacrifice.

ABP

WHAT I'M THANKFUL FOR . . .

Jesus, thank You for dying on the cross and for forgiving me for the many things I do wrong. Help me to show Your love to others and tell them about the rescue You offer.

THE BLOOD OF JESUS CLEANS US FROM OUR SIN.

THE BATTLE'S OVER. REALLY!

BIBLE: ROMANS 6:1-14
We were . . . buried with him (V.4).

For twenty-nine years after World War II ended, Hiroo Onoda hid in the jungle, refusing to believe his country had surrendered. Japanese military leaders had sent Onoda to a remote island in the Philippines with orders to spy on the Allied forces. Long after a peace treaty had been signed and the war ended, Onoda stayed hidden on the island. In 1974, Onoda's commanding officer travelled to the island to find him and convince him the war was over.

Onoda lived a cut-off, lonely life because he refused to surrender—refused to believe that the war was done. We make a similar mistake. Paul tells us the stunning truth that "all of us who were baptised into Christ Jesus were baptised into his death" (ROMANS 6:3). On the cross, in a powerful, mysterious way, Jesus put to death our old, sin-sick selves. The Bible teaches that Jesus' death was also our death (V.8). But this was a transforming death leading to life. Because we're now "dead to sin," we're also "alive to God" (V.11). Yet we often live as if the battle still rages. Rather than receiving the victory Jesus has already secured, freeing us from the power of sin and death, we mistakenly live as though sin still has the upper hand.

While we'll still wrestle with sin in this life, freedom comes as we recognise that Jesus has already won the battle with it. May we live in that truth!   *wc*

TO PRAY ABOUT . . .
Jesus, I know that You've won the battle over sin and darkness.
Please help me to live this out. By Your Spirit may I keep making the
choice to live for You, not for myself.

**JESUS HAS ALREADY WON.
IT'S TIME TO LIVE IN VICTORY!**

REFINED IN THE FIRE

BIBLE: 1 PETER 1:6-9
These trials will show that your faith is genuine (V.7 NLT).

Twenty-four karat gold is 100% gold with no impurities. But that percentage is difficult to get to. Refiners most commonly use one of two methods for the purification of gold. The Miller method is the quickest and least expensive, but the resulting gold is only about 99.95% pure. The Wohlwill process takes a little more time and costs more, but the gold is 99.99% pure at the end.

In Bible times, refiners just used fire to purify gold. The heat made impurities rise to the surface, so the impurity was easier to get rid of. In his first letter to Christians throughout Asia Minor, the apostle Peter used the gold refining process as a picture for the way trials work in our lives. When he wrote his letter, many Christians were being attacked by the Romans for their trust in Jesus. Peter knew what that was like too. But persecution, Peter explained, brings out the "genuineness of [our] faith" (1 PETER 1:7).

Perhaps you feel like you're in a fire right now—feeling the heat of school pressure, illness or other problems. But these things are often the way God purifies the 'gold' of our faith. Difficult situations cause the impurities in us to rise to the surface; we find ourselves doing and saying things that are not godly. When we admit those impurities to God, He cleanses them away. What's left is a little bit more pure.

He knows what's best for us, even when life hurts. Keep connected to Jesus and we will see Him transform our lives, especially in the hard times.   *LW*

WANT MORE . . . ?
Check out *How can we face our trials?* online at
ourdailybread.org/lookingdeeper

GOD USES TRIALS TO MAKE OUR TRUST IN HIM STRONGER.

A NEW LIFE

BIBLE: 2 TIMOTHY 1:6-14

He has saved us and called us to a holy life (V.9).

As a teenage gang leader, Casey and his gang broke into homes and cars, robbed corner shops and attacked other gangs. Eventually, he was arrested and sentenced. In prison, he became a 'shot caller', someone who handed out homemade knives during riots.

Sometime later, he was put in solitary confinement. While daydreaming in his cell, Casey experienced a 'movie' or vision replaying key events of his life—and of Jesus, being led to and nailed to the cross. In his vision, Jesus told him, "I'm doing this for you." Casey fell to the floor crying and admitted his sins. Later, he told the prison chaplain what had happened. The chaplain explained more about Jesus and gave him a Bible. "That was the start of my journey of faith," Casey said. Eventually, Casey was released into the mainline prison population, where he was bullied and attacked for his new belief in Jesus. But he felt at peace, because he "had found a new calling: telling other inmates about Jesus."

The apostle Paul talks about the power of Jesus to change lives in his letter to Timothy: God moves us from a life of selfishness to a life of following and living for Jesus (2 TIMOTHY 1:9). When we trust Him and see Him changing us, we'll want to tell others. The Spirit inside us helps us to talk about Jesus and to keep going when we suffer in our mission to share the good news (V.8). Like Casey, let's live out our new life for Jesus.

AK

THINKING IT OVER . . .

Read 2 Corinthians 4:5-18. When have you shared the gospel with someone? Did you feel attacked for your beliefs? How do Pauls words in verses 7-11 challenge and encourage you? What reasons does he give to "not lose heart" (V.16)?

WE WHO ARE ALIVE ARE ALWAYS BEING GIVEN OVER TO DEATH FOR JESUS' SAKE, SO THAT HIS LIFE MAY ALSO BE REVEALED IN OUR MORTAL BODY.
2 CORINTHIANS 4:11

KEPT SAFE

BIBLE: DEUTERONOMY 31:1-8
The LORD himself goes before you (V.8).

In my part of the world we have scary, poisonous snakes. One time I was in the garden and kicked aside some weeds that were growing . . . and leapt into the air! A venomous copperhead snake lay hidden in the grass—an inch to the left and I would have kicked it by mistake. I saw its colourful markings as soon as I moved the clump of weeds.

When my feet hit the ground a few feet away, I thanked God I hadn't been bitten. And I wondered how many times He had kept me from dangers I never knew were there.

God watches over His people. Moses told the Israelites before they entered the Promised Land, "The LORD himself goes before you and will be with you; he will never leave you nor forsake you. Do not be afraid; do not be discouraged" (DEUTERONOMY 31:8). They couldn't see God, but He was with them all the same.

Sometimes things happen that we don't understand. We ask God why our plans have got interrupted, why we didn't get the grades we worked so hard for, why we didn't get picked for a team. While these things hurt, maybe can we also think about the fact that God may be keeping us safe from unseen dangers when things like this happen. Perhaps He is guiding us along a specific path that will keep us close to Him and away from stuff that might lead us totally the wrong way in life.

The Bible reminds us that His perfect care remains over us every day. He is "always" with us (MATTHEW 28:20).

JB

WHAT I'M THANKFUL FOR . . .
Faithful Father, thank You for watching over me every day. Even when confusing things happen, thank You that You are in control and keeping me safe.

GOD KNOWS THE DANGERS OF THIS WORLD BETTER THAN WE DO.

HATERS

BIBLE: NEHEMIAH 6:1-15

They were all trying to frighten us, thinking, "Their hands will get too weak for the work, and it will not be completed." But I prayed, "Now strengthen my hands" (V.9).

Josh Evans never existed. Still, he made friends with 13-year-old Megan online. After a little while, he sent this message, "I don't know if I want to be friends with you. You're not nice to your friends." Josh posted more and more bullying messages until Megan committed suicide. As it turned out, 'Josh' was actually the mum of one of Megan's friends, pretending to be a teenage boy so she could hurt her.

Nehemiah understood all about living under the shadow of bullies who hated him and wanted to hurt him. When he and the Israelites were rebuilding Jerusalem's wall (after they returned from exile), he said his bullies were "trying to frighten us" (NEHEMIAH 6:9).

Sanballat and Geshem sent messages asking Nehemiah to meet with them so they could stop his work. Then they threatened to tell the king that Nehemiah was planning a rebellion.

Bullies are everywhere—at school, online and even at home. When they are attacking us and we feel overwhelmed, let's copy Nehemiah. We don't need to solve the problem ourselves or fight back or believe the things they say. We need to talk to God, because His words are the truth. Then we will be confident, as Nehemiah was: "Nothing like what you are saying is happening; you are just making it up out of your head" (V.8). Nehemiah then prayed, "Remember, O my God, all the evil things that [they] have done" (V.14 NLT).

No one can stand against us when we belong to God (ROMANS 8:31-33). Nehemiah proved it. When he and the Israelites finished the wall, his bullies were the ones who were "afraid and lost their self-confidence, because they realised that this work had been done with the help of our God" (NEHEMIAH 6:16).

JBS

WANT MORE . . . ?

Check out *How should I stand up to bullies?* online at **ourdailybread.org/teen**

IN GOD I TRUST AND AM NOT AFRAID. WHAT CAN MAN DO TO ME? PSALM 56:11

Seven Days with . . . King David

TRAINING DAYS

BIBLE: I SAMUEL 17:32-37

The LORD who rescued me from the paw of the lion and the paw of the bear will rescue me from the hand of this Philistine (V.37).

It's been more than sixty years since Brother Andrew first smuggled Bibles into anti-Christian countries. But he didn't just become brave overnight. His confidence in God, especially in very dangerous places, grew over time.

David was out looking after his dad's sheep when the prophet Samuel anointed him as God's chosen king of Israel (1 SAMUEL 16:12-13), but it took years of training before he became one of the nation's greatest rulers. His first public test ended in that famous victory over the giant Goliath (17:49-50), but other challenges had also helped prepared him to fully trust God.

King Saul doubted David's ability against a man who'd "been a warrior from his youth" (V.33). But David promised Saul that his ability to protect his dad's sheep against predators had prepared him for the fight against the giant who was challenging God's people (VV.34-36). He confidently said, "The LORD who rescued me from the paw of the lion and the paw of the bear will rescue me from the hand of this Philistine" (V.37).

God brings training days into our lives to prepare us for what lies ahead. Let's press on and grow in our trust in Him.

ROS

COMPLETING THE PICTURE . . .

David was born about 1,000 years before Jesus. He was marked out (anointed) as God's chosen king when he was a teenager. Not long after, he took down Goliath and soon became a warrior in King Saul's army (1 SAMUEL 18:12-15). King Saul was jealous of David and tried to kill him—a lot (19:9-10,11,14-15; 23:26-29; 24:1-7)! After Saul totally rejected God (28:16-19), he was killed in battle—and David finally became Israel's King David around fifteen years after Samuel first anointed him (2 SAMUEL 5:1-5).

GOD IS ALWAYS TRAINING US FOR THE CHALLENGES THAT LIE AHEAD.

Seven Days with . . . King David

LAVA IN PARADISE

BIBLE: 2 SAMUEL 6:1-9

Since we are receiving a kingdom that cannot be shaken, let us be thankful, and so worship God acceptably with reverence and awe, for our "God is a consuming fire" (HEBREWS 12:28-29).

All is quiet, except for slow-moving rivers of hissing lava. The people stand grim-faced yet amazed. Most days they call this place 'paradise'. On this day, however, the fiery lava in Hawaii reminded everyone that God made these islands through untameable volcanic power.

The ancient Israelites knew about untameable power too. When King David brought the ark of the covenant back to Jerusalem (2 SAMUEL 6:1-4), a celebration broke out (V.5)—until Uzzah died suddenly when he grabbed hold of the ark to steady it on the oxen-drawn cart (VV.6-7).

This may make us think of God as being as unpredictable as a volcano, just as likely to create as He is to destroy. However, it helps to remember that God had given Israel specific instructions for how to handle the things set apart for worshipping Him, like the ark (SEE NUMBERS 4). Israel could be close to God, but His presence was too overwhelming for them to come to Him carelessly.

Hebrews 12 remembers Mount Sinai, "burning with fire," where God gave Moses the ten commandments for His people. That mountain terrified everyone (HEBREWS 12:18-21). But then we're told: "You have come to . . . Jesus the mediator of a new [agreement with God]" (VV.22-24). Jesus—God's Son—made the way for us to draw near to His all-powerful, yet loving Father. *TG*

COMPLETING THE PICTURE . . .

The ark of the covenant was a gold-covered wooden chest which held important symbols of God's relationship with His people, including the ten commandments (HEBREWS 9:4). The ark itself was a symbol of God's presence and was often where priests and kings spoke with him. After Uzzah died from touching the ark, "David was afraid" (2 SAMUEL 6:9). Yet when he continued taking the ark to Jerusalem, "David was dancing before the LORD with all his might" (V.14). This reminder of God's awesome presence didn't fill David with dread, but joy—he worshipped the almighty God who loved him.

HOW GREAT TO KNOW THAT OUR ALL-POWERFUL GOD LOVES US WITH INFINITE LOVE!

Seven Days with . . . King David

BACK WHERE WE SHOULD BE

BIBLE: 2 SAMUEL 11

If we confess our sins, he is faithful and just and will forgive us our sins and purify us from all unrighteousness (1 JOHN 1:9).

As a teenager, she had called her parents horrible names. Little did she know that would be the last thing she ever said to them. They died hours later in a car crash. Now, even after years of counselling, she can't forgive herself. Guilt and regret paralyse her.

We all live with regrets—some of them are massive. But the Bible shows us a way through the guilt. Let's look at one example.

There's no sugar-coating what King David did. It was the time "when kings go off to war", but "David remained in Jerusalem" (2 SAMUEL 11:1). Away from the battle, he slept with another man's wife and tried to cover it up with murder (VV.2-5,14-15). God stopped David's downward spiral (12:1-13), but the king would live the rest of his life with the burden of what he had done.

In the meantime the leader of his army, Joab, was winning the battle David should have been fighting (2 SAMUEL 12:26). Joab challenged David, "Now muster the rest of the troops and besiege the city and capture it" (V.28). David finally got back to the place God had put him—as the leader of his country and his army (V.29).

When we let our regrets and mistakes crush us, we're basically telling God His grace isn't enough. No matter what we've done, our Father offers His complete forgiveness to us. We can find, as David did, grace enough to get back to where we should be with God.

TG

COMPLETING THE PICTURE . . .

The Bible calls David "a man after [God's] own heart" (1 SAMUEL 13:14). Yet when he was king, David committed adultery and murder. David clearly struggled with sin just as much as us. What made him "a man after [God's] own heart" was his genuine love for God. So David didn't fall into sin and love it; when he was selfish and made a mess of things, he hated it and wanted to get right with God again (2 SAMUEL 12:13). And so he was promised: "The LORD has taken away your sin. You are not going to die" (V.14).

OUR SIN DOESN'T DEFINE US; GOD'S LOVE DOES.

Seven Days with . . . King David

WHERE ARE YOU HEADED?

BIBLE: 2 SAMUEL 12

Then Nathan said to David, "You are the man!" (V.7).

In northern Thailand, the Wild Boars youth football team decided to explore a cave together. After an hour they turned to go back and found that the entrance to the cave was flooded. Rising water pushed them deeper into the cave, day after day, until they were finally trapped more than two miles inside. Once they had been heroically rescued two weeks later, people started asking how they had become so hopelessly trapped. The answer: one step at a time.

Nathan confronted King David for killing his loyal soldier, Uriah. How did the man "after [God's] own heart" (1 SAMUEL 13:14) become guilty of murder? One step at a time. David didn't go from hero to murderer in one afternoon. He warmed up to it, over time, as one bad decision bled into others. It started with a second glance that turned into a lustful stare at Bathsheba (Uriah's wife). He abused his kingly power by sending for Bathsheba, then tried to cover up her pregnancy by calling her husband home from the war David should have been fighting in. When Uriah refused to visit his wife while his fellow soldiers were fighting, David decided murder was his only option.

We may not be guilty of murder, or be trapped in a cave of our own making, but we're either moving towards Jesus or towards trouble. Big problems don't develop overnight. They sneak up on us gradually, one step at a time.

MW

COMPLETING THE PICTURE . . .

When Nathan confronted David, the king was quick to realise he had messed up. He came back to God straightaway to receive forgiveness. But he still had to face the consequences of his actions: the child of David's affair died (2 SAMUEL 12:15), and David's family was filled with infighting, death and traumas for the rest of his life after. What did David do once these things started happening? "He went into the house of the LORD and worshipped" (V.20). Even though he'd made a mess of everything—and had to live through it—David loved, trusted and focused on God, who faithfully brought him through it all.

IF WE'RE NOT RUNNING TO JESUS, WE'RE RUNNING AWAY.

Seven Days with . . . King David
CLEAN SLATE

BIBLE: PSALM 51

Wash away all my iniquity and cleanse me from my sin (V.2).

After being released from prison, Michael was ready for a fresh start. He wanted to remove the gang tattoos that covered his body. They were reminders of the way he'd lived before spending fifteen years in prison. Getting rid of them helped him begin a new life.

When we go to God for forgiveness, we begin a new life too. He cleans us up on the inside—removing all the 'tattoos' of our sin, mess and wrongs.

The psalmist, King David, talked about how God had cleaned him from sin in Psalm 51. After his affair with Bathsheba (and then murdering her husband), he knew he had "done what is evil in [God's] sight" (PSALM 51:4). David asked God to wash away those stains: "Cleanse me with hyssop, and I will be clean; wash me, and I will be whiter than snow" (V.7). God was willing to clean even those deep, dark 'tattoos'. When we ask God for new life with Him, there is nothing He won't forgive.

When we trust Jesus' sacrifice, where He became our sin and paid for it in full, we can be confident that we've been washed clean (2 CORINTHIANS 5:21). Even though there may be consequences—the son born from David's adultery died—we are made completely free from the 'tattoos' of our past. There is no judgement left for us to face (ROMANS 8:1)! Jesus, we too have done evil in Your sight. Please wash us clean!

KH.

COMPLETING THE PICTURE . . .

David was a great king. But he messed up a lot. Yet through David's family line, God promised to provide the true King of the world. This King wouldn't ever mess up; and He would rule a kingdom that would never end. That promised King's name? Jesus, the "Son of David" (SEE MATTHEW 1:1; 12:23; 20:30).

David realised that, on our own, we can never make things right with God when we sin: "You do not delight in sacrifice . . . [but] a broken and contrite heart you, God, will not despise" (PSALM 51:16-17). We need to come to God as we are; knowing we need His forgiveness and depending on the sacrifice *He provided* in Jesus, the perfect King, to pay for our sin in full.

JESUS WASHES US CLEAN.

Seven Days with . . . King David

NIGHT WATCHES

BIBLE: PSALM 63

On my bed I remember you; I think of you through the watches of the night (v.6).

During one summer holiday, I lived and worked on a farm. Everyone there was signed up on the "Night Watch" rota. Night watches meant staying up all night watching out for things like forest fires, intruders or distressed animals—while everyone else slept.

At first the night watches were really boring and tiring. But soon they became unique opportunities for me to be still before God, talking with Him, singing praise and thinking about things I had read recently in the Bible.

King David loved spending time with God and would "earnestly" look to make time with Him (PSALM 63:1), even from his bed and through the "watches of the night" (v.6). This psalm makes it clear that David was troubled. It's possible he was thinking about his deep sadness over his son Absalom's rebellion. Yet the night became a time for David to find help, strength and comfort in the "shadow of [God's] wings" (v.7).

Are you going through something that's keeping you awake at night? Why not use those sleepless times as your own night watches. Look for God, sing to Him, talk with Him and "cling to [him]" (v.8). And from those night watches with God, you'll be strengthened for the days ahead.

EM

COMPLETING THE PICTURE . . .

One of the consequences of King David's adultery was disruption and chaos in his family. David's son Absalom was a key figure in this chaos. He murdered his older brother Amnon in an act of revenge (SEE 2 SAMUEL 13:1,14,20,28). Then he made plans to take his dad's place as king (14:10), which led to King David having to run away (14:14) and a battle between them at the forest of Ephraim (2 SAMUEL 18). Absalom was killed (VV.9-15) and David grieved: "O my son Absalom! My son, my son Absalom! If only I had died instead of you" (V.33).

DURING DIFFICULT TIMES, SET UP YOUR OWN NIGHT WATCHES WITH GOD.

Seven Days with . . . King David

OUT OF THE PIT

BIBLE: PSALM 40

He put a new song in my mouth, a hymn of praise to our God. Many will see and fear the LORD and put their trust in him (V.3).

When King David looked back on his life, he remembered many painful things and lots of times that he'd messed up. In Psalm 40, he thought about one particular situation, a time when he felt as if he had sunk deep into "the slimy pit" (PSALM 40:2).

In his helplessness David had kept asking God for rescue. God faithfully provided for him, lifting him out of the "mud and mire" and setting his feet on "a rock" (V.2). Thinking about the ways God had rescued him, David broke out into this hymn of praise and thanks!

Do you find yourself stuck in a pit? Did you fall out with a friend? Mess up big time with your parents? Get found out? Are you feeling lost in anger, guilt or depression?

Keep asking God for rescue. And more than that, expect him to "put a new song in [your] mouth, a hymn of praise to our God" (V.3). All His works in our lives are good and worth praising. When we give our attention to Him, as David did, we will remember that nothing compares with our awesome God (V.5). As our friends and family see God provide for us, time and again, may they "see and fear the LORD and put their trust in him" (V.3).

VG

COMPLETING THE PICTURE . . .

David wrote many psalms (which are songs and prayers) during his life, from his teenage years as a shepherd to his last days as an old king. The Bible says about half of its psalms were written by David. Through all his ups and downs David remained "a man after [God's] own heart" (1 SAMUEL 13:14) because he never lost sight of the fact that he was "poor and needy" and always dependent on God, his "help" and "deliverer" (PSALM 40:17). Let's use David's words to tell God, "None can compare with you; were I to speak and tell of your deeds, they would be too many to declare" (V.5).

GOD NEVER LEAVES HIS CHILDREN IN THE PIT. HE IS OUR RESCUER!

THE SAME GOD

BIBLE: JOSHUA 7:16-26

"He himself bore our sins" in his body on the cross, so that we might die to sins and live for righteousness; "by his wounds you have been healed" (1 PETER 2:24).

People sometimes ask, "How come the God of the Old Testament seems so harsh compared to the God of the New Testament?" To start with, we need to know the God of the Old and New Testaments is the same God. He's "the same yesterday and today and for ever" (HEBREWS 13:8). And His stance towards sin has always been the same: it must be judged.

Achan hid things in his tent that God had said to stay away from (JOSHUA 7:20-22). He died for this along with all his family. This punishment seems incredibly harsh (V.25). But we need to grasp how seriously God views all sin. The death of Achan's family shows that our holy, perfect God will not put up with sin. Ever.

This is the same in the New Testament. Yet we see the answer to how God can destroy sin, yet love us—sinners. Before He went to the cross, Jesus said to God the Father, "Take this cup from me" (LUKE 22:42). What was this "cup"? It is the cup of God's anger and judgement towards sin (SEE ISAIAH 51:17-22; REVELATION 14:10). Jesus took the full punishment for everything we have done wrong. All our sins filled the cup that Jesus then 'drank' in full for us. God spared Him nothing as He died on a cross because "God loved the world"—loved us (JOHN 3:16).

Once we realise what sin deserves (and has always deserved, from the beginning of the Bible's story), then and only then are we able to stand in awe of Jesus' amazing sacrifice and rescue! There's no judgement left for those who trust in Jesus (ROMANS 8:1), because in love "He himself bore our sins" (1 PETER 2:24).

RF

WANT MORE . . . ?

Check out *Is God the same in the Old and New Testament?* online at
ourdailybread.org/lookingdeeper

BUT GOD DEMONSTRATES HIS OWN LOVE FOR US IN THIS: WHILE WE WERE STILL SINNERS, CHRIST DIED FOR US. ROMANS 5:8

PLANS

BIBLE: PROVERBS 16:1-9

In their hearts humans plan their course, but the LORD establishes their steps (V.9).

When I went to Bible college straight out of school, I started out on a course for young church leaders. I could picture myself preaching and leading a church just as my home church pastor was doing. Then, after hearing inspiring stories from missionaries who shared the good news of Jesus all over the world, I even thought about giving my life to an overseas mission.

But God had a different plan for me. The opportunities He gave me were in Bible teaching—but mostly in writing. He is using the gifts He gave me, but not how I had expected.

Most of us have plans. We think ahead and dream about what we might do in the future and what life might look like. But in most cases things don't go as planned. Some doors close, while others open. If this happens to you, it may be that God has something completely different in mind.

It's good to plan and dream and think ahead. But we must always be open to God-appointed changes in direction. "Humans plan their course," King Solomon wrote, "but the LORD establishes their steps" (PROVERBS 16:9).

God will never lead us the wrong way. When we trust Him, He will direct our paths (3:5-6). His way is always best.   *DE*

TO PRAY ABOUT . . .

Dear God, please help me to trust You with my hopes, dreams and plans. With You as my safety and security, I will be ready for the changes in direction You lead me through.

WHEN WE TRUST OUR PLANS TO GOD, WE'RE READY TO FOLLOW HIM WHEREVER HE LEADS.

PEER PRESSURE

BIBLE: I SAMUEL 24:1-10

The wisdom that comes from heaven is first of all pure; then peace-loving
(JAMES 3:17).

All of Kiera's friends were having sex with their boyfriends. One boy she'd gone on a date with had told her he couldn't handle a relationship that didn't have sex involved. She was sure people were talking about her because she was still a virgin. And her friends were starting to really put her under pressure. Maybe life would be easier if she had sex with someone . . .

David knew about peer pressure. David and his friends were hiding from King Saul (who was trying to kill them) in a cave (1 SAMUEL 24). Saul came into the cave but he couldn't see them. In the darkness, David's friends tried to pressurise David into killing Saul (vv.4,10). But David said "No". He knew Saul was in the wrong, but he also knew that Saul was "the LORD's anointed [the person God had chosen to be king]" (v.6). What God said came first.

Our friends will sometimes want us to do things they think are a good idea. Especially when it comes to sex; we're told we can't be living a complete life if we're not having sex! But there's a difference between what seems like a good idea to people and what actually pleases God (1 CORINTHIANS 2:6-7). Wisdom from God "is first of all pure, then peace-loving, considerate, submissive, full of mercy" (JAMES 3:17). If we're being pressurised to do anything that doesn't match what God says, then it's probably not a good idea.

When others are pushing us to do anything that is against the Bible, we need to remember that pleasing Him is what counts. And if we get laughed at for following His ways, He promises to be our strength during those times (MATTHEW 5:10-11).

JBS

THINKING IT OVER . . .

Are your friends pressurising you about sex? Do you find it easy or difficult to say "No" to your friends? What's the difference between pleasing people and pleasing God? (GALATIANS 1:10).

AM I NOW TRYING TO WIN THE APPROVAL OF HUMAN BEINGS OR OF GOD? GALATIANS 1:10

KNOCKED DOWN, NOT KNOCKED OUT

BIBLE: 2 CORINTHIANS 4:1-9

We are hard pressed on every side, but not crushed; perplexed, but not in despair (V.8).

Amy tried to end her life after years of abuse and heartbreak. She was six when her parents divorced and her stepmum began abusing her. At thirteen she was sexually assaulted and blamed for the crime. At eighteen her father committed suicide. Addiction and more pain and abuse followed. Yet Amy's trust in Jesus allowed her to survive. In time, she started a support group for people with similar struggles—The Semicolon Project. Its message is simple, but powerful: "A semicolon is used when an author could have chosen to end their sentence, but chose not to. The author is you, and the semicolon is your life."

Paul once opened up about some intense struggles in his life. He talked about being "hard pressed on every side" (2 CORINTHIANS 4:8). He was hated and beaten for loving Jesus. He suffered health issues. He was hunted down and jailed. Sometimes he went without food and sleep (6:5; 12:7).

Yet he wasn't "crushed". Living within us is the same life-giving Spirit that raised Jesus from the dead (ROMANS 8:11). And Paul said we can "overflow with hope by the power of the Holy Spirit" (15:13).

Despite the abuse she went through, Amy's message today is: "Stay strong; love endlessly; change lives." Hope involves trusting that God can bring good out of even the worst things (GENESIS 50:20; ROMANS 8:28). When we depend on His strength, getting knocked down is different from getting knocked out. Paul said, "We get knocked down, but we are not destroyed" (2 CORINTHIANS 4:9 NLT).   JBS

THINKING IT OVER . . .

Why do we sometimes keep our struggles to ourselves? What can happen when we share our pain with others (GALATIANS 6:2)? How might God want to use a painful experience you've been through to help someone else (2 CORINTHIANS 1:3-4)?

GOD WILL ALWAYS GIVE US THE STRENGTH WE NEED TO KEEP GOING.

PERSPECTIVE FROM ABOVE

BIBLE: ISAIAH 48:1-11,17
I will not yield my glory to another (V.11).

When he was a young boy, using a metal detector was only a hobby for Peter. But for the last thirty years he's been leading people from around the world on metal-detecting daytrips. They've made thousands of discoveries—swords, ancient jewellery, coins. They use Google Earth to look for patterns in the landscape on farmland throughout the UK. It shows them where roads, buildings and other structures may have been centuries ago. Peter says, "To have a perspective from above opens a whole new world."

God's people in Isaiah's day needed "a perspective from above". They said they depended on God but in reality thought they and their fake gods were in charge. God had another perspective. Even though they were stubborn and rebellious towards Him, God said He would rescue them from captivity to Babylon. Why? "For my own sake . . . I will not yield my glory to another" (ISAIAH 48:11). God's perspective from above is that life is for His glory and purpose—not ours. Our attention is to be given to Him and His plans—and to inviting others to praise Him too.

Having God's glory as our own perspective opens a whole new world. Only God knows what we will discover about Him and what He has planned for us. He'll teach us what is good for us and lead us along the paths we should follow (V.17).   AC

TO PRAY ABOUT . . .
God, I want my life to be about You and not myself. Teach me and change me.

IF WE'RE FOCUSED ON JESUS, WE WON'T BE SO FOCUSED ON OURSELVES.

WHO YOU ARE

BIBLE: PSALM 8

What is mankind that you are mindful of them? (V.4).

His name is Dnyan and he calls himself a student of the world. And "this is a very big school," he says—talking about all the cities and towns he's passed through. He's on a four-year, world-wide journey on his bicycle to meet and learn from people. When there's a language barrier, he finds that sometimes people can understand just by looking at each other. He also depends on a translation app on his phone to chat with them. He doesn't measure his journey in the miles he's travelled or the sights he's seen. Instead, for him it's all about the people who've left an imprint on him: "Maybe I do not know your language, but I would like to find out who you are."

We all want to be known. The psalmist David was in awe of God when he thought about all the works of His hands: the making of the heavens, the moon and the stars (PSALM 8:3). He wondered, "What is mankind that you are mindful of them, human beings that you care for them?" (V.4). It's a very big world, yet God knows everything about it and the people in it—fully and completely.

God knows you more thoroughly than anyone else possibly can—and He cares for you. We can only say, "LORD, our Lord, how majestic is your name in all the earth!" (VV.1,9).

AC

THINKING IT OVER . . .

How does it make you feel that God knows all about you and loves you?
What does believing this truth look like in your life today?

GOD KNOWS YOU BETTER THAN YOU KNOW YOURSELF.

IS GOD HIDING?

BIBLE: ISAIAH 8:12-18

I will wait for the LORD, who is hiding his face . . . I will put my trust in him (V.17).

Lela was dying of cancer. Tim couldn't understand why a loving God would let her suffer. She had been a Bible teacher and a mentor to many people in the church. "Why did You let this happen?" he cried. Yet Tim continued to trust God, even though he couldn't understand why this was happening.

"So why do you still believe in God?" I asked him frankly. "What keeps you from turning away from Him?"

"Because of what has happened before," Tim replied. While he couldn't 'see' God now, he explained, he remembered the times in his life when God helped and protected him. These were signs that God was still there caring for his family. "I know the God I believe in will come through in His own way," said Tim.

Tim's words echo Isaiah's of trust in God. Even when God was "hiding his face" from Israel, they would "wait for the LORD." They could trust in God because of the signs He'd given of His continuing love and provision (ISAIAH 8:17-18).

There are times when it feels as if God is hiding. That's when we rely on what we can see of His work in our lives, in the past and present. They are the visible reminder of an invisible God—a God who is always with us and will answer in His own time and way.

LK

THINKING IT OVER . . .

What signs can you see of God working in your life? How do they remind you that you can still trust Him, even when things don't make sense?

THE GOD WE CAN'T SEE IS ALWAYS AT WORK IN THE STUFF WE DO SEE.

LOVING OUR WORST ENEMIES

BIBLE: MATTHEW 5:43-48

Love your enemies and pray for those who persecute you, that you may be children of your Father in heaven (V.44).

During World War II, a fifty-year-old church leader named Henry Gerecke became a military chaplain. After the war, when others returned home, Henry spent time with twenty-one Nazi war prisoners during their trial at Nuremburg, entering each cell to talk and pray with every man. How could he serve his country's worst enemies? Henry learned to see every man—criminal that he was—as an important person God had made.

We don't like the thought of looking out for and caring for abusive people, hurtful people, even the weird kids in class—anyone who seems different or horrible. Yet Jesus challenges, "Love your enemies, and pray for those who persecute you" (MATTHEW 5:44). Jesus is telling us to live out a God-like love that looks to bring good even to those who hate us. Surprisingly, Jesus goes on to say that loving our enemies results not just in their good, but in our good as well: "Love your enemies . . . that you may be children of your Father in heaven" (VV.44-45).

As we care about and pray for people who hate us, we copy the love God has for us. Once we ourselves were enemies of God (ROMANS 5:10) and now we are his children (1 JOHN 3:10). If God can do that for us, can we learn to see our enemies as God sees them? Children who He wants to bring into His family. EM

TO PRAY ABOUT . . .

Dear God, thank You for moving me from Your enemy to Your child. Help me to see my worst enemies the way You do, as people You are ready to bring into Your family.

WHEN WE LOVE OUR ENEMIES, WE LOVE LIKE GOD DOES.

RENAMED

BIBLE: RUTH 1:19-22

"Don't call me Naomi," she told them. "Call me Mara, because the Almighty has made my life very bitter" (V.20).

Riptide. Batgirl. Jumpstart. My friends have all sorts of strange nicknames! Given to them because of funny stories from their past, embarrassing moments, something about the way they look or weird habits they have.

Nicknames are not limited to our friendship groups—we even find them used in the Bible. For example, Jesus called the apostles James and John the "sons of thunder" (MARK 3:17). It is rare in the Bible for someone to give themselves a nickname, yet it happened when a woman named Naomi asked people to call her "Mara," which means bitterness (RUTH 1:20). Both her husband and two sons had died. She felt that God had made her life bitter (V.21).

The nickname Naomi gave herself didn't stick, however, because her losses were not the end of her story. In her sadness, God gave her a loving daughter-in-law, Ruth, who eventually remarried and had a son, creating a family for Naomi again.

Although we might sometimes be tempted to give ourselves bitter nicknames, like "failure" or "unloved", based on hard stuff we've gone through or mistakes we've made, those names are not the end of our stories, either. We can replace those labels with the name God has given each of us, "beloved child" (ROMANS 9:25-26), and look for the ways He is providing for us in even the most challenging of times.

LS

THINKING IT OVER . . .

God often gives people new names as a sign of their new identity when they trust Him. Abram was renamed Abraham (GENESIS 17:5). Jacob was renamed Israel (32:28). Simon was renamed Peter (JOHN 1:42). Saul was renamed Paul (ACTS 13:9). What will be special about the "new name" we receive in heaven (REVELATION 2:17)?

WE MAY GET CALLED MANY NAMES, BUT ONLY THE NAME GOD GIVES US MATTERS: "CHILDREN OF THE LIVING GOD" (ROMANS 9:26).

MAKING HIS MUSIC

BIBLE: 2 CORINTHIANS 3:17-18

We all . . . are being transformed into his image (V.18).

Arianne spent her childhood sitting on her hands—to hide them. She had been born with fingers missing or fused together. She also had no left leg and was missing toes on her right foot. But one day her choir teacher asked her to conduct—which made her hands quite visible. From that moment she grew in confidence, going on to conduct church and university choirs. "My teacher saw something in me," she explains.

Her inspiring story can make us ask, *What does God, our holy teacher, see in us, despite our 'limits'?* More than anything else, He sees Himself. "So God created human beings in his own image. In the image of God he created them; male and female he created them" (GENESIS 1:27 NLT).

As His "image", when others see us, we should reflect Him. For Arianne, that meant God's Spirit, not her hands—or her lack of fingers—mattered most. The same is true for all Christians. "And we all, who with unveiled faces contemplate the Lord's glory, are being transformed into his image" (2 CORINTHIANS 3:18).

Similar to Arianne, we can live by His Spirit's leading (v.18), not by what makes sense to us. When we are focused more on God than our limits, we have the chance to display Him better to the people around us. *PR*

THINKING IT OVER . . .

What limits, issues or insecurities impact the way you see yourself? Think about and focus on God and His awesome power and ability to use you beyond what you "ask or imagine" (EPHESIANS 3:20). How does that challenge you to let people see God at work in you?

GOD MADE US AS HIS IMAGE —TO MAKE HIM KNOWN TO THE WORLD.

LEAVING TO FOLLOW

BIBLE: MATTHEW 4:18-22

At once they left their nets and followed him (V.20).

As a teenager, I imagined myself marrying my high school boyfriend—until we broke up. My dreams felt shattered and I struggled with what to do next when I left school. After a while I felt like God was telling me that moping around wasn't doing anyone any good. Instead He wanted me to start looking out for others, rather than just feeling sorry for myself. So I signed up for a course at a Bible college. Then the reality hit me that I'd be moving away from my friends and family. In order to do what I felt God was telling me, I had to leave.

Jesus was walking beside the Sea of Galilee when He saw Peter and his brother Andrew casting nets into the sea, fishing for a living. He invited them to "Come, follow me . . . and I will send you out to fish for people" (MATTHEW 4:19). Then Jesus saw two other fishermen, James and his brother John, and gave them the same invitation (V.21).

When these disciples came to Jesus, they also left something. Peter and Andrew "left their nets" (V.20). James and John "left the boat and their father and followed him" (V.22). Luke puts it this way: "So they pulled their boats up on shore, left everything and followed him" (LUKE 5:11).

Following Jesus means giving up our old life of living for ourselves. But even as we live for Jesus, He will lead us to do things, meet people and go to places that mean we have to give up other specific things and dreams. Why do we give things up in our life with Jesus? Because He is worth it!   *EM*

TO PRAY ABOUT . . .

Loving God, help me understand what I might need to give up or leave behind so that I can closely follow Jesus.

WHEN WE FOLLOW JESUS, HE IS THE MOST IMPORTANT PERSON IN OUR LIVES.

NOT COMING BACK

BIBLE: LUKE 14:25-33

Whoever does not carry their cross and follow me cannot be my disciple (V.27).

"One thing you knew about a man walking out of town with a cross on his back: he wasn't coming back!"

When I read that from a Christian writer, I thought he sounded a bit flippant about Jesus carrying His cross to His death. But the writer didn't mean it that way. He wanted to hit home what our commitment to follow Jesus means—because we're following the One who tells us to also carry our cross as well.

It must have been confusing for Jesus' listeners when he said, "Whoever does not carry their cross and follow me cannot be my disciple" (LUKE 14:27). The crowds had enthusiastically followed Him and now He offered them what? A form of torture and execution? This wasn't something they would have expected from Him. Why would He lead them to such an awful punishment? It's possible the crowd thinned out a bit at that point!

Jesus also talked about "hating" our own family (v.26). Now we can get around this one quite comfortably by saying that our love for Jesus should be so great that, in comparison, all other love is hatred. But let's think about these things a little more. Jesus wants all of our attention, every scrap of our lives. By taking up the cross ourselves to follow Him, we're saying that we have died, are dying and will die each day to all that we want, all our agendas, hopes, dreams and plans. Why? Because of our love for Him, our understanding of our need for Him and our certainty that we will spend forever with Him.

What a huge challenge the crowd heard from Jesus that day—a huge challenge for us too. But Jesus' loving example makes sense of it all. He "laid down his life for us" (1 JOHN 3:16). By His power, may we do the same for Him and others! RF

THINKING IT OVER . . .

Read Galatians 2:20. What do you think it means that we have been crucified with Jesus? How does this verse describe the life we now live as Christians?

TAKING UP YOUR CROSS MEANS YOU'RE NOT COMING BACK TO YOUR OLD LIFE.

WHEN IT'S HARD TO PRAY

BIBLE: PSALM 25:1-22

In you, LORD my God, I put my trust (V.1).

Sometimes we can feel guilty about our prayer lives. No matter how much we pray, we're sure it's not enough. We think we should pray more, but then something comes up; our parents give us a job to do, homework needs to be done or we're just too tired.

Where could you turn in the Bible to find help with praying? The book of Psalms. But the psalms are more than prayers. God's people would also sing the psalms with others. Their prayers were meant to be sung. Think about Psalm 25, a song that includes things that make up a healthy prayer life.

Praising God: "Good and upright is the LORD" (PSALM 25:8). "All the ways of the LORD are loving and faithful" (V.10). "The LORD confides in those who fear him" (V.14).

Admitting sin: "Do not remember the sins of my youth" (V.7). "For the sake of your name, LORD, forgive my iniquity, though it is great" (V.11).

Asking for God's help: "Show me your ways, LORD, teach me your paths." (V.4). "Relieve the troubles of my heart and free me from my anguish" (V.17).

There will be days when it's hard to pray. So why not turn to the psalms, like Psalm 25. Use these words to help you focus on God, praise Him, trust Him and rely on Him.

MW

WHAT I'M THANKFUL FOR . . .

Thank You, Father, for the psalms in the Bible. Thank You that they can help me talk honestly with You and praise Your goodness.

GOD HAS GIVEN US THE PSALMS TO HELP US PRAY.

BIBLE: EXODUS 3:1-15

"Do not come any closer," God said. "Take off your sandals, for the place where you are standing is holy ground" (V.5).

A friend asked me, "How many gods are there in this world?" I got out my phone to see what Google said. Let me be clear, I believe there's only one true God. But Google gave me this clever answer: seven billion gods. There are seven billion people in this world. And everyone has (or is) their own god.

The ancient Greeks worshipped Zeus, Poseidon, Apollo and lots of other gods. We do the same. Sure, we don't have lots of statues and temples. But we still live for things like popularity, good grades, a boyfriend or girlfriend, money, the number of Instagram followers we have. These are not 'named gods'—but they are the same thing really.

It might be helpful to ask ourselves, "What is the name of the God—or god—I love most?" That's the question Moses asked when God appeared to him: who are you? "What is [your] name?" (EXODUS 3:13). "God said to Moses, 'I AM WHO I AM . . . This is my name for ever'" (VV.14-15).

"I AM" tells us God has always been, will always be and has no limits. He is the one King in the universe who isn't dependent on anything else for His existence. He's the Creator and Sustainer of all that exists. He'll never change who He is. He "is the same yesterday and today and for ever" (HEBREWS 13:8).

Just as God told Moses, "Take off your sandals, for you are standing on holy ground" (EXODUS 3:5), it's vital for us to live only for God—in awe of the one, true God; and not looking for god (or gods) anywhere else. For wherever He is, that place is good. May we "worship at his footstool; he is holy" (PSALM 99:5).   KTS

THINKING IT OVER . . .

Read Isaiah 6:1-8. How is God described (VV.1-4)? How did Isaiah react to being in the presence of God (V.5)? What did God do for Isaiah (V.7)? Why not spend some time thinking about this awesome description of God's power, love and mercy.

NO GOD COMPARES TO THE ONE TRUE GOD!

KNOW HIS VOICE

BIBLE: JOHN 10:1-15

I am the good shepherd; I know my sheep and my sheep know me (V.14).

Does your church run holiday Bible clubs during the summer holidays? They're normally a week of Bible stories, games and activities for younger kids.

My church did one once where they decided to bring in a sheep from a local farm. They thought it would be something a bit different for the kids—and it would help them remember the theme of the week: Jesus as our good Shepherd (SEE PSALM 23; JOHN 10:11).

On the first day the Bible club leader had to practically drag the sheep by a rope into the church hall. But as the week went on, it became less reluctant to follow him. By the end of the week, he didn't have to hold the rope anymore; he just called the sheep and it followed, knowing it could trust him.

In the New Testament, Jesus compares Himself to a shepherd, explaining that His people—His sheep—will follow Him because they know His voice (JOHN 10:4). But those same sheep will run from a stranger or thief (VV.5,10). Like sheep, we get to know the voice of our Shepherd through our relationship with Him. And as we do, we will get to know Him better and learn to trust Him.

As we get to know God through the Bible, we will get to know His ways, priorities, mission, love, promises and plans (so, His voice). And as we listen to His voice, we'll be prepared to run from the "the thief [who] comes only to steal and destroy" (V.10)—so, anything that tries to distract us from God.

There are a lot of 'voices' in the world. We need to be making time to listen to the voice of our Shepherd who will always lead us well.   JS

THINKING IT OVER . . .

What have you learned about God's character recently through reading the Bible? How did that impact you? How does it help you to recognise good and bad influences in your life?

THE Lord IS MY SHEPHERD, I LACK NOTHING. PSALM 23:1

BEAUTIFUL TO GOD

BIBLE: PSALM 8:4-9

What is mankind that you are mindful of them, human beings that you care for them? (V.4).

W hen Denise began dating her boyfriend, she tried to make herself look as good as possible: keeping herself slim, wearing fashionable clothes outside of school, experimenting with different make-up. She believed she would be more attractive to him if she did those things. After all, it was what all the online blogs said you should do. It was only much later that she found out what he really thought: "I liked you just as much when you chilled out about how you looked and you didn't worry about what you wore."

Denise realised then how subjective beauty is. Our view of beauty is so easily influenced by others. It's often all about how we look, forgetting the value of who we really are. But God sees us in only one way—as His beautiful, loved children. I like to remember that when God created the world, He left the best for last—us! Everything He created was good, but we're extra special because we're made in the image of God (GENESIS 1:27).

God thinks we're beautiful! "What is mankind," one of the psalm-writers asked, "that you are mindful of them, human beings that you care for them?" (PSALM 8:4). Yet God chose to give us a special place in His world that nothing else has (V.5).

This should give us great reason to praise Him (V.9). No matter what others think of us—or what we think of ourselves—know this: we are beautiful to God.

LK

TO PRAY ABOUT . . .

Father, You know how insecure I can feel about myself and how I look.
Thank You for the assurance that You love me and made me just as I am.

INNER BEAUTY IS THE ONLY BEAUTY THAT WILL LAST.

TRUE FRIENDS

BIBLE: I SAMUEL 18:1-4; 19:1-6
A friend loves at all times (PROVERBS 17:17).

In school, I had a 'sometimes' friend. We were friends at our small church (where I was nearly the only girl her age), and sometimes we hung out together outside of school. But at school, it was a different story. If she met me by herself, she might say hello; but only if no one else was around. Realising this, I didn't try to get her attention within school walls. I knew the limits of our friendship.

We've probably all experienced the pain of disappointingly one-sided or narrow friendships. But there's another kind of friendship—one that goes the distance, not matter what. It's the kind of friendship we have with our best friends; people we totally 'click' with.

David and Jonathan were friends like this. Jonathan was "one in spirit" with David and loved him "as himself" (1 SAMUEL 18:1-3). Although Jonathan would have been next in line to rule after his dad Saul's death, he was loyal to David, God's chosen replacement. Jonathan even helped David to escape two of Saul's plots to kill him (19:1-6; 20:1-42).

Despite being on opposite sides, Jonathan and David stayed true friends—living out Proverbs 17:17: "A friend loves at all times." Their friendship also gives us a glimpse of the loving relationship God has with us (JOHN 3:16; 15:15). Through friendships like theirs, our understanding of God's love is deepened.   *AK*

THINKING IT OVER . . .
Who are your true friends? Why? How is it comforting to know that God is our truest friend? What does James 2:23 and 4:4 tell us being a friend of God looks like?

OUR LORD JESUS CHRIST HAS MADE US FRIENDS OF GOD. ROMANS 5:11 NLT

WALK LIKE A WARRIOR

BIBLE: JUDGES 6:1-16

When the angel of the LORD appeared to Gideon, he said,
"The LORD is with you, mighty warrior" (V.12).

Eighteen-year-old Emma talks about Jesus on social media, even though trolls have humiliated her with angry and rude posts because of her love for Him. Some also simply attack her about how she looks. Others say she must be stupid because she believes in God.

Even though the hateful words upset her, Emma continues to share the good news about Jesus with confidence, because she knows He can use her social media to impact lives in the best way possible.

Sometimes, though, she's tempted to believe her identity and worth are affected by the posts she reads. If people don't like her, she feels like more of a failure than when people thank her for what she shares. When that happens, she asks God for help remembering that she is His child no matter what. Nothing can change that identity she has been given as an heir to God's kingdom—with every right to it (EPHESIANS 1:13-14). So she prays for the people attacking her, thinks about the promises God gives in the Bible, and keeps on using her social media for Jesus.

Gideon faced a scary enemy—the Midianites (JUDGES 6:1-10). Though God called him a "mighty warrior", Gideon struggled to let go of his doubt and insecurities (VV.11-15). More than once he questioned God's plans and his own ability. But finally he chose to trust what God said.

When we trust God, we can live like we believe what He says about us is true. Even when others make us doubt our identity, our loving Father reminds us we are His children through the Bible and His Spirit in us (GALATIANS 4:6). XD

WANT MORE . . . ?

Check out *How can I make God the centre of my social media?* online at
ourdailybread.org/teen

BEING A CHILD OF GOD IS THE HIGHEST HONOUR IN THE WORLD.

NO LONGER AFRAID

BIBLE: ZEPHANIAH 3:9-17

They will eat and lie down and no one will make them afraid (V.13).

When the Ethiopian police found her, a week after she was taken, three black-maned lions surrounded her, guarding her as though she was their own. Seven men had kidnapped the twelve-year-old girl, carried her into the woods and beaten her. Miraculously, however, a small pride of lions heard the girl's cries, came running and chased off the attackers. "[The lions] stood guard until we found her and then they just left her like a gift and went back into the forest," the police officer said later.

There are days when the messed up things in our world make us feel completely alone and terrified, without any hope or protection. At one point in their history the people of Judah felt the same way. They were invaded by enemy armies and unable to imagine ever escaping. They were deeply afraid. However, God promised His people: "The LORD, the King of Israel, is with you; never again will you fear any harm" (ZEPHANIAH 3:15). Even when our mess comes from our own mistakes or bad choices, God still comes to our rescue. "The LORD your God is with you," we hear, "the Mighty Warrior who saves" (V.17).

Whatever mess we land ourselves in, whatever is done to us, Jesus—the Lion of Judah—is with us. No matter how alone we feel, our strong Saviour always holds us. No matter what we are afraid of, our God promises us that He is by our side.   *wc*

TO PRAY ABOUT . . .

Mighty Warrior God, I need You. I need a Mighty Warrior to stand with me and make me less afraid. I'm choosing to trust You.

OUR MIGHTY WARRIOR IS WITH US, SO WE DO NOT NEED TO BE AFRAID.

MINISTER OF LONELINESS

BIBLE: HEBREWS 13:1-8
Keep on loving one another as brothers and sisters (V.1).

More than nine million British people (15% of the UK population) say they often or always feel lonely. Now we even have a minister for loneliness in the Government to find out why so many of us feel lonely—and work out what can be done to help.

We can feel lonely for loads of reasons. We struggle to be open with people because we've been hurt in the past. We feel awkward talking face to face, so we stick to just messaging online. Maybe bullies have cut us off at school. Maybe we just don't know where to start when it comes to making friends.

I feel lonely sometimes, and you may too. This is one reason we need other Christians. The book of Hebrews encourages us to meet together regularly (HEBREWS 10:25). We belong to the family of God, so we're to love "one another as brothers and sisters" and "show hospitality to strangers" (13:1-2).

Jesus has promised to never leave nor forsake us (V.5), and we can use His friendship to fuel our love for others. Are you lonely? What ways can you find to look out for the people in your church and youth group—not just when you meet, but during the week as well? The friends you make in Jesus last forever, through this life and beyond.   *MW*

THINKING IT OVER . . .
Who needs your friendship? Who can you look out for in youth group or school this week? If you are feeling lonely, what activities or events can you get involved in at your church? And why not talk with your youth group leader and let them know how you are feeling.

THE FAMILY OF GOD IS A GREAT ANSWER TO OUR LONELINESS.

BIBLICAL PRESCRIPTION

BIBLE: PROVERBS 17:19-22

A cheerful heart is good medicine, but a crushed spirit dries up the bones (V.22).

One family I know have a "Joke Night" every week. And the whole family get involved. If something funny happened at school that week, or one of them heard a good joke, they share it during dinner together. They have all said that laughter, and simply messing about together, is good for them and makes them feel loads better—especially during rubbish weeks.

I remember reading something a Christian author wrote, "The sun looks down on nothing half so good as a household laughing together over a meal." And this idea is even in the Bible itself. Proverbs 17:22 tells us, "A cheerful heart is good medicine, but a crushed spirit dries up the bones." This proverb offers a 'prescription' to help our health and general wellbeing—allowing joy and happiness to fill us.

We all need this biblical prescription. But laughter and happiness don't just happen. They come from good, healthy relationships with others—especially other Christians. They can help us keep our bad days, bad grades or stressful school projects in perspective. Other Christians lift us up from the gloom of life, reminding us that with Jesus we have every reason to laugh and know we are well loved.

Do you need more laughter in your life? Remember, even the Bible tells us to have "a cheerful heart" as we enjoy knowing God and spending time with His people.

LS

WHAT I'M THANKFUL FOR . . .

Almighty God, thank You for Your gift of peace, assurance and joy. Thank You that even in difficult times You promise to fill us up with laughter.

LAUGHTER IS A GIFT OF GOD—ENJOY IT!

AT HOME IN JESUS

BIBLE: JOHN 15:1-11
Remain in me, as I also remain in you (V.4).

Our black cat is called Juno. She's a great pet and she does a good job of controlling the mice population in our house! She came from the local animal shelter—but she is more comfortable living outdoors.

When we first brought her home, the staff at the animal shelter told us how to set up a good feeding routine so that Juno would quickly learn that our house was now her home. A good routine would show her that our house was where she belonged and would always have food and safety. That way, even if Juno might wander off for a few days, she would always come home at some point.

If we don't know our true home, we'll always be tempted to wander about searching for happiness, love and meaning. To find our true home, Jesus said, "Abide in me" (JOHN 15:4 NASB). One Bible teacher explained how "abide" (like a similar word: "abode") brings a sense of family and home. So the teacher translated Jesus' words as: "Stay at home in me."

To really make His point clear, Jesus used the illustration of branches attached to a vine. Branches, if they want to live, must always stay at home, fixed (abiding) where they belong.

There are many things, people and groups around us, offering to fix our problems or provide us with all the excitement and meaning we could possibly want. Yet none of these things ever meet our deepest needs for long. If we're to truly live, we must remain in Jesus. We must stay at home.   *wc*

WANT MORE . . . ?
Check out *What does it take to be happy?* online at
ourdailybread.org/lookingatlife

HOME IS WHERE WE ARE MOST COMFORTABLE AND MOST 'OURSELVES'; ARE YOU 'AT HOME' IN JESUS?

NOT ABOUT ME

BIBLE: ROMANS 6:5-14

Now if we died with Christ, we believe that we will also live with him (V.8).

David grew up in a violent home. Early on in his childhood, he decided, "There's nothing wrong with me, it's everyone else who has a problem. I'm the only smart, sane one." With this perspective, along with his mental-health issues, he felt no guilt after he tried to kill his dad. As an atheist, he believed that, after all, people are only "sacks of molecules".

In jail, David met a Christian who gave him a Bible. As he read, he began to understand that he wasn't the "best, most advanced human being" ever. Jesus was far superior! Over time David put his trust in Jesus and became a Christian. His outlook changed radically through his belief in Jesus—and he began to rebuild his life and relationships in a healthy, God-dependent way.

When we choose Jesus, we also leave behind the belief that we're at the centre of the universe. We're no longer slaves to sin (our self-centred, Godless instincts), as Paul told the Romans, for our "old self was crucified" with Jesus (ROMANS 6:6). With sin no longer in charge of us (V.14) and with the Spirit's strength, we begin to change and look outside ourselves to live for God and the people He has made.

As you think about David's story of real change, ask God to remind you how He's transforming you as well. And if you haven't experienced any change, talk to Him about it! We are not to follow "the pattern of this world, but be transformed by the renewing of your mind" (12:2).   *ABP*

THINKING IT OVER . . .

Do you truly believe that God can change people? Where has God been working in your life? Where do you feel like giving up? Who can you ask to pray with you and help you keep going as God brings about real change?

IT IS GOD WHO WORKS IN YOU TO WILL AND TO ACT IN ORDER TO FULFIL HIS GOOD PURPOSE. PHILIPPIANS 2:13

Seven days with . . . Solomon
GROWING WISE

BIBLE: I KINGS 3:5-15

Give your servant a discerning heart to govern your people and to distinguish between right and wrong (V.9).

Solomon was a young man. But he had the responsibility of ruling one of the most prosperous kingdoms in the ancient Near East. Israel was a significant power then, extending from the Euphrates River to the border of Egypt. Responsible for so much, Solomon knew he needed help. So when God asked the young king what He could do for him, Solomon did not ask to be healthy or wealthy. He asked to be wise (1 KINGS 3:9). "The LORD was pleased that Solomon had asked for this" (V.10).

God said to him, "Because you have asked for this . . . I will do what you have asked. I will give you a wise and discerning heart" (VV.11-12).

When Solomon asked God for a "discerning heart" (V.9), he was literally asking for "hearing" (which is what the original word meant). God gave Solomon a hearing heart that would listen firstly to God, so he could judge the people, and "distinguish between right and wrong".

Wise people hear God through the Bible. They read other books, of course, but they judge them all by the words of God. There is no greater wisdom.

If you want wisdom, ask God for it. The apostle James said, "If any of you lacks wisdom, you should ask God, who gives generously to all without finding fault, and it will be given to you" (JAMES 1:5).

DR

COMPLETING THE PICTURE . . .

Solomon was the son of King David, and third king over Israel (after Saul and David). He was born to Bathsheba (who David had originally had an affair with). He reigned over Israel for forty years (1 KINGS 11:42) during the peak of Israel's history, when the nation was something of a superpower. "King Solomon was greater in riches and wisdom than all the other kings of the earth. The whole world sought audience with Solomon to hear the wisdom God had put in his heart" (1 KINGS 10:23-24; SEE ALSO VV.1-9). Solomon wrote much of the wisdom books of the Old Testament: Ecclesiastes, the Song of Solomon and most of Proverbs.

GOD GIVES HIS WISDOM TO THOSE WHO ASK FOR IT.

Seven days with . . . Solomon

AMBITIOUS FOR GOD

BIBLE: I KINGS 8:54-63

May he turn our hearts to him, to walk in obedience to him (V.58).

Is it good to be an ambitious person? We want to work hard and do well at exams—that kind of ambition is good. But we live in a world where ambition often means pushing others out of the way to get what we want. God tells us to live differently. We are to "do nothing out of selfish ambition" (PHILIPPIANS 2:3). Instead, our ambition should be to love and follow God. There is a test for our ambition that never fails: "Do it all for the glory of God" (1 CORINTHIANS 10:31).

After the flood in Noah's day, a group of people decided to build a tower because of their ambition to "make a name" for themselves (GENESIS 11:4). They wanted to be famous! But they were not doing it for God's glory; they were not ambitious for Him to be loved, known and praised.

Yet when King Solomon finished building the temple, he said, "Just as the LORD promised, I have built the temple for the Name of the LORD" (1 KINGS 8:20). Then he prayed, "May he turn our hearts to him, to walk in obedience to him and keep the commands" (V.58).

When God is the centre of our lives, we'll want to bring glory to Him. He will make us driven, ambitious people; not ambitious for ourselves, but ambitious for His great name to be known by our friends and family. May our "hearts be fully committed to the LORD our God, to live by his decrees and obey his commands" (V.61).

KO

COMPLETING THE PICTURE . . .

David planned the temple in Jerusalem, where God's presence would dwell in the inner room (SEE 1 CHRONICLES 28). Solomon completed the work. Yet Solomon asked: "But will God really dwell on earth? The heavens, even the highest heaven, cannot contain you. How much less this temple I have built!" (1 KINGS 8:27). The temple was, in the end, an illustration of Jesus, who said of the temple: "'Destroy this temple, and I will raise it again in three days' . . . But the temple he had spoken of was his body" (JOHN 2:19-21). Now we don't need to find God at a temple. When we trust Jesus we are always 'in' His temple (SEE JOHN 4:19-24; HEBREWS 4:16) and actually part of it (1 CORINTHIANS 6:19-20; EPHESIANS 2:19-22). The temple of Jerusalem was destroyed in AD 70.

DO EVERYTHING FOR THE GLORY OF GOD.

Seven days with . . . Solomon

GOOD FOR YOU

BIBLE: PROVERBS 24:13-14

Wisdom is like honey for you: if you find it, there is a future hope (V.14).

Worldwide, people spend an estimated £80 billion on chocolate each year. That's a lot of money! But maybe it's not all that surprising. Chocolate, after all, is the best food in the world (as far as I'm concerned!). And all of us choc-a-holics celebrated when it was found to have significant health benefits too. Chocolate contains flavonoids that provide some protection against ageing and heart disease. Never has a health prescription been so well received (in moderation, of course!).

Solomon says there's another "sweet" that has even better benefits: wisdom. He compared having wisdom to eating honey (PROVERBS 24:13-14). It tastes good and is good. If we spend time in God's wisdom in the Bible, we'll find it enjoyable, exciting and everything we need for our learning and training in godliness for "every good work" (2 TIMOTHY 3:16-17).

Wisdom is what allows us to make smart choices and understand the world around us. And it is worth investing in and sharing with others—as Solomon wanted to when he wrote part of the book of Proverbs. The Bible is a treat that we can enjoy without limit—no need for moderation! *God, thank You for the teaching of Your words, they help me live my best life!*

KH

COMPLETING THE PICTURE . . .

Wisdom isn't about intelligence, your IQ score or how smart you are. It's about knowing God, doing life with Him and trusting Him more than you trust yourself (PROVERBS 3:5-8). The ancient philosopher Aristotle once said, "The beginning of all wisdom is knowing yourself." Whereas the Bible clearly teaches, "The fear of the LORD is the beginning of knowledge" (1:7) and "The LORD gives wisdom" (2:6). These two starting points are totally opposite. The world's wisdom starts with what works for *me*; but real wisdom starts with the awe (or "fear") of God. These two wisdoms are incompatible. So the world looks at those of us who trust Jesus like we are "foolish" (SEE 1 CORINTHIANS 1:18-31).

REAL WISDOM IS KNOWING GOD'S MIND –WHAT HE THINKS ABOUT THINGS.

Seven days with . . . Solomon

THE RIGHT WAY TO LIVE

BIBLE: PROVERBS 3:1-8

Trust in the LORD with all your heart, and lean not on your own understanding (V.5).

My friend is a 'good' person. Her goal in life is to live the right way, to be authentic, to do good things, to respect others, and to ultimately live her best life. I admire her. Yet she also believes that God's existence makes no real difference. As I listen to her, I wonder: *How can we know what the right way is on our own? How can we follow our own instincts when we so often think, feel and do bad things? How do we define good without an absolutely correct standard to measure it with?*

King Solomon, guided by God, gave answers to these questions in the book of Proverbs. His advice was to "trust in the LORD with all your heart and lean not on your own understanding; in all your ways submit to him, and he will make your paths straight" (PROVERBS 3:5). This means we can't just rely on our own five senses. They will misdirect us sometimes. They don't lead us down "straight" paths, but off into all sorts of places—some which are no good for us at all!

Solomon said we need an objective truth to follow—and that truth is God. He didn't say, "Trust with a little bit of your heart," but "Trust in the LORD with *all* your heart and lean *not* on your own understanding." We need to give everything we are to God and follow Him, no longer just doing whatever makes sense to us.

One Bible translation writes Proverbs 3:5 (AMP) like this: "Do not let mercy and kindness and truth leave you [instead let these qualities define you]." The only way to have genuine mercy, kindness and truth in our lives is to trust the Giver of these things.

EPE

THINKING IT OVER . . .

How have you been learning to trust God's ways first? Where are you still tempted to go with your own 'gut'?

"WHY DO YOU CALL ME GOOD?" JESUS ANSWERED, "THERE IS NO ONE GOOD EXCEPT GOD ALONE." MARK 10:18

Seven days with . . . Solomon

THE RIGHT PLACE

BIBLE: SONG OF SOLOMON 7:10-13

"I am my beloved's, and my beloved is mine" (Song of Solomon 6:3).

I was at a family member's wedding recently. She turned to the groom during the vows and promised to love him, comfort him, honour him and, *forsaking all others, keep faithful to him as long as they both shall live*. A few minutes later, the service leader announced they were husband and wife.

As King Solomon grew in wisdom, it meant he learned to live life by God's good ways and by His perfect design. And God has designed every part of our lives, including sex. Solomon saw the plan God had for sex as so special that he wrote a whole book about it: the Song of Solomon!

God's design for sex is that we give ourselves to just one person, in marriage. It gives us the purity and simplicity of being able to say, "I am my beloved's, and my beloved is mine" (Song of Solomon 6:3).

When a man and woman are united in marriage and in Jesus, they can share spiritual, emotional and physical closeness with happiness and freedom. There is no pressure or messy complications. So sex is to be "stored up" for marriage (V.13).

God's designs are always given for a reason. Sex is a powerful thing, connecting couples in a dynamic way. So let's take it seriously, give it the respect it deserves and be wise. We'll find God's plan for sex far better than the world's.

TF

THINKING IT OVER . . .

In your own words, how would you explain why God gave sex only for marriage? Have a look at Genesis 2:23-25, 1 Corinthians 6:12-20 and Ephesians 5:21-33. How do these passages help you understand the greater purpose and goal of marriage? Read 1 Corinthians 7:25-35: the pressure to be 'getting together' with people is all around us. But what does Paul say our primary focus should always be (VV.32-35)?

GOD'S DESIGNS ARE ALWAYS GOOD AND ALWAYS HAVE A PURPOSE.

Seven days with . . . Solomon

SMART HOUSE

BIBLE: ECCLESIASTES 2:1-11

Through wisdom a house is built, and by understanding it is established
(PROVERBS 24:3).

I'd love to live in a fully-functioning smart house. Imagine being able to control everything with your phone and your voice. You could start the shower, turn the lights on and make a drink from your bed—before even opening your eyes!

Living in a smart house would give me a taste of the life of King Solomon. In his day, he had everything a person could want. He wrote, "I denied myself nothing my eyes desired; I refused my heart no pleasure . . . [Yet] everything was meaningless, a chasing after the wind; nothing was gained under the sun" (ECCLESIASTES 2:10-11).

When Solomon filled his life with luxuries, he also filled it with emptiness (V.11). When he lived for whatever he could get his hands on, he ran into all sorts of problems. Money and possessions didn't seem to make him happy, but miserable. No matter what he had, he realised that life without God wasn't worth living.

The end of Ecclesiastes gives us Solomon's conclusion about life: "Fear God and keep his commandments, for this is the duty of all mankind. For God will bring every deed into judgement, including every hidden thing, whether it is good or evil" (12:13-14). It doesn't matter what we have now; it matters what we have when we stand before God on the final day. Will we have His unending friendship and a welcome into His home?

A real dream home is any house, no matter how big or small, that is built on the wisdom of God—Jesus Christ Himself (SEE PROVERBS 24:3; 1 CORINTHIANS 1:30).

MDH

THINKING IT OVER . . .

Read Matthew 7:21-29. Why is listening to Jesus' words and obeying them like building a house with a strong foundation (V.25)? What sort of "storms" are you facing? What difference does it make to be built on Jesus, our "rock" (1 PETER 2:6-8)?

OUR LIVES WILL HAVE PURPOSE AND MEANING WHEN THEY ARE BUILT ON JESUS.

Seven days with . . . Solomon
THE WORLD'S LIBRARY

BIBLE: I KINGS II

As Solomon grew old, his wives turned his heart after other gods, and his heart was not fully devoted to the LORD his God, as the heart of David his father had been (V.4).

Many years ago, one of the guys who actually came up with the internet had a vision for it to be "the great library." He then said, "It is now technically possible to live up to the dream of the Library of Alexandria." He was referring to a huge collection of writings in ancient Egypt that was said to house the world's knowledge.

I guess his vision has pretty much come true. You can search for literally anything online! It's easy to become an expert in whatever you want.

But knowing lots is not the same as wisdom. In the end, King Solomon was a man of knowledge (1 KINGS 4:29-34). At his best, he had shown wisdom, following God and relying on Him for everything. But "as Solomon grew old, his wives turned his heart after other gods, and his heart was not fully devoted to the LORD his God" (11:4). Solomon had 700 wives and 300 concubines, all from other nations with false gods. Despite 'knowing' better, Solomon showed we can have all the knowledge in the world and still misunderstand the purpose of life (ECCLESIASTES 1:16-18).

His lack of devotion to the one true God led to God's anger (1 KINGS 11:9) and split the nation of Israel (VV.31-33). Solomon's life is a warning to us. It is so easy to fall down the slippery slope of selfishness and sin. The clever things we know won't keep us on the right path; but the God we know will—let's stick close to Him. That's real wisdom.

MDH

COMPLETING THE PICTURE . . .

King Solomon's life had a sad end. He had been the wisest man on earth (1 KINGS 4:30), yet became like "the fool [who] says in his heart, 'There is no God'" (PSALM 141). God just became one of hundreds of gods for him. The end of Solomon's reign marked the end of Israel's golden era. Israel was then split into the Northern Kingdom (Israel) and the Southern Kingdom (Judah). It remained this way until the kingdoms ended up in exile because of their rejection of God. Despite Israel's poor choices and rebellion, God never abandoned His people. He stayed true to His promise to provide a Saviour to the world through them (SEE 1 KINGS 11:34-36).

NO MATTER HOW CLEVER WE ARE, IDOLATRY MAKES FOOLS OF US.

PROTECT YOUR HEART

BIBLE: PROVERBS 4:20-27

Above all else, guard your heart, for everything you do flows from it (V.23).

During World War II mathematician Abraham Wald joined the military to look for ways to protect the planes flying over enemy lines. He and his team were asked to figure out how to better armour the military aircraft to withstand enemy fire. They began by examining returning aircraft to see where they were most damaged. But Abraham Wald realised something pretty key: returning planes only showed where a plane could be hit *and still survive* (pretty obvious once you think about it!). The areas on the planes that most needed additional armour were the places they could see no damage. Planes hit in the most vulnerable parts—like the engine—had gone down and not made it home, and so couldn't be examined.

Solomon teaches us about protecting our most vulnerable part—our heart. He says: "Above all else, guard your heart, for everything you do flows from it" (PROVERBS 4:23). God's instructions guide us through life, steering us away from bad decisions and teaching us where to focus our attention.

If we armour our most vulnerable part by prioritising reading the Bible and looking for God's direction, we'll be more likely to "keep [our feet] from evil" and remain strong in our journey with God (V.27). We walk into enemy territory every day (in the world around us, at school and sometimes even at home), but with God's ways guarding our hearts we can stay focused on our mission, stick close to Jesus and live well for Him.　　　　*KH*

TO PRAY ABOUT . . .

God, please protect me from the dangers that threaten me and the things that tempt me. I choose to hide myself in You and the truth of the Bible.

KNOWING GOD THROUGH THE BIBLE IS LIKE ARMOUR FOR OUR HEARTS.

KEEP YOUR RADIO ON

BIBLE: I SAMUEL 3:I-IO

The LORD came and stood there, calling as at the other times, "Samuel! Samuel!"
Then Samuel said, "Speak, for your servant is listening" (V.10).

If the radio had been on, they would have known the Titanic was sinking. Cyril Evans, the radio operator of another ship, had tried to get a message to Jack Phillips, the radio operator on the Titanic—letting him know they had just navigated through an ice field. But Phillips was busy relaying passengers' messages and rudely told Evans to be quiet. So Evans turned off his radio and went to be bed. Ten minutes later, the Titanic hit an iceberg. Their distress signals went unanswered because no one was listening.

In 1 Samuel we read that the priests of Israel were dishonest, living for whatever they could get for themselves and ignoring God completely. "The word of the LORD was rare; there were not many visions" (1 SAMUEL 3:1). But God wouldn't give up on His people. He began to speak to a young boy called Samuel who was being raised in the priest's household. Samuel, whose name means "God hears", would now need to learn how to hear God.

"Speak, for your servant is listening" (V.10). If we want to hear, we also need to be people who are "listening". May we also choose to listen to and obey what God has said in the Bible. Let's give our lives to Him and take the time to read, enjoy and think about His words. We need to be people who have our 'radios' turned on.

GP

WHAT I'M THANKFUL FOR . . .

Dear Jesus, thank You that You're a speaking God. Thank You for the Bible that speaks Your words to me.

GOD IS ALWAYS SPEAKING . . . ARE WE LISTENING?

BEAT AGAIN

BIBLE: JUDGES 5:19-21

March on, my soul; be strong! (V.21).

After removing a patient's heart to repair it, the heart surgeon returned it into the chest and began gently massaging it back to life. But the heart wouldn't restart. So he started pumping it harder, but the heart still wouldn't beat. Finally, the surgeon knelt next to the unconscious patient and spoke to her: "Miss Johnson," he said, "this is your surgeon. The operation went perfectly. Your heart has been repaired. Now tell your heart to beat again." Her heart began to beat.

The idea that we could tell our hearts to do something might seem strange, but it's actually what the Bible teaches. "Why, my soul, are you downcast?" one psalm-writer says to himself. "Put your hope in God" (PSALM 42:5). "Return to your rest, my soul," says another, "for the LORD has been good to you" (116:7). After beating Israel's enemies in war, Deborah, a judge (the judges ruled Israel before they had kings), said that she too had spoken to her heart during battle. "March on, my soul," she told it, "be strong!" (JUDGES 5:21)—because God had promised victory (4:6-7).

God, our spiritual Surgeon, has fixed us on the inside, repairing our selfish hearts (PSALM 103:3). So, when worry, depression or guilt come, be ready to talk to yourself with words of truth from the Bible: March on! Be strong! "The LORD has been good to you" (PSALM 116:7).

SV

THINKING IT OVER . . .

How often do you remind yourself of truths from the Bible? Read Ephesians 1 and highlight all the powerful truths about your relationship with God that you can be telling yourself, particularly on bad days.

WHEN WE TALK TO OURSELVES, LET'S REMIND OURSELVES OF EVERYTHING THAT GOD HAS DONE FOR US.

THE BELL

BIBLE: MATTHEW 16:13-20

I tell you that you are Peter, and on this rock I will build my church, and the gates of Hades will not overcome it (V.18).

Jack dreamed of joining the navy from when he was a little kid—an ambition that led to years of exercise, discipline and self-sacrifice. When he was old enough, he faced exhausting tests of strength and survival.

Jack wasn't able to complete the demanding training, and finally rang a bell to tell the commander and other trainees that he had decided to quit the programme. For most of us, this kind of thing would feel like failure. But even though he was really disappointed, Jack was able to see his 'failed' military experience as good life-training for whatever God had in store for him next.

Peter, one of Jesus' first followers, went through his own time of failure. He boasted to Jesus and the other disciples that he would stay loyal to Jesus even to prison or death (LUKE 22:33). Yet later he wept because he'd denied knowing Jesus to save his own skin (VV.60-62). But God had plans to use even this failure. Before Peter messed up big time, Jesus had told him, "I tell you that you are Peter, and on this rock I will build my church, and the gates of Hades will not overcome it" (MATTHEW 16:18; SEE ALSO LUKE 22:31-32).

Are you struggling with a mess you've made? Do you feel like a failure and unable to move on? Don't let the ringing bell of failure make you miss God's plans for you. He can use even our bad days to prepare us for what's coming next.

EM

WANT MORE . . . ?

Check out *Ever wanted to start over?* online at **ourdailybread.org/lookingatlife**

GOD CAN USE EVERY CIRCUMSTANCE, EVEN THE BAD STUFF, TO SHAPE US FOR WHAT LIES AHEAD.

INVISIBLE

BIBLE: 1 THESSALONIANS 5:16-24
Do not quench the spirit (V.19).

When I looked round an art gallery, I saw one painting called *The Wind*. The piece showed a storm moving through a wooded area. Tall, thin trees leaned to the left. Bushes thrashed in the same direction.

In an even more powerful sense, the Holy Spirit is able to move Christians in the direction of God's goodness and truth. If we go along with the Spirit, we can expect to become braver and more loving. We will also become more self-controlled and better able to spot things that are bad for us, even though they look good (2 TIMOTHY 1:7).

In some situations when the Spirit nudges us towards spiritual growth and change, we say, "No." Continually blocking or ignoring what the Holy Spirit is doing in us is what the Bible calls "quench[ing] the Spirit" (1 THESSALONIANS 5:19). Over time, things we once knew were wrong become not quite as bad. Pretty soon they become normal. All because we deliberately ignored the warnings of the Holy Spirit.

When our relationship with God seems distant and disconnected, this may be because we've been repeatedly brushing aside the Spirit's voice or convictions. The longer this goes on, the harder it is to see where we're going wrong. Thankfully, we can pray and ask God to show us our sin. If we turn away from sin and re-trust ourselves to Him, God will forgive us and help us to live under the influence of His Spirit within us.

JBS

TO PRAY ABOUT . . .
God, please show me how I have ignored Your Holy Spirit. Help me to listen when You speak. I want to be right with You again.

GOD WILL ALWAYS TELL US EXACTLY WHERE WE'VE GONE WRONG AND GET US BACK ON TRACK—IF WE ASK.

HATRED

BIBLE: I PETER 4:7-11

Hatred stirs up conflict, but love covers over all wrongs (PROVERBS 10:12).

"Hatred destroys the container that carries it." These words were spoken by a politician at the funeral of a world leader. Trying to describe his friend's kindness, the politician remembered how the leader had chosen humour and love, rather than hatred, as the way he would manage his responsibilities and relationships.

I really get his quote. I do so much damage to myself when I hold onto hatred!

Even some medical research agrees. We actually hurt our bodies when we cling to anger, grudges and hatred. Our blood pressure rises. Our hearts pound. Our muscles tense and ache. Our bodies are strained.

In Proverbs 10:12, King Solomon wrote, "Hatred stirs up conflict, but love covers over all wrongs." Our hatred doesn't just hurt us, it makes us look for revenge against the people we hate. It stops us being able to connect with them in a healthy, normal way.

God's way of love, however, covers—or forgives—all wrongs. That doesn't mean we ignore the bad things other people do, sweep arguments under the carpet or let others do whatever they want without consequence. But it does mean that we stop holding onto the wrong when someone is truly sorry. And if they never apologise, we still trust the issue to God and His perfect justice. We who know that "God is love" (1 JOHN 4:16) are to "love each other deeply, because love covers over a multitude of sins" (1 PETER 4:8).

EM

THINKING IT OVER . . .

Read 1 John 2:9-11. If we insist on hating people, what might that show about our relationship with Jesus (V.9)? What is the danger of holding onto hatred (V.11)? Why is it so important to actively live in an attitude of love (V.10)? If you struggle with holding grudges, how does 1 John 2:1-2 encourage you? How does this verse strengthen and inspire you to forgive the people you want to hate?

HATRED IS LIKE DRINKING POISON AND HOPING IT HURTS THE OTHER PERSON.

INSTAGRAM CHRISTIANITY

BIBLE: PSALM 13

How long, LORD? Will you forget me for ever? How long will you hide your face from me? (V.1).

When I visited Mount Rainier, one of the highest points in America, I hoped to see some amazing views. But for the entire time I was there the mountain was covered in clouds. So instead of taking pictures, I googled photos of the view instead.

My holiday made me think about the way I show my Christian life to the people around me. Do I give an 'Instagram' view of Christianity? You know what I mean by that, right? Do I only share with other people when God answers prayer, when I've got a new favourite praise song or when I've been doing really well at spending regular time with God? Do I give the impression that my view of God is always clear and that everything's going really well, all the time? Because the reality is that I struggle a lot, I have big questions, I don't always feel in sync with what God's doing and I struggle to maintain a regular prayer life.

David didn't live out Instagram Christianity. In Psalm 13 he admitted that he couldn't see God and didn't understand what He was doing (PSALM 13:1). But by the end of his prayer, he could say with certainty that God was still there and still good; even though he couldn't see clearly (VV.5-6).

Christians are like people living at the foot of a mountain. They've seen the mountain before, so they know it exists even when clouds are covering it.

When suffering or confusion stops us seeing God clearly, we can be honest with others about our doubts, rather than pretending everything is fine. But we can also have confidence that God is still there by remembering times we've seen His love and goodness. That's better than Instagram Christianity.

JAL

THINKING IT OVER . . .

When are you most tempted to fake your Christian walk? Who can you be more open with at your church when things aren't so straightforward?

BEING A GOOD WITNESS FOR GOD DOESN'T MEAN WE HAVE TO BE FAKE.

BIBLE: PSALM 27

Hear my voice when I call, LORD; be merciful to me and answer me (V.7).

Frustrated and disappointed with church, seventeen-year-old Oscar began looking for answers. But nothing he explored seemed to satisfy him or answer his questions.

His journey did draw him closer to his parents. Still, he had problems with Christianity. During one conversation, he said, "The Bible is full of empty promises." We've probably all felt like that at one time or another.

Another man faced disappointment and hard times that fuelled his doubts. But as David ran from the enemies who wanted to kill him, his response was not to run from God but to praise Him. "Though war break out against me, even then I will be confident," he sang (PSALM 27:3).

Yet David's poem still hints at doubt. His cry, "Be merciful to me and answer me" (V.7), sounds like a man with fears and questions. "Do not hide your face from me," David pleaded. "Do not reject me or forsake me" (V.9).

David didn't let his doubts paralyse him, however. Even in those doubts, he said, "I will see the goodness of the LORD in the land of the living" (V.13). Then he addressed his readers: you, me and the Oscars of this world. "Wait for the LORD; be strong and take heart and wait for the LORD" (V.14).

We won't find fast, simple answers to our huge questions. But we will find—when we wait for Him—a God who can be trusted.

TG

THINKING IT OVER . . .

What do you do with your big questions? Where have you seen answers "in the land of the living" (PSALM 27:13), and where are you still waiting for answers?

FEELING GUILTY

BIBLE: I JOHN 3:16-20

If our hearts condemn us, we know that God is greater than our hearts, and he knows everything (V.20).

God knows us better than we know ourselves. He's knows all about our issues, our anxieties and the ways we keep messing up again and again. He knows that we struggle to forget and move on from the shame of the stuff we've done wrong. He knows the fights we have with our parents, the loneliness we feel even with our family and friends, and the people who pressurise us into doing stupid and dangerous things. He knows it all.

We look at that list and we judge ourselves. We fill up with guilt and stress. We can't get over the failures, the problems and the huge obstacles in our way. We're weighed down with the pain and the regrets. "Our hearts condemn us" (1 JOHN 3:20)—we look at ourselves as worthless and useless.

But here's the thing: "God is greater than our hearts" (V.20). If we trust Jesus, God sees us (even clearer than we do, warts and all) and He loves us. He doesn't condemn us. In fact, John tells us, "This is how we know what love is: Jesus Christ laid down his life for us" (V.16). Jesus paid for all our mess in full. There is now nothing for us to be feel ashamed of, afraid of or guilty about. God knows my shame when I fail and is quick to forgive when I admit it to Him (1 JOHN 1:9). This wonderful truth gives us rest when we are tempted to give ourselves a hard time. There is no reason to wallow in guilt—Jesus has set us free from it all.   *DR*

WANT MORE . . . ?

Check out *Can I be forgiven?* online at **ourdailybread.org/lookingdeeper**

GUILT IS A WEIGHT GOD NEVER MEANT FOR US TO CARRY.

DISASTER

BIBLE: LUKE 13:1-5

Those eighteen who died when the tower in Siloam fell on them—do you think they were more guilty than all the others living in Jerusalem? I tell you, no! But unless you repent, you too will all perish (VV.4-5).

Some Christians can be quick to label things like terrorist attacks, murders, earthquakes, floods and other disasters as "acts of God" or "acts of judgement". That's not what the Bible teaches.

In Luke 13, Jesus was asked about some people who were murdered, and about eighteen people who died when a tower collapsed on them. The crowd asking the questions were wondering if the people who died in those situations were worse sinners than others. Was that why they suffered and died in those terrible ways? "I tell you, no!" said Jesus, "But unless you repent, you will all perish" (LUKE 13:3,5).

Terrible things happen in our world. It's no longer good and perfect, as God made it. It is damaged by human sin and selfishness. And so the bad, upsetting things that go on in our world are not necessarily signs of God's anger or judgement. But Jesus' explanation shows us there is a way to understand these things: they are warnings to us that we too might suffer and die at any time. So we need to make sure we are right with God through trusting Jesus, and looking to help others meet Jesus too.

The bad things in our world are not good in themselves, but they can be a wake-up call to us to remember Jesus is our only security in this world. And they can also be good opportunities to tell others about the hope He gives. *HVL*

TO PRAY ABOUT . . .

Dear God, please help me to focus on You, not the bad stuff I see in the world. I am never alone or helpless with You by my side. You are my security, no matter what happens.

WHEN THINGS LOOK BAD, LISTEN TO GOD'S WAKE-UP CALL.

WHEN YOU'RE DOWN

BIBLE: PSALM 6

I am worn out from my groaning. All night long I flood my bed with weeping and drench my couch with tears . . . The LORD has hear my cry for mercy (VV.6,9).

Sometimes it doesn't take much to get us down, does it? Our friends making fun of us, a bad day at school, having nothing to watch on TV, finding yourself home alone for the evening. As a Christian, maybe you think you should feel peace no matter what. But somehow you never really do. Everything seems against you; you can't get outside the gloom of your own head; and even simple things are a struggle.

David must have been feeling that way when he wrote Psalm 6. He felt weak and sickly (PSALM 6:2), troubled (V.3), abandoned (V.4), tired (V.6) and full of sadness (V.7). But he knew what to do when he was down. He looked up and trusted God to take care of him and to see him through.

When we look up and focus on God, something good happens. We get our eyes off ourselves and gain a new appreciation of Him.

Next time you're down, try looking up to God. He is King (PSALM 47:8); He loves you (1 JOHN 4:9-10); He says you are so special (MATTHEW 6:26); He has a purpose for your life, even in the tough times (JAMES 1:2-4).

Yes, things can seem way too dark at times. But don't let it keep you down and unable to get outside your own head space. Think about God's goodness, talk to Him and know that He hears you (PSALM 6:9). That will give you strength to get up when you're down.

DB

TO PRAY ABOUT . . .

Father, You know when I'm feeling really low. Please help me to turn to You and lift my thoughts to Your goodness and love. Help me to get up when things knock me down.

WHEN LIFE KNOCKS YOU TO YOUR KNEES, YOU'RE IN A GOOD POSITION TO PRAY.

THE MIRACLE OF PRAYER

BIBLE: 2 CHRONICLES 30:21-27

The priests and the Levites stood to bless the people, and God heard them, for their prayer reached heaven, his holy dwelling-place (V.27).

Have you ever thought of group prayer as a miracle? That thought came to my mind one evening at church after we broke into small prayer groups. As someone in each group prayed, I heard several people talking to God at the same time. It sounded like a jumble of words. But that's the miracle. God was hearing each prayer—along with millions of others being lifted to Him around the world in many different languages.

I get confused when I've got more than one friend messaging me at the same time! I end up sending the wrong message to the wrong person and getting all my conversations in a muddle. It really is amazing that God can give His full attention to all of us at the same time.

Think about the story of Hezekiah's Passover celebration. He told the Israelites to join him in Jerusalem for praise and prayer (2 CHRONICLES 30:1). Huge crowds came for what turned into a two-week-long praise service. All those people rejoiced and praised God at the same time (V.25). As the religious leaders prayed, "their voice was heard; and their prayer came up . . . to heaven" (V.27).

The miracle goes on. Today, throughout the world, millions of people are praying to God. Let's rejoice in knowing that He hears each prayer.   *DB*

WANT MORE . . . ?

How should I pray? What should I pray about? Check out answers to questions like this in *Big questions about . . . prayer* online at **ourdailybread.org/teen**

WE WILL NEVER HAVE ANY DIFFICULTY KEEPING GOD'S ATTENTION—HIS EYES ARE ALWAYS ON US.

PAIN AND GAIN

BIBLE: HEBREWS 12:1-11

No discipline seems pleasant at the time, but painful. Later on, however, it produces a harvest of righteousness and peace for those who have been trained by it (V.11).

I used to be a really anxious Christian. When I began spiralling downwards emotionally, God didn't stop me. He knew I needed to reach the end of myself and my strength. When I finally hit rock bottom, the "rock" on which I fell was Jesus Christ (PSALM 18:2; 1 CORINTHIANS 10:4).

God immediately began looking after me, showing me powerful truths from the Bible to teach me to trust Him—not myself. Slowly He helped me to be a more joyful, God-dependent person—just as He made me to be. Through this painful but necessary experience, I learned that when God disciplines us, our greatest gain isn't what we *get* but what we *become*.

In Hebrews 12, we read that our heavenly Father loves us too much to let us stay as we are—filled with insecurity, anxiety, selfishness and a fuzzy understanding of who He us. Like any loving Father, He disciplines, corrects and trains us—often through difficult situations. God uses our times of struggle to help us grow and bring us closer to Him (HEBREWS 12:10-11).

Most of the time we're looking to make things as easy as possible for ourselves. We try to avoid pain at all costs. But the life God leads us through will involve tough times as He helps us to realise He alone is our strength and hope.

Growth and change are often unsettling, but the growth of our relationship with God is worth it.

JY

THINKING IT OVER . . .

Read James 1:2-4. Why do you think James tells us to approach trials with "pure joy" (V.1)? What is the end result of keeping going with God through hard times (V.4)? Is this the goal you have in mind when you face something difficult?

GOD USES SETBACKS TO HELP US MOVE FORWARD.

WHO PACKED YOUR PARACHUTE?

BIBLE: 1 SAMUEL 30:1-25

The share of the man who stayed with the supplies is to be the same as that of him who went down to the battle. All shall share alike (V.24).

Anton was sitting in a restaurant when a random guy came up to him and said, "You're Anton. You flew a jet fighter for the RAF. You were shot down!"

"How in the world did you know that?" asked Anton.

The man, who had served in the RAF at the same time, answered, "I packed your parachute." Then he added, "I guess it worked."

That night Anton thought about this guy who had stood at a table carefully folding parachutes for men whose lives might depend on them. Anton wondered, *How many times did I pass this guy but didn't even say good morning because I was a jet pilot and he was just some low-ranking soldier?*

This story makes me think of David's words in today's Bible reading. Two hundred of his men became too tired to keep marching and fight the Amalekites. So they stayed behind to guard the supplies. When David returned from battle, he made no distinction between them and his fighting men. He said, "They shall share alike" (1 SAMUEL 30:24).

In God's family there are no high and low people, no important or unimportant jobs. We all work together in the church, depending on one another.

HVL

THINKING IT OVER . . .

Read 1 Corinthians 12:12-27. How does this image of a body help you think about the way we are to 'fit together' with our church family? What should the attitude be of everyone in this body (VV.24-26)?

YOU ARE THE BODY OF CHRIST, AND EACH ONE OF YOU IS A PART OF IT. 1 CORINTHIANS 12:27

THE BIG SHUFFLE

BIBLE: EPHESIANS 2:4-10

It is by grace you have been saved, through faith—and this is not from yourselves, it is the gift of God (V.8).

As a bus driver, the woman showed great care towards the kids she drove to school each day—quizzing them on homework and making a big deal of their successes. "I want to see these kids make it in life," she said. But there was another motivation for how she lived her life.

When she was a teenager the words of an aunt had shaken this woman to her core. "She'd tell us that we had to do something God would notice," she explained, "or else we'd get lost in the big shuffle!" Worried at the idea of hell after the "big shuffle" of judgement, this woman had come up with ways to "get God's attention"—going to church so "He'd see me being loyal" and working hard to serve others so God might "hear from others what I was doing."

I was so sad reading her words. Why had no one told this woman that she already had God's attention (MATTHEW 10:30)? How had she not heard that Jesus took care of the big shuffle for us, offering freedom from judgement forever (ROMANS 8:1)? How had she missed that salvation can't be bought with a 'good' life but is a gift to anyone who trusts Jesus (EPHESIANS 2:8-9)?

Jesus' life, death and resurrection take care of our future with God and set us free to live for Him now with joy. *SV*

THINKING IT OVER . . .

Why is it easy to mistakenly believe we must do good things to be accepted by God? How does understanding the freeing truth of the gospel help us to love others better?

WE DON'T NEED TO TRY TO GET GOD'S ATTENTION OR IMPRESS HIM.

HIDING PLACE

BIBLE: PSALM 34:4-8

Taste and see that the LORD is good; blessed is the one who takes refuge in him (V.8).

In this world of storms and stress, there is only one safe shelter: God Himself. "He shields all who take refuge in Him" (PSALM 18:30).

The phrase "to take refuge in" is another way of saying "to hide in" or "to hide with". It suggests a secret place where we can't be found or attacked.

When we're worn out by trying to get by in our own strength, when we're confused by our problems, when we're left out by our friends, when we're bullied by our class, we can hide ourselves in God. There is no safety in this world that even comes close to being with Him.

If we were to find our security in our popularity, our grades, our health or our family life, we'd never know true peace and safety. What would happen when these things change or let us down? But God's love and protection never changes, never fails, never forgets us and never gets beaten. He gives us the peace, happiness and security we were made for.

The only safe place is God Himself. When storm clouds gather and everything seems to be going wrong, we must run to Him in prayer and take our time there (PSALM 57:1).

One Christian once said, "That person is perfect in faith who can come to God in their utter misery . . . and honestly say to Him, 'You alone are my refuge.'" How safe and secure we are!

DR

WHAT I'M THANKFUL FOR . . .

Thank You, Father, for always being with me. Thank You for describing Yourself as my Rock, Fortress, Refuge and Strong Tower. There is nowhere else I'd rather be than in Your presence.

SAFETY IS NOT FOUND IN AVOIDING DANGER BUT IN KNOWING GOD.

MOVING ON FROM GOD

BIBLE: 2 CHRONICLES 26

He sought God during the days of Zechariah, who instructed him in the fear of God. As long as he sought the LORD, God gave him success (V.5).

Uzziah started out really well in his life with God. He had been made king as a teenager (when he was sixteen!). Despite being young, we read that "He did what was right in the eyes of the LORD . . . He sought God during the days of Zechariah, who instructed him in the fear of the LORD. As long as he sought the LORD, God gave him success" (2 CHRONICLES 26:4-5). This "success" wasn't that Uzziah had a super easy life necessarily—but that he got to know God better and saw God work in his life and in the nation as a whole.

This meant Uzziah's fame spread and his army grew stronger (V.8). He had 2,600 chief officers and 307,500 soldiers who helped him defeat his enemies (VV.12-13).

But we then read, "After Uzziah became powerful, his pride led to his downfall" (V.16). Uzziah started to forget that God had given him success, and that he had relied on God-centred people to make wise and loving decisions. He rejected God when he burned incense in the temple, and God gave him leprosy (VV.16-19). "King Uzziah had leprosy until the day he died. He lived in a separate house—leprous, and excluded from the temple of the LORD" (V.21).

We also need to listen to the warning in Proverbs 16:18, "Pride goes before destruction, a haughty spirit before a fall." As soon as we start thinking we've got things sorted and we can do stuff on our own, we're in trouble. Jesus tells us clearly: "apart from me you can do nothing" (JOHN 15:5). Let's make a habit of thanking God for what He's doing in our lives and remembering how much we need Him. That will keep us from forgetting Him and just relying on ourselves. AL

THINKING IT OVER . . .

In the Bible skin diseases, like leprosy, are a picture of sin. That's why God gave King Uzziah leprosy. It kept him out of God's presence (2 CHRONICLES 26:21) and should have shown Uzziah clearly what rejecting God had done to his relationship with Him. Read Leviticus 13:45-46 to see what life with leprosy looked like. Why is this a good picture for what sin really is? How does Jesus' reaction to a leper (MATTHEW 8:1-4) help show you what He came to earth to do?

DEPENDENCE ON GOD IS HARDEST WHEN LIFE IS EASY.

LET'S TALK ABOUT IT

BIBLE: MATTHEW 18:15-20

Let love and faithfulness never leave you; bind them round your neck, write them on the tablet of your heart (PROVERBS 3:3).

A woman complained to the police because she was getting annoying phone calls. In the middle of the night a person would phone her, bark like a dog and then hang up. The police soon discovered that one of her neighbours was making the prank calls. He said that whenever he was woken up by the barking of her dog, he wanted to make sure she was awake too.

The Bible says there are better ways to handle disagreements and fights. Sometimes the only thing to do is face our problems, or difficult people, head-on (MATTHEW 18:15-20). At the right time and in the right attitude (kind, understanding and generous), an honest conversation is so often the best way to move forward.

Yet such a loving, open approach is hard work. It goes against our every instinct and sense of justice. Instead of trusting God and walking into tense situations wanting to bring peace, we prefer to 'play games'. We gossip, we blank people, we tell our friends to pick sides, we whinge and moan, we try to get even somehow. I think that is one of the reasons we're told, "Let love and faithfulness never leave you" (PROVERBS 3:3).

Our problems with other people can't just be smoothed over by burying our anger or ignoring our pain. And pain will only increase as we fight back. But knowing the love and faithfulness God has shown us, we can make the choice—the hard choice—to talk honestly with the people we have issues with and try to bring peace.

MDH

TO PRAY ABOUT . . .

Dear God, please help me to be a generous, kind, loving person, even when people hurt me. I know how much I want to fight back when others are unkind. Help me to focus on Your love for me so that I can be better prepared to show that same love, even when things are tense.

FORGIVE AS THE LORD FORGAVE YOU. COLOSSIANS 3:13

NOTHING BUT THE TRUTH

BIBLE: PROVERBS 12:17-22

The LORD detests lying lips, but he delights in people who are trustworthy (V.22).

I came across some unusual and funny reasons people gave to their insurance companies when explaining car accidents they had been in:

"An invisible car came out of nowhere, hit my car and vanished."

"I had been driving my car for forty years when I fell asleep at the wheel and had the accident."

"The pedestrian had no idea which direction to go, so I ran him over."

"The telephone pole was approaching fast. I attempted to swerve out of its path when it hit my front end."

"The guy was all over the road. I had to swerve a number of times before I hit him."

"The reason for this accident was a little guy in a small car with a big mouth."

These 'excuses' might bring a smile to your face today, and some were probably meant to. But they also remind us of how quick we are to dodge the blame and come up with excuses, especially when it can get us out of trouble.

The book of Proverbs tells us: "The LORD detests lying lips, but he delights in people who are trustworthy" (PROVERBS 12:22). Why? Because being honest, even when we've made a mess of things, shows we're trusting in God to bring us through the situation. Lies are just another way for us to try and save ourselves. But we belong to Jesus now, who is our Saviour in everything. So let's be careful to stick to the truth—and trust ourselves to God!

RDH

THINKING IT OVER . . .

When are you most likely to tell lies? Do you see this as a big deal or not?
How does this reading challenge you about your attitude, but encourage you
to trust God with the truth—even if it may make you look bad?

HONESTY IS ANOTHER EXAMPLE OF OUR RELIANCE ON GOD.

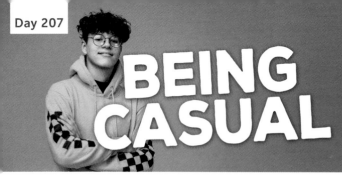

BEING CASUAL

BIBLE: MALACHI 1:6-14

"When you bring injured, lame or diseased animals and offer them as sacrifices, should I accept them from your hands?" says the LORD (V.13).

"I am not pleased with you." This was God's stinging rejection of His people through the words of Malachi (MALACHI 1:10). God was angry with their careless, 'casual' and half-hearted way of living for Him. The animals they brought for sacrifice were not acceptable to Him because they were not the best of the herds and flocks. Instead, they offered Him stolen, lame and sick animals (V.13).

What about us? What does our life with God look like? Are we giving Him the best of all that we are? Are we loving Him as the very centre of who we are? Or are we getting a bit casual and complacent towards Him? Are things cooling off between us and God?

A friend of mine said something really challenging to me the other day: "When I shop for simple stuff like new music, I hardly think about it. But when I'm looking for a new smartphone, I shop very carefully. I browse online, read reviews, watch videos and compare specs for hours to make sure I get something that's just right for me." Then she added, "I should pay that same attention when I am living for God. But sometimes I approach Him as casually as if I were just buying a packet of crisps on the way home from school."

When we're singing about God at church, we might not always give Him our full attention. When we're praying, our minds often wander. When we're doing life, maybe we don't think about God all that regularly. A life of worship—the kind of life that we're made to live—is about focusing on God in all that we do! When we give Him all that we are, we won't slip into casual Christianity. *DE*

WANT MORE ... ?

Check out *What is worship?* online at **ourdailybread.org/lookingdeeper**

CASUAL CHRISTIANITY FORGETS JUST HOW GOOD IT IS TO BELONG TO GOD!

AND IT WAS SO

BIBLE: GENESIS 1:1-13

God said, "Let the water under the sky be gathered to one place, and let dry ground appear." And it was so (V.9).

These words are repeated loads of times in Genesis 1, the story of God making the world: "And it was so."

Whatever God said—it happened. "Let there be light . . . Let the land produce vegetation . . . Let the water teem with living creatures . . ." (GENESIS 1:3,10,20). Then, each time, the words: "And it was so." God spoke the words, and it became a reality. That is how powerful His words are!

As I read about this beginning of our world and the power of God, I started to think about some other things God and His Son Jesus have said—things we can count on.

When Jesus was talking about us, His followers, He said, "I give them eternal life, and they shall never perish; no one will snatch them out of my hand" (JOHN 10:28). If we have put our trust in Him, we can be confident that we have unending life with Him, right now. And we will live with Him forever. We know because He has said so. And no one can undo or unsay God's powerful words!

The book of Hebrews tells us, "Be content with what you have, because God has said, 'Never will I leave you; never will I forsake you'" (HEBREWS 13:5). We can be sure that our needs will be met and that we won't be left alone. Because God has said so!

One of Jesus' most comforting promises is "I will come back and take you to be with me that you also may be where I am" (JOHN 14:3). He said it; we can believe it and wait confidently for that day. Count on God's words. It will be so.

AC

WHAT I'M THANKFUL FOR . . .

Thank You, God, for Your powerful words. Whatever You say is true.
Thank You that the Bible is full of Your incredible promises. And they
are all certain because You said them!

GOD SAID IT. I BELIEVE IT. THAT SETTLES IT.

SLOWLY BEING COOKED

BIBLE: LUKE 22:54-62

So, if you think you are standing firm, be careful that you don't fall!
(1 CORINTHIANS 10:12).

You might have heard what happens when a frog is put in a pan of slowly heating water. The frog doesn't realise it's being cooked! The body temperature of the cold-blooded frog changes to match with the temperature of its environment, so it is unaware of the slowly increasing temperature. When it finally realises it is dying in boiling water, it's already too late!

That picture is a little gross. But it is a helpful way of thinking about how sin can take over, without us realising. Let's think about the time Peter crashed out and denied knowing Jesus. He didn't just suddenly flip out and lose it; this rejection of Jesus was a build up over time.

It started when Peter was proud and overconfident, boasting at the evening meal, "Lord, I am ready to go with you to prison and to death" (LUKE 22:33).

Then, in the garden, he slept when he should have been praying (VV.45-46). He was totally tuned out to the idea that Jesus would have to suffer and die. As soldiers arrested Jesus, Peter instinctively drew his sword to fight in his own strength (V.50; SEE ALSO JOHN 18:10). Finally, scared for his life and shocked by what had happened, he denied knowing Jesus to save his own skin (LUKE 22:56-62).

Peter was like a frog in heating water. He relied on himself, thought he knew better, ignored Jesus words and finally—when things were at boiling point—realised it was too late. He found himself lost in his own mess and out of options.

Sin, selfishness and self-reliance creep up on all of us like this. That's why we have to stay awake and alert with Jesus (V.46), focusing on Him in the Bible and being more aware of our surroundings and the things that want to drag us away from God.

MDH

THINKING IT OVER . . .

Read Hebrews 4:12-13. Why is it so important to read the Bible if we want to keep our eyes open to where sin is trying to get a hold of us?

WE END UP IN A BIG MESS ONE SMALL COMPROMISE AT A TIME.

THE SHIELD

BIBLE: PSALM 3:1-5
You, LORD, are a shield around me (v.3).

On the international space station, astronauts have a bigger challenge than orbiting earth at 17,500 miles per hour! It's the return trip home. Their tiny capsule must get through the earth's atmosphere at a precise angle and speed. Our atmosphere is a bit like a shield, designed by God, to protect our planet's life from space. It screens us from ultraviolet radiation and it also stops meteors and space debris from hurtling down on us in a fiery rain.

As Christians, we have an even better shield around us. That shield is God Himself. He protects us from temptations, doubts, worries, lies, guilt and other dangers. "But you, LORD, are a shield around me," said David. "My glory, the One who lifts my head high" (PSALM 3:3).

David prayed those words while enemy soldiers surrounded him. They served Absalom—David's rebellious son—who wanted to kill David and take his throne. Needing a shield, David trusted in God our King and slept peacefully during his crisis. "I lie down and sleep; I wake again, because the LORD sustains me" (v.5).

In our journey through life, problems and issues are sure to come. But God hears and sees us. He is with us in every trial and crisis. Can you say with David that God is your trusted shield, your heavenly protector who you rely on? He is our shield! He says so! But are we taking shelter in Him, or still trying to figure stuff out for ourselves? When we trust Him, our enemies, issues and problems don't rule. God does. *PR*

THINKING IT OVER . . .
What situation is attacking you today? How can you approach this challenge with God as your shield? What will that look like and how will it change the problems you face?

NOTHING CAN GET PAST OUR HEAVENLY SHIELD.

Seven days with . . . Elijah
CHIRPY

BIBLE: 1 KINGS 17:2-6

The ravens brought him bread and meat in the morning and bread and meat in the evening, and he drank from the brook (V.6).

For twelve years, Chirpy, a seagull, has made daily visits to a guy who helped him recover from a broken leg. John got Chirpy's attention with dog biscuits and was then able to help mend his leg. Though Chirpy only lives on Instow Beach in Devon between September and March, he and John find each other easily. Chirpy flies straight to him when he arrives at the beach each day, even though he won't go anywhere near another human. It's a strange relationship for sure!

John and Chirpy remind me of another strange relationship between a person and birds. When Elijah, one of God's prophets, was sent into the wilderness to "hide in the Kerith Ravine" during a time of drought, God said he was to drink from the brook, and He'd send ravens to give him food (1 KINGS 17:3-4). Despite the drought, Elijah would have his needs met. Ravens were odd food suppliers—yet that's the way God chose to provide.

It may not surprise us that a guy would help a bird, but when birds provide for a man with "bread and meat in the morning and bread and meat in the evening," it can only be explained by God's power and care (V.6). Like Elijah, we too can trust in His provision for us.

KH

COMPLETING THE PICTURE . . .

We first meet the prophet Elijah in 1 Kings 17:1 when he suddenly appears to challenge Ahab, an evil king who ruled the northern kingdom (after Israel split) from around 874 to 853 BC. Elijah prophesies a drought to come on the whole land because of Ahab's evil (1 KINGS 17:1-7). Warned by God, Elijah then hid near the brook of Kerith, being fed by ravens until it was time to move on.

GOD MAY NOT PROVIDE IN WAYS WE EXPECT —BUT HE WILL ALWAYS PROVIDE!

Seven days with . . . Elijah

GOD'S WAYS

BIBLE: 1 KINGS 17:1-16

How unsearchable his judgements, and his paths beyond tracing out!
(ROMANS 11:33).

- -

After the rivers and brooks started drying up in Israel, because of the drought God had sent, God told Elijah to go to Zarephath where he would find food and somewhere to stay. I wonder if Elijah was surprised to find out that the widow who was to look after him was extremely poor! In fact, she only had enough food to feed her and her son one last meal, "that we may eat it— and die" (1 KINGS 17:12).

Yet Elijah knew better. God's words were the truth of the matter and He was their true provider, no what the widow saw in her empty food cupboards. So Elijah said, "First make a small loaf of bread for me from what you have and bring it to me, and then make something for yourself and your son" (V.13).

The widow had a choice: eat her one last meal and live a few more hours, or give up her meal and trust her life, and her food supply (V.14), to God.

We often only see what's going on around us. School pressure, exam stress, family issues, homework . . . and we forget to 'look up' and remember that God is at work in it all. The widow was able to look away from her empty cupboards and trust what God said. Can we do the same? Can we trust God's care and provision, even when it feels like we don't have enough?

Our heavenly Father knows exactly what He is doing. Although His ways are sometimes hard to understand (ISAIAH 55:9), He promises us that everything will work out for our good if we trust Him (ROMANS 8:28).   HB

TO PRAY ABOUT . . .

Loving God, please help me to trust in You to meet my needs no matter how things look. Help me make the choice to focus on Your words instead of what I see around me.

GOD'S WAYS ARE ALWAYS GOOD AND TRUSTWORTHY, EVEN WHEN THEY ARE HARD TO UNDERSTAND.

Seven days with . . . Elijah
POWERFUL PRAYERS

BIBLE: I KINGS 18:30-45

The prayer of a righteous person is powerful and effective (JAMES 5:16).

Do you ever feel like praying is a bit pointless? Like you're just talking to yourself—and nothing ever really changes?

The Bible writer James looked back at the life of Elijah to reassure us that, "The prayer of a righteous person is powerful and effective" (JAMES 5:16). Being a "righteous person" isn't about being super-human or 'good enough' for God to hear us. It's about being right with Him by putting our trust in Jesus. Our prayers aren't powerful because of who we are, but because of who He is!

We see this when God told Elijah, "I will send rain on the land" (1 KINGS 18:1), promising to end a drought in Israel that had lasted three and a half years. Even though God had promised rain, a short time later "Elijah climbed to the top of Carmel, bent down to the ground and put his face between his knees"—praying for the rain to come (V.42). Then, while he continued to pray, Elijah sent his servant to go and look out over the ocean "seven times", scanning the horizon for any sign of rain (V.43).

"Elijah was a human being, even as we are" (JAMES 5:17). He was nothing special, yet through his prayers God sent a drought for three and a half years, and then He sent the rains. No matter how small we feel, or how difficult we might find it to pray, God uses our prayers in amazing ways. Not only does God use our prayer times to focus us back on Him and who He is, but he will meet our needs and guide us through our difficulties.

JB

COMPLETING THE PICTURE . . .

King Ahab was one of the most evil kings of Israel (1 KINGS 16:30). He married Jezebel, who hated God and His people. They worshipped the false god Baal, and made the northern kingdom of Israel do the same (VV.31-33). Elijah challenged the prophets of Baal on Mount Carmel (1 KINGS 18:17-40). The false prophets couldn't get Baal to light an altar. Then Elijah built an altar which he drenched in water. God then sent fire down from heaven, burning the sacrifice, the wood, the stones and licking up the water in the ditch. God proved He was more powerful than false gods. Elijah then killed all of the false prophets of Baal (SEE DEUTERONOMY 13:5).

OUR PRAYERS AREN'T POWERFUL BECAUSE OF WHO WE ARE, BUT BECAUSE OF WHO WE'RE TALKING TO!

Seven days with . . . Elijah

A BAD PRAYER

BIBLE: 1 KINGS 19:1-10

The LORD is near to all who call on him, to all who call on him in truth (PSALM 145:18).

Have you ever prayed a bad prayer? In school I often selfishly asked God to help me get better grades than my friends in my essays and tests. There's nothing wrong with asking God to help us do well, but I really just wanted to get one over on my friends and hide my insecurities behind my good results. But while God didn't always seem to answer these prayers, He also didn't punish me.

Elijah gives us a great example of God dealing with a bad prayer. Elijah had seen God do some amazing things, like sending fire from heaven (1 KINGS 18:30-40) and sending rain after a three year drought (VV.41-45).

But when Queen Jezebel sent a messenger to threaten Elijah's life, "Elijah was afraid and ran for his life" (19:2). Instead of trusting God, Elijah ran away into the wilderness. There he prayed a bad prayer. He asked to die (VV.3-4).

What was God's response? He showed amazing kindness and love, giving Elijah food and rest. Then He encouraged the prophet and set him up with the next steps of the plan (VV.5-18).

We all pray bad prayers sometimes—prayers that are selfish or that just forget to be in line with God's love and good ways (SEE JOHN 16:23). But even a bad prayer has some good if it shows our need for God. So let's talk to Him no matter what our feelings. If we talk with Him honestly, He will change us to be more like He is, helping us to pray and live by His ways (COLOSSIANS 1:9). *HVL*

COMPLETING THE PICTURE . . .

Ahab told his wife, Jezebel, about God's victory over Baal on Mount Carmel (1 KINGS 19:1). Rather than turn to God, Jezebel vowed to kill Elijah. Hearing of this, Elijah fled to the wilderness, where he prayed for God to take his life. But God made Elijah feel better with food, drink and sleep instead. Then Elijah took a forty-day journey to Mount Horeb (V.8). There Elijah hid in a cave, still feeling sorry for himself. Yet God spent time with him there and gave him what he needed to keep going as a voice for God in the northern kingdom, which had largely forgotten Him (SEE 1 KINGS 16:29-33; 18:3-5,22; 19:10).

GOD IS NEVER PUT OFF BY OUR HONEST PRAYERS

Seven days with . . . Elijah

STILL SMALL VOICE

BIBLE: I KINGS 19:11-18

Be still, and know that I am God (PSALM 46:10).

When God spoke to Elijah on Mount Horeb, He could have done so in the wind, earthquake or fire (1 KINGS 19:11-12). But He didn't. He spoke with a "gentle whisper" (V.12). God asked, "What are you doing here, Elijah?" (V.13), as he hid from Jezebel who had threatened to kill him.

Elijah's reply highlighted what God already knew—the depth of Elijah's fear. Elijah said, "I have been very zealous for the LORD God Almighty . . . I am the only one left, and now they are trying to kill me too" (V.14). Or, in other words: "What do I get for being the only one standing up for You?"

Was Elijah really the only one living for God in Israel? No. God had "seven thousand in Israel . . . whose knees have not bowed down to Baal" (V.18).

Maybe you are the only person who loves Jesus in your family. You might be the only person following Him at school. But you are not alone. Psalm 46:10 reminds us to "be still, and know" who God is. Just as God spoke to Elijah, He wants to speak with us too through the Bible to encourage us. And He will speak to us through our church family and youth group. They are also on our side to pray for us, teach us and support us. The sooner we focus on God and His love—rather than letting our circumstances direct our feelings—the quicker we will find relief from our self-pity and worry.   *AL*

THINKING IT OVER . . .

Read Romans 8:31-39. What encouragement do you get from these verses? How do they help change your perspective on the things and people who are making life hard for you at the moment? Can anything you face today separate you from the love of Jesus (VV.35-39)?

IF GOD IS FOR US, WHO CAN BE AGAINST US?

ROMANS 8:31

Seven days with . . . Elijah

GOOD ROLE MODEL

BIBLE: 2 KINGS 2:1-6

As surely as the LORD lives and as you live, I will not leave you (V.6).

My youth leader was always looking out for me—and everyone in the group. He had an 'open house' policy, so we knew we were always welcome to go over for a chat or to pray about anything. And he helped me to read the Bible, get into a habit of praying and become more involved at church.

Elijah played a huge role in Elisha's growth as well. Elijah found him ploughing a field and told Elisha to follow him as his successor (1 KINGS 19:16,19). The young man watched Elijah do incredible miracles and follow God no matter what. God used Elijah to prepare Elisha for a lifetime of living for God. Towards the end of Elijah's life, Elisha had the chance to leave. Instead, he chose to stick close to his mentor. Three times Elijah offered to release Elisha from his duties, yet each time he refused, saying, "As surely as the LORD lives and as you live, I will not leave you" (2 KINGS 2:2,4,6). As a result, he too was used by God in amazing ways.

We all need someone who models what it means to follow Jesus. May God give us godly men and women who help us grow. And may we too, by the power of His Spirit, show others what it means to belong to God. *EPE*

COMPLETING THE PICTURE . . .

When Elisha and Elijah were walking, "a chariot of fire and horses of fire appeared and separated the two of them, and Elijah went up to heaven in a whirlwind" (1 KINGS 19:11). Elisha continued as God's prophet to the people in Elijah's place (V.15). Elisha performed lots of miracles—and some seemed to be glimpses of what God's promised King would do when He arrived (SEE 2 KINGS 4:42-44 AND MATTHEW 16:9-10; 2 KINGS 5:1-15 AND MATTHEW 8:1-4). Elisha was a prophet in Israel for about sixty years.

GOOD ROLE MODELS SHOW US WHAT IT MEANS TO STICK CLOSE TO GOD.

Seven days with . . . Elijah

LISTEN TO HIM

BIBLE: MARK 9:1-8

A voice came from the cloud, saying, "This is my Son, whom I have chosen; listen to him" (LUKE 9:35).

A guy in his late teens got his first car. It needed a bit of work, but he was excited about having a go. His dad was a mechanic. But he didn't want to listen to his dad—he was more interested in listening to his friends (who didn't know any more about cars than he did!).

That guy reminds me of Peter. Jesus took him, with James and John, up a mountain to pray. As Jesus talked with the heavenly Father, "his clothes became dazzling white" (MARK 9:3). Then Moses and Elijah appeared and talked with Jesus (V.4). Peter was so amazed and scared at the same time, that he started saying all sorts of weird things about building altars for the three of them (VV.5-6)!

At that point, the voice of God could be heard, saying, "This is my Son, whom I have chosen; listen to him" (LUKE 9:35). In this experience, Moses and Elijah represented the Old Testament. The law was often called the Mosaic Law, because Moses brought it down from Mount Sinai. And Elijah, being the most famous prophet, represented the prophets of the Old Testament. Peter wanted to turn his attention to them, but that would have been listening to the wrong people. Jesus came to fulfil the law and the prophets (SEE MATTHEW 5:17; LUKE 24:44).

The important thing is to "listen" to Jesus and focus on Him. There are many things demanding our attention. And lots of them are good. But none of them are Jesus, the One who the whole Bible points to as our only hope and Saviour. Knowing Him is our first priority, so "listen to him".   *DE*

COMPLETING THE PICTURE . . .

Elijah's story didn't end after he was taken up to heaven (1 KINGS 19:11). Not only did he appear in the story of Jesus' transfiguration (MARK 9:1-8), but the Old Testament promised he would come before Jesus, to make Him known (MALACHI 4:5-6). Jesus said this prophecy was fulfilled by John the Baptist (MATTHEW 17:10-13). In a sense, John the Baptist was the handover from the Old Testament (defined by the law and the prophets) to the New Testament where Jesus makes it clear that He is the only way to heaven (JOHN 14:6). The law and the prophets like Elijah were there to help us realise our need for a rescue, and to clearly identify Jesus as the promised Saviour.

THE BIBLE TELLS JESUS' STORY, MAKING US "WISE FOR SALVATION THROUGH FAITH" (2 TIMOTHY 3:15)

RUN AWAY!

BIBLE: I CORINTHIANS 6:12-20

You were bought at a price. Therefore honour God with your bodies (V.20).

"Parry four!"

When I started fencing, my coach would shout what I had to do next to defend ("parry") against the move he was making. When he tried to attack me with his weapon, I had to listen and do what he said if I wanted to defend myself.

That active listening reminded me of the quick action the Bible tells us to have when we face temptations we know we really struggle with. Paul tells us to "flee the evil desires" (2 TIMOTHY 2:22). "Evil desires" are anything that put us and what we want above God; like sleeping around, lying, gossiping, cheating. There are lots of ways we can misuse our desires.

Sometimes we are to "stand firm" against problems and trials (GALATIANS 5:1; EPHESIANS 6:11). But because it is so easy to misuse our desires and make a mess of things, the Bible simply shouts: "Run away!"

Quick action will stop temptations hanging around too long in our minds. Once we start thinking too much about it, we'll find fighting temptation really hard to do. A glance in the wrong place online, a nasty word in a friend's ear— each are steps that take us where we shouldn't go and put distance between us and God. The answer to temptation is simple: run far away from it.

When we run away, God also gives us a place to run to. Through Jesus' death on the cross for our sins, He offers us hope, forgiveness and a new beginning— no matter where we've been or what we've done. When we run to Jesus in our weakness, He helps us to live in His strength.   JB

THINKING IT OVER . . .

How easy or hard do you find it to run away to God when you are tempted?
How does your time with God each day help prepare you for these challenges?

WE WIN THE BATTLE OF TEMPTATION WHEN WE DECIDE TO IMMEDIATELY SHUT THE DOOR ON WRONG THOUGHTS.

MY WAY

BIBLE: 2 KINGS 5:1-15

Now I know that there is no God in all the world except in Israel (v.15).

Two kids were playing a game together. After a few minutes the older boy turned to his friend and said angrily, "You're not doing it properly. This is my game, and we play it my way. You can't play anymore!" Lots of us had conversations like that when we were little. And even now, we still want to have things our own way!

Naaman was used to having things his way. He was commander of the army of the king of Syria. But Naaman also had an incurable disease. One day his wife's servant girl, who had been captured from the land of Israel, suggested that he looked for Elisha, the prophet of God, who might be able to help. Naaman was desperate enough to do this, but he wanted the prophet to come to him. He expected to be treated with great ceremony and respect. So when Elisha simply sent a message that he should wash seven times in the Jordan River, Naaman was furious! He refused (2 KINGS 5:10-12). Only when he finally humbled himself and did it God's way was he cured (VV.13-14).

We've probably all had times when we've said "I'll do it my way" to God. But His way is always the best way. So let's ask God to give us the humility to put our own instincts and pride to one side so that we can willingly choose His way, not our own.

MS

TO PRAY ABOUT . . .

Father, forgive me for my pride and for so often thinking I know best.
Help me to be humble and willing to follow Your way in everything.

HUMILITY IS SEEING OURSELVES AS WE REALLY ARE: PEOPLE WHO NEED GOD!

BEING A BRIDGE

BIBLE: PROVERBS 13:18-21
Walk with the wise and become wise (V.20).

David, a church leader, believes friendship is a key way to help former prisoners get back into normal life (and not just return to the lifestyle and choices that landed them in prison in the first place). He says, "No significant change in life comes without a significant relationship." David's church offers those kinds of relationships, coming alongside people trying to start a new life after being released. David and others from his church hope to be the bridges—friends and mentors—these former prisoners need to rebuild their lives and head in a better direction with God.

We find a similar idea in the book of Proverbs where the writer noticed that those who "walk with the wise . . . become wise" (PROVERBS 13:20). On the other side of things, people who only have selfish and godless friends are more likely to keep messing up and making bad choices.

We'll never have all the answers to the problems our friends, family and classmates have. But as we keep reading the Bible and getting to know God's ways better, we can let others know about the life, security and hope He offers them. God's wisdom helps us as we see others facing challenges of all kinds. We can, like the people in that church, be bridges. We can give our time and attention to the people around us who are struggling, not to just try and solve their problems, but to keep introducing them to Jesus, who will walk with them through every trial and lead them in a better way of life. *KH*

THINKING IT OVER . . .
When you see a friend is struggling, how likely are you to bring God into the conversation? How does Colossians 4:2-6 help you think about the way we can be bridges to God in our relationships?

BE WISE IN THE WAY YOU ACT TOWARDS OUTSIDERS; MAKE THE MOST OF EVERY OPPORTUNITY. COLOSSIANS 4:5

CHANGING THE WORLD

BIBLE: I THESSALONIANS 4:1-12

Make it your ambition to lead a quiet life (V.11).

Sometimes we might feel like we need to change the world for God. We feel pressured to transform our school single-handedly for Jesus! But is that really what God expects of us?

Paul says we "please God" when we're holy (set apart for God and focused on Him) and love each other (1 THESSALONIANS 4:1-10). In a sense, this is seen most clearly in the basic, ordinary stuff. He adds, "Make it your ambition to lead a quiet life: you should mind your own business and work with your hands, just as we told you, so that your daily life may win the respect of outsiders" (VV.11-12).

This doesn't sound like a command to change the whole world ourselves—which is a relief! Only Jesus can truly change it. And because He did (when He died and came back to life—making the way for each of us to be right with God), we don't have to. The pressure is off; we can simply focus on knowing Him and taking the opportunities He gives us. It might be something small like telling a friend we're praying for them if they're having a hard time. It might be something no one ever sees, like praying for our classmates in the privacy of our bedroom. Whatever we do, let's do it for Him (COLOSSIANS 3:17).

We want to do the best we can and see people deciding to trust Jesus in our family and school. But it's not all on us to make this happen. We just need to do our part each day, no matter how small that may seem.

So thank God for the big things He does through us, and thank Him for the small, quiet stuff as well. Simply do whatever God leads you to do. *MW*

TO PRAY ABOUT . . .

Jesus, I want my normal, ordinary stuff to be all about You. In everything, big or small, public or private, may I live for You.

WHATEVER WE DO, LET'S DO IT FOR JESUS.

BIBLE: 1 THESSALONIANS 5:12-28

Rejoice always, pray continually, give thanks in all circumstances (VV.16-18).

Do you feel like you are always online? Even when we're not looking at our screens, our phones are in our bags or pockets, ready to buzz with messages or alerts for us to look at. One writer came up with the phrase "continual partial attention" to describe the way we always need to know what's happening 'out there', to make sure we're not missing anything. But this continual alertness to our phones can lead to quite serious anxiety.

Although the apostle Paul struggled with anxiety for different reasons, he understood our souls are wired to find peace in God. Which is why, in a letter to new Christians who'd gone through persecution (1 THESSALONIANS 2:14), he told them to "rejoice always, pray continually, give thanks in all circumstances" (5:16-18).

Praying "continually" might sound impossible. But then, how often do we check our phones? What if we instead let that urge to go online be a prompt to talk to God? To say thank you, lift up a prayer request or praise Him? If our minds can be continually connected to the online world, then we are able to be continually focusing on God.

What if we learned to swap the need to always be in 'the know' for continual, prayerful rest with God? Always checking our phones and listening out for them can lead to anxiety and restlessness. But talking to God frequently during the day can lead to peacefulness and the confidence that we already have everything we really need to know in the Bible. *AH*

THINKING IT OVER . . .

How would you say your smartphone impacts your daily routine, your mental health and you relationship with God, both in good ways and bad? What can you do to develop an ongoing conversation with God throughout each day?

THE BEST CONTINUAL CONNECTION WE HAVE IN OUR DAY IS WITH GOD, NOT OUR PHONES!

LIFE TO THE FULL

BIBLE: JOHN 10:7-15

The thief comes only to steal and kill and destroy; I have come that they may have life, and have it to the full (V.10).

The year was 1918, near the end of World War I, and photographer Eric Enstrom was putting together some of his most striking photos. He wanted to include one that gave a sense of fullness in a time that felt quite empty to so many people. The photo he chose showed a bearded old man sitting at a table with his head bowed in prayer. On the table is just a book, a pair of glasses, a bowl of porridge, a piece of bread and a knife. Nothing more, but also nothing less.

Some might say the photograph shows the old man didn't have very much. But Enstrom's point was the opposite: here is a full life, one lived in thankfulness, one you and I can experience as well no matter what our circumstances are.

Jesus announced the good news: "life . . . to the full" (JOHN 10:10). We totally misread this verse when we think "full" means having lots of stuff. The fullness Jesus talked about isn't measured in what we have or what grades we get. It is all about who we are with God; it's about the state of our heart, mind, soul and strength. Are we full of thankfulness that our good Shepherd gave "his life for the sheep" (V.11) and cares for us and our every need. This is a full life—enjoying a close, personal relationship with God—that's possible for every one of us. JB

THINKING IT OVER . . .

Would you say that right now you're living "life to the full"? Why or why not?
Are you tempted to think of "full" as having lots of stuff?

THE FULLEST LIFE IS THE LIFE THAT LIVES OUT THE PURPOSE FOR WHICH IT WAS CREATED.

GROWING

BIBLE: LUKE 3:21-22

The Holy Spirit descended on him in bodily form like a dove. And a voice came from heaven: "You are my Son, whom I love; with you I am well pleased" (**V.22**).

For many people at the time, it must have seemed like Jesus turned up out of the blue. He rocked up with everyone else and was baptised by John the Baptist. But when He came out of the water, He heard His Father say, "You are my Son, whom I love; with you I am well pleased" (**LUKE 3:22**).

What had Jesus been doing that pleased God the Father so much? He had not yet done a single miracle; He had not preached a single sermon; He had not healed one leper. In fact, it seemed like He hadn't done anything to really stand out.

What had He been doing in Nazareth during those thirty silent years? He was growing "in wisdom and stature, and in favour with God and men" (**2:52**).

What's done in the quiet place with God is what matters. It's in the personal hours with God that we're shaped and moulded and made into people He can use—people He is well-pleased with because of all Jesus went on to do for us.

You might be thinking, *I'm in a place where I can't be useful.* You may feel too small, too quiet, too weak, too slow, too overwhelmed. But your place, wherever it is, is a place to grow. Spend time reading the Bible and talking with God. Grow where you are, and your Father will be pleased with you—and will use you for His great plans. *DR*

WHAT I'M THANKFUL FOR . . .

Thank You, Father, that even here—even with my issues, even in my confusion—I can grow to know You better. May this be my focus and goal. Thank You that You are well pleased with me because of Jesus.

EVERY PLACE YOU FIND YOURSELF IS SOMEWHERE YOU CAN FIND OUT MORE ABOUT GOD.

IDOLATRY

BIBLE: 1 CORINTHIANS 10:1-14
My dear friends, flee from idolatry (V.14).

In ancient times, idolatry was easy to spot—dancing around the golden calves; bowing before images of dragons; setting up shrines and altars to all sorts of false gods . . . Even when the apostle Paul wrote to Christians in first-century Corinth, pagan idolatry was openly practised. He warned them to avoid going anywhere near it (1 CORINTHIANS 10:14).

But idolatry isn't just a problem of the past. It is still a danger to us today, though it isn't always so easy to spot. Today's idols are more subtle—but they still come from the same place as the ancient idols: our hearts.

If we want to know our idols, we need to ask God to help us see the thoughts, needs, urges, insecurities and demands of our hearts that are getting in the way of our relationship with Him. As soon as we're being driven by whatever's going on in our hearts or minds, we're letting something other than God direct our lives . . . it means we're being idolatrous. We may not think of ourselves 'bowing down' to something like insecurity, but if that is deciding how we live and blocking our view of God, then it is our idol.

Only God can satisfy the deepest needs of our hearts and make us truly alive. That's why we need to think clearly about who or what we are living for. If God is not our focus, then we can be sure something else is; and it won't lead us the right way. We need to listen to Paul: "My dear friends, flee from idolatry."

DR

THINKING IT OVER . . .
Read Exodus 32:1-8. Why did the people of Israel make an idol when Moses was up Mount Sinai (V.1)? The golden calf was clearly an idol, but what do you think the 'idol' was in their hearts that blocked their view of God in the first place? Could it be they were driven by insecurity to make a 'god' they could see so they would feel more in control of the situation?

AN IDOL IS ANYTHING WE PUT BEFORE GOD.

CHOOSING TO FORGIVE

BIBLE: LUKE 1:76-79

Father, forgive them, for they do not know what they are doing (LUKE 23:34).

At school, Patrick felt God had chosen him for something special. But what? Later he survived a horrific high school massacre where thirteen people were killed and twenty-four injured, including Patrick. That's when he began to understand the task he had been given.

Through his long recovery, Patrick learned that clinging to bitterness only makes us worse. God showed Patrick that the key to forgiveness is to stop focusing on what others have done *to* us and to focus on what Jesus has done *for* us. Jesus' prayer on the cross, "Father, forgive them, for they do not know what they are doing" (LUKE 23:34), fulfilled Zechariah's prophecy of Luke 1:77. And through Jesus' example, Patrick discovered God's purpose for him: to show what forgiveness looks like.

While most of us will not go through something this awful, we all have stuff to forgive. Friends gossip about us. Parents fight. We get in trouble over something that wasn't our fault. How do we move forward? We look to the example of Jesus. Even though He was being murdered, He forgave. It is through Jesus' forgiveness of our sins that we, ourselves, find salvation, which includes the ability to forgive others. And like Patrick, we can choose to let go of our bitterness as we trust Jesus, and allow ourselves to be examples of God's forgiveness.

EM

TO PRAY ABOUT . . .

Dear God, show me who I need to forgive today, and give me the strength to offer the forgiveness You died to provide.

FORGIVENESS DOESN'T JUST HAPPEN; IT IS A CHOICE WE CAN MAKE BECAUSE OF ALL JESUS HAS DONE FOR US.

DOES HE CARE?

BIBLE: MATTHEW 6:25-34

The life I now live in the body, I live by faith in the Son of God, who loved me and gave himself for me (GALATIANS 2:20).

Atheism, and a lot of modern thinking today, says we are insignificant specks. We're just bags of molecules; random, unintended, unloved, without consequence or purpose . . . But if you are ever tempted to write yourself off as insignificant among the billions of people on earth, remember this truth: you are a one-of-a-kind creation of God (PSALM 139:13-14). That's true even of identical twins. There never has been and never will be another person exactly like you.

Even more important, God values you (MATTHEW 6:26-30) and has gone to great lengths to show you His love. The Bible says that His Son Jesus loves you so much that He gave His life for you (GALATIANS 2:20).

If you were to ask a loving mum of a large family which child she would be willing to give up, I'm sure she would think your question was ridiculous. Susannah Wesley, for example, had nineteen sons and daughters! Among them were John and Charles, who famously preached the gospel in the 18th century. Yet if you were to read the letters she wrote to each of her children, you would see she loved all her children equally, knowing their unique personalities and problems. It was as if each child was her one and only.

That's a picture of how much God cares about you. If you are ever tempted to wonder if He knows you exist or cares what happens to you, remember what Jesus did for you on the cross. That's how much He loves you. *VG*

THINKING IT OVER . . .

Read Psalm 18:1-19. What does this psalm show you about the lengths God will go to for just one of His people when they are in trouble?

GOD LOVES YOU AS MUCH AS IF YOU WERE HIS ONLY CHILD.

WHAT ARE YOU LOOKING FOR?

BIBLE: JOHN 1:35-42

Jesus saw them following and asked, "What do you want?" (V.38).

How would you answer if Jesus were to ask you, "What do you want?" (JOHN 1:38). Would you ask Him for better looks? More friends? A bigger Instagram presence? Good grades? To be better at sport?

For two disciples of John the Baptist, this situation was more than an interesting idea. Jesus literally asked them this question! One day while they were with John, Jesus walked by and John announced, "Look, the Lamb of God!" (V.36). Instead of continuing to follow John, his two disciples started following Jesus.

When Jesus saw them, He asked, "What do you want?" (V.38). It seems like John had prepared them well to meet Jesus, because their answer showed that they were not interested in just getting more stuff or better lives—they wanted Jesus Himself. They wanted to know where Jesus was staying. Not only did Jesus show them the place, He spent the rest of the day with them.

I wonder how often we miss an opportunity to spend time with Jesus because we're looking for something other than Him to fulfil us. I know from experience that the more time I spend with Jesus, the less desire I have for a lot of things that once seemed very important. *JAL*

WANT MORE . . . ?

Why do I need Jesus? How do I follow Jesus? Check out answers to questions like this in *Big questions about . . . why we need Jesus* online at **ourdailybread.org/teen**

WHAT WOULD YOU ASK JESUS FOR?

STEPS TO NOWHERE

BIBLE: JOHN 3:5-16

For God so loved the world that he gave his one and only Son, that whoever believes in him shall not perish but have eternal life (V.16).

Most religions are about our effort to reach up to God and please Him or get His attention through our good works. In China, for example, some people climb a mountain called Taishan. They struggle up 7,000 steps, first passing through the "middle gate", then through "heaven's southern gate".

Finally they reach the Temple of the Azure Cloud. Here they offer sacrifices, which they believe will earn them God's love. But these efforts, as impressive as they are, don't bring them any closer to God than when they took the first step.

Christianity, on the other hand, begins with the Creator reaching down to us. In His holiness He is so far out of reach of us that only He Himself could cross the gap and make the connection with us. And that's exactly what He did. He became a Man and gave Himself as a once-and-for-all sacrifice for our sin (HEBREWS 7:27). Then, after rising from the dead, He went back to heaven. And He did it all for us. Our part is to admit that we are sinners, to give up all efforts to earn our salvation, and to trust Jesus as our only Saviour.

Those still climbing endless steps of self-effort to prove themselves may as well give up. They lead nowhere. Instead, take that all-important step of trusting Jesus. It's the only step that leads to heaven. *DDH*

WANT MORE . . . ?

Check out *Aren't all religions just the same thing really?* online at
ourdailybread.org/lookingatlife

SALVATION ISN'T SOMETHING WE ACHIEVE; IT'S SOMETHING WE RECEIVE.

NOT SHAKEN

BIBLE: PSALM 16

I will praise the LORD, who counsels me; even at night my heart instructs me. I keep my eyes always on the LORD. With him at my right hand, I shall not be shaken (VV.7-8).

We opened an email that was sent to Our Daily Bread Ministries. It didn't have a name at the bottom, and it looked like it had been sent from a 'fake' email address (meaning the sender didn't want a reply). The email simply said, "By the time you read this, I will have committed suicide. I trusted Jesus two years ago. But lately my world has been crumbling around me. I can't take it anymore. I can't fall again or be 'bad' anymore. God and I have drifted apart . . . Lord, help me."

Most people who take their own lives do so when they are deeply depressed. Reality has become distorted, and they can't see any other way out or forward. But God wants to be our safety and refuge (PSALM 16:1), just as He has been for all of His people through the ages. David continued in Psalm 16 by saying he was "glad" (V.9) even in his struggles. Why? "I keep my eyes always on the LORD. With him at my right hand, I shall not be shaken" (V.8).

If you feel like despair is closing in and you are out of options, God is here to be your way forward. If you are at the end of your strength, rely on His. He has great plans for you: "You make known to me the path of life; you will fill me with joy in your presence" (V.11).

DDH

THINKING IT OVER . . .

List all the things about God that make David glad and secure in Psalm 16. Why not reflect on some of these things this week. What is the danger of running "after other gods" or anything that isn't God to try and sort ourselves out (V.4)?

WHEN WE ARE MOST READY TO GIVE UP, GOD IS MOST READY TO HELP US.

SAMSON'S FLAW

BIBLE: JUDGES 14

"Must you go to the uncircumcised Philistines to get a wife?" But Samson said to his father, "Get her for me. She's the right one for me" (VV.3-4).

A girl I know may die young if she doesn't control her eating habits. And a teenage guy I met the other day is in a bad downwards spiral because his drinking and gambling habits are out of control. How do we land ourselves in this kind of mess? Maybe part of it is our lack of self-discipline.

In the Bible, Samson had absolutely no self-discipline or self-control. It led him to make mistakes which ended with him being captured by the Philistines, who cut out his eyes and enslaved him. His downward spiral began when he wanted to marry a Philistine woman (rather than a woman from among God's people). His demand, "Get her for me. She's the right one for me" (JUDGES 14:4) set the pattern of selfishness that destroyed his life (16:15-21).

Without self-control, we are "like a city whose walls are broken through" (PROVERBS 25:28). We are open to be invaded and taken over by whatever needs, wants, urges and desires are running riot in our minds. Paul teaches us instead to be people who "take captive every thought to make it obedient to Christ" (2 CORINTHIANS 10:5).

People who do well in sport (for example) do so because they eat properly, exercise and practise regularly. Likewise, people who know God read the Bible, pray, obey Him and bring every thought and desire to Him. Selfishness and indulgence only ever leads to a downward spiral; self-control comes from looking to God first, rather than our own hearts.

HVL

TO PRAY ABOUT . . .

Dear God, please help me to live a self-controlled life by the power and strength of Your Spirit within me. You have made me a brand new person to live for You, not controlled by my own instincts and desires.

THE FRUIT OF THE SPIRIT IS LOVE, JOY, PEACE, FORBEARANCE, KINDNESS, GOODNESS, FAITHFULNESS, GENTLENESS AND SELF-CONTROL.
GALATIANS 5:22-23

CITIZENS OF HEAVEN

BIBLE: PHILIPPIANS 3:17-21

Our citizenship is in heaven. And we eagerly await a Saviour from there,
the Lord Jesus Christ (V.20).

As Christians, the Bible says we are now citizens of heaven. Our true home is with God in heaven—yet all too often we act as if this world is where we really belong.

A guy visited his friend, a British military officer stationed in an African jungle. One day when the friend entered the officer's hut, he was surprised to see him dressed in a suit and tie (despite the heat) and seated at a table laid with stuff from home: silverware and fine china plates and cups. The guy asked what was going on. The officer explained, "Once a week I dress like the people back home and lay the table like they do to remind myself of who I am—a British citizen. I want to remember the lifestyle of my real home and live by the codes of British life, no matter how those around me live."

Christians should have a similar outlook. Our true citizenship is in heaven, so we must be careful not to just live as the people around us do—driven by a 'me first' culture rather than living according to God's ways (SEE ROMANS 12:2). We are not to take on this world's ways or adopt its values. We need to live in such a way that others will see that we are different. We are strangers in this world and citizens of heaven.

RDH

TO PRAY ABOUT . . .

Father, please help me to remember that my true home is with You in heaven. My identity and culture come from You now, not the world. Please help me to stand out and show to the people around me how much better it is to belong to You.

OUR TRUE HOME IS HEAVEN.

FEARING THE GOD YOU LOVE

BIBLE: PROVERBS 14:26-27

The fear of the LORD is a fountain of life, turning a person from the snares of death (V.27).

Jesus commands us to love God (MATTHEW 22:37), yet Paul also tells us to fear Him (COLOSSIANS 3:22). But if we love God, shouldn't we be free from fear?

My own experience can help answer this. I love God, but I still feel fear when I think of the day I will stand before Him. I'm not afraid He will send me to hell; I know that Jesus paid the price for my sins. Yet the thought of standing in the presence of a holy God awes me. This awesome fear (not terrified fear) helps me to want to live in a way that pleases God. Having an awesome fear of God is actually very positive and healthy for us as His people.

The Bible tells us that this fear of God is the "beginning of knowledge" (PROVERBS 1:7), that it is "pure" (PSALM 19:9), that it gives us "a secure fortress" (PROVERBS 14:26) and that it is "a fountain of life" (V.27).

Moses showed this kind of fear when God spoke to him from a burning bush. Moses "hid his face, because he was afraid" (EXODUS 3:6). Daniel must have experienced that same feeling. His love for God was great, yet when he met God in a vision he collapsed in fear (DANIEL 8:15-27). One glimpse of God's holiness overwhelmed him. These examples are here partly to help us remember just who our God is. Yes, we love Him and find our security in Him; but He is the awesome King of the universe who holds our every breath in His hands (ACTS 17:25).

Love God, but also stand in awe of who He is. This mix of love and fear is the key to living life well.

HVL

THINKING IT OVER . . .

Read Hebrews 12:25-29. What reasons are given here for us to "worship God acceptably with reverence and awe" (V.28)?

FOR THE LORD MOST HIGH IS AWESOME, THE GREAT KING OVER ALL THE EARTH. PSALM 47:2

CHARTING OUR COURSE

BIBLE: JEREMIAH 8:1-8
Each pursues their own course (V.6).

Edward Teach, also known as the famous pirate Blackbeard, has been shown in a new light by some modern historians. Although he is well known for his pirating, which involved raiding merchant ships and towns, some historical sources say he actually avoided fighting whenever possible. He preferred to create a threatening reputation so that people would be frightened into surrendering. Those who gave up without a fuss were shown mercy by Blackbeard.

The facts and myths about Blackbeard show a man who lived by his own set of rules and morals. Why can't we live like pirates and make up our own rules based on what seems right to us? The Israelites in Jeremiah's day suffered as they set "their own course like a horse charging into battle" (JEREMIAH 7:30-31; 8:6). This every-man-for-himself mentality resulted from idolatry, pride and a wrong understanding of God's laws. Eventually, the Israelites also rejected Jeremiah's warnings (VV.2,6-9).

We can't always trust our own judgement because we are fundamentally sinful and selfish (17:9). What we can trust is God's guidance, which is backed by His pure character. His goodness, faithfulness and perfection lead us to this conclusion: "The instructions of the LORD are perfect . . . The decrees of the LORD are trustworthy" (PSALM 19:7 NLT). We can rely on the Bible and His Spirit to help us chart a good course for our lives.

JBS

WANT MORE . . . ?
Check out *What does it mean to be free?* online at **ourdailybread.org/teen**

WHAT SEEMS GOOD TO US ISN'T NECESSARILY THE SAME AS WHAT'S GOOD.

NEVER ENOUGH

BIBLE: ECCLESIASTES 1:1-11
The eye never has enough of seeing (V.8).

Frank Borman led the first space mission that circled the moon. He wasn't impressed. The trip took two days both ways. Frank got motion sickness and threw up. He said being weightless was cool—for thirty seconds. Then he got used to it. Up close he found the moon boring to look at. His crew took pictures of the grey wasteland, then lost interest.

Frank went where no one had gone before. It wasn't enough. If he quickly got bored of an incredibly unique experience, perhaps we should expect the same thing to happen to us. King Solomon, the writer of Ecclesiastes, explained that no experience can give us the ultimate joy and satisfaction we're looking for. "The eye never has enough of seeing, nor the ear its fill of hearing" (ECCLESIASTES 1:8). We may feel moments of happiness, but it soon wears off and we look for the next thing to excite us.

Frank had one cool moment, when he saw the earth rise from the darkness behind the moon. Like a blue and white swirled marble, our world sparkled in the sun's light. In a similar way, lasting happiness comes from the Son shining on us. Jesus is our life, the only real source of meaning, love and purpose. Our deepest satisfaction isn't found in this world—we can go all the way to the moon, yet still not go far enough. We need to look out of this world to the One who made it.

MW

THINKING IT OVER . . .
When are you at your happiest? Why doesn't it ever last? How do you feel when you spend time with God in the Bible? There might be times when you feel bored reading the Bible—but trust that you are getting to know God day by day. Ask God to remind you how amazing it is to know Him.

NOTHING IN THIS WORLD WILL EVER TRULY SATISFY US.

WHO IS HE?

BIBLE: PSALM 24

Who is he, this King of glory? The LORD Almighty—he is the King of glory (V.10).

On our way home from holiday, my family and I waited to check in our luggage at the airport. I suddenly pointed to a man standing a few feet away.

They didn't look impressed. "Who is he?"

I excitedly rattled off the actor's most famous roles, then walked up and asked him for a selfie. I still enjoy sharing the story of the day I met a movie star.

Recognising a famous actor is one thing, but there's Someone more important I'm thankful to know personally. "Who is this King of glory?" (PSALM 24:8). The psalmist David tells us God is our Creator, Sustainer and Ruler of all. He sings, "The earth is the LORD's, and everything in it, the world, and all who live in it; for he founded it on the seas and established it on the waters" (VV.1-2). In awestruck wonder, David says God is above all, yet so close and personal (VV.3-4). We can know Him, be strengthened by Him and trust Him to fight for us as we live for Him (V.8).

God provides opportunities for us to talk about Him as the only Famous One truly worth sharing with others. As we show His character in how we live, those who don't know Him will have more reasons to ask, "Who is He?" Like David, we can point them to God with joyful amazement and tell His story!   XD

WHAT I'M THANKFUL FOR . . .

Dear God, thank You for the privilege of knowing You for myself and for giving me opportunities to show You and talk about You with others every day.

IF WE'RE AMAZED BY OUR GOD, THEN WE'RE READY TO TELL OTHERS WHO HE IS.

SURE HOPE

BIBLE: 1 PETER 1:3-9

In his great mercy he has given us new birth into a living hope . . . and into an inheritance that can never perish, spoil or fade (VV.3-4).

Alan remembers being six-years-old and seeing his alcoholic dad punch his mum. He started shoplifting at nine, and later robbed people at knife-point. In and out of prison for years, he began sniffing glue and taking drugs to numb the pain. After stabbing another inmate, he was sent to solitary confinement where he broke down and asked God to change him. After several years God used a Christian book to tell Alan about Jesus, and he asked Jesus to be his Saviour.

Alan still has struggles, but his trust in God continues to grow. He thanks God for rescuing him "from a very dark and destructive lifestyle, and for giving me a future filled with hope and eternal salvation."

Alan has experienced a "new birth into a living hope" and will enjoy an inheritance in heaven that will never break, grow old or fade away (1 PETER 1:3-4). We too, when we trust Jesus as our Saviour, have the sure promise of salvation, even though we may have to go through hard things in our earthly lives (V.6). Even in the difficulties we can be filled with "glorious joy" because of our love for Him and His certain promises to us (V.8).

As we look forward to the amazing inheritance of heaven that belongs to us, may our love for God and confidence in Him grow all the more, drawing others to Him as well.

ABP

THINKING IT OVER . . .

How does having an inheritance in heaven affect the way you live day by day?
How could you share your confidence with someone else today?

GOD PROMISES US HIS HOME AS OUR INHERITANCE.

SUCCESS AND SACRIFICE

BIBLE: 1 JOHN 3:11-18

This is how we know what love is: Jesus Christ laid down his life for us (V.16).

The class was set reading as their homework. The book was about a boy who wanted to climb an Alpine mountain in Switzerland. Training for the climb took up most of his time. When he finally set off for the summit, things didn't go as planned. Partway up the slope, a teammate became sick and the boy decided to stay behind to help him instead of reaching the top.

In the classroom, the teacher asked, "Was the main character a failure because he didn't climb the mountain?" One student said, "Yes, because he never did what he set out to do." But another kid disagreed. He reasoned that the boy was not a failure, because he gave up something important to help someone else.

When we set aside our plans and care for others instead, we're acting like Jesus. Jesus sacrificed having a home, a job and a comfortable life to travel Israel's dusty roads sharing God's truth. Ultimately, He gave up His life to free us from sin and show us God's love (1 JOHN 3:16).

Our understanding of success is often very different from success in God's eyes. He values the compassion that makes us come alongside and care for people who are upset, lost, lonely and struggling in some way (v.17). He loves it when we decide to look out for others. With God's help, we can live by His ways and show the love of Jesus wherever we go. This is what living our best life really looks like.

JBS

TO PRAY ABOUT . . .

Dear God, I want to be successful in Your eyes.
Teach me how to love others the way You love me.

SUCCESS IS BECOMING MORE LIKE JESUS.

WHY DID HE CROSS THE LAKE?

BIBLE: MARK 5:1-21

The man went away and began to tell in the Decapolis how much Jesus had done for him. And all the people were amazed (V.20).

Cyndi comes from a difficult family life. Her parents fight, her siblings bring different drugs into the house, and they often have the police or social services knocking on the door. Cyndi drinks a lot, tries the various drugs her family have and spends many of her nights with guys she doesn't really want to be with. So she finds being on her own less painful. On her bad days, her thoughts always become dark and hopeless.

When Jesus and His disciples crossed the Sea of Galilee after a long day, a hopeless guy in a dark mood met them. Possessed by demons, this man had often been chained up, but he snapped the chains and lived "among the tombs and in the hills" (MARK 5:5).

Jesus stepped in to this man's life with a radical change. While others tried to imprison the man to protect themselves, Jesus drove out the demons, freeing him to reach out to others. "Those who had seen it told the people what had happened to the demon-possessed man . . . Then the people began to plead with Jesus to leave their region" (VV.16-17). Perhaps the peopled feared Jesus' power, shown both in driving out demons and changing this man's life.

But the man himself wanted to follow Jesus (V.18). Jesus replied, "Go home to your own people and tell them how much the Lord has done for you" (V.19). Then we read that Jesus *crossed back over the lake* (V.21)! Apparently Jesus only crossed the lake to transform and free this one, hopeless case. The guy who was in a desperate mess and had no one looking out for him was Jesus' sole focus!

TG

THINKING IT OVER . . .

Check out the rest of Mark 5 (VV.22-43) to see more examples of Jesus connecting personally with people and meeting their needs. How does Jesus' love for each individual He met help show you that when He died for the sin of the world, He also very specifically and deliberately died for you? How do these stories encourage you that Jesus is able to save absolutely anyone?

OUR GOD IS A GOD WHO SAVES; FROM THE SOVEREIGN LORD COMES ESCAPE FROM DEATH. PSALM 68:20

FAMILY REJECTION

BIBLE: 2 TIMOTHY 1:5-10; 3:10-17

If anyone comes to me and does not hate father and mother, wife and children, brothers and sisters—yes, even their own life—such a person cannot be my disciple (LUKE 14:26).

Graeme was part of a group of Satanists at my school. He came to know Jesus during a church event. From that point he always came to youth group meetings. He read his Bible and loved his new life with God. But one day I noticed he looked really down. When I asked why, he said his parents didn't like of his new way of life. They wanted him to go back to how he was before. They were more comfortable with his clubbing, drinking and dark rituals than they were with his Bible reading, praying and church involvement.

I wonder if Graeme's story helps us make sense of Jesus' statement: "If anyone comes to me and does not hate father and mother, wife and children, brothers and sisters—yes, even their own life—such a person cannot be my disciple" (LUKE 14:26). Does Jesus really want us to hate our families? No, I don't think that is quite what He's saying. The point is that our love for Him is to be so strong, that by comparison every other love seems like hate. It means that when life with our parents is hard (maybe because they don't like us being Christians) we still follow Jesus and listen to Him first. It means we value what He says about us more than what anyone else may say.

The Apostle Paul challenged Timothy to "not be ashamed of the testimony about our Lord" because "the Spirit God gave us does not make us timid, but gives us power, love and self-discipline" (2 TIMOTHY 1:7-8). Jesus needs to come first in our lives, even when we face pressure to change—that way we'll continue to be His witnesses, even to our families. And then we can pray that He'll use our witness to change their lives too.   _TG_

TO PRAY ABOUT . . .

Father, please help me to keep Jesus at the very centre of my life, even when my friends or family want me to change. Your words and Your Spirit keep me steady when life is hard.

WE LOVE OUR FAMILIES BEST WHEN WE LOVE JESUS FIRST AND LIVE FOR HIM.

GOD IS WITH ME IN MY PANIC ATTACKS

I was hanging out with some of my friends. We went to get something to eat and were having fun together. I was enjoying myself, laughing and cracking jokes.

Then suddenly I looked around at all the people around our tables—friends and strangers who were all filling the café. I became uncomfortably aware of all the conversations, the sound of people chewing food, utensils clattering and food orders being yelled in the kitchen. The smells of the different foods around me became too much to take in and I started getting dizzy.

Knots tightened in my stomach and it was becoming difficult to breathe calmly. I quickly got up from my chair and made straight for the exit. It wasn't much better outside though, since we were in the city centre and it was a busy evening. People and cars seemed to be swarming all around me. Within seconds it had all completely overwhelmed me; it was something I had zero control over. I simply couldn't handle the busyness and noise anymore.

The tears started coming and I felt myself going down another one of my dark spirals of fear, confusion and insecurity. I walked and walked until I found a small, lonely alley and tried to calm down enough to do the breathing exercises I had been taught. Standing in that alley trying to ground myself in reality again felt like it took forever, but the intense fear finally faded and I felt safe again.

That kind of thing has happened many times in the three years since my battle with anxiety started. It has happened in cafés, in shops, in church, in friends' homes, on the bus and other places. I panic when my brain realises it can't control its surroundings and the way they make me feel.

The struggle is constant. Panic comes unexpectedly and for no obvious reason. Often I'm frustrated with myself—why can't I be like the rest of my friends who can just go out and enjoy themselves without falling apart?

God Comforts Me

But even in the fear and confusion, I am increasingly realising that God is near. No matter what we're going through, God always has what we need (PSALM 91:15). And He has been teaching me to listen to His voice, even when I feel anxious and overwhelmed, so that I can push past my feelings and hear what He has to say.

God created me, and He knows all my weaknesses and problems. As I learn to trust Him through my hardships, I see more of His generosity and love. He has surrounded me with close friends who understand my struggles, who know when to keep me company or talk me through my panic. I do not take this for granted.

Each time I have a panic attack, I also discover how much comfort even the simplest prayer or insight can bring. One day a friend shared with me a quote from a Christian author: "I get the invitation every morning when I wake up to actually live a life of complete engagement . . . it's brought in by a sunrise, a bird's song or the smell of coffee drifting lazily from the kitchen. It's the invitation (from God) to actually live, to fully participate in this amazing life for one more day."

I'm starting to realise that my senses and feelings are a gift from God so that I can experience His amazing creation. God wants me to take hold of His gifts and enjoy His goodness which is everywhere to be found (SEE ISAIAH 6:3 AND ROMANS 1:20). My senses don't have to control me; I can use them to focus on my God who is always with me in everything I see, and who is my "ever-present help in trouble" (PSALM 46:1).

Learning to Love Others

With this in mind, I am learning how to take my panic-attack triggers, turn them around and practise seeing God in them. Most of my triggers are people-related (crowds, outdoor noises and busyness), so I am trying to see past my difficulty and love people around me more.

After a panic attack, I will often focus on being useful or kind to people around me, largely so I can take my mind off my panic. Sometimes I pray for anyone I can see. Other times I stop and look for someone I can help (which can be anything from giving a person directions, to helping clear away the table after a meal).

It's amazing what happens when we take time to look around us and see how we can serve others. This is what Jesus did (MATTHEW 14:13-14), and as His followers, we're to do the same. This can be very hard to do when we're caught up in our own issues. It is difficult for me to even see light at the end of the tunnel most days. I have often found great relief and peace by focusing on other people and looking out for them, rather than myself.

Be Willing to Ask for Help

Improving mental health is a process. If you are struggling with panic attacks or anxiety, please know that getting better really is possible, even if it takes time. Prayer and Bible reading have been vital for me, but they were not enough on their own. I had a one-to-one mentor for some time, to help me learn to start breaking the cycle that led to panic. God also uses doctors and other medical professionals—and there is no shame in getting help from them. Whatever we do, and whoever we talk to, the most important thing is that we do talk. The worst thing we can do is keep our battles to ourselves. Who can you open up with about your mental and emotional battles?

Through all our struggles, God is right here with us. Even in our darkest places, we can come close to Him. We just have to be open to Him—spend time with Him and make it a priority to talk with Him throughout our day. Don't push away those who care for you and want to be there for you. Everyday day there are invitations to experience God's love and grace.

Even on your worst day, there is still a God of love and power holding you and seeing you through it all: "When you pass through the waters, I will be with you . . . For I am the LORD your God, the Holy One of Israel, your Saviour" (ISAIAH 43:2-3).

Seven days with . . . the prophets
RESTORED

BIBLE: JOEL 2:18-27

I will repay you for the years the locusts have eaten (V.25).

One year an infestation of Mormon crickets (really big insects!) spread across certain parts of America, eating loads of their crops (costing about £25 million!). There were so many of these big bugs that people couldn't walk anywhere without stepping on them—which just sounds gross! The grasshopper-like insects eat so much that they can quickly destroy whole farms and farming communities within days.

The Old Testament prophet Joel talked about a swarm of similar insects destroying the entire nation of Judah because they had ignored and rejected God. He told them about an upcoming invasion of locusts (which was a picture for the foreign Babylonian army that was going to take them captive into exile). This invasion was going to be like nothing the nation had seen before in its history (JOEL 1:2). The 'locusts' would lay waste to everything in their path, driving the people into famine and poverty. If, however, the people would turn from their sinful ways and ask God for forgiveness, Joel said God would "repay [them] for the years the locusts have eaten" (2:25).

We too can learn from Judah's lesson: like insects, our wrongdoings eat away at the good, Jesus-centred life God intends for us. When we keep Him at the centre, and turn away from our past choices, He promises to remove our shame and help us live a new life of growth, not destruction. *KH*

COMPLETING THE PICTURE . . .

Because of their rejection of God, the northern kingdom of Israel was invaded by the Assyrian Empire around 700 BC. About 100 years later, the southern kingdom of Judah was attacked and defeated by Babylon several times. Many of the people were taken captive back to Babylon during these attacks. Joel was one of the prophets who warned of this coming invasion. In 597 BC Babylonian's King Nebuchadnezzar, "carried all Jerusalem into exile . . . Only the poorest people of the land were left" (2 KINGS 24:14). And then around ten years later Nebuchadnezzar stopped a rebellion (V.20), completely destroying Jerusalem, including the temple, important buildings and city walls (25:8-15).

GOD'S FORGIVENESS REPLACES OUR SELF-DESTRUCTIVE SIN WITH NEW LIFE AND PURPOSE WITH JESUS.

Seven days with . . . the prophets

ANOTHER CHANCE

BIBLE: MICAH 7:1-20

You will again have compassion on us; you will tread our sins underfoot and hurl all our iniquities into the depths of the sea (V.19).

At the Second Chance Bike Shop near where I live, volunteers **rebuild** bikes that have **been** chucked away or donated to them—and give **them** to families who can't afford to buy them. Shop founder Ernie Clark **also gives** bikes to the homeless, the disabled and ex-military personnel struggling to make it in non-army life. Not only do the bikes get a second chance but sometimes the people get a new start too. One ex-soldier used his new bike to get to a new job.

Second chances change lives, especially when the second chance comes from God. The prophet Micah talked about this **during a** time when the nation of Israel was filled with bribery, violence and lies (MICAH 6:9-12). Micah described the nation like this: "The faithful have been swept from the land; not one upright person remains" (7:2).

God would **rightly punish** their selfishness, Micah knew. But being loving, He would give another chance to those who truly said sorry and turned back to Him. Humbled by such love, Micah asked, "Who is a God like you, who pardons sin and forgives the transgression?" (V.18).

We too can be in thankful awe that if we ask for forgiveness, God doesn't give up on us despite our mess. As Micah said to God, "You will again have compassion on us; you will tread **our sins** underfoot and hurl all our iniquities into the depths of the sea" (V.19).

God's love gives second chances to all who trust Him.

PR

COMPLETING THE PICTURE

Micah talks about the coming destruction of both the northern **kingdom** of Israel and the southern kingdom of Judah. Yet he also gives hope, talking **about** God's people returning from exile to live with God again (MICAH 7:12). But **the greatest** hope is the promise he gives of God's ultimate rescue, which would **come out of** Bethlehem: "Out of you will come for me one who will be ruler over **Israel**, whose origins are from of old, from ancient times" (5:2; SEE MATTHEW 2:6).

EVEN IN OUR BIGGEST MESS, GOD WON'T GIVE UP ON US!

Seven days with . . . the prophets

A BRAVE TEENAGER

BIBLE: DANIEL I

To these four young men God gave knowledge and understanding of all kinds of literature and learning (V.17).

Imagine yourself in Daniel's position. King Nebuchadnezzar, the king of Babylon, has told you, a Jewish teenager, what you're going to eat and drink from his table. But there's a problem: God has said that the food on the menu goes against His law. What would you do?

Some people don't think teenagers have what it takes to do what's right in similar situations—where it would cost them to take a stand for God. Daniel, a teenager who was abducted from his home and forced to serve a foreign king, is an example of Paul's words: "Don't let anyone look down on you because you are young, but set an example for the believers in speech, in conduct, in love, in faith and in purity" (1 TIMOTHY 4:12).

I think Daniel, the young guy who was challenged to stand up to the king in God's name, must have had people who taught him to make right choices. And it showed, because he "resolved not to defile himself with the royal food and wine" (DANIEL 1:8).

Because Daniel kept God at the centre of his life, and chose to follow His ways in a place that expected the opposite, God used him and his friends (V.17). In fact, these teenagers were ten times better at their work than anyone else who served the king (V.20).

CW

COMPLETING THE PICTURE . . .

Daniel read the words of the prophet Jeremiah and discovered that God's people would be exiled in Babylon for seventy years (DANIEL 9:2) before returning to Jerusalem. Also, "Daniel could understand visions and dreams of all kinds" (1:17). This was a key part of King Nebuchadnezzar's journey to trust God for himself (SEE 2:26-28; 4:19-37). Daniel had visions from God, which take up chapters 7-12. Some of them seem to predict the coming kingdoms on the earth, but even more important are the descriptions of God's kingdom (7:27; SEE ALSO 2:44). The visions and prophecies are hard to understand without guidance from study guides and our church leaders. But what we can see in Daniel's visions is the promise of the coming King who has all power and authority, and who will reign without end (7:13-14).

GOD HONOURS THOSE WHO HONOUR HIM.

Seven days with . . . the prophets
PROMISES

BIBLE: MICAH 5:1-5

But you, Bethlehem Ephrathah, though you are small among the clans of Judah, out of you will come for me one who will be ruler over Israel, whose origins are from of old, from ancient times (V.2).

Isaiah, Micah and many of the other prophets predicted and promised many details of Jesus' birth, life and death hundreds of years before they were fulfilled. One American mathematician worked out the probability of just eight of these prophecies being fulfilled by just one person. He said, "The chance that any man might have fulfilled all eight prophecies would be just one in 100,000,000,000,000,000."

He then came up with an image, to show just how unlikely it would be. He said that if we took that many silver coins and laid them across Texas they would cover the state two feet deep. Then, to emphasise his point, he said, "Mark one of these silver coins and stir the whole mass thoroughly. . . . Blindfold a man and tell him he can travel as far as he wishes, but he must pick up [that one marked silver coin.] What chance would he have of getting the right one?"

So what this all means is that if Isaiah and the others were making up their promises about the coming King, it would be pretty much impossible for someone to fulfil them all perfectly. Yet Jesus did fulfil them perfectly. And not just eight, but all of them—which is over three hundred prophecies! He is the real deal—the King that God promised through the prophets.   *DDH*

WANT MORE . . . ?

Check out *Who is Jesus?* online at **ourdailybread.org/lookingdeeper**

PROPHECY IS HISTORY WRITTEN AHEAD OF TIME.

Seven days with . . . the prophets
WHY HE DIED

BIBLE: ISAIAH 53:1-10

He was pierced for our transgressions, he was crushed for our iniquities; the punishment that brought us peace was on him, and by his wounds we are healed (V.5).

Jesus died so we could live. His death on the cross was not an accident or a surprise to God. It was His plan for our salvation. And it had always been His plan (EPHESIANS 1:4).

From the very first moment that people rebelled against Him, God said that death is the consequence for sin (GENESIS 2:17). And every person since Adam and Eve has sinned (ROMANS 3:23). Yet, in love He made a way for us to be rescued. God could not simply say, "I feel sorry for you. I love you. I will just save you, ignore your sin and forget about it." No, an absolutely holy and perfect God could not treat rejection of His love and goodness so lightly. The penalty for sin must be paid; guilt must be removed.

Here's what is so amazing: Jesus Christ, God's Son, took our sin, carried it to the cross, paid the penalty in full and came back to life on the third day. Jesus, who was completely perfect, took on the guilt of our sin, as promised by the prophet Isaiah (ISAIAH 53). His resurrection was the proof that the Father accepted His sacrifice in our place and that justice had been done.

That was 2,000 years ago, long before you and I were born. It was all prepared by God. It was all because of His love. It is His gift to us. All we have to do is accept it by trusting Jesus for ourselves. God's offer today is "whoever believes in [Jesus] shall not perish but have eternal life" (JOHN 3:16).   *MDH*

COMPLETING THE PICTURE . . .

The prophetic books in the Bible all talk about promises to do with God's people of Israel. Many of the judgement prophecies were fulfilled by the exile; and many of the rescue prophecies were fulfilled by the people's return. However, the proper fulfilment of all the promises of God's judgement and rescue are found in Jesus—which is why there are so many specific prophecies of His life in the Old Testament (such as in Isaiah 53). Paul explains, "For no matter how many promises God has made, they are 'Yes' in Christ" (2 CORINTHIANS 1:20). So while many prophecies find immediate fulfilment in the history of Israel, they find their true "yes" in Jesus, who took our judgement and is our rescue.

SAVING US THROUGH THE CROSS WAS ALWAYS GOD'S PLAN.

Seven days with . . . the prophets

GOD'S LAST WORDS

BIBLE: MALACHI 4

See, I will send the prophet Elijah to you before that great and dreadful day of the LORD comes (V.5).

M alachi 4 gives us God's final words to Israel in the Old Testament, after they had returned home from their exile. Then He would remain silent for 400 years until they heard "A voice of one calling in the wilderness, 'Prepare the way for the Lord, make straight paths for him'" (MATTHEW 3:3).

The last verses of Malachi are a strange mix of threat and promise, or so it sounds to us. But the point was that the next thing to happen in God's story was . . . Jesus! God Himself was about to step onto the stage of human history. "I will send my messenger, who will prepare the way before me. Then suddenly the Lord you are seeking will come to his temple" (MALACHI 3:1). John the Baptist was this "Elijah" like messenger (4:5), preparing the way for Jesus.

The question for the people of Israel was, in effect: *Are you ready?* That would determine if Jesus' coming was a threat or a promise.

God's final prophetic words to us in the New Testament do the same thing: "[Jesus] who testifies to these things says, 'Yes, I am coming soon'" (REVELATION 22:20). God's last words to Israel and Jesus' last words in the Bible give us hope—if we trust Him. That's what makes us ready to meet Him face to face.

DDH

THINKING IT OVER . . .

Read Matthew 2:1-12. What were the reactions to Jesus' birth in Jerusalem (V.3)? How does this compare with the reactions of Simeon and Anna (LUKE 2:25-38)? What made Simeon and Anna different (VV.25,37-38)?

THE GOD WHO INSPIRES THE PROPHETS, SENT HIS ANGEL TO SHOW HIS SERVANTS THE THINGS THAT MUST SOON TAKE PLACE. REVELATION 22:6

Seven days with . . . the prophets

ARE YOU READY?

BIBLE: LUKE 12:31-40

So you also must be ready, because the Son of Man will come at an hour when you do not expect him (MATTHEW 24:44).

- -

A teacher told his class that he would be going away for a few weeks. They'd have a few different supply teachers while he was away—and so he promised to give a prize to the student whose desk was the tidiest when he came back. But he didn't actually tell them which day he'd be back at school.

Each kid in the class was excited about the prize. One girl said, "I plan to clean my desk every Monday from now on!"

"But," someone said, "what if he comes back on a Friday?"

For a moment she was silent. Then she said, "I know what I'll do. I'll just keep it clean!"

Jesus has said a similar thing to us: "I am coming soon" (REVELATION 22:20). We might think "soon" is an odd way to describe what has become a 2,000 year wait! But we should understand this statement to be less about 'speed' and more about the certainty of Jesus' return. In other words, Jesus' second coming is not *pending*, but *active*—right now. He *is* coming!

So we are to "eagerly" wait for Him (PHILIPPIANS 3:20). Eagerly waiting for Jesus means that even today—an ordinary and maybe boring day—we can be excited about meeting Jesus face to face. Is that what defines your days? Is that what you are looking forward to? Because if you're excited about Jesus' return, it'll show in how you live. "You ought to live holy and godly lives as you look forward to the day of God" (2 PETER 3:11-12). That's something of what it means to "be ready" (MATTHEW 24:44).

HB

COMPLETING THE PICTURE . . .

When Jesus calls Himself "the Son of Man" (MATTHEW 24:44) He is actually referring back to one of Daniel's visions of Him. Daniel wrote: "In my vision at night I looked, and there before me was one like a **son of man**, coming with the clouds of heaven . . . He was given authority, glory and sovereign power; all nations and peoples of every language worshipped him . . . His kingdom is one that will never be destroyed" (DANIEL 7:13-14). By using this title, Jesus was telling people He is God's promised King!

JESUS COULD COME AT ANY TIME—ARE WE LOOKING FORWARD TO HIS RETURN ALL THE TIME?

IT'S UP TO GOD

BIBLE: MATTHEW 6:5-15
Your will be done (V.10).

Nate and Sherilyn enjoyed their stop at an *omakase* restaurant while on holiday. Omakase is a Japanese word for "I will leave it up to you." It means customers let the chef choose their meal. Even though it was their first time to try this type of food and it sounded risky, they loved everything the chef chose and made for them.

That idea could carry over to our attitude towards God in our prayer requests: "I will leave it up to You." The disciples saw that Jesus "often withdrew to lonely places" to pray (LUKE 5:16), so they asked Him one day to teach them how to pray. He told them to ask for their daily needs, forgiveness and the way out of temptation. Part of His teaching also showed an attitude of surrender: "Your will be done, on earth as it is in heaven" (MATTHEW 6:10).

We can give all our needs to God because He wants to hear what's on our minds—and He loves to give. But being human and limited, we don't always know what's best, so it only makes sense to ask for God's provision as we submit to whatever His will and plan might be. We can leave the answer to Him, confident that He's trustworthy and will lead us the right way, even if it isn't what we would have chosen for ourselves.

AC

WHAT I'M THANKFUL FOR . . .
Thank You, God, for carrying me and my needs close to Your heart.
I surrender my life and those I love to Your care.

SURRENDERING TO GOD MEANS LETTING HIM LEAD THE WAY.

GOD'S SPECIAL TREASURE

BIBLE: I PETER 2:4-10

But you are . . . God's special possession (V.9).

Imagine a throne room. Seated on the throne is a great king. A large, impressive chest sits at the king's feet. From time to time the king reaches down and runs his hands through the contents. What's in it? The rarest, most expensive jewels, gold and gemstones you've ever seen! This chest holds the king's treasures, a collection that brings him great happiness.

The Hebrew word for this treasure is *segulah*, and it means "special possession". That word is found in such Old Testament passages as Exodus 19:5, Deuteronomy 7:6 and Psalm 135:4, where it refers to the people of Israel. But that same image shows up in the New Testament in Peter's first letter. He's describing the "people of God", those who "have received mercy" (1 PETER 2:10), a collection of people now beyond the nation of Israel. In other words, he's talking about those who believe in Jesus, both Jew and gentile. And he writes, "You are . . . God's special possession" (V.9).

Imagine that! The great and powerful King of heaven thinks of you as an important part of His special treasure. He has rescued you from the grip of sin and death. He claims you as His own. The King's voice says, "This one I love. This one is mine." *JB*

THINKING IT OVER . . .

Can you think of a time when someone genuinely called you "special"? How did it make you feel? What does it mean for you to know that this is exactly how God thinks of you?

GOD LOVES TO CALL YOU HIS OWN SPECIAL POSSESSION!

HOLY!

BIBLE: PSALM 48

Holy, holy, holy is the LORD Almighty; the whole earth is full of his glory
(ISAIAH 6:3).

God can do nothing that goes against His good, perfect, pure character—in other words, His holiness. Since He is holy by nature, everything He says and does comes from that perfection. Think about these things:

1. As a holy God, He is perfect. This means we can completely trust Him with our lives, no matter what is going on. We can surrender to His plans and leading because we are confident of the answer to Abraham's question, "Will not the Judge of all the earth do right?" (GENESIS 18:25).

2. As a holy God, He is perfect in His justice and judgement. Those of us who trust Jesus will "receive what is due to us for the things done while in the body, whether good or bad" (2 CORINTHIANS 5:10). Whereas for those who are determined to reject Jesus, we read: "Anyone whose name was not found written in the book of life was thrown into the lake of fire" (REVELATION 20:15).

3. As a holy God, He is perfect in His truthfulness. We can take Him at His Word. Numbers 23:19 says, "God is not human, that he should lie, not a human being, that he should change his mind. Does he speak and then not act? Does he promise and not fulfil?" If God says it, then it is true. So no matter how we feel about ourselves, the Bible reveals the truth of who we are (1 JOHN 3:1).

4. As a holy God, He is perfect in His faithfulness. We read, "Because of the LORD's great love we are not consumed, for his compassions never fail. They are new every morning; great is your faithfulness" (LAMENTATIONS 3:22-23).

We can have total confidence in our good, just, truthful and faithful God. He is holy.

RDH

THINKING IT OVER . . .

How do you feel about God's holiness? Is it something that scares you?
Comforts you? Strengthens you? Inspires you?

FOR THIS GOD IS OUR GOD FOR EVER AND EVER.
PSALM 48:14

WHO KILLED JESUS?

BIBLE: ACTS 2:22-39

Fellow Israelites, listen to this . . . you, with the help of wicked men, put him to death by nailing him to the cross (VV.22-23).

During the Middle Ages, some parts of the badly misguided church killed Jews on their way to free Jerusalem from the Turks. These religious wars are often called The Crusades. The crusaders thought the Jewish people were guilty of Jesus' death and wrongly called them "Christ-killers".

Feelings can run deep even today about the question of who actually killed Jesus. But what does the Bible say? According to Matthew's retelling, it seems like that the Romans were responsible. The Roman governor Pilate allowed Jesus' death, even while saying He was innocent. And Roman soldiers took Him to the cross and executed Him. Yet Peter, preaching several weeks later in Jerusalem, accused the Jews themselves of crucifying Him (ACTS 2:22-24).

But the bigger point is that we are all responsible for Jesus' death. On the cross, Jesus paid the penalty for the sins of both Jews and Romans, as well as for ours (1 PETER 2:24). He died for every person who has fallen short of God's holiness (2 CORINTHIANS 5:15). That is why people who trust Jesus as their Saviour need to remember this truth: it is because of us—personally—that Jesus died.

Jesus died for all of us. Our sins cost Him His life. But by trusting Him, we now have forgiveness, peace with God and unending life with Him.   *DE*

WANT MORE . . . ?

Check out *What happened to the soldiers who killed Jesus?* online at
ourdailybread.org/lookingdeeper

WE ARE ALL RESPONSIBLE FOR JESUS' DEATH; BUT EVEN IF WE WERE THE ONLY PERSON IN THE WORLD, HE STILL WOULD HAVE DIED FOR US.

FULLY KNOWN

BIBLE: JEREMIAH 1:1-8
Before I formed you . . . I knew you (V.5).

"You shouldn't be here right now. Someone up there was looking out for you," the accident-recovery driver told my mum after he had pulled her car from the edge of the road—right next to a steep, rocky drop! Mum was pregnant with me at the time. As I grew up, she often told me the story of how God saved both our lives that day, and explained to me that God valued me even before I was born.

None of us escape our omniscient (all-knowing) Creator's attention. Over 2,500 years ago He told the prophet Jeremiah, "Before I formed you in the womb I knew you" (JEREMIAH 1:5). God knows us more deeply than any person ever could and is able to give our lives purpose and meaning unlike any other. He not only made us through His wisdom and power, He provides for every moment of our lives—including the details we often don't even notice: from the beating of our hearts to the breaths we take. Reflecting on how our heavenly Father holds together every aspect of our lives, David said, "How precious to me are your thoughts, God!" (PSALM 139:17).

God is closer to us than our last breath. He made us, knows us and loves us. He is always worthy of our worship and praise.

JB

WHAT I'M THANKFUL FOR . . .
You are amazing, God! Thank You for holding me up and getting me through every moment of the day!

IN HIM WE LIVE AND MOVE AND HAVE OUR BEING.
ACTS 17:28

RIGHT BESIDE YOU

BIBLE: DEUTERONOMY 4:5-8
The LORD our God is near us whenever we pray to him (V.7).

Each day at a post office in Jerusalem, the staff sort through piles of letters. But many end up in a box which has been labelled: "Letters to God".

About a thousand of these letters reach Jerusalem each year, addressed simply to God or Jesus. Unsure what to do with them, one member of staff began taking the letters to Jerusalem's Western Wall to have them placed between its stone blocks with other written prayers. Most of the letters ask for a job, a partner or good health. Some want forgiveness, others just offer thanks. One man asked God if his wife who had died could appear in his dreams because he wanted to see her again. Each sender believed God would listen, if only He could be reached.

The Israelites learned much as they travelled through the wilderness. One lesson was that their God wasn't like the other gods of the surrounding nations—distant, deaf, limited or found only in certain places. No, "the LORD our God is near us whenever we pray to him" (DEUTERONOMY 4:7). What other people could claim that? This was life-changing news!

God doesn't live in Jerusalem. He's close by us, wherever we are, whoever we are (ACTS 17:27). Some still need to discover this amazing truth. If only each of those letters could be sent this reply: God is right beside you. Just talk to Him.

SV

THINKING IT OVER . . .
God's closeness to us is an amazing gift. How can you avoid taking it for granted?
Who in your life needs to know of God's readiness to hear their prayers?

GOD HEARS OUR EVERY PRAYER, BECAUSE HE IS RIGHT HERE WITH US.

TOGETHER WE WIN

BIBLE: EXODUS 17:8-13

Two are better than one . . . If either of them falls down, one can help the other up (ECCLESIASTES 4:9-10).

In the middle of the night, Pastor Samuel Baggaga got a phone call asking him to come to the home of someone in his church. When he arrived, he found the house was on fire. The man who had called him, though burned, had re-entered the home to rescue his child—and came out with his unconscious daughter. The hospital, in this rural Ugandan setting, was six miles away. With no cars or public transport, the pastor and the dad started running to the hospital with the girl. When one of them got tired from carrying her, the other one took over. Together they made the journey; the dad and his daughter were treated and then fully recovered.

In Exodus 17:8-13 God created a great victory that included the efforts of Joshua, who led the soldiers on the battlefield; and Moses, who kept his hands raised to heaven while holding the staff of God. When Moses's hands grew tired, Aaron and Hur helped him by each holding up one of his hands until the setting of the sun and the defeat of the enemy.

The value of working together can never be underestimated. God, in His kindness, puts people in our lives for us to support and be supported by. Listening ears; helping hands; correcting words; loving prayers—we can give and receive these essential gifts. Together we win and God gets the glory!   *AJ*

WHAT I'M THANKFUL FOR . . .

Father, thank You for the people You've put in my life and for those You've allowed me to share my life with. Thank You that I never have to walk alone.

CHURCH IS MADE UP OF ALL OUR TEAMMATES!

WHEN WE PRAISE

BIBLE: ACTS 16:25-34

At once all the prison doors flew open, and everyone's chains came loose (V.26).

When nine-year-old Will was kidnapped from his front garden he sang his favourite praise song over and over again. During the three-hour abduction, Will ignored the kidnapper every time he told him to be quiet as they drove around. Eventually, the kidnapper let Will out of the car unharmed. Later, Will said that he felt his fear turn into peace as he sang, while the kidnapper seemed to just get more and more agitated.

Will's reaction to his scary situation reminds me of a situation Paul and Silas found themselves in. After being beaten and thrown into jail, they reacted by "praying and singing hymns to God, and the other prisoners were listening to them. Suddenly there was such a violent earthquake that the foundations of the prison were shaken. At once all the prison doors flew open, and everyone's chains came loose" (ACTS 16:25-26).

When he saw this awesome display of power, the jailer believed in the God of Paul and Silas, and his entire household was baptised along with him (VV.27-34). Through their praise, both physical and spiritual chains were broken that night.

When we're in trouble, we may not always experience such a dramatic rescue like Paul and Silas, or like Will. But we know that God answers the praises of His people! When we focus on Him, through our prayers and songs, He gives us His peace and strength for what lies ahead.   RO

THINKING IT OVER . . .

What lessons do you learn from Paul and Silas' decision to sing praise to God during their imprisonment? How do you normally react when things are going wrong? What can you do to copy their attitude when times are hard?

"[GOD], YOU ARE HOLY, ENTHRONED IN THE PRAISES OF ISRAEL" PSALM 22:3 NKJV

DESTROY THIS HOUSE

BIBLE: JOHN 2:13-25

Destroy this temple, and I will raise it again in three days (V.19).

A demolition company bulldozed the wrong building. It turns out the owner of the house that was meant to be demolished nailed his own house number on to a neighbour's house so the company would destroy that home instead!

Jesus did the opposite. He was on a mission to let his own 'house' be torn down for the sake of others. Imagine the scene and how confused everyone must have been, including Jesus' own disciples. Picture them eyeing one another as He challenged the religious leaders: "Destroy this temple," Christ said, "and I will raise it again in three days" (JOHN 2:19). The leaders replied in fury, "It has taken forty-six years to build this temple, and you are going to raise it in three days?" (V. 20). But Jesus knew He was referring to the 'temple' of His own body (V. 21). They didn't.

They didn't understand He had come to show that the harm we do to ourselves and to one another would ultimately fall on Him. He would pay for it in full.

God has always known our hearts far better than we do. So He didn't trust the fullness of His plans even to those who saw His miracles and believed in Him (VV. 23–25). Then, as now, He was slowly revealing the love and goodness in Jesus' words that we couldn't understand even if He told us. *MDH*

TO PRAY ABOUT . . .

Father in heaven, please help me to believe that You are always working in the background doing far more—and much better—than I know or understand.

EVEN KNOWING HOW BAD WE CAN BE, JESUS LOVES US ENOUGH TO TAKE THE BLAME IN FULL.

A WIDE, SWEEPING GRACE

BIBLE: ISAIAH 44:21-23
I have swept away your offences (V.22).

Alexa, Amazon's voice-controlled assistant, has an interesting feature: it can delete everything you say. Whatever you've asked Alexa to do, whatever you've asked Alexa to find out, one simple sentence ("Delete everything I said today") sweeps it all clean—as if it never happened. It's too bad that the rest of life doesn't have this function! Every mean word, every selfish act, every moment we wish we could delete—we'd just speak the words, and the entire mess would disappear.

There's good news though. God does offer each of us a clean start. Only, He goes far deeper than just deleting our mistakes or dark secrets. God provides *redemption*, a deep healing that transforms us and makes us brand new. "Return to me," He says, "I have redeemed you" (ISAIAH 44:22). Even though Israel rebelled and disobeyed, God reached out to them with amazing mercy. He "swept away [their] offences like a cloud, [their] sins like the morning mist" (V.22). He gathered all their shame and sin and washed them away with His wide, sweeping grace.

God will do the same with our guilt and wrongs. There's no mistake He can't mend, no hurt He can't heal. God's mercy cleans and redeems the most painful places in our lives—even the ones we've hidden away. His mercy sweeps away all our guilt, washes away every regret.

wc

THINKING IT OVER . . .
Where are you most aware that you've messed up? How does the picture of God sweeping away all your sin and shame give you hope? Why not spend some time this week reflecting on 2 Corinthians 5:21.

THERE IS NOTHING IN OUR LIVES THAT JESUS CAN'T PAY FOR ON THE CROSS. BUT HAVE WE TRUSTED HIM TO SAVE US YET?

DRIVING THROUGH LOOPHOLES

BIBLE: MARK 7:6-13

You have let go of the commands of God and are holding on to human traditions (V.8).

A police officer asked a driver if she knew why he had stopped her. "No idea!" she said in surprise. "You were texting while driving," the officer told her. "No, no!" she protested, holding up her phone as evidence. "It's an email."

The law says people can't text while driving; but that doesn't mean there is a loophole that allows them to email! The point of the law isn't to stop texting, but to stop distracted driving in general.

Jesus accused the religious leaders of His day of coming up with even worse loopholes. "You have a fine way of setting aside the commands of God," He said, quoting the command to "Honour your father and mother" as evidence (MARK 7:9-10). Pretending to be religious and godly, these greedy leaders were ignoring the needs of their families. They simply said their money was "devoted to God"—and ta-dah!—suddenly they didn't have a penny to spare to help out Mum and Dad in their old age. Jesus quickly got to the heart of the problem. "You nullify the word of God by your tradition," He said (v.13). They weren't honouring God; and they were dishonouring their parents.

Rationalising our own selfishness can be subtle. We can be so quick to avoid responsibilities, explain away selfish behaviour and apply the Bible's commands to others rather than ourselves. If that sounds familiar, then maybe we should spend some time asking God to help us change. Jesus offers us the opportunity to swap our selfishness for love, willingness and the strength of His Spirit so we can follow His good ways.

TG

TO PRAY ABOUT . . .

Dear God, I need Your help to live in a way that is genuine, kind and loving. I am so tempted to be selfish and excuse myself from looking out for others. Help me to live in step with Your Spirit of love, truth and holiness.

WE ARE EITHER SERVING GOD OR OURSELVES IN HOW WE LIVE. WHO DO YOU LIVE FOR?

DEATH ZONE

BIBLE: 2 SAMUEL 11:1-17

But David remained in Jerusalem (V.1).

In 2019, a climber saw his last sunrise from the peak of Mount Everest. He survived the dangerous climb, but the high altitude squeezed his heart, and he died on the way back down. One medical expert warns climbers not to think of the summit as their journey's end. They must get up and down quickly, remembering "they're in the Death Zone."

David survived his dangerous climb to the top. He killed lions and bears, defeated Goliath, dodged Saul's spear and army, and conquered Philistines and Ammonites to become king.

But David forgot he was in the death zone. At the peak of his success, as "the LORD gave David victory wherever he went" (2 SAMUEL 8:6), he committed adultery and murder. His mistake? He stayed on the mountaintop. When his army set out for new challenges, he "remained in Jerusalem" (11:1). David once had volunteered to fight Goliath; now he relaxed in the victory and comforts of his triumphs.

It's hard to stay grounded when everyone, including God, says you're special (7:11-16). If we've done well at something, let's celebrate it and thank God, giving Him the praise. And let's remember that in the best moments of our lives we're also in the Death Zone. If we stay there too long, we may well get comfortable with feeling that good and start making very selfish choices to keep the feeling going.

Let's remember to come down the mountain, looking for the next challenge or opportunity God has planned for us (EPHESIANS 2:10).   *MW*

THINKING IT OVER . . .

Are you climbing a mountain or near the top?
How can you avoid the dangers that come with doing well?

EACH MOUNTAIN IS THERE TO PREPARE US FOR THE NEXT ONE; THEY'RE NOT THERE FOR US TO GET COMFY ON.

PROTECT THE IMAGE

BIBLE: JAMES 3:7-12

With the tongue . . . we curse human beings, who have been made in God's likeness (V.9).

- -

Emma handed out invitations for her party to her classmates. Everyone thanked her except Tom, who grabbed the invitation and ripped it in half. Emma yelled, "What are you doing?!" "I'm not going to come to your party," said Tom, "so why pretend?" Emma replied, "Because that's not how you treat people!"

Emma's right. That's a horrible way to treat another person. But it's also how we sometimes treat God. James noticed how we praise God and then turn around and "curse human beings, who have been made in God's likeness" (JAMES 3:9). Our gossip, mean comments and name-calling attack other people who are the image or picture of God.

Many religions guard the image of their gods. Only the true God lets His image loose in the world. His image carriers—us—are weak and often mess up. It's way too easy to attack each other and put our classmates down.

We would never rip up the picture of a friend. Yet we slash at the image of God every time we hurt others with our words. Thankfully this works both ways. If mean words scar the image of God, then kind words uphold and protect it.

How we treat others can be a good indicator of how we view God's image. Do we respect others as being God's creation? Or do we remove God from the picture?

MW

THINKING IT OVER . . .

How do you feel when you learn that others are gossiping about you? How might your words and actions change if you remembered people are the image of God?

OUR WORDS EITHER PROTECT OR ATTACK THE IMAGE OF GOD.

ONE WEEK

BIBLE: MARK 10:32-34

You are looking for Jesus the Nazarene, who was crucified. He has risen! He is not here. See the place where they laid him (MARK 16:6).

What would you do if you only had one week to live? Would you go somewhere special? Spend time with your friends and family?

Knowing He had less than a week to live, Jesus acted very differently than many of us would—bravely making the journey to Jerusalem where He would be killed, while preparing His friends for His death.

On Sunday, the crowds cheered His entrance into Jerusalem (MARK 11:1-11). Monday, He chased thieves out of the temple—calling it "a house of prayer" (V.17). Tuesday, the temple leaders questioned His authority (VV.27-28). The Pharisees and other religious leaders also questioned Him about paying taxes and the greatest commandment (12:13-34). On Wednesday, one of Jesus' disciples, Judas Iscariot, began to plot His death (14:10-11).

On Thursday, after a Passover meal during which Jesus prepared His disciples for life after His death, Judas betrayed Him to the religious leaders who had Him arrested (VV.43-46). On Friday, they handed Jesus over to the Roman authorities who had Him beaten and then crucified on a cross (15:15).

As the reality of Jesus' death hit His followers on Saturday, so did despair— their hopes died with Him. But then came His amazing resurrection on Sunday morning (16:1-7)!

The events of Jesus' last week show that because of Jesus and His love we can face the trials of today in His strength. Jesus' resurrection gives us the ultimate confidence that even the most difficult things in life—even our worst weeks—will not have the final say.

JO

WHAT I'M THANKFUL FOR . . .

Thank You, Jesus, for going to the cross for me. You knew that was how Your week in Jerusalem would end, yet You kept walking towards it because You were determined to save me and make me Yours. Thank You that nothing can defeat You. Now I am Yours, nothing can defeat me either.

JESUS' RESURRECTION SHOWS HE ALWAYS HAS THE LAST WORD.

NOT SO!

BIBLE: LUKE 23:49-56

All those who knew him, including the women who had followed him from Galilee, stood at a distance, watching these things (V.49).

"I wanted somehow to make it not so," said the man, talking about a friend who had died. His words hit home with me. Death stuns and scars us all. We want to undo what can't be undone.

The longing to "make it not so" might well describe how Jesus' followers felt after His death. The gospel accounts say little about those awful hours, but they do tell us about the actions of a few faithful friends.

Joseph, a religious leader who secretly believed in Jesus (SEE JOHN 19:38), suddenly found the bravery to ask Pilate for Jesus' body (LUKE 23:52). Think for a moment what it would take to remove a body from a grisly crucifixion and prepare it for burial (V.53). Think too of the love and bravery of the women who stayed with Jesus every step of the way, even to the tomb (V.55).

These followers weren't expecting a resurrection; they were coming to terms with their loss. The chapter ends without hope, "Then they went home and prepared spices and perfumes [to embalm Jesus' body]. But they rested on the Sabbath in obedience to the commandment" (V.56).

Little did they know that the stage was set for history's most dramatic scene. Jesus was about to do the unimaginable: He would make death itself "not so".

TG

WANT MORE . . . ?

Check out *How can I get through my grief?* online at
ourdailybread.org/lookingdeeper

JESUS MAKES DEATH "NOT SO"!

HOLY BIBLE

LIFE-CHANGING WORD

BIBLE: ISAIAH 55:10-13

So is my word that goes out from my mouth: It will not return to me empty (V.11).

Lily, a Bible translator, was flying home to her country in Asia when she was detained at the airport. Her phone was searched, and when the officials found an audio copy of the New Testament on it, they confiscated the phone and questioned her for two hours. At one point they asked her to play the Bible app, which happened to be set at Matthew 7:1-2: "Do not judge, or you too will be judged. For in the same way you judge others, you will be judged, and with the measure you use, it will be measured to you." Hearing these words in his own language, one of the officers turned pale. Later, she was released and no further action was taken.

We don't know what happened in that official's mind at the airport, but we know that the Bible always achieves what God wants (SEE ISAIAH 55:11). Isaiah spoke these words of hope to God's people when they were captives in a foreign land, promising them that even as the rain and snow make the earth flower and grow, so too does the Bible achieve God's purposes (VV.10-11).

As those who follow Jesus, we can read this bit of the Bible to increase our confidence in God. We may feel that we're facing really tough situations, like Lily with the airport officials, but we can trust that God will act in our lives through the Bible's words to change us and the people around us!

ABP

WANT MORE . . . ?

What is the Bible and what's in it? Why should I trust the Bible? Check out answers to questions like this in *Big questions about . . . the Bible* online at **ourdailybread.org/teen**

GOD IS ALWAYS AT WORK CHANGING LIVES THROUGH HIS WORDS IN THE BIBLE.

ESCAPE

BIBLE: PSALM 55

Cast your cares on the LORD and he will sustain you; he will never let the righteous be shaken (V.22).

A n online news report caught my eye: "Increase in suicide rates in Singapore: male suicides double that of female." The report explained, "According to some psychiatrists, the higher number of suicides among men is not unusual . . . When it comes to dealing with their problems, men don't often look for help, so they end up pushing themselves into a deeper depressive spiral."

David was under terrible strain and pressure as he suffered the attacks of his enemies (PSALM 55:3-5,9-11). But his enemy wasn't some distant nation or army. It was someone who had been his good friend, who he described as "a man like myself, my companion, my close friend, with whom I once enjoyed sweet fellowship at the house of God" (VV.13-14). Having his friend turn against him was a pain that felt too hard to cope with.

David's gut reaction was to escape. He wanted to run away! He wanted to "flee far away" to a "place of shelter" (VV.7-8). I can't help wondering if suicide was one escape option David thought about in his depression.

Thankfully, David chose a different way, because suicide is a permanent solution to temporary problems. He looked for help from God, his real "place of shelter", crying out, "Listen to my prayer, O God . . . My thoughts trouble me and I am distraught" (VV.1-2).

Are you feeling hopeless, distraught or depressed by life's pressures and pain? Do you wish that you could just fly away (V.6)? Then it's time to pray and to fly into the loving arms of God, who rescues you and keeps you safe (VV.16-18). Listen to David's advice: "Cast your cares on the LORD and he will sustain you; he will never let the righteous be shaken" (V.22). *KTS*

THINKING IT OVER . . .

Read about David's betrayal by his son Absalom and his close friend and advisor Ahithophel (2 SAMUEL 15:1-12; 16:15-23). How does this backstory help you understand the pressure and pain he faced? How does David's prayer in Psalm 55 encourage you to find your strength, shelter and hope in God?

RATHER THAN RUNNING AWAY, LET'S RUN TO GOD.

ROYALTY

BIBLE: JOHN 1:9-14

To all who did receive him, to those who believed in his name, he gave the right to become children of God (V.12).

It seems like the closer someone in the British royal family is to the throne, the more we hear about them. Others are almost forgotten. The royal family has a line of succession that includes nearly sixty people. One of them is Lord Frederick Windsor, who's forty-ninth in line for the throne (at time of writing!). Instead of being in the limelight, he quietly goes about his life. Though he works as a financial analyst, he's not considered a 'working royal'—one of the more high-profile family members who are paid for representing the family.

David and Bathsheba's son Nathan (2 SAMUEL 5:14) is another royal who lived outside the limelight. Very little is known about him since his brother Solomon became king. But while the genealogy of Jesus in Matthew mentions Solomon—tracing Joseph's line (MATTHEW 1:1)—Luke's genealogy, which many Bible teachers believe is Mary's family line, mentions Nathan (LUKE 3:31). Even though Nathan didn't rule, he still had a role in God's kingdom.

As Christians we're also royalty. The apostle John wrote that God gave us "the right to become children of God" (JOHN 1:12). Though we may not be in the spotlight, we're children of the King! God says each of us is important enough to represent Him here on earth and to one day reign with Him (2 TIMOTHY 2:11-13). Like Nathan, we may not wear an earthly crown, but we still have a key part to play in God's kingdom.

LW

THINKING IT OVER . . .

How does knowing you're royalty—God's child—make you feel? As a child of the King, what do you see as your responsibilities to the people around you?

WE ARE A KEY PART OF THE GREATEST ROYAL FAMILY TO EVER EXIST.

CHEATERS

BIBLE: MALACHI 3:6-12

Should people cheat God? Yet you have cheated me! But you ask, "What do you mean? When did we ever cheat you?" You have cheated me of the tithes and offerings due to me (VV.8-9 NLT).

As the teacher read through his pupils' exam papers it became clear that the class had cheated and copied each other's answers. So he told them: "Admit that you have cheated, and then the remainder of your classwork will decide your final grade at the end of the year. The school will keep no record of your cheating." Everyone in the class admitted they had cheated.

God told the people of Judah to come clean too. They had been cheating Him (MALACHI 3:8-9). The people, having returned from exile in Babylon, were half-hearted in their relationship with God. The small offerings and tokens of 'love' they were throwing God's way showed how disinterested they really were in Him. Instead of giving God the best of everything as a sign of their love and dependence on Him, they were giving the dregs.

You can almost hear the people of Judah saying, *Hey God, we've been through some tough times lately. Give us a break!* I think we sometimes do the same thing—allowing hard days and difficult situations to be an excuse to push God to the back of our minds while we get on and sort stuff out. But when we do this, we're cheating Him. We are still to give Him the best of us, even on our worst days.

God told His people that He would "open the floodgates of heaven and pour out so much blessing that there will not be room enough to store it" (V.10). And He will do the same for you and me. Even in our tough times. So let's keep Him as our focus, even when we feel like we don't have time, and we will be able to experience the peace of knowing He is with us and leading us through. *TF*

TO PRAY ABOUT . . .

Father, when things are hard and I feel like I don't have time for You, please help me to slow down and focus back on Jesus. You are my shield, strength and provider. Help me to give You my best, even when I'm at my worst, so I can rest in Your goodness.

**EVEN AT OUR WORST,
LET'S NOT CHEAT GOD OUT OF OUR BEST.**

EXAM STRESS

BIBLE: PSALM 23

The LORD is my shepherd, I lack nothing (V.1).

A few of the youth group were preparing for their GCSE exams. And they were stressing out. Their youth leader didn't tell them off for being worried about their exams. At first he just listened. And then he had an idea.

He said to them, "Instead of saying 'I'm worried', stop and say the first line of Psalm 23. Then try and add, 'So I'm worried to death' at the end."

The teenagers turned to that psalm and instantly laughed at how ridiculous it sounded to say, "The Lord is my shepherd, I lack nothing. So I'm worried to death." His advice to them was to keep reading their Bibles every day, even with the pressure of revision, and to make time to reflect on Psalm 23. And when they felt overwhelmed, instead of saying, "I'm stressed out!" or "I'm worried!", they should instead say the opening verse of Psalm 23 first. And then see how their worry sounded.

Later that week, the youth leader got a message from one of the teenagers who had been most stressed out. She had been worrying over a particular exam she had been dreading to take. Her message read, "As I froze with worry, I remembered to say, 'The Lord is my Shepherd . . . so I'm afraid I'll fail!' Suddenly I felt the strangest peace of mind. I laughed at myself, then I took the exam—I think it went well. But it was good to be reminded that God was there with me!"

JY

WANT MORE . . . ?

Check out *Help! My exams are stressing me out!* online at
ourdailybread.org/teen

OUR BIGGEST WORRIES ARE TINY COMPARED TO GOD.

KING OF THE COSMOS

BIBLE: COLOSSIANS 1:15-20

He is before all things, and in him all things hold together (V.17).

As you read this, the moon is circling the earth at 2,300 miles per hour. Even at that speed, it will take it nearly a month to make a full rotation. Meanwhile, despite circling the sun at 66,000 miles per hour, the earth will take a whole year to make one orbit. And our sun is just one of 200 million other suns spinning around the Milky Way at 483,000 miles per hour—it will take them 225 million years to do one circuit. And the Milky Way is but one of 100 billion other galaxies shooting through space at over a million miles an hour. The universe is massive!

The hugeness of our universe reflects God's own awesomeness. It is He who stretched out the stars of heaven, covered the earth with the seas and made the mountains rise (PSALM 104:1-9). "Through everything God made," Paul says, "[we] can clearly see his invisible qualities—his eternal power and divine nature" (ROMANS 1:20 NLT).

Paul knew nothing of the universe being 100 billion galaxies large, but think about what he wrote about Jesus: "In him all things were created: things in heaven and on earth" (COLOSSIANS 1:16). All those galaxies were made by and for Jesus, and He holds them all together in His hands (V.17).

This is mind-boggling! The One who walked this earth 2,000 years ago is the same One who keeps the galaxies spinning today. Jesus isn't just the God of you and me. He's the King of the cosmos. *SV*

THINKING IT OVER . . .

Read Ephesians 4:10, Hebrews 1:2-3 and Revelation 4:11 and spend some time reflecting on Jesus' glory as the Creator of heaven and earth.

LIFE IS NEVER BORING WHEN WE KNOW THE ONE WHO FLUNG THE STARS INTO SPACE!

INNOCENCE

BIBLE: 2 CORINTHIANS 5:14-21
See what great love the Father has lavished on us, that we should be called children of God! (1 JOHN 3:1).

"I'm not who I once was. I'm a new person."

Those simple words from Geoff, spoken to kids at a school assembly, describe the change God made in his life. Once addicted to heroin, Geoff judged himself by his sins and mistakes. But now he sees himself as a child of God.

The Bible encourages us with this promise: "If anyone is in Christ, the new creation has come: the old has gone, the new is here!" (2 CORINTHIANS 5:17). No matter who we've been or what we've done in our past, when we trust Jesus for our salvation and receive the forgiveness offered through His cross, we become someone new. Once the guilt of our sins separated us from God, but He has now "reconciled us to Himself through Christ", "not counting" our sins against us (VV.18-19). We are His dearly loved children (1 JOHN 3:1-2), washed clean and made new in the likeness of His Son.

Jesus makes us brand new. The innocence we have lost through our selfish choices is found again in Him. He frees us from sin and its power, and a new life opens wide before us—where we don't have to live for our misguided, damaging instincts and desires, but "for him who died for [us] and was raised again" (2 CORINTHIANS 5:15). This transforming love means we now live with a new identity and purpose—we show others who Jesus is, so they too can be made brand new!

JB

WHAT I'M THANKFUL FOR . . .
Father, thank You for sending Your Son to save me so that I could be Your child. Please send me to someone who needs to come home to You today!

LOST INNOCENCE IS FOUND AGAIN IN JESUS.

BIBLE: ROMANS 6:13-23

Do not offer any part of yourself to sin as an instrument of wickedness, but rather offer yourselves to God as those who have been brought from death to life (V.13).

Her Christian friends at youth group were all talking about a TV show they'd been watching. So Beth decided to check it out. After just two episodes she was shocked by the show's explicit sex scenes. She stopped watching the show, but couldn't understand why they continued to watch it.

As Christians, the Bible tells us that "Christ has set us free" (GALATIANS 5:1). But how do we live out this freedom—especially as we live for a perfect and holy God who wants us to be like Him? Does our freedom in Jesus mean that it no longer matters what we watch on TV? Or what we look up online? Are films with sex and nudity in something to just shrug our shoulders at and watch anyway?

Paul offered guidelines in the Bible that are still true today. He reminds us that we are only Christians because of God's love and grace. But he also says that this grace of God doesn't mean we can just do whatever we want, knowing we'll be forgiven anyway (ROMANS 6:1-2).

Our lives are no longer enslaved to sin and death (V.22), but our freedom is to be used to show Jesus to the world around us—in every situation and circumstance (including the movies we choose to watch with our friends). Yes we have freedom in what we watch, where we go and what we choose to do with our time . . . But all these things should still be used to please God and show Him at work in our lives. In everything we do, we either offer ourselves to sin or to God. So let's "count [ourselves] dead to sin but alive to God in Christ Jesus" (V.11).   RF

THINKING IT OVER . . .

Read Matthew 6:22-23. What are you filling your eyes with when you watch TV or go online? Is your life being filled with "light" or "darkness"? What sort of things do you think fall into each category? Don't be surprised if you're more easily tempted by the things you fill your mind with.

LIVE AS FREE PEOPLE, BUT DO NOT USE YOUR FREEDOM AS A COVER-UP FOR EVIL; LIVE AS GOD'S SLAVES. 1 PETER 2:16

Seven days in . . . Jesus' mission

WHAT'S IN A NAME?

BIBLE: MATTHEW 1:18-25

She will give birth to a son, and you are to give him the name Jesus, because he will save his people from their sins (V.21).

Gip Hardin, a preacher, named his son after the famous preacher John Wesley, hoping his baby boy would be like his namesake. John Wesley Hardin, however, chose a different path. Claiming to have killed forty-two men, Hardin became one of the most notorious gunfighters and outlaws of the late 1800s.

In the Bible, as in many places today, names hold special meaning. Announcing the birth of God's Son, an angel told Joseph to name Mary's child "Jesus, because he will save his people from their sins" (MATTHEW 1:21). The meaning of Jesus' name—"God saves"—explained His mission to rescue us from sin.

Unlike Hardin, Jesus completely lived up to His name. Through His death and resurrection, He completed His rescue mission. When John came to the end of his retelling of Jesus' life, he said: "These are written that you may believe that Jesus is the Messiah, the Son of God, and that by believing you may have life in his name" (JOHN 20:31). The book of Acts invites everyone to trust Him, for, "Salvation is found in no one else, for there is no other name under heaven given to mankind by which we must be saved" (ACTS 4:12).

Everyone who trusts Jesus' name can enjoy the forgiveness, new life and unending future only He provides. Have you trusted Him?   BC

THINKING IT OVER . . .

If you were named after your purpose in life, what would your name be? Why do you think Jesus promises His people a "new name?" (REVELATION 2:17).

JESUS' NAME IS ALSO HIS MISSION —TO SEEK AND TO SAVE THOSE WHO ARE LOST.

Seven days in . . . Jesus' mission

CORNER OF YOUR EYE

BIBLE: LUKE 9:51-62

As the time approached for him to be taken up to heaven, Jesus resolutely set out for Jerusalem (V.51).

Peripheral vision allows us to be aware of our surroundings while remaining focused on what is in front of us. What we see from 'the corner of our eye' can be useful. But it can become a distraction!

When I read Jesus' story in the gospels, I am always amazed by His determination as He headed towards Jerusalem one last time. Why did He "resolutely set out for Jerusalem" (LUKE 9:51)—or "set His face" (V.51 NKJV)? He was going there to die for me and you.

"As the time approached for him to be taken up to heaven, Jesus resolutely set out for Jerusalem" (V.51). From that moment on, Jesus' eyes were on the cross: His death for us and His resurrection afterwards. Everything else became part of His peripheral vision.

A few people on the road said they wanted to follow Him (VV.57-62). Jesus said to them: "No one who puts a hand to the plough and looks back is fit for service in the kingdom of God" (V.62). The point was that we can't move ahead while looking at what we've left behind. If we're following Jesus, He has to be our focus.

Neither the praises of the people (19:37-38) or their shouts of hatred (23:21) could keep Jesus from His goal "to give his life as a ransom for many" and to pay the price to set us free (MATTHEW 20:28). Where is our focus today?   DM

THINKING IT OVER . . .

What is your focus on generally? Is it Jesus or something else? What do you think it means to be people of light who "put aside the deeds of darkness" (ROMANS 13:12). How do we "clothe [ourselves] with the Lord Jesus Christ" so that we don't focus on our selfish desires (V.14)?

WHOEVER WANTS TO BE MY DISCIPLE MUST DENY THEMSELVES AND TAKE UP THEIR CROSS AND FOLLOW ME. MATTHEW 16:24

Seven days in . . . Jesus' mission

THE HOLY SPIRIT

BIBLE: JOHN 16:7-15

When he, the Spirit of truth, comes, he will guide you into all the truth (V.13).

As I got on the aeroplane to fly to a country over a thousand miles from my home and family, I felt nervous and alone. But during the flight, I remembered how Jesus promised His followers the comforting presence of the Holy Spirit.

Jesus' friends must have felt confused when He told them, "It is for your good that I am going away" (JOHN 16:7). Having witnessed His miracles and learned from His teaching, how could they possibly be better off without Him? But Jesus told them that if He left, then the Helper—the Holy Spirit—would come.

Jesus, nearing His last hours on earth, talked with His disciples in John 14-17 (during their last meal together). He wanted to help them understand what was about to happen: His death, resurrection and return to heaven. Central in this conversation was the coming Holy Spirit (14:16-17) who would be with them (15:15), teach them (V.26), keep pointing them to Jesus as their Saviour and hope (V.26), and guide them (16:13).

If we have put our trust in Jesus, we have been given this gift of His Spirit living within us—that's what it means to be "born again" into a brand new life (JOHN 3:3). From Him we get so much: He helps us see our sin so we can say sorry to God and change how we live. He brings us comfort when we are hurting, strength when temptation is attacking us, the eagerness to listen to (and understand) God's teaching in the Bible, confidence in our future, and a new way of dealing with other people (SEE GALATIANS 5:22-23). We probably won't see these changes overnight—the Holy Spirit will be working in us and transforming us the rest of our lives! But we can thank God that He always lives in us by His Spirit.

ABP

WANT MORE . . . ?

What does the Holy Spirit do? What does it mean to be filled with the Holy Spirit? Check out answers to questions like this in *Big questions about . . . the Holy Spirit* online at **ourdailybread.org/teen**

WITHOUT THE HOLY SPIRIT,
WE COULD NEVER LIVE THE CHRISTIAN LIFE.

Seven days in . . . Jesus' mission

THE CROSS

BIBLE: HEBREWS 12:1-4

For the joy that was set before him he endured the cross, scorning its shame, and sat down at the right hand of the throne of God (V.2).

One time I was in Australia I got to see the Southern Cross. It was a clear night, and the constellation of stars was really bright. Seafarers began relying on it as early as the 15th century for direction through the seas. It's quite a small collection of stars, but it is visible most of the year.

Isn't it amazing to think that the very God who created those stars actually allowed Himself to be hung on a wooden cross to die for the people He created? Hebrews 12:2 tells us to "[fix] our eyes on Jesus, the pioneer and perfecter of faith. For the joy that was set before him he endured the cross, scorning its shame, and sat down at the right hand of the throne of God."

The wonder of the cross is that while we were still in our sins—enemies of God (EPHESIANS 2:1-5)—our Saviour died for us (ROMANS 5:8). Now, as soon as we put our trust in Jesus, we are made right with God, even being called His children (1 JOHN 3:1). He gives us a brand new life, identity, purpose and future— right now! He comes and makes His home in us (JOHN 14:23) so that we can live our best life (JOHN 10:10). All because Jesus died in our place. What incredible love! What an amazing gift!

BC

WHAT I'M THANKFUL FOR . . .

Thank You, Jesus, for taking my place on the cross. I don't deserve Your love; I've done nothing to earn it. I am so in awe that You would take it on Yourself to save me and make me Your own. Thank You that Your resurrection gives me new life now with You—and new life forever in Your home!

JESUS' DEATH AND RESURRECTION ARE THE VERY CENTRE OF WHO WE ARE.

Seven days in . . . Jesus' mission

JESUS' GRAVE

BIBLE: LUKE 24:1-12
He is not here; he has risen! (V.6).

In one documentary a guy claimed there was evidence that disproved Jesus' resurrection. He said that the words "Jesus son of Joseph" found on a tomb near Jerusalem are referring to Jesus of the Bible. He also claims to have identified Jesus' DNA.

How valid are his thoughts? The Israel Antiquities Authority calls them "nonsense". Other secular and religious scholars agree. Jesus and Joseph were common names in first century Judea. And the guy would need actual DNA samples from Jesus to compare with the bones he's found in the tomb! Obviously, that's impossible!

But the arguments in favour of Jesus' resurrection are pretty strong. Most amazing is the fact that every original follower of Jesus (except John) was killed for their belief in Him and His resurrection. They changed from being confused and grieving to being ablaze with the news that Jesus had risen again. Their message about Jesus coming back to life was very offensive to people; and they faced horrible opposition and even death (ACTS 2:29-32). If Jesus had not been raised from the dead, why did His friends choose to die for a lie?

Two thousand years ago, Jesus' friends were eyewitnesses to the real tomb of Jesus—and that there was no body to be found. The angels told them, "Why do you look for the living among the dead? He is not here; he has risen! " (LUKE 24:5-6). When they met Him after His resurrection, their lives were never the same again (JOHN 20:24-29)!

DF

WANT MORE . . .
Check out *Did Jesus really rise from the dead?* online at
ourdailybread.org/lookingdeeper

THE RESURRECTION IS A FACT OF HISTORY THAT DEMANDS A DECISION.

Seven days in . . . Jesus' mission

THE ASCENSION

BIBLE: HEBREWS 4:9-16

Since we have a great high priest who has ascended into heaven, Jesus the Son of God, let us hold firmly to the faith we profess (v.14).

Jesus' ascension back into heaven (ACTS 1:9-11) is probably the bit of His story we think about the least. It was probably a big moment for His friends to watch Him rise up into the sky and disappear behind a cloud—but is there any more to the story than their amazement?

I recently read these words from one Christian writer: "The ascension is not only a great fact of the New Testament, but a great factor in the life of Jesus and us. We can't have a complete view of Jesus unless the ascension and its consequences are included."

He then went on to talk about what the ascension actually means for us. It shows Jesus completed His rescue mission. He has now "sat down at the right hand of the throne of the Majesty in heaven" (HEBREWS 8:1), because the work of salvation is done! He is now the "head over everything for the church" (EPHESIANS 1:22), our representative in heaven (1 TIMOTHY 2:5), with us by His Spirit (MATTHEW 28:20) and working through us to bring people from all over the world into His family (VV.19-20).

Think of it! Jesus not only died, but He came back to life, went back to the Father, represents us in heaven right now and will return as He went (ACTS 1:11).

RDH

COMPLETING THE PICTURE . . .

The Most Holy Place in the temple was a special place of God's presence. This chamber could only be entered by the high priest on the Day of Atonement each year (SEE LEVITICUS 16). The priest would enter the Most Holy Place with smoke (from the altar of incense) to help shield his view and sprinkle blood as payment for sin (HEBREWS 9:7). Anyone who entered this chamber when they were not supposed to would die.

Jesus has entered heaven (the real Most Holy Place) as the High Priest who "truly meets our need—one who is holy, blameless, pure, set apart from sinners, exalted above the heavens. Unlike the other high priests, he does not need to offer sacrifices day after day, first for his own sins, and then for the sins of the people. He sacrificed for their sins once for all when he offered himself" (HEBREWS 7:26-27). Now we can enter and live in God's presence "with confidence" (4:16).

JESUS WHO DIED TO SAVE US NOW LIVES TO KEEP US.

Seven days in . . . Jesus' mission

JESUS IS COMING

BIBLE: 1 THESSALONIANS 4:13-18

For the Lord himself will come down from heaven, with a loud command, with the voice of the archangel and with the trumpet call of God (V.16).

I heard one Christian speaker once say, "The topic of the Jesus' return in the New Testament is like a mountain range that takes over the whole view of the landscape."

He went on to say, "No matter what road you take, no matter what paths you tread, you will find the mountain bursting on your vision at every turn of the way, and at every parting of the hills. What first struck me in reading the New Testament was this: whatever topic, issue or passage I was thinking about, I found it always pointing me towards (and being fulfilled by) Jesus' return. Everything in the Christian life and the Bible's teaching leads to that mountain."

Did you know that there are more than 300 references to Jesus' return in the New Testament? One fact is clear—Jesus is coming back. Each day we are getting closer to that moment. Today could be the day!

Are you ready? Knowing that Jesus could return at any moment is a great hope and a comfort to all who trust in Him (1 THESSALONIANS 4:18; 5:11; TITUS 2:13). But He is also coming in fiery judgement on those who don't know Him and who reject the gospel (2 THESSALONIANS 1:7-9). If you have trusted Jesus, there is nothing to fear in His return—but it gives us a real sense of urgency to share the gospel with the people we know.

RDH

WANT MORE . . . ?

What did Jesus teach? Is Jesus the only way to heaven? Check out answers to questions like this in *Big questions about . . . Jesus' story* online at
ourdailybread.org/teen

[ENCOURAGE] ONE ANOTHER—AND ALL THE MORE AS YOU SEE THE DAY APPROACHING. HEBREWS 10:25

WHEN IT'S NOT FAIR

BIBLE: I SAMUEL 24:1-19

May the LORD judge between you and me. And may the LORD avenge the wrongs you have done to me, but my hand will not touch you (V.12).

My anger burned inside me when a friend hurt me, blamed me for everything and then gossiped about me. I wanted everyone to know what she'd done. I wanted her to hurt in the same way she had hurt me. I was so full of bitterness and anger that I got a tension headache which made my head feel like it was about to explode. But as I began praying for my pain to go away, the Holy Spirit challenged me. How could I look to get my own back while at the same time asking God for relief? If I believed God would care for me, why wouldn't I trust Him to handle this situation? Knowing that hurting people often hurt other people, I asked God to help me forgive my friend. Though our friendship ended, God gave me peace.

The psalmist David understood the difficulty of trusting God while being unfairly treated. Though David did his best to be loving and serve well, King Saul was jealous of him and wanted to murder him (1 SAMUEL 20:27-32; 24:1-2). David suffered a lot during those years before God finally gave him the throne—but still he chose to trust God instead of trying to get even or sort things out himself (VV.3-7). He did his part to offer peace in his relationship with Saul—and then left the results in God's hands (VV.8-22)

It is hurtful and frustrating when life is unfair and people get away with doing bad things to us. But by trusting God and knowing He takes care of us (and the people who have hurt us), we can forgive as He's forgiven us and live in the peace only He can give.

XD

THINKING IT OVER . . .

How can trusting that God is perfect, loving, good and in control help us when it feels like other people are just getting away with how they treat us? Who do you need to forgive and trust to God's mighty and merciful hands? When will you do this?

WHEN THINGS AREN'T FAIR, WE CAN TRUST GOD, THE GOOD AND PERFECT JUDGE OF THE EARTH.

WE NEED EACH OTHER

BIBLE: HEBREWS 10:19-25

He went to Nazareth, where he had been brought up, and on the Sabbath day he went into the synagogue, as was his custom. He stood up to read (LUKE 4:16).

W hat's the point of going to church? Have you ever wondered about why we go each Sunday, and meet for Bible studies and youth group during the week? After all, we can get everything we need on our phones and laptops: there are sermons, Bible reading plans, forums for our questions, blogs of people's journeys with God . . . It can be tempting to stop meeting up with other Christians altogether.

How different from Jesus! He regularly went along to the synagogue, where the Jews held their services and read the Bible (LUKE 4:16). But today, many people ignore the example He lived out. They settle for a way of life where they try to go it alone, without other people to pray with them, share their struggles, help them read the Bible and give them godly advice.

Meeting with other Christians is uplifting and reassuring when we share openly and honestly. It may not be that Sunday services always offer this freedom and support, but that's why smaller mid-week meet-ups are so important. Through services, Bible studies, youth group, prayer meetings and one-to-ones we get the teaching, inspiration and personal support we need to keep close to Jesus through everything.

We need our own personal time with God. But the Bible also warns us not to "[give] up meeting together" (HEBREWS 10:25). We need to spend time together to "spur one another on towards love and good deeds" (V.24). We need to make it our habit to spend time with other Christians. We need each other. *VG*

WANT MORE . . . ?

Check out *Do I have to go to church?* online at **ourdailybread.org/teen**

THE CHRISTIAN LIFE WAS NEVER MEANT TO BE LIVED ALONE.

FOR BAD PEOPLE

BIBLE: EPHESIANS 2:1-10

It is by grace you have been saved, through faith—and this is not from yourselves, it is the gift of God—not by works, so that no one can boast (VV.8-9).

Lots of us probably know the song "Amazing Grace". But do we know what "grace" is? Could you explain it if someone asked?

One day when one Christian preacher was studying the meaning of God's grace, he ran into the street and shouted to the first guy he saw, "Do you know grace?" Confused, the man replied, "Grace who?" The preacher then explained what he had learned: God has compassion on sin-sick people and freely offers them forgiveness and new life through trusting Jesus, even though they don't deserve it. That's grace!

I heard about a guy who had lived a hard life and died without understanding the message of God's grace. A church leader had talked to him and encouraged him to come to church, but he always said, "I'm too bad." He didn't know that God's grace is for the bad, the messy, the absolute worst!

In Paul's letter to the Ephesians, he bluntly described their pre-Christian lives as being "dead in . . . sins" (EPHESIANS 2:1). Then he used two hope-filled words: but God (V.4). Paul explains that even though we are dead and deserve judgement, God's mercy and grace provide forgiveness and new life through Jesus. Salvation is through trusting Jesus, not through being good enough (VV.8-9). God's grace means anyone—absolutely anyone—can be rescued and made new by Jesus, no matter what they have done.

Let's help others to understand that God's salvation is for bad, messed up people—and that includes all of us. That's what makes God's grace so amazing!

JY

THINKING IT OVER . . .

How would you explain what God's grace is in your own words? How does it encourage you that you have been saved by Jesus' works and not your own?

THE FIRST STEP TO RECEIVING A NEW LIFE WITH JESUS IS TO ADMIT THAT WE DON'T DESERVE IT.

LIVING PEACEFULLY

BIBLE: GENESIS 26:14-22

If it is possible, as far as it depends on you, live at peace with everyone
(ROMANS 12:18).

Isaac lived amongst the Philistines, who turned out to be bad-tempered neighbours. He had grown so rich and powerful that they felt intimidated by him and asked him to leave their lands. Being "too powerful" for them (GENESIS 26:16), Isaac could have said "No" and done whatever he wanted. But he agreed to move into a nearby valley where his father Abraham had dug some wells years before.

The Philistines had stopped up the wells after Abraham died. Each time Isaac reopened a well they took it for themselves, even though they had not been using it. They were just being sneaky and bad-tempered. But Isaac kept moving on until he found a place where the Philistines were happy to leave him alone.

I've met people like that. When my brothers and I played catch as kids, we had to be very careful about our throws, because our next-door neighbour would keep any balls that went into his garden.

It's difficult to like those kind of people, but Jesus went so far as to say that we must love them, pray for them and be good to them (MATTHEW 5:44). It may not be easy, and those argumentative people may not change. Yet, according to Romans 12:18, we must still do all we can to live peacefully with everyone. *HVL*

TO PRAY ABOUT . . .

Dear God, please help me to do my best to live at peace with everyone, even when other people seem like they are out to get me. Give me the patience to follow Isaac's example and move on when others are looking to just wind me up.

TRY TO LIVE AT PEACE WITH OTHERS EVEN THOUGH THEY MAY WANT TO FIGHT WITH YOU.

THE BEACON

BIBLE: MARK 6:45-52

He saw the disciples straining at the oars, because the wind was against them.
Shortly before dawn he went out to them, walking on the lake (V.48).

When a helicopter crashed on a steep, cold mountainside, the pilots survived but were seriously injured. The frozen afternoon stretched towards an even more freezing night. The situation seemed hopeless—until a rescue helicopter appeared, its searchlights lighting up the darkness. It spotted the wreckage, landed nearby and carried them off to safety.

"How did you know where we were?" an injured man asked. "The homing beacon on your aircraft," the rescuers told him. "It went off automatically when you went down. All we had to do was follow it."

The disciples of Jesus also knew the joy and relief of being rescued. They had been struggling as they rowed their boat against wind and waves during a dark night on the Sea of Galilee (MARK 6:45-47). Then Jesus came to them, walking on the water, and calmed the sea (VV.48-51).

We all go through times when everything feels dark and hopeless. We can't help ourselves, and it seems that no one else can either. Maybe we feel like no one really understands how terrified and exhausted we are. No one, that is, except Jesus.

When we've messed up, feel lonely or are spiralling into depression, Jesus knows it. Our cries for help are beacons that bring Him to our side—right when we need Him most. *DE*

THINKING IT OVER . . .

How did the disciples react when they first saw Jesus in this story (MARK 6:50)? How did Jesus calm and reassure them (V.50)? What was their fear replaced with (V.51)? How do you react to Jesus' power and control? How can focusing on His rescuing power change the way you view dark times?

JESUS ANSWERS EVEN THE QUIETEST CRY FOR HELP.

FOCUS

BIBLE: COLOSSIANS 3:1-11
Set your minds on things above, not on earthly things (V.2).

A pilot explained, "One of the most difficult lessons to teach new pilots about landing on short, hazardous airstrips is to keep their eyes on the good part of the strip rather than on the hazard at the end of it. The natural tendency is to concentrate on the obstacle, the danger, the thing the pilot is trying to avoid. But experience teaches us that pilots who keep their eyes on the hazard will hit it dead centre."

This makes me think of a key truth the Bible teaches us about how we are to live our Christian lives. Instead of concentrating on the sins and selfish things we want to avoid, we are told to focus on our relationship with Jesus—filling our minds with all that He is, all He has done, all He promises. Paul wrote: "Set your minds on things above, not on earthly things" (COLOSSIANS 3:2). We are to get rid of our old ways of thinking, which are all about *me* and what *I* want (VV.5-9) and instead to "put on" new ways of living that are all about knowing Jesus (VV.10-17).

That pilot summed up by saying that experienced pilots focus their attention only on the place they want the plane to land. When Jesus and His ways are the focus of our lives, He will direct how we live and how we grow. It's only when we fill our minds with other stuff, or listen to all the things that want to distract our attention, that we end up way off course. Let's keep reading the Bible and spending quality time with God, as first importance each day. Then we'll have "our eyes on Jesus" (HEBREWS 12:2) and "throw off everything that hinders and the sin that so easily entangles" (V.1).

DM

THINKING IT OVER . . .
What 'hazards' sometimes turn your attention away from Jesus? How can you more deliberately focus on Jesus when other things want to get in the way?

WHEN OUR EYES ARE FIXED ON JESUS, WE'LL BE LESS DISTRACTED BY OTHER THINGS.

HOT OR COLD

BIBLE: REVELATION 3:14-22

I know your deeds, that you are neither cold nor hot. I wish you were either one or the other! So, because you are lukewarm—neither hot nor cold—I am about to spit you out of my mouth (VV.15-16).

I like soup when it is steaming hot and a fizzy drink when it is icy cold. I can't stand either one lukewarm. Jesus has the same attitude towards us. He hates lukewarmness. When speaking to the half-hearted church of Laodicea, He said He wished they would be either cold or hot (REVELATION 3:15).

Some people understand the word "cold" here to mean rejection of Jesus and the gospel, while "hot" means a love for Him. But I don't believe Jesus prefers people to reject Him outright. Instead, in His message to the church in Laodicea, Jesus may have had in mind two springs in the area—the hot mineral springs at Hierapolis and the pure cold water springs in Colosse.

The hot springs were soothing, especially to those who were ill or had aches in their bodies. The cold springs were refreshing to drink. The Christians in the church at Laodicea brought neither healing nor refreshment in how they lived. They were lukewarm and of no use to anyone.

You and I must ask ourselves these questions about what our lives with Jesus look like: do I offer refreshment to other Christians by giving them encouragement? Do I bring healing to others by praying for them, supporting them and offering them hope from the Bible?

We can't help anybody if we are lukewarm. What does that show others about Jesus? If we are not that bothered by Him, why should they be? Jesus wants our relationship with Him to change how we live!

HVL

THINKING IT OVER . . .

What is Jesus' encouragement to the church at Laodicea (REVELATION 3:19)? What is the answer to half-heartedness (VV.19-20)? What would it look like for you to spend some time sitting and 'eating' with Jesus this week?

IF WE'RE HALF-HEARTED ABOUT OUR LIFE WITH GOD, WE NEED TO GO BACK TO THE BIBLE TO BE REMINDED WHO HE IS.

BIBLE: MATTHEW 5:11-16
You are the salt of the earth (V.13).

- -

It's common, cheap and found on lots of dinner tables. Historically it has caused wars, determined global trade routes and paid the salaries of soldiers. Today it is mainly used as a preservative and as seasoning. What is it? Salt!

Jesus, who often used ordinary, everyday things to teach deep truths, talked about salt when He was teaching His disciples how they were to live as people of His kingdom. He said, "You are the salt of the earth" (MATTHEW 5:13).

So how are we to be like salt? We can preserve (look after and protect) the people around us. And we can stand out in this world like seasoning does on our food. As we live for Jesus, we show a completely different (and attractive) way of living to our school, friends and family.

Salt that's put away on a shelf is not doing anyone any good. In a similar way, unless we are actively at work sharing the love, welcome and forgiveness of Jesus, we're not being the salt this world needs. After all, the best place for salt is in the 'mix' of the lives around us.

It can be easy to complain when things go wrong, moan when our friends let us down and point out when others mess up. But salt doesn't work from a distance; salt gets involved and brings a completely different flavour to these situations—the flavour of God's love. *VG*

TO PRAY ABOUT . . .
Father, when I am tempted to hang back or just make comments at a distance, help me to step forward to show Jesus' love in the situations I find myself in.

WE ARE JESUS' PRESENCE ON THE EARTH, SO LET'S GET INVOLVED SO PEOPLE CAN GET TO KNOW HIM!

BEHIND THE SCENES

BIBLE: ESTHER 4:1-4,12-17

Who knows but that you have come to your royal position for such a time as this? (V.14).

One church made a video for YouTube. In the clip, a guy wakes up covered in wrapping paper. As he rips it off, he gives thanks for his life and breath and all the other gifts in his life: his family, food, clean water and many other things we so often take for granted.

Although God isn't mentioned in the video, He's the reason behind the guy's thankfulness. The Bible shows God at work behind the scenes providing every good gift in our lives (JAMES 1:17).

The Bible book of Esther, similarly, is a story that never openly mentions God, yet we see Him clearly working behind every scene. In an unlikely series of events, Esther, a young Jewish woman, becomes the queen of Persia. Later, an official named Haman plots to destroy the Jewish people as revenge for Esther's uncle Mordecai refusing to honour him (ESTHER 3:1-10). Ultimately, what Mordecai tells Esther proves true: "Who knows but that you have come to your royal position for such a time as this?" (4:14). Chapters 5-10 show how God saved His people through her actions and trust in Him.

God is always busy at work in our stories. Even when He seems distant, He is working behind the scenes to provide for us, help us grow and use us for the things He has planned.

AK

WHAT I'M THANKFUL FOR . . .

Dear God, we praise You for all You have given us and for all You have done and continue to do in our lives.

GOD IS THE AUTHOR AND DIRECTOR OF OUR LIVES, EVEN WHEN HE SEEMS SILENT.

A SIN BY ANY OTHER NAME

BIBLE: GENESIS 39:1-9

No one is greater in this house than I am. My master has withheld nothing from me except you, because you are his wife. How then could I do such a wicked thing and sin against God? (V.9).

Joseph found himself in a tricky situation one day when his master's wife tried to get him to sleep with her (GENESIS 39:7). How tempting she must have been to this young guy! Joseph could sleep with her, without anyone knowing . . . or say "No" and face her anger. It must have been hard to do the right thing, yet Joseph flatly refused her. She asked him "day after day" (V.10), even grabbing him by his clothes, "but he left his cloak in her hand and ran out of the house" (V.12). How was he able to turn away from such obvious sexual temptation—especially when it was shoved in his face every day?

Joseph's ability to say "No" came from his clear view of sin and from his love and awe of God. He said to her, "How then could I do such a wicked thing and sin against God?" (V.9).

To Joseph, sin was not just "a mistake". Nor was it a "slip of the tongue" or a "one-off" in a "moment of weakness". These are the sorts of words we sometimes use to make sin seem smaller. But Joseph saw sin for what it was—a serious offence against God, the One who would provide him with what he needed so that he didn't need to grab it for himself. He understood the seriousness of sin.

God's standards are absolutely perfect. It is only when we see that sin is our enemy, not our friend, that we will be motivated to stand against it—even stuff we do in private or think about in the quiet of our own minds. It is our love for God that weakens our love of sin.

Calling sin by a softer name will not change what it is: a rebellion against God that Jesus died to pay for. *CPH*

TO PRAY ABOUT . . .

Dear Jesus, thank You for paying for my sin in full. Help me to see it for what it is, so that my love for You will grow and my love for sin will fade.

THERE'S NO EXCUSE FOR EXCUSING SIN.

CONFESSING

BIBLE: NUMBERS 5:5-8

Any man or woman who wrongs another in any way and so is unfaithful to the LORD is guilty and must confess the sin they have committed (VV.6-7).

Researchers at one university have found that people who have a guilty conscience experience "a powerful urge to wash themselves". To understand this urge, the researchers asked half the study volunteers to talk about things they had done in the past that they were still ashamed of. They were then asked to wash their hands as a symbol of cleaning their conscience. Those who had talked about their shame washed their hands at "twice the rate of those who had not talked about their past".

The Bible tells us about the only way of properly dealing with sin—confession. In the Old Testament, one of the ways the Israelites were supposed to clean themselves and have purity before God and in their community was by confessing their sins (NUMBERS 5:5-8). To confess means: "to speak the same"; "to agree with". When the people confessed to God, they were agreeing with Him that what they did was wrong. But their confession showed the change they wanted to make in their lives, and their trust in God to forgive them and make them clean again. Those who refused to admit their sins just allowed sin to take deeper root within their lives and community.

Admitting our sin means we can know true forgiveness, joy and peace. If we confess our sins, God is faithful to forgive (1 JOHN 1:9).   *MW*

WANT MORE . . . ?

Check out *What does it mean to repent?* online at
ourdailybread.org/lookingdeeper

CONFESSION IS AGREEING WITH GOD ABOUT OUR SIN AND TRUSTING HIM TO MAKE US CLEAN.

UNSEEN

BIBLE: 2 CORINTHIANS 4:16-18

We fix our eyes not on what is seen, but on what is unseen (V.18).

A couple of years ago there was a rare phenomenon called a supermoon. The moon's orbit reached its closest point to the earth in over sixty years, so it looked much bigger and brighter than usual. But as per usual, it was cloudy where I live that day. Although I saw photos from friends in other places, when I looked up, I just had to trust that it was there somewhere, hiding behind the clouds.

The apostle Paul taught the church at Corinth something similar. Even though they were surrounded by difficulties and persecution, he told them to focus firstly on what is unseen, because that is what will last forever. He said their "momentary troubles" achieve "an eternal glory" (2 CORINTHIANS 4:17). So they could fix their eyes "not on what is seen, but on what is unseen" because what is seen will soon fade, but what is unseen will never end (V.18). Paul wanted to see the people in Corinth grow in their trust of God, no matter what they were facing. They might not be able to see Him, but they could believe He was with them and looking after them day by day (V.16).

When I looked at the clouds that day I thought about how God is unseen, yet always with us. And I hoped the next time I was tempted to believe that God was far from me, I would fix my eyes on what is unseen. *ABP*

TO PRAY ABOUT . . .

God, sometimes I feel like You're far from me. Help me to believe the truth that You are always near, whether I feel Your presence or not.

GOD IS ALWAYS NEAR US.

TOUGH TRAINING

BIBLE: 1 TIMOTHY 4:1-9
For physical training is of some value, but godliness has value for all things (V.8).

During my last year of school, I realised I was so unfit that I couldn't run more than thirty seconds before I was totally exhausted. So I made some time each week to work out and use a climbing wall. Near the end of the year, I went for a run, thinking I'd only make it a few minutes. I lasted two miles! The physical training paid off. But it wasn't easy, and I didn't always want to do it. To be completely honest, I sometimes feel the same way about reading and studying the Bible.

In his letters, Paul often used physical training as a picture for godly 'training'. In 1 Timothy 4, he warned Timothy about false teaching: "Have nothing to do with godless myths . . . rather, train yourself to be godly" (1 TIMOTHY 4:7). He then explained what he meant: physical training has some value, "but godliness has value for all things, holding promise for both the present life and the life to come" (V.8).

Through training in godliness—learning to live like Jesus through studying and applying the Bible's words—Timothy and those he led in his church would be "nourished on the truths of the faith and of the good teaching that [they had] followed" (V.6). Although this kind of training can be tough, it helps us to live well and make God-centred choices as our minds are filled with the truth of the Bible.

JS

THINKING IT OVER . . .
In what ways do you struggle with training in godliness?
What are some practical ways you can train regularly?

TRAINING IN GODLINESS MAKES AN IMPACT IN EVERY AREA OF OUR LIVES.

NO MISUNDER-STANDING

BIBLE: ROMANS 8:26-30

We know that in all things God works for the good of those who love him (V.28).

Alexa, Siri and other voice assistants in our smart devices sometimes misunderstand what we're saying. A six-year-old talked to her family's new device about cookies and a dollhouse. Later her mum got an email confirming an order of seven bags of cookies and a £200 dollhouse were on their way to her home. Even a talking parrot in London, whose owner had never bought anything online, somehow ordered a package of golden gift boxes without her knowledge. One person asked their device to "turn on the living room lights," and it replied, "There is no pudding room."

There's no misunderstanding on God's part when we talk with Him. He's never confused, because He knows our hearts better than we do. The Spirit both searches our hearts and understands God's will.

Paul told the churches in Rome that God promises He will accomplish His good purpose of maturing us and making us more like His Son (ROMANS 8:28). Even when, because of "our weakness", we don't know what we need in order to grow, the Spirit prays according to God's will for us (VV. 26–27).

Confused about how to talk to God? Not sure what or how to pray? Say what you can with honesty. The Spirit will help us; and God will never misunderstand. He knows us perfectly.

AC

THINKING IT OVER . . .

What's on your mind right now that you should share with God?
How are you encouraged by the truth that He knows and
understands what you're facing?

GOD UNDERSTANDS EVERY WORD, EVERY GROAN AND EVERY WHISPER WE BRING TO HIM.

STANDING TOGETHER

BIBLE: DANIEL 3:1-30

As iron sharpens iron, so one person sharpens another (PROVERBS 27:17).

In school some of my friends were a bad influence on me, and my need to fit in with them made me act like everyone but Jesus. Around that time, I became friends with a girl from my church who wasn't impressed with the things I did with my school friends. It didn't take long before I noticed that her life stood out in a completely different way—she showed Jesus to the people around her. And soon I realised I wanted to do that too!

My friend helped me keep my focus on Jesus in a world that doesn't look or act like Him. Paul understood this challenge well and warned Christians not to "conform to the pattern of this world" (ROMANS 12:2).

Living like our school friends is often easier than living like Jesus. But it's not impossible to be different, especially with the help of other Christians. For example, together Shadrach, Meshach and Abednego (exiled Jews in Babylon) refused to bow down to the image King Nebuchadnezzar had set up for his people (DANIEL 3:12). They stood for God—no matter the cost. "If we are thrown into the blazing furnace, the God we serve is able to deliver us from it, and he will deliver us from Your Majesty's hand. **But even if he does not,** we want you to know, Your Majesty, that we will not serve your gods or worship the image of gold you have set up" (DANIEL 3:17-18).

The writer of Hebrews encouraged Christians to think about "how we may spur one another on towards love and good deeds" (HEBREWS 10:24). Let's make it a focus this week to help other Christians we know to keep standing out for Jesus, and use their support and the strength of the Holy Spirit to do the same ourselves!

JS

THINKING IT OVER . . .

How are your friends being a good or a bad influence on you? How can you make sure you are also regularly spending time with Christians for prayer and encouragement?

WHO WE SPEND OUR TIME WITH MAKES A MASSIVE DIFFERENCE TO WHO WE ARE.

SATISFIED

BIBLE: PSALM 119:129-138

The teaching of your word gives light, so even the simple can understand
(V.130 NLT).

The more I speak with my friends and take an honest look at my own life, the more I wonder if we dive into things like gossip, sexual relationships, getting drunk or picking on the weird kids at school just as a way to mask our own pain and insecurities. We look to these things as easy ways to fill the emptiness we sometimes feel.

Whatever we try to fill our lives with, it never gives us the peace or fulfilment we're looking for. We often end up feeling emptier than we started.

It may be hard to understand how the Bible can bring real satisfaction to our lives when the world around us is screaming that we need sex, money, Instagram followers and fame to feel complete. But it's only when we spend time with God and put our confidence in Him and the Bible that we can know a peace "which transcends all understanding" (PHILIPPIANS 4:7) and a satisfaction that isn't reliant on how well life is going (VV.11-13).

In Psalm 119, the psalm writer—who went through bullying, hunger, loneliness and all sorts of suffering—says that true encouragement and sturdy hope is found in the Bible. There's so much to be gained from the "wonderful things" His words teach us (PSALM 119:18).

Try to prioritise spending time with God. Turn to the Bible and allow yourself the space to read and reflect on the things it teaches. Only there will you find the peace and satisfaction you are looking for.

RR

THINKING IT OVER . . .

Follow the psalm writer's example this week and ask God to: help you understand His instructions (PSALM 119:130); give you a desire to read the Bible (V.131); keep you safe from temptation (V.133); help you obey what the Bible teaches (V.134); feel the Holy Spirit's sadness and conviction when you go against God's ways (V.136); and trust that everything He says is good and trustworthy (V.138).

TRUE FULFILMENT IS NOT FOUND IN INDULGING OURSELVES; BUT IN DOING THINGS GOD'S WAY.

REASON TO LIVE

BIBLE: JOB 2
Shall we accept good from God, and not trouble? (V.10).

When Charlie, a church leader, found out he had a fatal disease called Creutzfeldt-Jakob, he wrote the following message: "What does a Christian do . . . when the doctors have told him that his disease is destroying his brain, and that his whole personality may be warped? . . . After two days of self-searching, it comes to me that ultimately and finally Christians are to always view life as a gift from God . . . and it is not ours to smash."

Charlie decided that suicide was out of the question because of his deep trust in the God who "created my inmost being; you knit me together in my mother's womb" (PSALM 139:13) and who planned our days in His book (V.16). But he still asked God to bring him quickly to heaven. God answered Charlie's prayer, and he died a short while later.

Job faced a similar situation. Although he was suffering with a painful illness and lost everything he had, Job trusted God enough to reject his wife's suggestion that he should "curse God and die!" (JOB 2:9).

Some people in our world hold up death as a way out of our difficulties and serious illnesses. While we should never downplay the pain some people are in, we can learn from Job and from Charlie about what trusting God looks like, even when life is at its worst. They knew that life comes from the Creator, and it is not ours to take away.   HVL

TO PRAY ABOUT . . .
Father, sometimes it doesn't feel simple to say that life is Your gift, especially when I'm in pain or depressed. Please help me to remember that my life, breath and everything else are in Your hands; my days have been written in Your book. I choose to trust You, even in the pain.

WITHOUT JESUS WE'RE NOT READY TO DIE; WITH JESUS WE HAVE EVERY REASON TO LIVE.

IN GOD'S IMAGE

BIBLE: GENESIS 1:26-31

God created mankind in his own image, in the image of God he created them; male and female he created them (V.27).

When her beautiful brown skin started losing its colour, a young teen felt scared—as if she were disappearing or losing herself. With heavy makeup, she covered up "my spots" as she called them—patches of lighter skin caused by a condition called vitiligo. It's a loss of skin pigment called *melanin* which gives skin its colour tone.

Then one day, she asked herself, *Why am I hiding?* Relying on God's strength to accept herself, she stopped wearing heavy makeup. Soon she began getting attention for her self-confidence. Eventually she became the first spokesmodel with vitiligo for a global cosmetics brand.

"It's such a blessing," she said, explaining that her trust in God, along with the support of her family and friends, gives her the courage to be the person God made her to be.

This woman's story is a powerful reminder that we each are created in God's image. "God created mankind in his own image, in the image of God he created them; male and female he created them" (GENESIS 1:27). No matter what we look like on the outside, all of us are image-bearers of God. As His created people, we show His glory; and as Christians we are being transformed to look more and more like Jesus in how we live.

Do you struggle to love the skin you're in? Today, look in the mirror and tell yourself the truth: "I am made in God's image—just as He planned; just as He designed." And then let's ask God to make Jesus obvious to others when they look at us.

PR

THINKING IT OVER . . .

What's more important to you—how people see you or if they see God in you?
What are ways you can show God's image to your friends at school today?

GOD HAS MADE US TO BE HIS IMAGE-BEARERS.

UNTYING THE ROPE

BIBLE: GENESIS 33:1-11

But Esau ran to meet Jacob and embraced him; he threw his arms around his neck and kissed him. And they wept (V.4).

One Christian organisation's mission is to explain the healing nature of forgiveness. One of their videos shows a person who has been hurt strapped back to back with a rope to the person who hurt them. Only the person who has been wronged can untie the rope. No matter what they do, the person has got someone on their back. Without forgiveness—without untying the rope—they cannot escape.

Forgiving other people isn't about 'letting them off the hook' or saying what they have done doesn't matter. It is about releasing ourselves from the bitterness and hatred of the situation. When we don't forgive, our grudges just hold us closer to those people in our minds, making us more and more angry with them.

In Genesis, we see two brothers separated for twenty years after Jacob stole from Esau. After this long time, God told Jacob to return to his homeland (GENESIS 31:3). He obeyed, but nervously, sending gifts ahead to Esau (32:13-15). When the brothers met, Jacob bowed at Esau's feet seven times in humility (33:3). Imagine his surprise when Esau ran and embraced him, both of them enjoying the release of their forgiveness and reconciliation (V.4). No longer were they held by their hatred and bitterness.

Do you feel imprisoned by unforgiveness? Are there grudges constantly in your mind when you think of or spend time with certain people? Know that God, through His Son and Spirit, can release you when you forgive with His help. He will give you the strength to begin untying any ropes of bitterness. *ABP*

TO PRAY ABOUT . . .

Dear God, You want us to live with our families and friends in peace, but so often we mess things up and hurt each other. Help us to love others with the forgiveness You have given.

FORGIVENESS SETS US FREE.

GOD IS BIGGER

BIBLE: 1 SAMUEL 17:41-50

You come against me with sword and spear and javelin, but I come against you in the name of the LORD Almighty (V.45).

Giles, a South African game ranger, described the strange scene: two honey badgers were battling six lions! The two honey badgers refused to back down from the fierce predators, who were ten times bigger. The lions thought the kill would be simple, but Giles' video shows the badgers walking away with something like a swagger.

David and Goliath were an even more unlikely story. Young, inexperienced David confronted the fierce Philistine giant Goliath. Towering above his young opponent, Goliath had brutal strength and weaponry—bronze armour and a lethal, razor-edged javelin (1 SAMUEL 17:5-6). David, a shepherd boy, carried only a slingshot when he arrived at the battlefield with bread and cheese for his brothers (VV.17-18).

Goliath challenged Israel to fight him, but King Saul and "all the Israelites were . . . terrified" (V.11). Imagine the shock when David stepped into the scene. What gave him the bravery none of Israel's hardened warriors could find? For everyone else, Goliath took up their vision. David, however, saw God: "The LORD will deliver [Goliath] into my hands" (V.46). While everyone else believed Goliath controlled the story, David knew God was the real Author. And, with a single stone to the giant's forehead, David's trust proved true.

We're tempted to believe that our 'Goliaths' (our troubles) direct the story. God is bigger, every time. He alone tells the story of our lives.   *WC*

THINKING IT OVER . . .

What 'giants' threaten to take over your story today?
How does God's reality, the fact that He's bigger, transform your view?

NO MATTER WHAT YOU FACE TODAY, GOD IS BIGGER.

PRECIOUS

BIBLE: PSALM 16
You are my Lord; apart from you I have no good thing (V.2).

"My precious . . ." In the *Lord of the Rings* films, Gollum has a maniacal obsession with the "precious" ring of power. In many ways he has become something of an icon for greed, addiction and even insanity.

It's also a troublingly relatable image. In his tormented love-hate relationship with both the ring and with himself, Gollum's voice echoes the needs and desires we all have. Whether it's directed at one thing in particular, or just a general need for more, we're sure that once we finally get our own 'precious', we'll be satisfied. But instead, what we thought would make us whole leaves us feeling even emptier than before.

There's a better way to live. As David explains in Psalm 16, when we feel like we're on a desperate hopeless hunt for satisfaction (PSALM 16:4), we can remember to turn to God for all we need (V.1). Apart from Him we have nothing (V.2).

And as our eyes stop looking for satisfaction 'out there' to look instead at simply who God is (V.8), we find ourselves finally finding true, lasting contentment—a life of the "joy [of God's] presence". And we can enjoy walking with Him each moment in "the way of life"—now and forever (V.11 NLT). Nothing's better!

MB

TO PRAY ABOUT . . .
God, forgive me for thinking I can find what I need in other places.
Thank You for always being there even when I forget to look for You.
Help me to stay close to You and to enjoy just knowing who You are.

NO MATTER WHAT WE THINK WE NEED, LET'S TURN TO GOD FIRST!

THE POWER OF PRAYER

BIBLE: MARK 11:20-24

"Have faith in God," Jesus answered. "Truly I tell you, if anyone says to this mountain, 'Go, throw yourself into the sea,' and does not doubt in their heart but believes that what they say will happen, it will be done for them" (VV.22-23).

Some people think that prayer itself is a source of power. If they pray hard enough, well enough, with the right words and in the right places, then hopefully God will do what they want.

In Mark 11, Jesus explained one of the secrets behind prayer: "Have faith in God" (MARK 11:22). That means the only place we put our trust is in God. We don't put faith in our prayers (relying on how good they sound or how genuine they are); our trust is in God alone. We have faith in the One we speak to; not in what we're saying.

Jesus told His disciples they could tell a mountain to be thrown into the sea, and if they believed it would happen, it would. Jesus then explained what that promise meant: "Whatever you ask for in prayer, believe that you have received it, and it will be yours" (V.24). Jesus was talking about answered prayer. We can ask and get answers only if our asking is directed to God in faith, trusting Him to act and do things in His own perfect and good way (1 JOHN 5:14). This doesn't mean God is a genie who will do whatever we ask; it means He *will* answer—our role is to trust Him, even before we see Him at work.

I've often wished that I could move mountains—the things that get in my way each day. But God has done something much more important: He has removed the mountains of worry, fear and regret in my life and thrown them into oblivion because I trust in Jesus. I know my prayers are powerful—not because of me or how well I speak—but because I speak to the One who's in control of every mountain. *JY*

WANT MORE ... ?

Check out *What is prayer?* online at **ourdailybread.org/lookingdeeper**

FAITH IS CONFIDENCE IN GOD TO DO WHAT HE SAYS HE WILL DO.

KEEP ASKING

BIBLE: LUKE 11:1-13

So I say to you: ask and it will be given to you; seek and you will find; knock and the door will be opened to you (V.9).

I heard one girl say that she never prayed more than once for anything. She didn't want to wear God out with her repeated requests.

Jesus' teaching on prayer in Luke 11 paints a very different picture! He told a story about a man who went to his friend's house at midnight and asked for some bread to feed his unexpected visitors. At first the friend refused, because he and his family were in bed. Finally he got up and gave him the bread—not out of friendship but because the caller was so persistent (LUKE 11:5-10).

Jesus used this parable to compare this reluctant friend with our generous heavenly Father. If an irritated neighbour will give in to his friend's persistence, how much more readily will our heavenly Father—who loves to provide for us—give us all we need!

It's true that God, in His great wisdom, may sometimes delay His answers to prayer. It's also true that we must pray in agreement with the Bible and God's plans and purposes. But within these things Jesus tells us to keep praying, keep asking and to keep trusting our needs to God (v.9). This way, we'll know we're looking to God for the answer, rather than being tempted to take matters into our own hands.

Don't worry about wearing God out. He will never get tired of our prayers! He loves it when we come to Him with our needs and trust them to Him! *JY*

WHAT I'M THANKFUL FOR . . .

Thank You, Father, that I can bring my every need to You—again and again and again. And I know You will answer in Your perfect ways and timing.

GOD NEVER GETS TIRED OF OUR ASKING.

Seven days with... Paul

I AM

BIBLE: 1 TIMOTHY 1:12-17

Christ Jesus came into the world to save sinners—of whom I am the worst (V.15).

There is a famous story that the London Times newspaper once asked a question to readers during the early 1900's: *What's wrong with the world?*

That's quite the question, isn't it? How would you answer? We might say, "Well, how much time do you have for me to tell you?" And that would be fair, as there seems to be so much that's wrong with our world.

The story continues that the newspaper received hundreds of responses, but one in particular caught everyone's attention. The English writer, poet and philosopher G.K. Chesterton is said to have written this four-word response:

"Dear Sirs, I am."

What do you make of that response? It's nothing but true. Long before Chesterton gave that answer, the apostle Paul admitted how much he had messed up: "I was once a blasphemer and a persecutor and a violent man" (1 TIMOTHY 1:13). After saying that Jesus came to save "sinners", he added very honestly: "of whom I am the worst" (V.15). Paul knew exactly what was and is wrong with the world. And he knew the only hope of making things right: "the grace of our Lord" (V.14).

Jesus didn't come into the world to judge us for our mess or to make us hang our heads in shame. He came to save us (JOHN 3:16-17)! In Jesus, we no longer need to be part of what's wrong with the world.

JB

COMPLETING THE PICTURE

Paul became a Christian when he met Jesus in a vision (ACTS 9). Before this, Paul had been a religious leader in Israel named Saul, and he had hated Jesus, Christians and the church (SEE PHILIPPIANS 3:1-14). He actively hunted Christians down, dragged them from their homes and threw them in prison (ACTS 8:3). When Paul later tried to join up with the apostles (Jesus' first followers, like Peter) in Jerusalem, "they were all afraid of him, not believing he really was a disciple. But Barnabas took him and brought him to the apostles" (9:26-27). Paul was also an apostle, being "sent not from men nor by a man, but by Jesus Christ and God the Father" to spread the gospel (GALATIANS 1:1).

WE MAY BE THE PROBLEM WITH THIS WORLD, BUT THANK GOD THAT JESUS IS THE ANSWER!

Seven days with . . . Paul

MAKING UP

BIBLE: COLOSSIANS 4:7-10
If he comes to you, welcome him (V.10).

Two best friends were very different from each other. Amos was loud, excitable and a big personality. Danny was quiet, shy and a bit of a loner. They laughed and hung out all the time. But then came the day they fell out. Danny said he'd had enough of Amos being so self-centred and that they were no longer friends.

Three days later, Amos called with terrible news. Doctors had found cancer and given him six months to live. Danny's heart broke. "We're friends," he said, "no matter what."

Paul was a hard-nosed visionary and Barnabas a gentle-hearted encourager. God put them together and sent them on a missionary journey (ACTS 13:2-3). They preached and started churches, along with Mark who they were mentoring—that is until their disagreement over Mark leaving them. Barnabas wanted to give Mark a second chance on their next journey, but Paul said he could no longer be trusted. So they split up (15:36-41).

Paul eventually forgave Mark. He closed three letters with greetings that included Mark's name, showing they were working together again (COLOSSIANS 4:10; 2 TIMOTHY 4:11; PHILEMON 1:24). We don't know what happened with Barnabas. Did he live long enough to make up with Paul? I hope so.

Whatever your situation today, try to reach out to those who you may have had a falling out with. Now is the time to show and tell them how much they mean to you.

MW

COMPLETING THE PICTURE . . .

After Paul became a Christian he went away into Arabia for three years, being taught "by revelation from Jesus Christ" (GALATIANS 1:11-18). During the book of Acts, Paul went on three missionary journeys (the first of which was with Barnabas and Mark). In the first he spent a lot of time in Galatia (modern-day Turkey), setting up new churches. In the second and third journeys he encouraged those churches (ACTS 15:36) and travelled as far as Greece, and spent quite a bit of time with the church at Ephesus (ACTS 19).

After these journeys Paul returned to Jerusalem, where he was arrested for talking about Jesus. He was sent to Rome to stand trial before Caesar (ACTS 25; 26:32). The book of Acts ends with Paul preaching in Rome under house arrest (28:30-31).

WHEN WE FORGIVE OTHERS, WE HAVE THE CHANCE TO DEEPEN OUR RELATIONSHIP WITH THEM TOO.

Seven days with . . . Paul

HAVING A WORD

BIBLE: GALATIANS 2:11-20

Wounds from a friend can be trusted, but an enemy multiplies kisses (PROVERBS 27:6).

I'll never forget what my friend said to me when I was seventeen. He had overheard me laughing at a dirty joke someone was telling at school. So he said he had admired my Christian beliefs, and was surprised that I would laugh at something so rude. Embarrassment swept over me. I admitted that I hadn't been very Jesus-like.

It's not nice when someone has to have a word with us about something we've said or done. I can imagine that the apostle Paul didn't like confronting Peter (GALATIANS 2:11). But he felt he had to, because Peter's hypocritical behaviour was hurtful and confusing to the gentile Christians at Antioch. Peter had freely eaten with them, but after some Christian Jews from Jerusalem came to the Antioch church, he separated himself from the gentiles, worrying about the Jews' disapproval.

I imagine that Peter felt shame, but he apparently accepted the telling off and changed his ways. He knew that Paul was a true friend who loved him. And in later years he referred to him as "our dear brother Paul" (2 PETER 3:15).

If you need to have a word with someone, do it gently. If you are told off, avoid getting angry; instead try to listen to the truth of what you're being told. You may be getting a needed "wound from a friend".

HVL

COMPLETING THE PICTURE . . .

The Galatian church (in modern-day Turkey) was made up of non-Jews (gentiles). They didn't have the Old Testament law as part of their culture, so they didn't follow its rules or traditions. Christian Jews would sometimes look down on Christian gentiles because of this. But Paul made it clear that everyone (whether Jew or gentile) comes to God through Jesus, who created "in himself one new humanity out of the two, thus making peace, and in one body to reconcile both of them to God through the cross" (EPHESIANS 2:15-16).

Peter's choice to eat only with the Jews wasn't a good example of Jesus' love. His actions suggested the Jews were somehow better. So Paul called him out on it, setting the record straight: "There is neither Jew nor Gentile, neither slave nor free, nor is there male and female, for you are all one in Christ Jesus" (GALATIANS 3:28).

A TRUE FRIEND WILL HELP US SHOW JESUS IN HOW WE LIVE

Seven days with . . . Paul

THE REASON AND THE RISK

BIBLE: 1 CORINTHIANS 9:18-23

What then is my reward? Just this: that in preaching the gospel I may offer it free of charge, and so not make full use of my rights as a preacher of the gospel (V.18).

It was the kind of moment that people have nightmares about. A tanker lorry filled with 2,500 gallons of propane gas caught fire while parked at a fuel storage warehouse. The flames shot out of the back of the lorry and quickly spread to a loading dock. The whole place was in danger of exploding.

The warehouse manager rescued the badly burned driver and then jumped into the blazing lorry and drove it away from the warehouse. His quick action and bravery saved many lives.

The apostle Paul also risked his life for others (2 TIMOTHY 2:10). He was stoned and left for dead (ACTS 14:19). Another time he was mobbed, whipped and imprisoned (16:22-23). Three times he was shipwrecked, and he was beaten many times with lashes and rods (2 CORINTHIANS 11:23-28). Why did Paul willingly go through such suffering? He knew that saving people from hell was worth the risk of pain and even his own death.

Do we see things as clearly as Paul did? Do we realise that the most important thing in the whole world is that people know Jesus for themselves? Do we have the same sense of purpose and urgency to tell people about Him? Are we part of Jesus' rescue mission, like Paul was? Are we willing to get laughed at and lose friends just to give them the opportunity to hear how much they need Jesus?

MDH

COMPLETING THE PICTURE . . .

Paul's attitude to his life is summed up pretty well in the first letter he wrote to the church at Corinth (in Greece): "I have made myself a slave to everyone, to win as many as possible" (1 CORINTHIANS 9:19). Paul taught in many different countries and cultures. He always tried to meet people where they were 'at', becoming "all things to all people so that by all possible means I might save some" (V.22). His second missionary journey gives us a great example of this. He preached a sermon in Athens using the idols, statues and poetry of the culture as a starting point for him to talk about Jesus in terms the people there would understand (SEE ACTS 17:16-34).

THE MOST IMPORTANT THING IN THE WHOLE WORLD IS THAT PEOPLE KNOW JESUS FOR THEMSELVES.

Seven days with . . . Paul

GATHERING STICKS

BIBLE: ACTS 28:1-10

You, my brothers and sisters, were called to be free. But do not use your freedom to indulge the flesh; rather, serve one another humbly in love (GALATIANS 5:13).

During a painful illness, Alan had to stop just about everything for a few months. But God taught him a lot during this time, drawing his attention to the story of Paul's shipwreck on Malta in Acts 28 (during his trip to Rome as a prisoner). There is more to the story than Paul's miraculous immunity to a poisonous snakebite (ACTS 28:3-6).

This apostle, preacher, miracle worker and writer of much of the New Testament was stuck on an island as a prisoner. Did he lie back and moan about his situation? Did he think he should be treated better because he was an apostle? No! The Bible tells us that he got involved with the work and helped the people he was with. It was cold and rainy, so Paul "gathered an armful of sticks" for a much-needed fire (V.3 NLT).

God never forgets about us; He never leaves us in places for no reason at all. Each of us is in a specific family, school, class, church and friendship group. There are people we are meant to meet, help out and share Jesus with. There is plenty of stuff for us to get involved with, even if it's as simple and uninspiring as "gather[ing] an armful of sticks". When we're ready to do what we can, God will use us to make Jesus known!   *DE*

COMPLETING THE PICTURE . . .

Even imprisoned (ACTS 28:11-16), Paul made the most of his time, writing letters to churches he had visited: Ephesus (EPHESIANS 3:1), Philippi (PHILIPPIANS 1:9-14) and Colossae (COLOSSIANS 4:18). He also wrote a personal letter to a good friend (PHILEMON 1:1). It seems like Paul was released from his house arrest, only to be imprisoned in Rome again sometime later (which led to his execution). During his last imprisonment Paul wrote to his friend Timothy (who he also had mentored): "I am suffering even to the point of being chained like a criminal. But God's word is not chained" (2 TIMOTHY 2:9).

Paul's church letters are: Romans, 1 and 2 Corinthians, Galatians, Ephesians, Philippians, Colossians and 1 and 2 Thessalonians. His personal letters are: 1 and 2 Timothy, Titus and Philemon.

GOD NEVER PUTS YOU IN THE WRONG PLACE.

Seven days with . . . Paul
GROWING TO KNOW

BIBLE: PHILIPPIANS 4:10-13
I can do all this through him who gives me strength (V.13).

I was seventeen and excited to be going to Germany as an exchange student. But I only had three months until I left for Germany, and I didn't know a single word in German. So I spent those months cramming—studying German for hours and even writing words on my hands to memorise them.

Months later I was in a classroom in Germany, fed up because I could barely understand what was being said around me. That day a teacher gave me some good advice: "Learning a language is like climbing a sand dune. Sometimes you feel like you're not getting anywhere. But just keep going and you will."

Sometimes I remember that advice when I think about what it looks like to follow Jesus. The apostle Paul said, "I have learned the secret of being content in any and every situation" (PHILIPPIANS 4:11). Even for Paul, having peace wasn't something that just happened overnight. It was something he learned, developed and grew into as he got to know and trust Jesus better. Paul explained: "I can do all this through him who gives me strength" (VV.12-13).

Life has its challenges. And there are plenty of reasons to not feel content or satisfied with the stuff we have to go through. But as we cling tightly to Jesus who has "overcome the world" (JOHN 16:33), we find He is always faithful to us and that nothing matters more than our closeness to Him. He alone makes us content, gives us peace and strengthens us for everything. *JB*

COMPLETING THE PICTURE . . .
The non-Christian Jews stirred up trouble against Paul because of his message about Jesus, often trying to kill him (FOR EXAMPLE SEE ACTS 13:45; 14:2,19; 17:13). In his second letter to the church in Corinth he listed all the trials, pains, abuse and attacks he had suffered because he kept telling people about Jesus (2 CORINTHIANS 11:23-33). Paul also had an illness that seriously affected his eyes (GALATIANS 4:12-16). And he had an issue or illness that he asked God three times to get rid of (2 CORINTHIANS 12:7-8). "But he said to me, 'My grace is sufficient for you, for my power is made perfect in weakness.' Therefore I will boast all the more gladly about my weaknesses, so that Christ's power may rest on me" (V.9).

DAILY COMMITMENT DOESN'T ALWAYS SEEM EXCITING, BUT WE ARE BECOMING MORE LIKE JESUS WHETHER WE FEEL IT OR NOT.

Seven days with . . . Paul

TIED UP

BIBLE: 2 TIMOTHY 2:1-13

I am willing to endure anything if it will bring salvation and eternal glory in Christ Jesus to those God has chosen (V.10 NLT).

Bulgarian lifeguard Yane Petkov won a world record for swimming with his hands and feet tied together. He swam 3,380-metres through the water! But apparently the whole thing wasn't quite challenging enough—so he also wrapped himself in a sack!

The patience and strength he must have had to keep moving while being so 'tied up' amazes me. The apostle Paul showed this kind of determination as he served God. Through all the challenges he faced, Paul continued to preach and write encouragement and teaching to churches and friends.

Paul wrote his last letter to Timothy when he was alone in a Roman prison, awaiting execution. Although chains kept him tied down, he thanked God that the good news about Jesus could never be chained (2 TIMOTHY 2:9). Nothing could stop it spreading and changing lives. Paul said, "I am willing to endure anything if it will bring salvation" (V.10 NLT).

Things like illness, injuries and disabilities need care and attention, but they can't stop God's plan for us or the way He can make Jesus known through us. As Paul came to understand, God's power is made perfect in our weakness, because that's when we have to rely on Him (2 CORINTHIANS 12:9). When we do, it'll show to the people around us. God will use us to make Jesus known—even if we feel 'tied up'!

JBS

COMPLETING THE PICTURE . . .

Paul was imprisoned again in Rome and many believe he was executed under Nero. During his last imprisonment he wrote to Timothy, who he had mentored, and who was now a church leader at Ephesus (1 TIMOTHY 1:3). In his last written words to Timothy, Paul told him to stick to the words of the Bible and sound teaching (2 TIMOTHY 1:13), that his life with Jesus was the most important thing for him to guard (V.14), to take his stand with Jesus as seriously as if he were a soldier (2:3-4), to avoid false teachers (VV.14-19), to expect persecution (3:12) and to use the Bible as his basis for everything (VV.16-17). Paul signed off by saying: "I have fought the good fight, I have finished the race, I have kept the faith. Now there is in store for me the crown of righteousness" (4:7-8).

OUR LIMITS DON'T LIMIT GOD.

I SPY

BIBLE: JOHN 21:1-7

Then the disciple whom Jesus loved said to Peter, "It is the Lord!" (V.7).

Did you ever play "I Spy" as a kid? I heard about a family who play the game slightly differently. If any of them see something in the world that shows God at work, they point to it and shout: "I spy!" It might be something a friend said, an answer to prayer or simply a great view out the window. The point is that they keep on the lookout for reminders of God's presence in the world and in their lives.

That game makes me think of Jesus' followers and their unsuccessful fishing trip (JOHN 21:1-7). Jesus had come back to life after His resurrection, yet some of his friends were unsure what to do next. So they went fishing. Early in the morning they saw through the mist a man standing on the shore, but they didn't know it was Jesus. "Friends, haven't you any fish?" He asked. "No," they answered. "Throw your net on the right side of the boat and you will find some," He said (VV.5-6). The fishermen did as He asked, and their net was filled with so many fish they couldn't draw it in. "It is the Lord!" shouted John, who often called himself "the disciple whom Jesus loved" (V.7). It was an "I spy" moment. John was the first to recognise Jesus.

Ask God to help you 'see' Jesus at work today—in your conversations, in the things your family say, in your classes at school, in your prayers and Bible reading. If you pay attention, you will see Him at work when others have no idea. Try playing "I spy" today and let God's constant presence reassure you of His love and care.   *DR*

THINKING IT OVER . . .

What do you think it means when Paul tells us, "We know that in all things God works for the good of those who love him, who have been called according to his purpose" (ROMANS 8:28)? How could this perspective help you to 'see' Jesus in the different situations you find yourself in?

YOU CAN SEE GOD AT WORK WHEREVER YOU GO.

WITNESSING FROM A WHEELCHAIR

BIBLE: MATTHEW 20:20-28

The Son of Man did not come to be served, but to serve (V.28).

Nancy put this ad on her social media feed: "If you are lonely or have a problem, call me. I am in a wheelchair and hardly ever get out. We can share our problems with each other. Just call. I'd love to talk." The replies to that ad have been incredible—she gets about thirty messages every week!

What made Nancy want to reach out from her wheelchair to help others in need? Nancy explained that before her paralysis she had been perfectly healthy but deep in depression. She had tried to commit suicide by jumping from her flat window, but instead she became paralysed from the waist down. In the hospital, totally frustrated, she sensed Jesus saying to her, "Nancy, you've had a healthy body but a crippled soul. From now on you will have a crippled body but a healthy soul." As a result of that experience, she gave her life to Jesus. When she was finally allowed to go home, she prayed for a way to share God's love with others, and the idea of the social media ad came to her.

All of us can do something to help the people around us. Limited as we may feel, we can still pray, call, blog and take whatever opportunities God gives us. No matter how small we feel, we can be effective for Jesus Christ if we copy His serving attitude.

VG

THINKING IT OVER . . .

What excuses do you sometimes use to not look out for others? How can you copy Jesus today, expecting to serve, rather than wanting to be served?

GOD PROVIDES OPPORTUNITIES FOR US TO SERVE. ARE WE LOOKING FOR THEM?

TELL ME A STORY

BIBLE: MARK 4:26-34

He did not say anything to them without using a parable (V.34).

---

*O*nce upon a time. Those four words might just be some of the most powerful in the entire world. My earliest memories as a kid are all about that phrase. My mum would read from a children's Bible storybook to me and my brother every evening before lights-out. Those four words introduced many of the stories about interesting people from history and the God who loved them. Those Bible stories helped shape how I saw the big, wide world, even as a kid.

Jesus was the greatest storyteller in the world. He knew we all carry inside us a love for stories, so that was the way He often chose to teach His good news. Once upon a time there was a man who scattered "seed on the ground" (MARK 4:26). Once upon a time there was "a mustard seed" (V.31), and on and on. Mark's gospel clearly shows that Jesus used stories in His everyday explanations about God and His kingdom (V.34). Although Jesus' parables are not always easy to understand straightaway, the truths they hold and pictures they give us allow us to see the world more clearly and understand more thoroughly the God who loves us. It's well worth exploring Jesus' parables; these stories are a great way to explore deep truths without getting overwhelmed.

JB

THINKING IT OVER . . .

Read Luke 15. This chapter has three parables all about lost things being found.
What does this teach you about God's love and attitude towards lost people?
What other details and emphasis does the final, longer parable bring?

JESUS TOLD STORIES TO HELP US EXPLORE MORE OF WHO GOD IS.

DIGITAL FOOTPRINT

BIBLE: 2 PETER 1:1-12

His divine power has given us everything we need for a godly life through our knowledge of him who called us by his own glory and goodness (V.3).

The online world can save time, keep us connected with our friends, help us with our homework and keep us entertained when we're bored. But like everything else, it can open up not only a world of information, but a world of temptation. The question I ask myself each day is, *If my digital footprint were a trail to follow, where would it lead others?*

Even with all there is to do and find online, it can't begin to compare with all that we have in Jesus because of His sacrifice: "everything we need for a godly life" (2 PETER 1:3). Sexual temptation and pornography are not the only dangers of the online world. With a screen to protect us, it's easy to become a bully, to gossip, to show a fake life on our social media and to get involved in all sorts of things that are opposite to growing in "our knowledge of [God]" (V.3). The screens in our pockets can be really good. But they can also drag us further into "the corruption in the world caused by evil desires" (V.4).

Today's reading reminds us that we can resist the temptations we face, digital or otherwise, only by God's "divine power" (V.3)—not by trying to follow a list of rules in our own limited strength. People who live by the promises of Jesus have faith in Him—and from that trust, their character, needs and wants change (VV.5-7). They don't just 'hope' they'll live well; they "make every effort" to trust their desires to Jesus (V.10).

Let's rely on God's Holy Spirit within us—one day at a time, one step at a time—by putting our focus on Jesus, not ourselves.   *RF*

THINKING IT OVER . . .

If your youth leader were to see your digital footprint, where would the trail lead them? Read Psalm 1:1-6 and ask the Holy Spirit to show you where your choices need to be directed by your love for Jesus and the Bible.

DOES OUR DIGITAL FOOTPRINT LEAD TO JESUS, OR TO SOMETHING ELSE?

TAKE YOUR GRIEF TO GOD

BIBLE: LAMENTATIONS 3:49-66

My eyes will flow unceasingly, without relief, until the LORD looks down from heaven and sees (VV.49-50).

An orca (a killer whale) named Talequah gave birth. Talequah's pod of killer whales was endangered, and her newborn was their hope for the future. But the calf lived for less than an hour. In her grief, Talequah pushed her dead calf through the cold waters of the Pacific Ocean for seventeen days before letting her go.

Sometimes Christians have a hard time knowing what to do with grief. Perhaps we worry that our sadness might look like a lack of hope or like we don't trust God. But the Bible gives us many examples of humans crying out to God in grief. Loss and hope can actually work together during any times of grief we go through.

Lamentations is a book of five poems about the sadness of people who have lost their home. They've been hunted by enemies and were near death (LAMENTATIONS 3:52-54), and they weep and call to God to bring justice (V.64). They cry out to God not because they have lost hope, but because they believe God is listening. And when they call, God does come near (V.57).

It's not wrong to feel the weight of grief when people die or we lose things or important relationships in our lives. God is always listening, and you can be sure that He will help comfort you in your loss and give you reason to hope. *AP*

TO PRAY ABOUT . . .

Loving God, help us to remember that it's right to cry over loss,
just as it is right to look to You for hope.

GOD SEES US AND IS WITH US IN OUR GRIEF.

THE ONE WHO SEES

BIBLE: NUMBERS 32:16-24

You may be sure that your sin will find you out (V.23).

"Oh no!" My voice rang out when I stepped into the kitchen. Our Labrador Retriever Max bolted from the room.

Gone were the snacks that had been sitting too close to the edge of the kitchen side. Max had eaten them all, leaving an empty plate. He tried to hide under a bed. But only his head and shoulders fitted. His uncovered rump and tail stuck out when I went to track him down.

I couldn't help laughing when I saw him trying to hide. "Oh, Max," I said, "Your sin will find you out." The phrase was borrowed from Moses, when he told two tribes of Israel to be obedient to God and keep their promises. He told them: "But if you fail to do this, you will be sinning against the LORD; and you may be sure that your sin will find you out" (NUMBERS 32:23).

Sin feels good for a moment. Like Max, we do something selfish—with no thought for God or others. It makes us feel good, but each sin is an act of rejection of God and His good ways and plan for us. Moses reminded the people of Israel that God misses nothing. "Everything is uncovered and laid bare before the eyes of him to whom we must give account" (HEBREWS 4:13).

Though seeing all, our holy God lovingly helps us to admit our sin, repent of it (turn from it) and walk with Him again (1 JOHN 1:9). Let's admit where we have been selfish and sinful, so that we can come close to Him and follow His good ways.

JB

THINKING IT OVER . . .

How does the truth that God sees everything we do and still loves us encourage you to turn from sin? What will you do today in response to His love and forgiveness?

GOD SEES ALL OUR SIN IN FULL YET LOVES US, THAT'S WHY HE SENT JESUS TO PAY FOR IT ON THE CROSS.

CLIMBING

BIBLE: HEBREWS 12:1-4

Let us run with perseverance the race marked out for us, fixing our eyes on Jesus (VV.1-2).

George Mallory was a mountain climber who was last seen heading towards the summit of Mount Everest in June 1924. We don't know if he made it to the top. He never came back down.

He was once asked why he wanted to climb Everest. His answer was simply, "Because it's there!" That may sound strange to us. For mountaineers, Everest's challenging peak is itself all the motivation they need to have a go at it.

The book of Hebrews teaches us that just as mountain climbers are focused on the mountain in front of them, we are to be focused on Jesus. The writer encourages us to look back at the examples of other Christians (in our lives and in the Bible's story), but not to look back on our past mistakes and sins (HEBREWS 12:1). He tells us to keep going and not give up by "fixing our eyes on Jesus" (V.2).

Jesus started our faith and He will keep us growing to be more like Him, completing the work when we are in heaven (V.2; PHILIPPIANS 1:6). As we read and think about Jesus' example, we'll realise that He went through so much more than us and so will help us to get through our own issues by His strength (HEBREWS 12:3-4).

When mountaineers get tired, they look at the goal—at the summit—and climb on. When we struggle, we can trust in Jesus who is preparing us a room in His home (JOHN 14:1-3).   RF

WHAT I'M THANKFUL FOR . . .

Thank You, Jesus, that I can put my focus on You. Your story is incredible—and all You did, You did for me. When I want to give up, You are my strength, my energy, my fuel for everything!

WHEN OUR FOCUS IS ON JESUS, WE CAN BE SURE WE'RE HEADING THE RIGHT WAY.

LIVING WORSHIP

BIBLE: ROMANS 12:1-2

I urge you, brothers and sisters, in view of God's mercy, to offer your bodies as a living sacrifice, holy and pleasing to God—this is your true and proper worship (V.1).

Our understanding of worship is often all about the songs we sing on a Sunday morning at church. There's nothing wrong with that—the psalms repeatedly tell us to praise God with songs, such as Psalm 96:1: "Sing to the LORD a new song; sing to the LORD, all the earth."

But in Romans 12, Paul helps show how much bigger worship is than just singing praise: "I urge you, brothers and sisters, in view of God's mercy, to offer your bodies as a living sacrifice, holy and pleasing to God—this is your true and proper worship" (ROMANS 12:1). What is a "living sacrifice" and what does it have to do with worship?

Worship is not only something we give to God, but a response throughout our whole life to "God's mercy" to us. Since Jesus offered His own body for us on the cross as an act of love and mercy, it's only fitting that we should do the same for Him.

Offering our whole selves to God might sound like it's way too hard. Maybe we need to break it down to today, to this hour, to this moment—and ask ourselves, *How can I do this for and with Jesus?* That's what it means to live a life of worship—a life that belongs to Jesus, not to ourselves.

The Bible reminds us that we live for Jesus now through the power of His Spirit—and that "Christ lives in [us]" (GALATIANS 2:20). We give ourselves to God in worship because Jesus gave Himself for all of us out of love. *PC*

THINKING IT OVER . . .

What does it mean for you to be a "living sacrifice" for God? How can we always keep in mind that Jesus did this first for us? Read Romans 5:8 to be reminded that not only did Jesus give up His body for us, but He did so when we deserved it least.

WORSHIP ISN'T A MOMENT, BUT A WAY OF LIFE.

I'VE GOT THIS

BIBLE: JOSHUA 7:1-13

Commit to the LORD whatever you do, and he will establish your plans
(PROVERBS 16:3).

I had been doing well in maths and assumed that the upcoming exam was no big deal. A chilled out complacency settled over me. You might sum up my attitude as 'I've got this'!

It turns out I really didn't 'have this'. My marks were the lowest in the class.

The story of Joshua also shows how Israel assumed their success with a 'we got this' attitude. As they prepared to cross the Jordan River and enter the Promised Land in Joshua 3, they looked for God's direction and followed the priests who carried the ark of the covenant (the ark represented God's presence with them). And in Joshua 6, as they got ready to attack Jericho, the ark was once again by their side (JOSHUA 6:6-7). So far so good.

But after God gave them the victory, a man ignored God's commands (VV.18-19) and took some of the spoils of war for himself (7:1). Then Israel got things wrong again. The men who went to scout out the next military target returned and said, "Not all the army will have to go up against Ai. Send two or three thousand men to take it and do not weary the whole army, for only a few people live there" (V.3). It doesn't look like Israel talked to God about any of this. Well, except for turning to Him after their humiliating defeat (VV.4-9)! Who knows what the outcome might have been if they had asked God first . . .

It seems like each one of us is a strange mix of insecurity and independence. But God created us to rely on Him for everything—for stuff that seems impossible and for things that seem easy. As we make it our habit to look to Him first, He tells us, "I've got this!"

TG

THINKING IT OVER . . .

What's the difference between God-centred confidence and self-centred complacency? In what situations are you more likely to be overconfident? Read Matthew 14:22-33. When does Peter get things right, and where does he get things wrong? Where is his focus in both these extremes (VV.29-30)?

ONLY GOD CAN TRULY SAY, "I'VE GOT THIS."

DO THE HARD WORK

BIBLE: I TIMOTHY 6:6-19

Fight the good fight of the faith. Take hold of the eternal life to which you were called when you made your good confession in the presence of many witnesses (V.12).

I've come to realise there are no quick-fixes. There's no "6 easy steps" to follow Jesus and never mess up. And any sermons, books, blogs or songs that say otherwise are sending us down a very dangerous path.

One Christian author told a story about an alcoholic guy who asked his church leader to pray for him to be rescued from his drinking problem. He thought this would be a quick and easy way to beat his addiction. Recognising his motive in asking for prayer, the church leader replied, "I've got a better idea. I will pray for you, but you need to go to Alcoholics Anonymous." He told the guy to follow the programme all the way through and to read his Bible every day. "In other words," the leader explained, "do the hard work."

Do the hard work—that's what Paul was saying to Timothy when he told him: "But you, man of God, flee from [selfishness], and pursue righteousness, godliness, faith, love, endurance and gentleness. Fight the good fight of the faith. Take hold of the eternal life to which you were called" (1 TIMOTHY 6:11-12). While Jesus has rescued us into God's family, and there is no work for us to do to earn our salvation, we are still to "fight the good fight". Changing our lives, beating addiction and creating new habits take time and effort. We have to keep committing ourselves to God and spending time with Him in the Bible each day.

Just as there is no easy path to beating something like alcoholism, there is no effort-free route to being more like Jesus. If we really want to become like Jesus, we must keep on making time for Him and putting in the effort to study the Bible.

HVL

TO PRAY ABOUT . . .

Father, please help me to change and become more like Jesus by the power of Your Spirit. Help me to put in the effort every day to focus on You and the work You are doing in my life.

BECOMING LIKE JESUS IS THE WORK OF A LIFETIME.

BEATING ENVY

BIBLE: ACTS 13:42-52

When the Jews saw the crowds, they were filled with jealousy. They began to contradict what Paul was saying and heaped abuse on him (**V.45**).

- - - - - - - - - - - - - - - - - - -

We can all get a bit envious at times. Some of our classmates are clearly smarter than us. Some are better looking and get loads of attention. Others have lots of friends, newer phones, nicer clothes, etc., etc.

Envy comes up a lot in the Bible too. Rachel envied Leah because she had children (**GENESIS 30:1**). Joseph's brothers hated him because he was their dad's favourite (**37:11**). And in today's reading, the Jews fought against Paul's preaching for the same reason—envy. They were jealous of how many people were willing to listen to Paul talk about Jesus (**ACTS 13:45**).

None of us are immune from envy. It is always at work in us, ready to point out people we wish we were like.

When one Christian spoke at a conference, huge crowds came to hear his messages. Then a really famous preacher came to speak at the same conference. Soon the people were going to hear his sermons instead. The first guy was envious. He said, "The only way I can beat my feeling is to pray for the person I am jealous of every day—which I do!"

To stop envy taking over our lives, we need to be aware of it, spot it when we become jealous and admit it to God. Envy only leads to us thinking about ourselves. But if we pray for the people we're jealous of, we force our minds away from selfishness and look instead to see what ways God might want us to love and look out for these other people.

DJD

WANT MORE . . . ?

Check out *What is the danger of comparing?* online at
ourdailybread.org/lookingdeeper

A HEART AT PEACE GIVES LIFE TO THE BODY, BUT ENVY ROTS THE BONES. PROVERBS 14:30

ON ALERT

BIBLE: EPHESIANS 6:10-18

Put on the full armour of God, so that you can take your stand against the devil's schemes (V.11).

One of the most elite military special operations forces in the world uses a colour-code system to explain the different levels of combat readiness. I think we could use their system for the Christian life as well:

White: Soldiers are relaxed and daydreaming. They can easily be attacked. Christians who live like this are not reading the Bible regularly or spending quality time with God. They are easy for the devil to distract and mislead.

Yellow: Soldiers are relaxed physically but alert mentally. For us, this is like we know and worry about the dangers of temptation and the way the devil distracts us from God, but we don't feel able to do anything about it.

Orange: Soldiers are physically prepared, mentally alert and ready to fight. Christians who have this alertness are engaging regularly with God, the Bible and other Christians. They are wearing the armour of God (EPHESIANS 6:11) because they are sticking close to Him, not just once a day, but throughout each day; talking with God, and trusting His Spirit within them to lead and provide in every situation (V.18).

Red: As in orange, soldiers are ready to fight. The difference is experience. This is the growth of the Christian life—as we rely on God for all things, we "stand firm" (V.14) in Jesus more naturally and instinctively because we see again and again that trusting in Him is the only way to win our battles.

Wherever we are—at school, in a shopping centre, on a football pitch, even at church—we need to be ready to stand firm "against the devil's schemes" (V.11). He is always looking to attack and distract us. So we must always be alert and ready to talk with God and rely on His strength.

DCE

THINKING IT OVER . . .

Which colour describes you at the moment? How have you been handling temptation recently? Are you reading and studying the Bible regularly?

WE WILL ONLY WIN OUR BATTLES WHEN WE ARE PREPARED FOR THEM.

HE SMELLS OF THE STABLE

BIBLE: MATTHEW 1:22-25

"The virgin will conceive and give birth to a son, and they will call him Immanuel" (which means "God with us"). (V.23).

A stable? What a place to give birth to God's promised King! Farmyard smells and sounds were Jesus' first human experience. Like other babies, He probably cried at the sounds of the animals and the strangers surrounding His temporary bed.

If so, they would have been the first of many tears. Jesus would come to know loss and sadness; hear the doubts His family had about Him; face rejection and hatred from many; and see the pain His mother experienced as He was tortured and killed.

All these hardships—and so much more—awaited the baby trying to sleep that first night. From His very first breath, Jesus was "God with us" (MATTHEW 1:23). He knew exactly what it meant to be human.

In order to bring salvation to us, Jesus became fully human. And because He became just like us, Jesus understands us completely: "For we do not have a high priest who is unable to feel sympathy for our weaknesses, but we have one who has been tempted in every way, just as we are—yet he did not sin" (HEBREWS 4:15). We can never say that no one gets what we're going through. Jesus does.

And He became like us so that through His life, death and resurrection, we can become like Him: perfect children of God: "children born not of natural descent, nor of human decision or a husband's will, but born of God" (JOHN 1:13). Let's thank Him for the life He lived for us so that we can "approach God's throne of grace with confidence, so that we may receive mercy and find grace to help us in our time of need" (HEBREWS 4:16).   RK

WANT MORE . . . ?

Check out *What is the reality of Christmas?* online at
ourdailybread.org/lookingdeeper

JESUS UNDERSTANDS EXACTLY WHAT WE'RE GOING THROUGH ALL THE TIME.

PLAYING GOD

BIBLE: ACTS 17:22-29

He himself gives everyone life and breath and everything else . . . God did this so that they would seek him and perhaps reach out for him and find him, though he is not far from any one of us (VV.25,27).

Apparently some scientists are hoping to 'resurrect' people by the year 2045 through artificial intelligence and nanotechnology. Their goal is "to store data of conversational styles, behavioural patterns, thought processes and information about how your body functions from the inside-out." Then they'll code this information, have it built into an artificial body, and use the brain of a "deceased human". It sounds like science fiction is becoming reality!

But, if it even becomes possible, is this a real resurrection? The Bible tells us that the one true God, the Creator and Sustainer of the universe, is the only One who has power to give life and breath to everything (ACTS 17:25). At best, it sounds like these scientists can only make a copy of people who have died.

These attempts are simply not the same as God-breathed life. But the motivation for resurrection through artificial intelligence shows a God-given desire to live forever. As Ecclesiastes 3:11 tells us, "[God] has also set eternity in the human heart." Although people might make their own attempts to live as long as possible, God tells us that we truly can live forever. He's placed within us the desire to share life with Him and those we love. And He's made it possible through His Son Jesus Christ. "For God so loved the world that he gave his one and only Son, that whoever believes in him shall not perish but have eternal life" (JOHN 3:16).

God alone is the source of our lives—and eternal life. As Paul said, "In him we live and move and have our being" (ACTS 17:28). And one day we will continue our lives forever in heaven with Jesus!

MG

THINKING IT OVER . . .

Read Genesis 11:1-9. How is this attempted A.I. resurrection similar to the story of the Tower of Babel? It reminds us that even people who don't believe in God want to live forever. How can this truth help you share Jesus with others?

**WE WANT TO LIVE FOREVER
–BECAUSE THAT'S HOW GOD DESIGNED US!**

GOOD SOIL

BIBLE: MARK 4:1-20

Still other seed fell on good soil. It came up, grew and produced a crop, some multiplying thirty, some sixty, some a hundred times (V.8).

John Chrysostom was one of the best preachers of the early Christian church. Yet he realised that even great speakers can't make people listen.

He explained, "My preaching is addressed to all . . . but it is the duty of each one of my listeners to take what is relevant for their situation. I do not know who are sick and who are healthy. So I discuss subjects of every sort."

In Mark 4, the parable of the sower and the soils teaches us about the importance of how we respond to the Bible. In the story, the seed is the Bible, and the different types of soil are the various people listening. The growth of the crop isn't really down to the skill of the farmer (like preachers or Bible teachers) but how receptive the soil is.

Some listeners are like rich soil, and the Bible's words take root in them. Other people are shallow in their interest (MARK 4:5,16) or too busy with other things in the world (VV.7,18-19). Even if they listened to the best speaker in the world, they would still soon forget the Bible truths they were told because they are not really that interested.

We need to 'drink in' the teaching of the Bible in our churches, youth groups and our own personal study times. While we should test everything we hear against the Bible's words (ACTS 17:11; 2 TIMOTHY 5:16-17; 1 JOHN 4:1-6), we also need to make sure we are receptive and willing. That's why Jesus said, "Consider carefully what you hear," (V.24). Whether or not you benefit from a sermon is largely up to you.

CHK

THINKING IT OVER . . .

What is your attitude towards sermons and Bible studies? Are you eager to hear what the Bible says, even if the speaker is someone you think is boring?

THE BEST BIBLE TEACHING WON'T MAKE ANY DIFFERENCE IF WE'RE NOT LISTENING.

RUNNING FOR OTHERS

BIBLE: PHILIPPIANS 2:1-11

Do nothing out of selfish ambition or vain conceit. Rather, in humility value others above yourselves (V.3).

Tom never won a race during school, even though he was part of the track team. Tom was a 'pusher'. It was his job to set the pace for his team mates, who would then beat him to the finish line. When he ran a successful race, he was helping another runner to win. Even though Tom never had enough energy for the final sprint to victory, the coach knew he was a very important member of the team.

In a similar way, the New Testament tells us to run our 'race' looking to help others succeed. "Do nothing out of selfish ambition or vain conceit. Rather, in humility value others above yourselves, not looking to your own interests but each of you to the interests of the others." (PHILIPPIANS 2:3-4). Why? Firstly, by living like this we give people a picture of Jesus Christ, who left the glory of heaven to share our humanity and die on the cross so that we could have unending life with Him (VV.5-8).

Secondly, because the most important thing—ever—is to see more and more people crossing the finish line. In other words, trusting Jesus for themselves and choosing to bow before Him so that they can know His love and forgiveness. Whatever other aims and dreams we have for our lives, they can never compare with helping others to 'run' for Jesus.

If our 'running' can help another person meet Jesus, we should praise God. We are not told to be 'winners' who get everything they want in life. We are to be pushers, helping others to take hold of the prize of knowing Jesus, just as we have.

_DM_

TO PRAY ABOUT . . .

Father, please help me to be looking for ways to share Jesus with the people I know. There are lots of things I want to achieve and enjoy in life—but may those things never get in the way of helping others find and follow Jesus for themselves.

YOU CAN'T LOSE WHEN YOU HELP OTHERS WIN.

DISCOVERING

BIBLE: PSALM 95:1-7
In his hand are the depths of the earth (V.4).

The Veryovkina Cave, in the country of Georgia, is the deepest known cave on earth. A team of explorers have probed the dark and mysterious depths of its caverns to over two kilometres—around 2,212 metres (7,188 feet) into the earth! Similar caves (around 400 of them) exist in other parts of the country and across the globe. More caverns are being discovered all the time and new depth records are regularly being set.

Even though new discoveries are always being made—changing and adding to our understanding of the planet we live on—we can trust one thing that doesn't change: the God who created it all. One psalm-writer tells us all to "sing for joy" and "shout aloud" to God because of His greatness (PSALM 95:1). God's work of creation—whether we've discovered it or not—is good reason for us to bow down to our awesome King (V.6).

He doesn't just know the vast, physical places of His creation, but also the personal thoughts and details of our minds. And not unlike the caverns of Georgia, we will go through dark and perhaps scary times in life. Yet we know that God holds even those times in His powerful and loving hands. In the words of Psalm 95, we are His people, the "flock under His care" (V.7).

KH

TO PRAY ABOUT . . .
God, help me to trust Your care for me in even the darkest places!

THE GOD WHO KNOWS EVERY DEEP, DARK CAVE KNOWS EACH OF US AND THE THINGS WE'RE GOING THROUGH.

FOUND ON THE EDGES

BIBLE: LUKE 19:1-10

For the Son of Man came to seek and to save the lost (V.10).

I was in the middle of the crowd at a motorcycle show. Riders were doing all kinds of exciting and dangerous stunts—but I found myself needing to stand on my tiptoes to see. Glancing around, I saw three kids perched in a nearby tree, because they also couldn't get to the front of the crowd to see the action.

Watching the kids peer out from their tree-top view, I couldn't help but think of Zacchaeus, who Luke tells us was a wealthy tax collector (LUKE 19:1). Jews thought of tax collectors as traitors, hating them for working for the Roman government and collecting taxes from fellow Israelites. They also made a habit of demanding extra money for themselves. So Zacchaeus probably wasn't popular in his neighbourhood!

As Jesus passed through Jericho, Zacchaeus wanted to see Him but was too short to get a good look from the middle of the crowd he found himself in. So he climbed into a sycamore tree to catch a glimpse (V.3). And it was there, on the outskirts of the crowd, that Jesus searched him out and announced He was going to be a guest at Zacchaeus' home (V.5).

Zacchaeus' story reminds us that Jesus came to "seek and to save the lost," offering His friendship and the gift of salvation to anyone (VV.9-10). Even if we feel lonely or pushed to the 'back of the crowd' like Zacchaeus, we can be confident that Jesus finds us even there.

LS

THINKING IT OVER . . .

Have you been pushed aside by friends or family? Do you struggle with loneliness or feeling left out in any way? In what ways has Jesus found you and invited you to spend time with Him?

JESUS SEES EVERY PERSON IN THE CROWD.

AGREEING WITH GOD

BIBLE: MATTHEW 15:1-9

These people honour me with their lips, but their hearts are far from me (V.8).

I was listening to a podcast where a guy was giving his opinion on religion. "I can't stand religious hypocrites," he said. "They talk about religion, but they're no better than I am. That's why I don't like all this religious stuff."

This guy didn't realise it, but he was agreeing with God. God has made it clear that He can't stand hypocrisy either. It's ironic, though, that something God also hates (people pretending to be good and religious) is used by some people as an excuse not to bother with Him.

Jesus said this about hypocrisy: "These people honour me with their lips, but their hearts are far from me. They worship me in vain; their teachings are merely human rules" (MATTHEW 15:8-9).

Notice what Jesus said to perhaps the biggest hypocrites of His day, the Pharisees (the religious leaders). In Matthew 23, He called them hypocrites— not once, not twice, but seven times! They were religious people who were putting on a big show, but God knew who they really were. He knew they were more interested in themselves than in Him.

Non-Christians who point out hypocrisy in us when they see it are right in doing so. They are agreeing with God, who also wants us to be the same inside and out. Our job is to make sure we keep examining ourselves before God and asking Him to help us become people who love Him, through and through. Then we will be able to be transparent to everyone—because no matter when, where or how they see us, they'll firstly see people who love and rely on Jesus.   DB

WANT MORE . . . ?

Check out *Who am I?* online at **ourdailybread.org/teen**

BEING RELIGIOUS IS NOT THE SAME AS BEING GOD-CENTRED.

FICKLE FANS

BIBLE: MATTHEW 27:15-23

The crowds that went ahead of him and those that followed shouted, "Hosanna to the Son of David!" (MATTHEW 21:9).

If you follow sports at all, you know that sports fans can change like the weather. A team's star player can hear a stadium of cheering voices if they do well—or a stadium of booing voices if they mess up.

Sports stars easily fall from grace because people are fickle—ready to follow whoever the latest big deal is or whoever will score the goals or win the points for their team. And the fans are always ready to turn against that very same person the moment they start playing poorly.

The Bible has a key example of fickleness that is way more serious. A huge crowd in Jerusalem praised and cheered for Jesus on the Sunday He entered the city, riding on a donkey (MATTHEW 21:6-11). But just a few days later, some of those same people were almost certainly in the crowd calling for Jesus' crucifixion (27:20-23). On Sunday they worshipped Him, but on Friday they actually shouted for His death.

Sometimes we can flip-flop in our relationship with Jesus. We sing praise loudly on Sunday, but then act like Jesus just gets in the way when we're with our friends at school. We tell Him on Sunday that we love Him, but then we don't talk to Him again for the rest of the week.

Let's not be fickle followers of Jesus. Let's worship and praise Him every day!

DB

TO PRAY ABOUT . . .

Dear Jesus, You are my God and my Saviour. I want to love You, hold tight to You and live for You every day. Please help me to keep You at the very centre of all I do.

LIVING FOR JESUS ISN'T JUST FOR WHEN IT'S CONVENIENT, BUT FOR EVERY DAY.

WHAT WOULD YOU PAY?

BIBLE: ACTS 19:11-20

When they calculated the value of the scrolls, the total came to fifty thousand drachmas (V.19).

"How much for this train?" The seller looked up, hardly daring to hope. He hadn't sold much that day, and he could use the money. "They usually cost £60, but make me an offer." The customer replied, "Will you take £5?"

The guy shook his head and the customer turned away. He had spent days making the wooden toy. Is that all people thought it was worth? Five pounds?

It's fun to get a bargain, but what we pay shows what we think something is worth. Especially with God. The Ephesians were so grateful to be freed from sin that they decided to destroy everything from their past lives. "A number who had practiced sorcery brought their scrolls together and burned them publicly. When they calculated the value of the scrolls, the total came to fifty thousand drachmas" (ACTS 19:19). That equals fifty thousand days of wages!

The ex-sorcerers could have sold their scrolls and banked the money, perhaps splitting the profits with the church. Instead they willingly paid such a high price because they knew the stuff on the scrolls was bad, and because their salvation was worth so much more. Jesus had given His life for them, and they would gladly give up anything for Him in return.

How much do you think Jesus is worth? You can tell by what you would give up to follow Him. If you have paid hard costs for obeying Jesus, then you actually have reason to give Him thanks. You have told Jesus just how much you value Him. And He will never forget it (REVELATION 22:12)!

MW

THINKING IT OVER . . .

What does your life show about the value you put on Jesus? What have you given up for Him? What things do you struggle to give up for Him? Why?

OUR SACRIFICES FOR JESUS SHOW WHAT WE THINK HE IS WORTH.

WAY OF ESCAPE

BIBLE: JOHN 11:45-53

So from that day on they plotted to take his life (V.53).

Agatha Christie's Hercule Poirot detective story *The Clocks* is all about a group of people who commit a series of murders. Although their initial plan was to kill just one victim, they began taking more lives to cover up the original crime. When confronted by Poirot, one of the group admitted, "It was only supposed to be the one murder."

Like the schemers in the story, the religious authorities came up with a murderous plan of their own. After Jesus raised Lazarus from the dead (JOHN 11:38-44), they held an emergency meeting and plotted to kill Him (VV.45-53). But they didn't stop there. After Jesus rose from the dead, the religious leaders spread lies about what happened at the grave (MATTHEW 28:12-15). Then they began a campaign to silence Jesus' followers (ACTS 7:57-8:3). What started as a plot against one man for the 'greater good' of the nation (JOHN 11:50) became a web of lies, cover-ups and attacks.

Sin drives us down a road that often has no end in sight, leading us deeper into mess and chaos. But God always gives a way of escape (1 CORINTHIANS 10:13). When Caiaphas the high priest said, "It is better for you that one man die for the people than that the whole nation perish" (JOHN 11:50), he didn't understand the truth of his words. The plot of the religious leaders would help complete Jesus' rescue mission.

Jesus saves us from sin's tightening grip. Have you received the freedom He offers?

RO

THINKING IT OVER . . .

Read James 1:2-4 and 14-15. What are the two 'roads' that James describes? What road are you going down at the moment? Are you becoming more "mature and complete" in Jesus (V.4) or is sin becoming more "full-grown" (V.15)? What do you need to admit to Him today?

GIVE SIN ROOM, AND IT WILL TAKE OVER YOUR LIFE.

LESSONS FROM A SHEPHERD

BIBLE: LUKE 15:1-7

Suppose one of you has a hundred sheep and loses one of them. Doesn't he leave the ninety-nine in the open country and go after the lost sheep until he finds it? (V.4).

Jesus' parable of the shepherd and the lost sheep has some important lessons for Christians about their responsibility to those who still don't know Jesus.

The shepherd wasn't satisfied with 99% of his sheep being safe within the fold. He did not say, "I'm only missing one. That's pretty good!" No, he felt personally responsible for that one missing sheep (LUKE 15:4).

Nor did the shepherd assume that it would come back on its own. That sheep was unaware of its lost state, and unable to help itself. So the shepherd took the initiative and went searching for it. And he did not give up until it was found (v.5).

The shepherd also wanted others to share his happiness in finding that one lost sheep (v.6). His friends and neighbours who celebrated with him must have also felt that to find a lost sheep was one of the most important and worthwhile things that the shepherd could do.

We also have a responsibility to look out for our friends, family and classmates who still don't know Jesus. They are lost, whether they realise it or not. They are helpless, whether they realise it or not. And telling them about Jesus is the most worthwhile thing we can do with our time. They need to meet Him for themselves—what can you do this week to help them get a better idea of who He is?

RDH

WANT MORE . . . ?

Check out *Why is it so hard to tell others about Jesus?* online at
ourdailybread.org/lookingdeeper

TELLING OTHERS ABOUT JESUS IS THE MOST WORTHWHILE THING WE CAN DO WITH OUR TIME.

Seven days in . . . Revelation

JUST A TOUCH

BIBLE: REVELATION 1:9-18

Then he placed his right hand on me and said: "Do not be afraid. I am the First and the Last" (V.17).

- -

It was just a touch, but it made all the difference to Jake. A few people from his church went to the local town centre to talk to passers-by about Jesus and offer to pray with them. Some of the youth group, including Jake, went too. But the whole thing started to really stress him out. That's when an older guy from the church came over, put his hand on Jake's shoulder and warmly encouraged him. For Jake it was an important moment—a powerful reminder that God was with him.

John, the close friend and follower of Jesus, was exiled as an old man to the remote island of Patmos because he kept telling people about Jesus. As a prisoner on the island, he heard "a loud voice like a trumpet" (REVELATION 1:10). That startling sound was followed by a vision of Jesus Himself, and John "fell at his feet as though dead" (V.17). But in that scary moment, he was given comfort and strength. John wrote, "[Jesus] placed his right hand on me and said: 'Do not be afraid. I am the First and the Last'" (V.17).

God takes us out of our comfort zone to show us new things, to stretch us, to help us grow. But He also gives us the bravery to go through every situation. He won't leave us alone in our trials. He has everything under control. He has us in His hands.

TG

COMPLETING THE PICTURE . . .

The book of Revelation is John's written record of the vision Jesus showed him (SEE REVELATION 1:9-11; 21:5). John was given this vision around 90 AD.

A lot of Revelation is hard to understand. It deals with "what must soon take place" (1:1). There's a lot of imagery and poetic language. In fact, it reads a lot like the Old Testament prophetic books, which only really make sense now we know the story of Jesus (which is what they were pointing to). So we probably have to accept we won't understand everything Revelation tells us about Jesus' return. But there are some concrete details we can focus on—like Jesus' appearance (1:12-16), judgement (20:11-15), our future home (21:1-5) and that Jesus is definitely returning (22:20).

NOTHING WE HAVE TO FACE CAN STAND UP TO THE FIRST AND THE LAST WHO IS WITH US.

Seven days in . . . *Revelation*

IN LIVING COLOUR

BIBLE: REVELATION 4:1-6

The one who sat there had the appearance of jasper and ruby.
A rainbow that shone like emerald encircled the throne (V.3).

When Xavier put on the glasses his aunt sent for his fifteenth birthday, he literally couldn't believe his eyes. Born colour-blind, Xavier had only ever seen the world in shades of grey, white and black. But with his new *EnChroma* glasses Xavier saw colour for the very first time. His happiness at being able to see the world like everyone else made his family feel like they'd been part of a miracle.

Colourful brilliance also brought a powerful reaction from John (REVELATION 1:17). After falling in front of the full glory of Jesus (1:12-16), John saw "a throne in heaven with someone sitting on it. And the one who sat there had the appearance of jasper and ruby. A rainbow that shone like an emerald encircled the throne . . . From the throne came flashes of lightning" (4:2-5).

In the Old Testament, Ezekiel had a similar vision, seeing "what looked like a throne of lapis lazuli", with a figure above the throne who "looked like glowing metal, as if full of fire" (EZEKIEL 1:26-27). This awesome figure was surrounded with rainbow-like radiance (V.28).

One day we will meet Jesus face-to-face. These visions give us just a tiny hint of His breath-taking and dynamic magnificence. As we enjoy the world God made here and now, let's live eagerly waiting for the far better experience of enjoying knowing Him perfectly.

RO

WHAT I'M THANKFUL FOR . . .

Father, words fail us when we try to imagine what we will experience when we meet You face to face. Thank You for the small hints of Your awesomeness You have placed in our world already.

WHO IS LIKE YOU, LORD GOD ALMIGHTY? YOU, LORD, ARE MIGHTY, AND YOUR FAITHFULNESS SURROUNDS YOU. PSALM 89:8

Seven days in . . . Revelation

OUR PRAYERS MATTER

BIBLE: REVELATION 8:1-5

May my prayer be set before you like incense; may the lifting up of my hands be like the evening sacrifice (PSALM 141:2).

"Prayers are deathless." These are the attention-grabbing words of one Christian writer. He wanted us to understand the power and lasting nature of our prayers: "The mouths that spoke them may be closed in death, the heart that felt them may have ceased to beat, but the prayers live before God, and God's heart is set on them. Prayers outlive the lives of those who spoke them; they outlive a generation, outlive an age, outlive a world."

Have you ever wondered if your prayers—particularly those you've said in real difficulty, pain and worry—ever make it to God? These insightful words remind us of the importance of our prayers and so does Revelation 8:1-5. The setting is heaven (REVELATION 8:1), the throne room of God and the control centre of the universe. Angels stand in God's presence (V.2) and one angel, like the priests of the Old Testament, offers Him incense along with the prayers of "all God's people" (V.3). How eye-opening and encouraging to have this picture of the prayers offered on earth rising to God in heaven (V.4). When we think that our prayers may have been lost or forgotten, what we see here reminds us that they will be answered. Maybe not today; and maybe we won't see the answer tomorrow. But on the Day that God makes all wrong things right, we know all our prayers will be fulfilled. It's an encouragement to keep on praying! Our prayers matter to God—every single one!

AJ

THINKING IT OVER . . .

Have you questioned whether God really listens to Your prayers? How can passages like Revelation 8:1-5 give you renewed enthusiasm for prayer? Why should thinking about the final Day make us more prayerful (1 PETER 4:7)?

OUR PRAYERS MATTER TO GOD—EVERY SINGLE ONE!

Seven days in . . . Revelation

THE LAMB WINS

BIBLE: REVELATION 19:1-21

Worthy is the Lamb, who was slain, to receive power and wealth and wisdom and strength and honour and glory and praise! (REVELATION 5:12).

I saw an unusual sign on the front of a church building recently. It read simply: "The Lamb Wins." It's a strange idea. A lamb is a small, weak animal—often the first to be picked off by wolves or wild animals, and the least likely to win anything!

Yet "the Lamb wins" is exactly what Revelation shows us. Jesus came to earth as "the Lamb of God, who takes away the sin of the world!" (JOHN 1:29). He came humbly as our sacrifice, to die in our place. He was "led like a lamb to the slaughter" (ISAIAH 53:7).

Yet we see His true strength in John's vision (REVELATION 19:11-16). Jesus was not our Lamb because He is weak, but because He *chose* to take our place on the cross. "Worthy is the Lamb, who was slain, to receive power and wealth and wisdom and strength and honour and glory and praise!" (5:12).

Jesus came as a Lamb. He will return as the Judge of the world. To Him will be "praise and honour and glory and power, for ever and ever!" (V.13) as He fulfils all the prophecies about God's King throughout the Bible (SEE DANIEL 7:12-13).

But the reign of God's King will not come peacefully. The imagery of Revelation 19 is full of God's fierce power and His terrible judgement. In that day the world will hold a great rebellion against God (REVELATION 19:19), but they will be destroyed in a moment (V.21).

HR

COMPLETING THE PICTURE . . .

The Day of Jesus' return is scary to read about. But the Bible is clear that the judgement is for the "destruction of the ungodly" (2 PETER 3:7)—or in other words, the people who absolutely refuse Jesus. They do not and will not accept the Lamb as their "sin offering" (LEVITICUS 4:32). Anyone who rejects this salvation must face God's wrath for themselves (SEE JOHN 3:18,36). Whereas "whoever believes in him is not condemned" (V.18)—there is no judgement for us to face; the Judge is on our side as the One who has already taken our judgement on the cross.

The Bible also tells us that God isn't rushing to bring this final Day, because "he is patient with you, not wanting anyone to perish, but everyone to come to repentance" (2 PETER 3:9).

THE LAMB WHO DIED IS THE LORD WHO LIVES.

Seven days in . . . Revelation

HEAVEN IS FAR BETTER

BIBLE: REVELATION 21:1-8

Look! God's dwelling-place is now among the people, and he will dwell with them (V.3).

One summer my family and I went on holiday to a little seaside town. I enjoyed walking past all the different boats and reading their names, like: "The Codfather", "Unsinkable II", "Buoyoncé" and "She Got the House".

But one name made me think a little deeper: "Heaven Can Wait". I guess that name kind of sums up how we might feel when we're doing something we love. The people on that boat probably felt heaven had little to offer compared to the feel of sailing freely across the sea.

To be honest, sometimes I find I'm enjoying my life so much that I'm not all that sure about the idea of heaven. But when that happens, I need to take some time in the last chapters of Revelation. Because the greatness of heaven isn't described in the stuff we'll do there or the things we'll have.

What makes heaven better is that it is God's home. We will literally live with Him. "We will be his people, and God himself will be with [us] and be [our] God" (REVELATION 21:3). And He will personally "'wipe every tear from [our] eyes. There will be no more death' or mourning or crying or pain, for the old order of things has passed away" (V.4).

It's great to have a good life here. God "richly provides us with everything for our enjoyment" (1 TIMOTHY 6:17), but let's not get so attached to it that we lose all interest in heaven. It's Jesus, not stuff and experiences, who really makes life worth living. To be with Him forever should be the most exciting thought we can have!

DE

COMPLETING THE PICTURE . . .

Heaven will be the fulfilment of the Old Testament temple, which had the inner Most Holy Place (EXODUS 26:33-34), representing God's presence with His people. Once a year one priest could enter. That was it. But this was "a copy and shadow of what is in heaven" (HEBREWS 8:5). In heaven Jesus will "present you before his glorious presence without fault and with great joy" (JUDE 1:24) so that we can stand in the very presence of God forever, enjoying Him and His love for us perfectly. When he saw heaven, John wrote: "I did not see a temple in the city, because the Lord God Almighty and the Lamb are its temple" (REVELATION 21:22).

NO MATTER HOW GOOD OUR LIFE MAY BE HERE, BEING WITH JESUS IN HEAVEN IS FAR BETTER.

Seven days in . . . Revelation

HAPPY ENDING

BIBLE: REVELATION 22:1-7

Then the angel showed me the river of the water of life, as clear as crystal, flowing from the throne of God and of the Lamb . . . On each side of the river stood the tree of life (VV.1-2).

The story of the Bible ends up very much where it began. The broken relationship between God and human beings has healed over at last, and the brokenness of Genesis 3 is finally fixed. Borrowing images from the Garden of Eden, Revelation pictures a river and a tree of life (REVELATION 22:1-2; SEE GENESIS 2:9-10). But this time a city replaces the garden—a city filled with people who love God. No death or sadness will ever darken that scene. When we wake up in the new heaven and new earth, we will have a happy ending at last.

Heaven is not an afterthought or an optional extra. It is the place we were made for. The Bible never minimises our pain, anxiety, depression, loneliness or issues. No book in history is as understanding and honest as the Bible. But it does add one key word: temporary. What we feel now, we will not always feel. The time for the new heaven and new earth will come. Every wrong will be made right. God's world will once again be "very good" (GENESIS 1:31).

If you feel trapped in your school, with the people you hang out with, in your family, in your mental health—heaven promises a future of health and wholeness and happiness and peace. The Bible begins with the promise of a Rescuer in the book of Genesis (3:15) and ends with that same promise (REVELATION 21:1-7)—a guarantee of future reality. The end will be the beginning.

PY

COMPLETING THE PICTURE . . .

In a sense, the story of the Bible is a tale of three trees. **The first tree:** In Genesis 3, Adam and Eve chose the tree of the knowledge of good and evil over the tree of life, because they wanted to be their own bosses. **The second tree:** Jesus came to pay for their sin (and our sin) in full. He took on the "curse" of sin for us by dying on the cross, "For it is written in the Scriptures, 'Cursed is everyone who is hung on a tree'" (GALATIANS 3:13 NLT). **The third tree:** Because of Jesus' sacrifice, we are now invited again to the tree of life in heaven. "The leaves of the tree are for the healing of the nations. No longer will there be any curse" (REVELATION 22:2-3).

HEAVEN PROMISES A FUTURE OF HEALTH AND WHOLENESS AND HAPPINESS AND PEACE.

Seven days in . . . Revelation
JESUS' RETURN

BIBLE: I THESSALONIANS 5:1-22

"Yes, I am coming soon." Amen. Come, Lord Jesus (REVELATION 22:20).

Nearly 2,000 years ago Jesus said, "I am coming soon" (REVELATION 22:20). Since then, some have wrongly tried to guess exactly when He will return. Others have given up waiting. Was Jesus wrong? Did something happen that He didn't expect?

Of course not! We view time from our own limited point of view. But to the God who is outside of time "a day is like a thousand years, and a thousand years are like a day" (2 PETER 3:8).

Jesus told His disciples that God has not given them specific information about "the times or dates the Father has set by his own authority" (ACTS 1:7). He wanted them—as He wants us—to live in an attitude of expectation. Paul echoed this when he told us to "eagerly" wait for Him (PHILIPPIANS 3:20). The point is we don't need to know *when* Jesus is coming back—it should be enough for us to simply know that He *is* coming back!

But how do we live eagerly and expectantly? Jesus told the disciples to tell the world His story (ACTS 1:8). And Paul said, "be awake and sober" (1 THESSALONIANS 5:6) so that we love each other (VV.12-15) and don't become complacent or distracted by the world around us. John told us to walk closely with Jesus (1 JOHN 2:28-3:3) so that we "may be confident and unashamed before him at his coming" (2:28).

Jesus' 'any-moment' return is not meant to make us calculate possible dates; it is meant to make us watchful, hopeful and expectant. Let's stay close to Him in everything we do, knowing that the next thing on His calendar is His return.

HVL

WANT MORE . . . ?

Check out *What difference does Jesus' return make to today?* online at
ourdailybread.org/lookingdeeper

THE PROMISE OF JESUS' RETURN MAKES US WATCHFUL, HOPEFUL AND EXPECTANT.

COMFORT FOOD

BIBLE: ROMANS 15:1-7

Whatever things were written before were written for our learning, that we through the patience and comfort of the Scriptures might have hope (V.4 NKJV).

I love comfort food! There's nothing like a burger and fries to put a smile on my face. Or having a big sharing bag of crisps all to myself. These are the kind of foods that make me feel like everything's alright in the world (even if they're not the healthiest things I could eat!).

Unfortunately, all is not well with the world, and no amount of crisps, fast food or fizzy drinks can make it right. Real comfort doesn't come from food, and it doesn't come from alcohol or drugs or money or sex or power. It is a much deeper need that requires a much deeper solution.

Paul told the church at Rome that the search for comfort really begins in the pages of the Bible. He wrote, "Whatever things were written before were written for our learning, that we through the patience and comfort of the Scriptures might have hope" (ROMANS 15:4 NKJV).

God has given us the Bible so that we can find our true comfort and satisfaction in Him alone. Through a relationship with Him, He gives us everything we need to live in a broken world, so that we don't have to keep on searching in all the wrong places.

BC

WANT MORE . . . ?

Will I have to give things up if I become a Christian? Can Christians still drink and go to parties? Check out answers to questions like this in *Big questions about . . . having fun* online at **ourdailybread.org/teen**

GOD'S COMFORT IS THE ONLY TRUE AND LASTING COMFORT.

THE WOULD-BE WOODCUTTER

BIBLE: 2 KINGS 6:1-7

Cast all your anxiety on him because he cares for you (1 PETER 5:7).

I spent one summer holiday cutting, stacking, selling and delivering firewood. It was a hard job, so I have sympathy for the unfortunate logger in today's story.

Elisha's school for prophets had grown, and their meeting place had become too small. Someone suggested they go into the woods, cut logs and make it big enough to fit the whole class. Elisha agreed and went with them. Things were going well until someone's axe head fell into the water (2 KINGS 6:5).

Some people have suggested that Elisha simply prodded about in the water with his stick until he found the axe head and dragged it into sight. That would hardly be worth mentioning, however. No, it was a miracle: the axe head was lost according to God's plans and began to float by His power so the logger could get it back (VV.6-7).

The simple miracle teaches us a powerful truth: God cares about the small things in life—lost axe heads, lost homework, lost glasses, lost phones—the little things that cause us to worry and stress. He doesn't always give us what we have lost, but He understands and can be fully trusted with each and every issue we face. He will be at work in everything and provide for us in ways we never expected.

Next to the confidence of our salvation, being confident of God's care is essential. Without it we would feel alone in the world and overwhelmed with every worry. It's good to know He cares and is involved in our every loss—small as they may be. Our concerns are His concerns.

DR

THINKING IT OVER . . .

What 'little' things are troubling you that you can cast on God right now? How does it encourage you to know that you can be confident in His daily care and love for you?

GOD IS INVOLVED IN EVEN THE SMALL STUFF.

MYSTERIOUS HELPERS

BIBLE: HEBREWS 13:1-3

Do not forget to show hospitality to strangers, for by so doing some people have shown hospitality to angels without knowing it (V.2).

Louise suffers from muscular dystrophy. While trying to leave a train station one day, she found herself facing a large flight of stairs without an elevator or escalator. In her helplessness she was about to start crying. Suddenly Louise saw a man walk up next to her, pick up her bag and gently help her up the stairs. When she turned to thank him, he was gone.

Michael was late for a meeting. Already stressed out with issues at home, he started battling London's traffic only to get a flat tyre. As he stood helplessly in the rain, a man stepped out of the crowd, opened the boot, jacked up the car and changed the wheel. When Michael turned to thank him, he was gone.

Who were these mysterious helpers? Kind strangers, or something more?

The popular image we have of angels as radiant or winged creatures is only half true. While some appear this way (ISAIAH 6:2; MATTHEW 28:3), others come with dusty feet, ready for a meal (GENESIS 18:1-5) and are easily mistaken for everyday people (JUDGES 13:16). The writer of Hebrews says that by looking out for people and helping strangers, we can show "hospitality to angels without knowing" (HEBREWS 13:2).

We don't know if Louise and Michael's helpers were angels. But according to the Bible, they could have been. Angels are at work right now, helping God's people (1:14). And they can seem as ordinary as anyone else. _SV_

WHAT I'M THANKFUL FOR . . .

Thank You, God, for Your provision—whether through angels, friends, family or anyone or anything else, You are always looking out for me

ANGELS ARE PART OF GOD'S PROVISION AND PROTECTION FOR US.

SLEEPING MOUNTAIN

BIBLE: GENESIS 6

The LORD saw how great the wickedness of the human race had become on the earth . . . So the LORD said, "I will wipe from the face of the earth the human race I have created . . . for I regret that I have made them" (VV.5,7).

A volcanic mountain in Mexico suddenly came alive, erupting with so much power that it became one of the world's largest active volcanoes. The 7,300-foot El Chichon giant had been quiet for hundreds of years. People assumed the volcano had gone extinct, becoming just a sleeping mountain instead.

People around us may well think the same thing about God: He is just a sleeping mountain now—there is nothing to worry about. Nothing could be further from the truth. God is fully involved in our world and our lives. And He is returning to judge the world (SEE HEBREWS 4:13). He hasn't returned yet—but that's not because He is sleeping, but because He has set the perfect time.

Jesus warned that His return, and the judgement He will bring, will be similar to "the days of Noah . . . People were eating, drinking, marrying and being given in marriage up to the day Noah entered the ark. Then the flood came and destroyed them all" (LUKE 17:26-27). Those people assumed God was a sleeping mountain, uninvolved and disinterested in their lives. Then suddenly they were wiped "from the face of the earth" (GENESIS 6:7).

But we are not to live like this. Paul reminds us: "You know very well that the day of the Lord will come like a thief in the night . . . But you, brothers and sisters, are not in darkness so that this day should surprise you like a thief" (1 THESSALONIANS 5:2,4).

When we are tempted to think God has forgotten about the world or that nothing is ever going to change, let's remember what the Bible teaches us: "The Lord's coming is near . . . The Judge is standing at the door!" (JAMES 5:8-9).   *cw*

WANT MORE . . . ?

Check out *Why doesn't God just sort out all the bad stuff?* online at
ourdailybread.org/lookingatlife

GOD IS NOT SLEEPING AND HIS JUDGEMENT SHOULD NOT BE UNEXPECTED.

BIBLE: LUKE 15:1-10

I tell you, there is rejoicing in the presence of the angels of God over one sinner who repents (V.10).

Do you ever feel like you're meant to be bringing everyone in your class to Jesus and transforming your entire school? Don't get me wrong, if God gives us the opportunity to make big changes like that—let's do it! But more often than not God gives us opportunities to talk about Jesus with individuals, rather than crowds.

Jesus taught crowds, fed thousands by the Sea of Galilee and was followed by huge numbers of people—yet many of the stories in the gospels are about Him connecting with and looking after individuals, one at a time.

I find it really encouraging that Jesus was never 'too big' to take time out for just one person. Like His conversation with one religious leader called Nicodemus (JOHN 3); His visit with one adulterous woman at a well in Samaria (JOHN 4); and His attention for one greedy, little man called Zaccheus, who was sitting up in a sycamore tree (LUKE 19). How amazed he must have been when Jesus singled him out and said, "Zacchaeus, come down immediately. I must stay at your house today" (V.5).

In Luke 15, Jesus told the parables of a shepherd and a woman who went searching for the one sheep and coin they had each lost. The stories of Luke 15 show our Father's perspective: every single person is vitally important to Him.

If you are ever feel like you're not sharing Jesus with enough people, remember Jesus' example and the stories He taught. There is rejoicing in heaven over each individual who trusts Him. So let's keep focused on the individuals (or individual) we know who God is giving us opportunities to speak with.

RDH

WHAT I'M THANKFUL FOR . . .

Thank You, Father, that every person is important to You. Thank You that I don't need to transform the world; I am part of Your rescue mission when I simply share Jesus whenever I have opportunities.

NEVER UNDERESTIMATE THE VALUE OF THE ONE PERSON YOU ARE ABLE TO SHARE JESUS WITH.

GETTING IN THE WAY OF JESUS

BIBLE: JOHN 3:26-36

He must become greater; I must become less (V.30).

- -

When our youth leader asked our group a difficult question about the life of Jesus, my hand shot up. I had just read the story, so I knew this one. And I wanted the others in the room to know that I knew it. Then I had a sudden panic: what if the answer wasn't what I thought? I didn't want to look stupid in front of my friends. So I lowered my hand. *Am I really this insecure?* I asked myself. Suddenly I realised all my thinking and motivation was about me and how I looked.

John the Baptist shows us a better way. When his disciples complained that people were beginning to leave him and follow Jesus, John said he was pleased to hear it. He was just the messenger. "I am not the Messiah but am sent ahead of him . . . He must become greater; I must become less" (JOHN 3:28-30). John realised the point of his existence was Jesus. He is "the one who comes from heaven" and "is above all" (v.31)—the Son who gave His life for us. He must receive all the glory and praise.

Any attention drawn to ourselves distracts others from Jesus. And since He is our only Saviour and the only hope for the world, any credit we steal from Him ends up hurting us and others.

There's no harm giving an answer we know in a Bible study. But let's also try to step out of the picture—to make sure what we say and do is about helping people see Jesus, and not ourselves. It's best for Him, for the world and for us.

MW

THINKING IT OVER . . .

When are you tempted to share the spotlight with Jesus?
How can you turn your attention to where it belongs?

IF WE'RE GETTING THE ATTENTION, THEN WE'RE JUST GETTING IN THE WAY.

THE TOUGHEST EXAM

BIBLE: 1 CORINTHIANS 11:23-34

Everyone ought to examine themselves before they eat of the bread and drink from the cup (V.28).

Lindsay was busily preparing for the toughest exam of her life. She was going over old exam questions to see how much she remembered and what kind of marks she was getting. She didn't rest until she could pass every one of the previous questions. When it came to the real exam, she passed it because she had tested herself so thoroughly.

Paul told the Corinthian Christians something about testing themselves that applies to us as well. When we come to take communion at church, we should examine ourselves (1 CORINTHIANS 11:28). Any issues, any selfishness, any grudges, any selfish things we've done need to be admitted to God before we take the bread and the wine of communion. Why? Because as Jesus' people we are accountable to Him. We can't just rock up to His table without a second thought. Communion is a place for us to remember just how, why and where Jesus saved us from all our sin.

So how do we prepare and test ourselves? We can begin by looking at two issues: firstly, are we actually living out our love for God and for His people (MATTHEW 22:36-40)? And secondly, are we looking to please God more than anything or anyone else (6:33)?

As Lindsay tested herself in order to be prepared for her exam, we too must test ourselves so that we can come to communion ready to remember all that Jesus has done to save us—and ready to commit our lives to Him again (1 CORINTHIANS 11:29-32).   *DCE*

WANT MORE . . . ?

Check out *What is communion all about?* online at
ourdailybread.org/lookingdeeper

COMMUNION CHALLENGES US TO STOP BEING COMPLACENT ABOUT JESUS' SACRIFICE FOR US.

IMPOSSIBLE FORGIVENESS

BIBLE: LUKE 23:32-43
Father, forgive them (V.34).

The following prayer was found crumpled among the remains of the Ravensbruck concentration camp where Nazis killed nearly 50,000 women: "O Lord, remember not only the men and women of goodwill, but also those of ill will. But do not remember the suffering they have inflicted upon us. Remember the [good things that have come] thanks to this suffering—our comradeship, our loyalty, our humility, the courage, the generosity, the greatness of heart which has grown out of this. And when they come to judgement, let all [these fruits] be their forgiveness."

I can't imagine the fear and pain inflicted on the woman who wrote this prayer. I can't imagine what kind of incredible love and forgiveness was needed for her to write these words. She did the unthinkable: she asked God to forgive the people who hated, imprisoned, tortured and probably killed her.

This prayer echoes Jesus' prayer. After being falsely accused, hated, beaten and humiliated, Jesus was "crucified . . . along with [two] criminals" (LUKE 23:33). Hanging from a rough-hewn cross—His body torn to bloody pieces as He gasped for breath—I would expect Jesus to judge the people who put Him there. Yet Jesus' prayer went against every human instinct: "Father, forgive them, for they do not know what they are doing" (V.34).

The forgiveness Jesus offers seems impossible, but He offers it to us. As we start to really appreciate the forgiveness He gives us (and what it cost Him), we will find the forgiveness we need to show becomes a little less impossible itself.

WC

TO PRAY ABOUT . . .
God, sometimes forgiveness seems like a strange, impossible thing to have to show to the people who hurt us the most. In our pain, help us to focus on Jesus' forgiveness. In that place, teach us to love like You do.

FORGIVENESS BECOMES POSSIBLE WHEN WE SEE THE MAN ON THE CROSS IN OUR PLACE.

TEMPTATIONS AND TRIALS

BIBLE: JAMES 1:1-15

Consider it pure joy, my brothers and sisters, whenever you face trials of many kinds (V.2).

It can be hard to tell the difference between trials and temptations. Are they just two words to describe the same thing? Even though they can happen at the same time, there is a fine line between them.

James 1:2 tells us to rejoice when we come up against various trials, but Jesus taught His disciples to pray that they wouldn't fall into temptation (MATTHEW 26:41). Trials are actually an opportunity for something very good; whereas temptations are always dangers to be avoided.

One preacher explained the difference like this: "Temptation says, 'Do this selfish thing; do not be put off by the fact that it is wrong.' Trials say, 'Do this right but hard thing; do not be put off by the fact that it is painful.'" Temptations are an opportunity to be selfish and focus on ourselves; trials are an opportunity to trust God and focus on Him.

Every difficulty has the potential to be a temptation and a trial. Even something ordinary like homework—it is a trial to knuckle down and get on with the work in a way that pleases God; and we can easily be tempted to do a half-hearted job so we can go and do something more fun instead!

Trials, if we let them, can help us get to know God better as we trust His strength, direction and provision, rather than relying on ourselves. Giving into temptations only ever drives us further away from Him. So next time you're up against an issue or problem, use it as an opportunity to stretch and grow your trust in God, so that "you may be mature and complete, not lacking anything" (JAMES 1:4).

DDH

TO PRAY ABOUT . . .

Dear God, help me to keep my focus on You when things are hard. Protect me from all the temptations and keep me close to You.

GIVING INTO TEMPTATION WILL ONLY EVER BRING US DOWN; TRIALS ARE OPPORTUNITIES TO GROW.

PHOEBE

BIBLE: ROMANS 16:1-16

I commend to you our sister Phoebe, a deacon of the church in Cenchreae. I ask you to receive her in the Lord in a way worthy of his people and to give her any help she may need from you, for she has been the benefactor of many people, including me (VV.1-2).

When a Bible teacher was asked what his favourite bit of the Bible was, he said, "It's the last chapter of Romans." The other person replied, "Seriously?! But it's just a bunch of names!"

"Yes," said the teacher. "The ones mentioned there were all different people, yet each had their own part to play. The Holy Spirit made sure their names were written down here to let us know they were individually loved and appreciated by God."

The apostle Paul began Romans 16 with "I commend to you our sister Phoebe" (ROMANS 16:1). He asked the Christians to help her however she needed them to because "she has been the [helper] of many people, including me" (V.2).

Too often we think that the most effective Christians are those who go off to share the gospel in other countries, or who lead churches and speak at international Christian events. But if this is our perspective, we won't notice the loving words and actions of the normal Christians in our churches and families whose names never get into the limelight. It's natural to look up to those who have become famous because of their walk with Jesus, but we must also remember to encourage and pray for people like Phoebe.

You may never become a world-renowned Christian author, speaker or missionary—but then, that's not the point, is it? Each one of us can be a Phoebe—someone who helps others get to know Jesus in our normal, everyday lives.

HB

THINKING IT OVER . . .

What Christians do you look up to? Do you look up to people in your church who love Jesus faithfully, yet never get into the limelight? Why are they a good example of the Christian life?

WE MIGHT NOT FEEL LIKE WE'VE DONE ANYTHING IMPORTANT, BUT OUR NAME IS STILL RECORDED IN HEAVEN!

IN OUR WEAKNESS

BIBLE: ROMANS 8:10-17,26-27
In the same way, the Spirit helps us in our weakness (V.26).

Anne Sheafe Miller died at the age of ninety, but she nearly died fifty years earlier from septicaemia following a miscarriage. Nothing the doctors did was making any difference to her condition. That's when another patient told the doctors he knew a scientist who'd been working on a new wonder drug. Anne's doctor managed to get a tiny amount for Anne. Within a day, her temperature was back to normal! Penicillin had saved Anne's life.

Since Adam and Eve messed up in the Garden of Eden, all human beings have experienced a fatal spiritual illness called sin (ROMANS 5:12). Only the death and resurrection of Jesus and the power of the Holy Spirit make it possible for us to be made brand new so we can live with God forever (8:1-2). The Holy Spirit allows us to enjoy life with God on earth, promising us that an unending life with Jesus awaits us in His home (vv.3-10). "And if the Spirit of him who raised Jesus from the dead is living in you, he who raised Christ from the dead will also give life to your mortal bodies because of his Spirit who lives in you" (v.11).

When you feel like you're making a mess of things and that your sinful instincts are still running the show, give your attention to Jesus again and the salvation He has secured for you. We are no longer lying on our death beds—we have been cured forever!

When you're struggling, let the Holy Spirit comfort, strengthen and redirect you through the Bible's teaching (vv.11-17). "The Spirit helps us in our weakness" and "[prays] for God's people in accordance with the will of God" (vv.26-27). We never have to go it alone, because God is right here with us by His Spirit.   ROS

WHAT I'M THANKFUL FOR . . .
Heavenly Father, thank You for the salvation Your Son won for me, and for the power of the Holy Spirit who helps me to enjoy new life with You.

WHEN WE ARE WEAK, WE NEED TO REMEMBER THAT OUR GOD IS NEVER ANYTHING LESS THAN STRONG.

WORK TO BE DONE

BIBLE: PSALM 112

Surely the righteous will never be shaken; they will be remembered for ever (V.6).

If our new life as Christians is all about loving and knowing God—and growing closer to Him—then why doesn't He just take us to heaven as soon as we choose to trust Him? Surely there's no better place to get to know Him!

One reason is simply that God has work for us to do. "We are immortal," one Christian philosopher said, "until our work is done."

The time of our death is not decided by anyone or anything here on earth. That decision is made by God alone. When we have done all that God has planned for us to do, then and only then will He take us home—and not one second before. As Paul put it, "When David had served God's purpose in his own generation, he fell asleep" (ACTS 13:36).

In the meantime there's plenty for us to do. "As long as it is day, we must do the works of him who sent me," Jesus said. "Night is coming, when no one can work" (JOHN 9:4). One day in the future (maybe way in the future) we will close our eyes on this world for the last time. And Jesus will open our eyes in heaven. This is absolutely certain—every day brings us closer.

For now, we should have our focus on the work God has prepared for us to do (EPHESIANS 2:10). Our lives are no longer about all the stuff we can get or experience. Now they are about living for Jesus, trusting the Holy Spirit to make us more like Him, and sharing His love and welcome wherever we can. "And whatever you do, whether in word or deed, do it all in the name of the Lord Jesus, giving thanks to God the Father through him" (COLOSSIANS 3:17).   *DR*

WHAT I'M THANKFUL FOR . . .

Thank You, God, that You want to use me to make Jesus known in my family, school, church and wherever else You put me.

WE ARE GOD'S HANDIWORK, CREATED IN CHRIST JESUS TO DO GOOD WORKS, WHICH GOD PREPARED IN ADVANCE FOR US TO DO. EPHESIANS 2:10

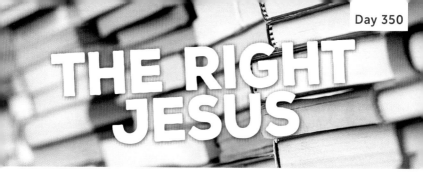

THE RIGHT JESUS

BIBLE: 2 CORINTHIANS 11:1-15

For if someone comes to you and preaches a Jesus other than the Jesus we preached . . . you put up with it easily enough (V.4).

The teacher started the lesson by summarising the plot of the book the class had been set to read as homework. As Jenny listened, it began to dawn on her how different this book sounded to the one she had read. Finally she had to put her hand up and admit to the teacher she had read the wrong book by accident. Although she had enjoyed it, it didn't help her much in class—she couldn't join in with the rest of her group as they discussed the 'right' book.

Paul did not want the Corinthian Christians to believe in a wrong Jesus. He explained that false Bible teachers had slipped into the church and were teaching them about a different 'Jesus' (2 CORINTHIANS 11:3-4). He also showed his distress that the people swallowed the lies "easily enough" (V.4).

Paul didn't describe exactly what these phony teachers tried to pass off as truth. In his first letter to the church, however, he went over some of the key facts about the real Jesus of the Bible. This Jesus was the promised King who "died for our sins . . . was raised on the third day . . . [and then] appeared to the Twelve, and finally to Paul himself" (1 CORINTHIANS 15:3-8). This Jesus had come to earth through a virgin named Mary and was named Immanuel (God with us) to show He was both fully God and fully human (MATTHEW 1:20-23).

Does this sound like the Jesus you know? Understanding and accepting the truth written in the Bible about Jesus is important. It shows us that we are on the right path—the only Way that brings us to God today and to heaven after we die (JOHN 14:6).

JBS

THINKING IT OVER . . .

How do I know that I believe the truth about Jesus? What might I need to investigate to make sure I understand what the Bible says about Jesus?

BEWARE OF PEOPLE WHO TALK ABOUT A 'JESUS' WHO DOESN'T MATCH THE JESUS OF THE BIBLE!

BLOOD NOT BRAVERY

BIBLE: ISAIAH 53

He was pierced for our transgressions, he was crushed for our iniquities; the punishment that brought us peace was on him, and by his wounds we are healed (V.5).

The death of Jesus Christ on the cross of Calvary was substitutionary—which means He died in our place, "the righteous for the unrighteous, to bring [us] to God" (1 PETER 3:18). He is our only hope for salvation—giving us new, forgiven life with God.

A chaplain had just finished praying with a dying soldier when a nurse came in and said, "You don't need to worry about anything; anyone who gives their life for their country is all right." The soldier smiled, but said, "You're wrong. When I lay out there on the battlefield, I knew I had given my all. But that didn't help me to face God. I wasn't fit to die, and I knew it. But this chaplain here has helped me realise that Jesus was punished for all my sins. I'm not afraid to die now, because I know that He has forgiven me."

That nurse meant well, but she didn't get it. She thought effort, brave acts and hard work are enough to make us pleasing to God. Yet the soldier understood the reality: no one, not even the best and bravest of us, is good enough to please God on our own. We all need Jesus to pay for our sin, our selfishness, our every failing, our lack of love—without Him, we have no hope "for all have sinned and fall short of the glory of God" (ROMANS 3:23).

We need to take time out every day to thank Jesus for dying on the cross and paying for our sins. He alone did it, and He did it alone.   PVG

WANT MORE . . . ?

Check out *Why did Jesus die?* online at **ourdailybread.org/lookingdeeper**

UNLESS OUR LIVES ARE PERFECT, THEY WILL NEVER BE GOOD ENOUGH. THAT'S WHY WE NEED JESUS.

REAL CHRISTIANITY

BIBLE: MATTHEW 5:3-12
Rejoice and be glad, because great is your reward in heaven (V.12).

I decided to volunteer in a Christian organisation a few years ago. When I first joined them, I was given a list of rules to do with the things I could and couldn't do when I was in their building. It included things like: no alcohol, no smoking, no social media, etc. One bit said: "We expect Christian behaviour from our employees." I found it easy to agree to this list because I didn't drink or smoke. And it wasn't a big deal for me to put my phone in a locker for the few hours I was there. But none of this had anything to do with my Christianity—the list just happened to match my lifestyle.

The list did make me think about the things that weren't on there. It didn't say: "don't be proud, insensitive, angry, hateful or critical." If those attitudes had made the list, I would have found it much harder to live up to!

Following Jesus can't be defined by a list of rules. It's a way of life and attitude that's difficult to describe, other than by using words like "love" and "serving".

Matthew 5:3-10 sums it up well though: those who rely on the Spirit of Jesus are humble (MATTHEW 5:3). They grieve over the bad things of this world, rather than joining in (V.4). They are gentle and kind (V.5). They love to know God better and share Him (V.6). They are merciful to those who make a mess of things (V.7). They are single-minded in their love for Jesus (V.8). They are peaceful and look to make peace no matter who they talk to (V.9). They are kind to those who hurt them, returning good for evil (V.10). And they are blessed, a word that means "happy" in the deepest sense.

This kind of life attracts the attention of others and belongs only to those who trust in Jesus—those who know they can't live like this on their own.   DR

THINKING IT OVER . . .
Which of the descriptions from Matthew 5:3-12 do you recognise the most in your life? Which others do you need more of? How can you grow in this way of life?

REAL CHRISTIANITY CAN ONLY BE LIVED OUT BY LETTING JESUS LIVE HIS LIFE THROUGH US.

BLESSED ARE . . .

BIBLE: 2 TIMOTHY 3:10-17

Blessed are those who are persecuted because of righteousness (MATTHEW 5:10).

In 1948, Harlan Popov, the pastor of an underground church in Bulgaria, was taken from his home for a "little questioning". He suffered around-the-clock interrogation and no food for ten days. Each time he denied being a spy, he was beaten. But Popov not only survived this torture, but also helped some of the other prisoners put their trust in Jesus. Finally, eleven years later, he was released and continued to share his love of Jesus. Two years after that he was able to leave the country and be reunited with his family. He spent the following years preaching and raising money to smuggle Bibles into countries which had made Christianity illegal.

Like countless Christians throughout the ages, Popov was persecuted because he refused to give up his Christian faith. Jesus, long before His own torture and death, said, "Blessed are those who are persecuted because of righteousness, for theirs is the kingdom of heaven" (MATTHEW 5:9). He continued, "Blessed are you when people . . . persecute you and falsely say all kinds of evil against you because of me" (v.10).

"Blessed"? What could Jesus have meant? He was talking about the wholeness, peace and comfort that we have in our relationship with Him—no matter how people might attack us (vv.4,8-10). Popov kept going because He was strengthened by his relationship with God, even in suffering.

Today, we know two things to be true: as Christians we will be attacked and made fun of (2 TIMOTHY 3:12); and as God's children He will provide the strength we need to keep going (ROMANS 8:37).

TG

WHAT I'M THANKFUL FOR . . .

Loving Father, we thank You for never leaving or giving up on us in our most difficult times.

PERSECUTION WILL COME; BUT WE WILL NEVER HAVE TO FACE IT ALONE.

GO-BETWEEN PRAYER

BIBLE: ROMANS 8:26-34
The Spirit intercedes for God's people (V.27).

Late one Saturday afternoon, my family stopped at a local restaurant for lunch. As the waiter brought the crispy fries and burgers to our table, we told him that we pray as a family before we eat. "Is there something we can pray for you about today?" Allen, the waiter, looked at us with a mixture of surprise and anxiety. A short silence followed before he told us that he was sleeping on his friend's sofa each night, his car had just broken down and he was completely broke.

As we prayed and quietly asked God to provide for Allen and show him His love, I thought about how our go-between prayer was similar to what happens when the Holy Spirit takes up our cause and connects us with God. In our moments of greatest need—when we realise we're no match for the stuff we're dealing with and we don't know how to say this to God, "The Spirit intercedes for God's people" (ROMANS 8:27). What the Spirit says is a mystery, but we're promised that it always fits with God's plan for our lives.

The next time you pray for God's answers, provision and protection in someone else's life, let that be a reminder to you that your needs are also being brought to God—who knows your name and cares about your problems.   *JBS*

THINKING IT OVER . . .
Is there anyone I can pray for today? How might I handle my problems
differently if I knew that the Holy Spirit was praying for me during the struggle?

WE CAN STAND BEFORE GOD ON BEHALF OF OTHERS.

THE BISCUIT TIN

BIBLE: EPHESIANS 5:1-14

Among you there must not be even a hint of sexual immorality, or of any kind of impurity, or of greed, because these are improper for God's holy people (V.3).

Sam's mum made biscuits and put them in the biscuit tin, telling him not to touch them until after lunch. Soon she heard the lid of the tin move, and she called out, "What are you doing?" A little voice called back, "My hand is in the biscuit tin, resisting temptation." As amusing as the idea is, we know that temptation is that much harder to say "No!" to when our hands are 'in the biscuit tin'.

This was the kind of challenge facing the early church in Ephesus. There were all kinds of open 'biscuit tins' for them to slip their hands into. One of which was sexual temptation. Paul understood that selfish, uncontrolled sexual activity was a huge problem for new gentile Christians in the early church to overcome. They had never had to control that part of their life before.

Paul wanted the Ephesians to stand against their instincts and the culture around them, and live out their identity as God's holy children. So he reminded them that sexual immorality—which makes sex a normal part of our relationships, when actually it is special and to be left for marriage—goes against what it means to live for Jesus in purity (EPHESIANS 5:3).

As followers of Jesus, God's plan is for us to stand out (so, to be holy) in this world. But keeping our hands in the biscuit tin when it comes to sex would mean allowing ourselves to daydream about sex, not putting safe-search controls on our phones or letting our relationships become more and more physical. These things will lead us into danger and regrets. Sex is powerful, good and—ultimately—tempting.

Standing out for Jesus means obeying the Bible, not our instincts (PSALM 119:9), living in self-control (1 THESSALONIANS 4:1-7), relying on God's Spirit (GALATIANS 5:16), and trusting God's good and proper limits for sex (1 CORINTHIANS 7:2,9). So let's keep well away from the biscuit tin! *TF*

WANT MORE . . . ?

Check out *What does the Bible say about sex?* online at **ourdailybread.org/teen**

WE WILL NEVER STAND UP TO SEXUAL TEMPTATION IF WE KEEP LOOKING TO BE TEMPTED.

JUST A LITTLE

BIBLE: GALATIANS 5:1-12

A little yeast works through the whole batch of dough (V.9).

One of China's popular 'hotpot' restaurants (where people dip vegetables and meat into boiling broth) lost more than £170 million after a customer found a small rat in his dinner! The guy filmed a video of the dead rodent held above the bowl with his chopsticks. The video went viral and, unsurprisingly, the company's reputation spiralled massively! Such huge damage—all from one tiny creature.

In Paul's letter to the Galatians, he warned them to be serious about seemingly small things which could spoil the freedom Jesus had won for them. "Stand firm," Paul said, telling them to reject anyone who said they needed to add religious rules or traditions to their relationship with Jesus (GALATIANS 5:1). The church may have found these rules familiar, and maybe even comforting—but allowing even the smallest 'add-on' in their Christian life would affect everything. A "little yeast works through the whole batch of dough," Paul said (v.9). Yeast is tiny, but even a sprinkle will make a whole batch of bread rise in the oven. Similarly, only a little sin, a little religious rule-keeping or a little self-reliance, starts to change everything, dragging our focus away from Jesus and back onto ourselves.

We may well hear some teachers or church leaders suggesting we must earn God's love or follow some kind of religious code in order to be His people. May God's Spirit within us speak loud and clear and help us realise these things are lies. The truth is that our salvation is complete in Jesus. We have incredible, astonishing freedom: no rules, just new life with Him! *wc*

TO PRAY ABOUT . . .

God, I've been letting false ideas, even small ones, spoil the freedom You've given me. Help me to know and enjoy the fullness of life that Jesus has already won for me.

IT IS FOR FREEDOM THAT CHRIST HAS SET US FREE.
GALATIANS 5:1

DEEP SPACE

BIBLE: MATTHEW 6:5-8

Your Father knows what you need before you ask him (V.8).

A group of scientists are looking up, but not to God. They have 'worked out' that as many as fifty million civilisations may exist somewhere in space, and they believe that some of them may have even invented ways to improve our lives and hold off death.

These scientists beamed a message to the outer edge of our galaxy. But even if that signal were picked up, they estimate that it would take 48,000 years for an answer to come back.

To Christians, these efforts seem crazy. Yet those scientists are serious about their efforts, while we—who do have contact with 'another world'— sometimes act as if our prayers are not heard. Every child of God can talk freely with the Creator and King Himself! We have close, personal 24/7 access to the One who stretched out all the galaxies. He hears us the instant we pray and answers in His perfect timing. Through the privilege of prayer, every Christian can come to One who is all-powerful, who listens in heaven, who meets our needs perfectly and is with us in all things.

We can send our messages to heaven with confidence, because we know personally that God listens—and it won't take 48,000 years for us to get His answers!

MDH

WHAT I'M THANKFUL FOR . . .

Thank You, Father, that I can bring every need to You and talk to You throughout my day. Thank You for always listening to me.

WHEN WE PRAY, WE SPEAK TO THE KING OF THE UNIVERSE—AND HE ANSWERS!

THE LIFE OF A LIE

BIBLE: PROVERBS 12:17-22

Truthful lips endure for ever, but a lying tongue lasts only a moment (V.19).

A university student became a local hero when word got around that he had rescued a girl from three attackers. But he got national attention when someone found out that his story was a lie. The embarrassed student admitted that he did not (as he had originally said) use martial arts to defend a girl. He had picked up his cuts and bruises being clumsy at home.

His short-lived fame proves what Solomon said about the life expectancy of lies. Lying to avoid trouble or embarrassment will only ever lead to more trouble.

Not telling the truth only delays the consequences of our lies. We end up just getting more and more entangled in them as we try to cover our tracks and make ourselves look better than we really are.

The truth always comes out in time. Proverbs 12 tells us why. God hates lies (PROVERBS 12:22) and He views them as weapons of violence (V.18). As a result, lies do not hold up very long (V.19). They are the tools of the trade of people who only rely on themselves to solve problems, and don't entrust their mess to God (V.20).

We can learn from today's reading and from the embarrassed student. A lie may seem like the easy way out, but it will end up causing more trouble in the long run.

MDH

TO PRAY ABOUT . . .

God, please help me to be truthful, even when it is painful and costs me something.
I know honesty pleases You and makes me rely on You, rather than myself.

THE TRUTH MAY HURT AT THE TIME, BUT AT LEAST IT LEADS TO PEACE LONG TERM.

PEACEMAKERS

BIBLE: I SAMUEL 25:14-35

Blessed are the peacemakers, for they will be called children of God
(MATTHEW 5:9).

Abigail was a true peacemaker! Her bravery and courage spared the future king of Israel from doing something terrible. Her story is in the Bible: David had been forced to live in the countryside to escape King Saul's jealousy. A group of about 600 men and their families had gathered around him. For several months they camped near Carmel where the flocks of Nabal (Abigail's husband) were grazing.

David's men had helped Nabal's shepherds protect the sheep from robbers. Now the shearing time had come, and David sent messengers to ask for some payment from Nabal, who was a wealthy man. But he refused and treated David's men with disrespect.

In anger David rashly decided to take revenge on Nabal and all the men in his household—and planned to attack them. When Abigail heard what had happened, she quickly gathered a large supply of food, met with David and his fighting men and humbly apologised for her husband's bad behaviour. David immediately realised that she had stopped him from carrying out a revenge which would have angered God, and he praised God for providing Abigail in the situation (1 SAMUEL 25:32).

Are we as quick to try and resolve our fights and arguments? Jesus said, "Blessed are the peacemakers, for they will be called children of God" (MATTHEW 5:9). *HVL*

THINKING IT OVER . . .

Read Ephesians 4:2-5. What do you think it would look like in your life if you made "every effort" to keep unity and peace (V.3)? How do the attitudes listed in verse 2 help makes us people of peace? What limits do you think there are to the unity and peace we offer (2 TIMOTHY 3:1-5; 2 JOHN 1:7-10)?

GOD'S PEOPLE ARE TO MAKE PEACE WHEREVER THEY CAN.

STARTING WITH TRUST

BIBLE: LUKE 1:31-38

When Joseph woke up, he did what the angel of the Lord had commanded him and took Mary home as his wife (MATTHEW 1:24).

When the angel Gabriel appeared to Mary and then to shepherds with good news for the world (LUKE 1:26-27; 2:10), was it good news to this teenage girl?

Perhaps Mary was thinking: *How do I explain my pregnancy to my family? Will my fiancé Joseph call off the wedding? What will everyone else say? How will I survive as a young single mum?*

When Joseph learned about Mary's pregnancy, he was really upset. He had three options. 1) Go ahead with the marriage. 2) Divorce her publicly and allow her to be publicly shamed. Or 3) break off the engagement quietly. Joseph chose option three, but God stepped in. He told Joseph in a dream, "Joseph son of David, do not be afraid to take Mary home as your wife, because what is conceived in her is from the Holy Spirit" (MATTHEW 1:20).

For Mary and Joseph, their journey began with trusting God with everything, despite the unthinkable challenges before them. They entrusted themselves to God and, in doing so, lived out the promise of 1 John 2:5: "If anyone obeys his word, love for God is truly made complete in them." May God's love give us the strength and confidence we need to live out our journeys with Him in the same way: through trusting everything He has said in the Bible.

AL

TO PRAY ABOUT . . .

Father, when things are hard, help me to copy Joseph and trust what You say. You are with me and bigger than all of the challenges I will ever face.

WE'LL FOLLOW GOD MORE READILY WHEN WE ENTRUST OURSELVES COMPLETELY TO HIM.

WHERE CHOICES LEAD

BIBLE: PSALM 1

The LORD watches over the way of the righteous (V.6).

With no phone signal and no map, we had just our memory of a fixed map at the start of the walking trail to guide us. More than an hour later, we finally found our way out of the woods and back into the car park. Having missed the turn-off that would have made for a half-mile hike, we ended up taking a much longer trek.

Life can be like that: we have to ask not simply if something is right or wrong, but where it will lead. Psalm 1 compares two ways of living—that of the righteous (those who love God) and that of the wicked (the enemies of those who love God). The righteous grow strong like a tree, but the wicked blow away in the wind (PSALM 1:3-4). This psalm shows what growing strong really looks like: depending on God for absolutely everything.

So how do we become that kind of person? Among other things, Psalm 1 tells us to step back from destructive friendships and selfish habits (V.1). These things can quickly block us from enjoying God's blessings in our lives (V.2). Ultimately, the reason for our growth and strength is God's daily care for us: "The LORD watches over the way of the righteous" (V.6).

Give all that you are to God, let Him redirect you from lifestyles that lead to nowhere, and instead plant yourself in the wisdom, direction and teaching of the Bible.

GP

THINKING IT OVER . . .

What friendships or habits do you need to make a break from? Where do you see your current lifestyle choices leading you? How can you create more time in your week to read the Bible?

EVERY CHOICE LEADS SOMEWHERE, SO LET'S MAKE SURE OUR CHOICES ALWAYS LEAD US TO JESUS.

COMPLETE

BIBLE: COLOSSIANS 2:6-12

So you also are complete through your union with Christ (V.10 NLT).

In a movie I watched recently, a marriage begins to fall apart. Trying to win his wife back, the husband looks into her eyes and says, "You complete me." It's a heart-warming message we see a lot at the cinema. It's the idea that each of us is a 'half' that must find our other half to be made complete.

The belief that a romantic partner completes us seems to be cemented into our thinking. But is it true? I've talked to many married couples who still feel incomplete for one reason or another. There's nothing wrong with their partner—but it turns out they're not the answer to their 'emptiness'. Ultimately, no human can fully complete us.

Paul gives another solution. "For in Christ lives all the fullness of God in a human body. So you also are complete through your union with Christ" (COLOSSIANS 2:9-10 NLT). Jesus doesn't just forgive us (VV.11-12) and free us from sin (VV.14-15), He *completes* us by bringing the life of God into our lives (V.13). He is the one we are each looking for!

Romance, dating and marriage are all good, but no matter how great being with another person is, they will never, ever make us whole. Only Jesus can do that. Instead of expecting a person or anything else to complete us, let's allow God's fullness to fill our lives more and more. *sv*

THINKING IT OVER . . .

How have you tried to find meaning and satisfaction through people instead of God? How does Jesus completing us change your view of dating, marriage and singleness?

ONLY JESUS BRINGS THE COMPLETION WE'RE LOOKING FOR.

SHALOM HOUSE

BIBLE: GALATIANS 5:16-25

The peace of God, which transcends all understanding, will guard your hearts and your minds in Christ Jesus (PHILIPPIANS 4:7).

In Perth, Australia, there is a place called *Shalom House* where men struggling with different addictions can go to find help. At *Shalom House* they'll meet caring staff members who introduce them to God's "shalom" (the Hebrew word for peace). Lives crushed under the weight of addictions to drugs, alcohol, gambling and other things are being transformed by the love of God.

Central to this transformation is the message of the cross. Through the resurrection of Jesus broken people find their own lives resurrected and made brand new. In Jesus we can find true peace and a real rescue.

Peace is not just being away from conflict; it is the presence of God's wholeness. All of us need this shalom, and it is only found in trusting Jesus and receiving His Spirit. This is why Paul directed the Galatians to the Spirit's transformational work. As the Holy Spirit works in our lives, He grows His "fruit" in us, which includes love, joy, patience and more (GALATIANS 5:22-23). He gives us that lifestyle of true, lasting peace.

As the Spirit helps us to live in God's shalom, we learn to bring our needs, addictions and issues to our heavenly Father. We don't need to try and sort them on our own. When we work through them with Him, we can experience "the peace of God, which transcends all understanding,"—the peace that "will guard your hearts and your minds in Christ Jesus" (PHILIPPIANS 4:7).   *BC*

WHAT I'M THANKFUL FOR . . .

God of shalom, thank You that Your plan is for peace to reign in my life.
Thank You for the work of Jesus to make peace available and the work of
the Spirit who helps me to live out a life of shalom.

WITH GOD'S SPIRIT WITHIN US, WE CAN KNOW TRUE PEACE.

AMAZING SKILL

BIBLE: PSALM 139:7-16

I praise you because I am fearfully and wonderfully made; your works are wonderful, I know that full well (V.14).

The leader of our church music group led the group and played the piano at the same time, skilfully balancing those two responsibilities. At the end of one service, he looked really tired, so I asked him if he was okay. He said, "I've never had to do that before." Then he explained. "The piano was so out of tune that I had to play the whole service in two different keys—my left hand playing in one key and my right hand in another!" I was blown away by his skill to be able to do something like that! And I was amazed at God, who creates humans to be capable of such things.

King David had an even bigger sense of wonder when he wrote, "Thank you for making me so wonderfully complex! Your workmanship is marvellous—how well I know it" (PSALM 139:14 NLT). Whether in people's abilities or simply the amazing world around us, everything in creation directs us to be in awe of our Creator.

One day, when we're with God in heaven, people from every corner of the earth will worship Him with the words, "You are worthy, our Lord and God, to receive glory and honour and power, for you created all things, and by your will they were created and have their being" (REVELATION 4:11). The amazing skills God gives us and the great world He has created are reason enough to praise Him.

BC

THINKING IT OVER . . .

What parts of God's creation make you praise Him? Why is it important for you to thank and praise God for the skills He's given you?

WE CAN PRAISE GOD FOR THE SKILLS HE HAS GIVEN US.

WHAT THEN?

BIBLE: MATTHEW 6:19-24

Riches do not endure for ever, and a crown is not secure for all generations
(PROVERBS 27:24).

- -

I read a story about a young guy in the 16th century who was talking to a Christian named Philip Neri. The young guy said excitedly, "My parents have finally agreed to let me study law!" Philip replied simply, "What then?"

The guy said, "Then I shall become a lawyer!"

"And then?" Philip repeated.

"Then I shall earn lots of money, buy a country house, get a carriage and horses, marry a beautiful woman and lead a happy life!"

Again Philip asked, "What then?"

"Then . . ." The guy began, suddenly thinking about death for the first time. He realised that he had not thought about God once in his plans.

The point of this story is not that plans, achievement and money are wrong. But if they become our central goal, we leave God out of everything. Jesus said it's impossible to love both money and God (MATTHEW 6:24), and He warned, "Do not store up for yourselves treasures on earth . . . but store up for yourselves treasures in heaven" (VV.19-20).

So next time you are making plans, put them to the "What then?" test. Are your plans made with God and His kingdom in mind? If so, they will stand up to the test!

JY

THINKING IT OVER . . .

What do you hope the future holds for your life?
How much is God at the centre of your plans?

**WE MAKE GOOD PLANS
WHEN GOD IS AT THE CENTRE OF THEM.**

GOD-CENTRED DATING

Does he like me? Did he just flirt with me? Does his reply mean something more?
Should I ask her? What does her silence mean? Should I admit how I feel to her?

When it comes to talking with the opposite sex, these questions will have probably crossed our minds before. After all, a friendship developing into more of a relationship is bound to make us a little uncertain: *Is he the one? Is she into me? What should I do?*

And with most of our conversations taking place through instant messaging and social media, we can miss out on the facial expressions, tone and body language that help us read how people feel about us. This means that miscommunications are more likely to happen, making us even more unsure about what our crush may have really said (or not said).

There's a whole dictionary of words to describe these *not-quite-relationships*. There isn't just *ghosting*—completely disappearing from someone's life after losing interest in them. There's also *benching*, where you become a plan B for someone who wants to keep their options open; and *cushioning*, where you're still in contact with potential partners even after committing to someone else. Not to mention *slow fading, breadcrumbing* . . . you get the point.

What does God think about these *situationships*—where it's more than a friendship but not quite a boyfriend/girlfriend relationship? While the Bible doesn't directly lay down laws for dating, it does give us principles that can help.

Firstly, if we are going to be dating, then as Christians we need to be looking to date other Christians. We only need to check out Solomon's example in the Bible to see the dangers of dating and committing to non-Christians: "his wives turned his heart after other gods, and his heart was not fully devoted to the LORD his God . . . so Solomon did evil in the eyes of the LORD" (1 KINGS 11:4,6). Loving God is the most important thing. People who don't know Him are only going to drag us away from Him. No matter how much we fancy them; the danger is just not worth it.

In fact, the greatest commandments in the Bible give us solid principles for our dating: "'Love the Lord your God with all your heart and with all your soul and with all your mind.' This is the first and greatest commandment. And the second is like it: 'Love your neighbour as yourself'" (MATTHEW 22:37-39).

In one Christian book about dating, I read this:

> "Dating requires us to honour God first. Many Christians approach dating mainly in terms of finding romance and meeting their emotional needs. Far too few think of it as an opportunity to honour God and grow more like Jesus. What about loving our neighbour? This commandment requires us to put our dating partner's holiness ahead of our happiness. If you are dating someone and the relationship does not grow into marriage, the least you can do as a Christian is to make sure that while dating you helped them stay close to God."

The point is, many people date for selfish reasons—they want to have their own desires and needs met. As Christians we need to put other people and their needs before ourselves. When we're dating, or thinking about dating someone, we need to ask ourselves: *What would the most loving action be towards him or her?* Here's two points that might be helpful to think about:

1. If you like (or don't like) someone, make it clear.
Don't leave someone hanging. There's nothing wrong with wanting to get to know someone better before talking about your interest in him or her. But be careful about what kind of impression you're making on the other person, and consider how he or she might be feeling in the meantime.

Also, if you don't like someone, make it clear. Don't flirt with them for the fun of it. The Song of Solomon 2:7 tells us not to "arouse or awaken love until it so desires". For example, if you know that someone is likely to feel hurt if you openly reject them, a more loving option might be to drop more subtle hints. This might mean politely turning down offers to meet or waiting longer periods before replying to their messages.

Similarly, you might want to consider gently and lovingly telling them that you're not interested in a relationship, if the situation calls for it.

While you might feel uncomfortable or afraid of hurting them, remember that it is our duty to respect them as a fellow Christian and child of God. If that means causing some hurt now, it's better than causing him or her even more hurt by only revealing it much later on.

Ask yourself: *Am I relating to the other person in a way that honours God and him or her? Are my responses clear when I talk about how I feel towards them? Or are my responses leading them to draw the wrong conclusion?*

On the other hand, if someone you like is sending you mixed signals—ignoring you one moment while flirting with you the next—you might want to consider two options. Either openly ask how he or she feels about you, or step away from the relationship if you feel that the other person isn't being straightforward.

Treat others as you would want to be treated (LUKE 6:31). Just as you don't want to be left hanging—or ghosted, breadcrumbed, cushioned or whatever—don't do these things to them either.

2. If you're unsure about how you feel, give it to God.

There may be times where the relationship isn't always so clear-cut. You might be unsure about how you feel about someone, especially where they might seem to want more. Do you really like him or her, or is it something else that's fuelling these feelings—insecurity, loneliness, lust?

I've felt this way many times over the years, thanks to the raging hormones of a teenage girl. How I pined and cried for the attention of one boy or another!

It was only when I became a Christian that I found that there was a better way: giving my cares and worries to Jesus, who loves us with a love no boyfriend or girlfriend can ever offer.

Before starting a relationship or even thinking about starting one, it's important to talk with God about how we feel, what His plans are for us and for peace about any decisions we make. It's important to remember there is no need to rush. There is always time to rest with God and talk things over with Him.

I wrote this in my diary a few years ago when I had a strong crush on a classmate I had just got to know:

> *"I find it so difficult to see a trace of that spark or non-spark; in that I cannot tell whether or not he feels the same way. Surely if he did, I could tell? Yet I see nothing (and so continue to believe everything). And this is the worst part: not knowing yet believing it to be so. Since he has shown neither interest nor dis-interest, I continue to hold on to this hope, which is a potentially devastating thing to do. Already I catch whiffs of him everywhere I go, and he is continually brought up again and again in my mind, growing the obsession.*
>
> *Where this friendship will lead me, I do not know. But I pray that God will keep and guide me, that ultimately He will give me His stamp of approval or rejection; and in the meantime will reveal to me more about this guy, that I may decide whether or not this can develop any further."*

God eventually did reveal something to me: this person was a non-Christian who already had a girlfriend, all of which I found out a few months later. Yet the process of committing this *situationship* to God daily—by choosing to commit my anxieties and uncertainties to Him, seeking His ways and will, and praying for Him to guard me— helped me to overcome the hurt and disappointment when I found out more.

It is tempting to spend hours thinking over whether your crush feels the same way—overanalysing every little thing they say or don't say. But don't take things into your own hands. If it is meant to be, God will reveal it to you and the other person (if he or she is a Christian). If it's not meant to be, God will reveal that too. I find that this is a simple but deeply comforting truth (as someone who's prone to overthinking and worrying!).

So trust God in everything, and He will answer whatever needs, worries and questions you have, in His perfect timing and in line with His perfect plans for you (PROVERBS 3:5-8). And always keep in mind that if God is preventing a relationship, it's because He's got something much better in mind for you!

EXPLORE THE BIBLE'S STORY IN A YEAR!

This 365 day reading plan takes you all the way from Genesis to Revelation. It won't overwhelm you with every chapter and verse of the Bible! But it covers all the main bits to help you get to know the full story . . .

☑

- [ ] Luke 4:16-30
- [ ] Mark 1:16-39
- [ ] Luke 5:1-39
- [ ] John 5:1-47
- [ ] Mark 2:23–3:19
- [ ] Matthew 5:1-16
- [ ] Matthew 5:17-30
- [ ] Matthew 5:31-48
- [ ] Matthew 6:1-18
- [ ] Matthew 6:19-34
- [ ] Matthew 7:1-12
- [ ] Matthew 7:13-29
- [ ] Luke 7:1-17
- [ ] Matthew 11:1-30
- [ ] Luke 7:36–8:3
- [ ] Matthew 12:22-50
- [ ] Mark 4:1-29
- [ ] Matthew 13:24-43
- [ ] Matthew 13:44-52
- [ ] Luke 8:22-56
- [ ] Matthew 9:27-38
- [ ] Mark 6:1-13
- [ ] Matthew 10:16-42
- [ ] Mark 6:14-29
- [ ] Matthew 14:13-36
- [ ] John 6:22-40
- [ ] John 6:41-71
- [ ] Mark 7:1-37
- [ ] Matthew 15:32–16:12
- [ ] Mark 8:22–9:1
- [ ] Luke 9:28-45
- [ ] Matthew 17:24–18:6
- [ ] Mark 9:38-50
- [ ] Matthew 18:10-22
- [ ] John 7:1-31
- [ ] John 7:32-53
- [ ] John 8:1-20
- [ ] John 8:21-59
- [ ] Luke 10:1-24
- [ ] Luke 10:25-42
- [ ] Luke 11:1-13
- [ ] Luke 11:14-32
- [ ] Luke 11:33-54
- [ ] Luke 12:1-21
- [ ] Luke 12:22-48
- [ ] Luke 12:49-59
- [ ] Luke 13:1-21
- [ ] John 9:1-41

- [ ] John 10:1-18
- [ ] Luke 13:22-35
- [ ] Luke 14:1-14
- [ ] Luke 14:15-35
- [ ] Luke 15:1-10
- [ ] Luke 15:11-32
- [ ] Luke 16:1-18
- [ ] Luke 16:19-31
- [ ] John 11:1-36
- [ ] John 11:37-57
- [ ] Luke 17:1-19
- [ ] Luke 17:20-37
- [ ] Luke 18:1-14
- [ ] Mark 10:1-16
- [ ] Mark 10:17-31
- [ ] Matthew 20:1-19
- [ ] Mark 10:35-52
- [ ] Luke 19:1-27
- [ ] John 12:1-11
- [ ] Matthew 21:1-17
- [ ] John 12:20-36
- [ ] John 12:37-50
- [ ] Mark 11:20-33
- [ ] Matthew 21:28-46
- [ ] Matthew 22:1-14
- [ ] Luke 20:20-40
- [ ] Mark 12:28-37
- [ ] Matthew 23:1-39
- [ ] Luke 21:1-24
- [ ] Luke 21:25-38
- [ ] Matthew 25:1-30
- [ ] Matthew 25:31-46
- [ ] Luke 22:1-13
- [ ] John 13:1-20
- [ ] John 13:21-38
- [ ] John 14:1-14
- [ ] John 14:15-31
- [ ] John 15:1-16
- [ ] John 15:17–16:4
- [ ] John 16:5-33
- [ ] John 17:1-26
- [ ] Mark 14:26-52
- [ ] John 18:1-24
- [ ] Matthew 26:57-75
- [ ] Matthew 27:1-10
- [ ] Luke 23:1-12
- [ ] Mark 15:6-24
- [ ] Luke 23:32-49

WHEN ONE HURTS, ALL HURT

ourdailybreadyouth TODAY'S READING...

📖 1 Corinthians 12:14-26

Key Verse: If one part suffers, every part suffers with it; if one part is honoured, every part rejoices with it (v.26)

When a teacher missed school for a week because he was sick, everyone started to get worried. After going to the hospital for a few days, he returned to school and showed us what the problem had been—a kidney stone. He'd asked his doctor to give him the stone so he could show us all. Looking at that stone grossed me out, but I was also sympathetic. It must have been

Coping with anxiety
What difference does God make to our battles with anxiety?

14
7
3

PICK A PLAN

TRENDING

BATTLING AGAINST ADDICTIONS

Battling against addictions

Can I trust the Bible?

THE S... OF JE...

The story of Jesus

EXAM STRESS

FIGH... TEMP...

BIBLE BASECAMP

We're here for you! Visit us at
ourdailybread.org/teen

Simply Trusting

Bible: Romans 3:19-4:8

A person is justified by faith apart from the
works of the law
ROMANS 3:28

...mply trust. This is one of the most difficult things for
...s to get our heads round. We have a hard time
...nderstanding that we can't do anything to earn God's
...ve. Jesus paid the penalty for all our sins when He
...ed on the cross. To enjoy God's forgiveness, a
...lationship with Him and a place in heaven forever, all
...e need to do is trust Him to save us. Paul put it this
...y: "To the one who does not work but trusts God
...o justifies the ungodly, their faith is credited as
...ghteousness" (ROM. 4:5).

...e person who understood this truth once wrote,
...r thirty years I had assumed that to swim I had to

If you enjoyed this Teen Edition, then come and check out
everything else we have to help you make sense of the Bible and
get to know Jesus better for yourself. That's why Our Daily Bread
Ministries exists! Get in touch at **europe@odb.org** and visit us at
ourdailybread.org/teen

Our Daily Bread
Ministries®

Our Daily Bread Ministries is committed to making the life-changing wisdom of God's Word understandable and accessible to all. We love to help others draw closer to God daily, which is why we create resources like this Teen Edition.

The best place to find out more about who we are, what we do and how you can get involved is at **ourdailybread.org**

On our website you will be able to see all the resources we have available to you, including all our apps, podcasts, websites, DVDs, CDs and booklets.

Ireland: Our Daily Bread Ministries, 64 Baggot Street Lower, Dublin 2, D02 XC62
ireland@odb.org ~ +353 (0) 1676 7315

UK & Europe: Our Daily Bread Ministries, PO Box 1, Millhead, Carnforth, LA5 9ES
europe@odb.org ~ +44 (0) 15395 64149

Many people, making even the smallest of donations, enable Our Daily Bread Ministries to reach others with the life-changing wisdom of the Bible. We are not funded or endowed by any group or denomination.